Honoré de Balzac

Eugenie Grandet and Other Stories

Honoré de Balzac

Eugenie Grandet and Other Stories

ISBN/EAN: 9783744751216

Printed in Europe, USA, Canada, Australia, Japan

Cover: Foto ©Thomas Meinert / pixelio.de

More available books at **www.hansebooks.com**

H. DE BALZAC

EUGÉNIE GRANDET

AND OTHER STORIES

TRANSLATED BY

ELLEN MARRIAGE

WITH A PREFACE BY

GEORGE SAINTSBURY

PHILADELPHIA
THE GEBBIE PUBLISHING CO., Ltd.
1897

CONTENTS.

	PAGE
PREFACE	ix
EUGÉNIE GRANDET	1
THE MARANAS	225
THE EXECUTIONER (El Verdugo)	297
FAREWELL (Adieu)	310
A SEASIDE TRAGEDY	359

LIST OF ILLUSTRATIONS.

"COME, NANON, TAKE AS MUCH AS YOU LIKE" . . *Frontispiece*

                                                                    PAGE

THE DOOR STOOD AJAR; SHE THRUST IT OPEN 125

"DO YOU HEAR WHAT I SAY? GO!" 170

HE WOULD SIT FOR WHOLE HOURS WITH HIS EYES FIXED ON THE LOUIS 195
Drawn by D. Murray Smith.

"IS THAT M. DIARD?" 293

PREFACE.

WITH "Eugénie Grandet," as with one or two, but only one or two others of Balzac's works, we come to a case of *Quis vituperavit?* Here, and perhaps here only, with "Le Médecin de Campagne" and "Le Père Goriot," though there may be carpers and depreciators, there are no open deniers of the merit of the work. The pathos of Eugénie, the mastery of Grandet, the success of the minor characters, especially Nanon, are universally recognized. The importance of the work has sometimes been slightly questioned even by those who admit its beauty: but this questioning can only support itself on the unavowed but frequently present conviction or suspicion that a "good" or "goody" book must be a weak one. As a matter of fact, no book can be, or can be asked to be, better than perfect on its own scheme, and with its own conditions. And on its own scheme and with its own conditions "Eugénie Grandet" is very nearly perfect.

On the character of the heroine will turn the final decision whether, as has been said by some (I believe I might be charged with having said it myself), Balzac's virtuous characters are always more theatrical than real. The decision must take in the Benassis of "Le Médecin de Campagne," but with him it will have less difficulty; for Benassis, despite the beauty and pathos of his confession, is a little "a person of the boards" in his unfailingly providential character and his complete devotion to others. Must Eugénie, his feminine companion in goodness, be put on these boards likewise?

I admit that of late years, and more particularly since the undertaking of this present task made necessary to me a more complete and methodical study of the whole works, including the most miscellaneous miscellanies, than I had previously given, my estimate of Balzac's goodness has gone up very much—that of his greatness had no need of raising. But I still think that even about Eugénie there is a very little unreality, a slight touch of that ignorance of the actual nature of girls which even fervent admirers of French novelists in general, and of Balzac in particular, have confessed to finding in them and him. That Eugénie should be entirely subjugated first by the splendor, and then by the misfortune, of her Parisian cousin, is not in the least unnatural; nor do I for one moment pretend to deny the possibility or the likelihood of her having

"lifted up her eyes,
And loved him with that love which was her doom."

It is also difficult to make too much allowance for the fatal effect of an education under an insignificant if amiable mother and a tyrannical father, and of a confinement to an excessively small circle of extremely provincial society, on a disposition of more nobility than intellectual height or range. Still it must, I think, be permitted to the *advocatus diaboli* to urge that Eugénie's martyrdom is almost too thorough; that though complete, it is not, as Gautier said of his own ill luck, "*artistement* complet;" that though it may be difficult to put the finger on any special blot, to say, "Here the girl should have revolted," or, "Here she would have behaved in some other way differently;" still there is a vague sense of incomplete lifelikeness—of that tendency to mirage and exaggeration which has been, and will be, so often noticed.

Still it is vague and not unpleasantly obtrusive, and in all other ways Eugénie is a triumph. It is noticeable that her creator has dwelt on the actual traits of her face with much more distinctness than is usual with him; for Balzac's extraordinary minuteness in many ways does not invariably extend to physical charms. This minuteness is indeed so great that one has a certain suspicion of the head being taken from a live and special original. Nor is her physical presence—abominably libeled, there is no doubt, by Mme. des Grassins—the only distinct thing about Eugénie. We see her hovering about the *beau cousin* with an innocent officiousness capable of committing no less the major crime of lending him money than the minor, but even more audacious because open, one of letting him have sugar. She is perfectly natural in the courage with which she bears her father's unjust rage, and in the forgiveness which, quite as a matter of course, she extends to him after he has broken her own peace and her mother's heart. It is perhaps necessary to be French to comprehend entirely why she could not heap that magnificent pile of coals of fire on her unworthy cousin's head without flinging herself and her seventeen millions into the arms of somebody else; but the thing can be accepted if not quite understood. And the whole transaction of this heaping is admirable.

Nanon is, of course, quite excellent. She is not stupid, as her kind are supposed to be; she is only blindly faithful, as well as thoroughly good-hearted. Nor is the unfortunate Madame Grandet an idiot, nor are any of the *comparses* mere dummies. But naturally they all, even Eugénie herself to some extent, serve mainly as set-offs to the terrible Grandet. In him Balzac, a Frenchman of Frenchmen, has boldly depicted perhaps the worst and the commonest vice of the French character, the vice which is more common, and certainly worse than either the frivolity or the license with which the nation is usually charged—the pushing, to wit, of thrift to the loathsome excess of an inhuman avarice. But he has justified himself to his country by communicating to his hero an unquestioned grandeur. The mirage works again, but it works with splendid effect. One need not be a sentimentalist to shudder a little at the *ta ta ta ta* of Grandet, the refrain of a money-grubbing which almost escapes greediness by its diabolical extravagance and success.

The bibliography of "Eugénie Grandet" is not complicated. Balzac tried the first chapter (there were originally seven) in *L'Europe Littéraire* for September 19, 1833; but he did not continue it there, and it appeared complete in the first volume of "Scènes de la Vie de Province" next year. Charpentier republished it in a single volume in 1839. The "Comédie" engulfed it in 1843, the chapter divisions then disappearing.

All the "Marana" group of stories appeared together in the fourth edition of the "Philosophical Studies," 1835–1837. Most of them, however, had earlier appearances in periodicals and in the *Romans et Contes Philosophiques*, which preceded the "Studies." And in these various appearances they were subjected to their author's usual processes of division and unification, of sub-titling and canceling sub-titles. "Les Marana" appeared first in the *Revue de Paris* for the last month of 1832 and the first of 1833; while it next made a show, oddly enough, as a "Scène de la vie Parisienne." "Farewell" (Adieu) appeared in the *Mode* during June, 1830, and was afterwards for a time a "Scène de la vie privée." "The Executioner" (*El Verdugo*) was issued by the *Mode* for January 29, 1830; and "A Seaside Tragedy" (*Un Drame au bord de la mer*) appeared nowhere except in book form with its companions until 1843, when it left them for a time (afterwards to return), and under another title accompanied several other stories in a separate publication. G. S.

EUGENIE GRANDET.

To Maria.

Your portrait is the fairest ornament of this book, and here it is fitting that your name should be set, like the branch of box taken from some unknown garden to lie for a while in the holy water, and afterwards set by pious hands above the threshold, where the green spray, ever renewed, is a sacred talisman to ward off all evil from the house.

IN some country towns there are houses more depressing to the sight than the dimmest cloister, the most melancholy ruins, or the dreariest stretch of sandy waste. Perhaps such houses combine the characteristics of all the three, and to the dumb silence of the monastery they unite the gauntness and grimness of the ruin, and the arid desolation of the waste. So little sign is there of life or of movement about them, that a stranger might take them for uninhabited dwellings; but the sound of an unfamiliar footstep brings some one to the window, a passive face suddenly appears above the sill, and the traveler receives a listless and indifferent glance—it is almost as if a monk leaned out to look for a moment on the world.

There is one particular house front in Saumur which possesses all these melancholy characteristics; the house is still standing at the end of the steep street which leads to the castle, at the upper end of the town. The street is very quiet nowadays; it is hot in summer and cold in winter, and very dark in places; besides this, it is remarkably narrow and crooked, there is a peculiarly formal and sedate air about its houses, and it is curious how every sound reverberates through it—the cobblestones (always clean and dry) ring with every passing footfall.

This is the oldest part of the town, the ramparts rise immediately above it. The houses of the quarter have stood for three centuries; and albeit they are built of wood, they are strong and sound yet. Each house has a certain character of its own, so that for the artist and antiquary this is the most attractive part of the town of Saumur. Indeed, it would hardly be possible to go past the house, without a wondering glance at the grotesque figures carved on the projecting ends of the huge beams, set like a black bas-relief above the ground floor of almost every dwelling. Sometimes, where these beams have been protected from the weather by slates, a strip of dull blue runs across the crumbling walls, and crowning the whole is a high-pitched roof oddly curved and bent with age; the shingle boards that cover it are all warped and twisted by the alternate sun and rain of many a year. There are bits of delicate carving too, here and there, though you can scarcely make them out, on the worn and blackened window sills that seemed scarcely strong enough to bear the weight of the red flower-pot in which some poor workwoman has set her tree carnation or her monthly rose.

Still further along the street there are more pretentious house-doors studded with huge nails. On these our forefathers exercised their ingenuity, tracing hieroglyphs and mysterious signs which were once understood in every household, but all clues to their meaning are forgotten now—they will be understood no more of any mortal. In such wise would a Protestant make his profession of faith, there also would a Leaguer curse Henry IV. in graven symbols. A burgher would commemorate his civic dignities, the glory of his long-forgotten tenure of office as alderman or sheriff. On these old houses, if we could but read it, the history of France is chronicled.

Beside the rickety little tenement built of wood, with masonry of the roughest, upon the wall of which the craftsman has set the glorified image of his trade—his plane—stands the mansion of some noble, with its massive round arched gateway; you can still see some traces above it of the arms borne by the owner, though they have been torn down in one of the many revolutions which have convulsed the country since 1789.

You will find no imposing shop windows in the street; strictly speaking, indeed, there are no shops at all, for the rooms on the ground floor in which articles are exposed for sale are neither more nor less than the workshops of the times of our forefathers; lovers of the middle ages will find here the primitive simplicity of an older world. The low-ceiled rooms are dark, cavernous, and guiltless alike of plate-glass windows or of showcases; there is no attempt at decoration either within or without, no effort is made to display the wares. The door, as a rule, is heavily barred with iron and divided into two parts; the upper half is thrown back during the day, admitting fresh air and daylight into the damp little cave; while the lower portion, to which a bell is attached, is seldom still. The shop front consists of a low wall of about elbow height, which fills half the space between floor and ceiling; there is no window sash, but heavy shutters fastened with iron bolts fit into a groove in the top of the wall, and are set up at night and taken down in the morning. The same wall serves as a counter on which to set out goods for the customer's inspection. There is no sort of charlatanism about the proceeding. The samples submitted to the public vary according to the nature of the trade. You behold a keg or two of salt or of salted fish, two or three bales of sail-cloth or coils of rope, some copper wire hanging from the rafters, a few cooper's hoops on the walls, or a length or two of cloth upon the shelves.

You go in. A neat and tidy damsel with a pair of bare red arms, the fresh good looks of youth, and a white handkerchief pinned about her throat, lays down her knitting and goes to summon a father or mother, who appears and sells goods to you as you desire, be it a matter of two sous or of twenty thousand francs; the manner of the transaction varying as the humor of the vendor is surly, obliging, or independent. You will see a dealer in barrel-staves sitting in his doorway, twirling his thumbs as he chats with a neighbor; judging from appearances, he might possess nothing in this world but the bottles on his few rickety shelves and two or three bundles of laths; but his well-stocked timber-yard on the quay supplies all the coopers in Anjou, he knows to a barrel-stave how many casks he can "turn out," as he says, if the vines do well and the vintage is good; a few scorching days and his fortune is made, a rainy summer is a ruinous thing for him; in a single morning the price of puncheons will rise as high as eleven francs or drop to six.

Here, as in Touraine, the whole trade of the district depends upon an atmospherical depression. Landowners, vine-growers, timber merchants, coopers, innkeepers and lightermen, one and all are on the watch for a ray of sunlight. Not a man of them but goes to bed in fear and trembling lest he should hear in the morning that there has been a frost in the night. If it is not rain that they dread, it is wind or drought; they must have cloudy weather or heat, and the rainfall and the weather generally all arranged to suit their peculiar notions.

Between the clerk of the weather and the vine-growing interest there is a duel which never ceases. Faces visibly lengthen or shorten, grow bright or gloomy, with the ups and downs of the barometer. Sometimes you hear from one end to the other of the old High Street of Saumur the words, "This is golden weather!" or again, in language which likewise is no mere figure of speech, "It is raining gold louis!" and they all know the exact value of sun or rain at the right moment.

After twelve o'clock or so on a Saturday in the summertime, you will not do a pennyworth of business among the worthy townsmen of Saumur. Each has his little farm and his bit of vineyard, and goes to spend the "week end" in the country. As everybody knows this beforehand, just as everybody knows everybody else's business, his goings and comings, his buyings and sellings, and profits to boot, the good folk are free to spend ten hours out of the twelve in making up pleasant little parties, in taking notes and making comments, and keeping a sharp lookout on their neighbors' affairs. The mistress of a house cannot buy a partridge but the neighbors will inquire of her husband whether the bird was done to a turn; no damsel can put her head out of the window without being observed by every group of unoccupied observers.

Impenetrable, dark, and silent as the houses may seem, they contain no mysteries hidden from public scrutiny, and in the same way every one knows what is passing in every one else's mind. To begin with, the good folk spend most of their lives out of doors, they sit on the steps of their houses, breakfast there and dine there, and adjust any little family differences in the doorway. Every passer-by is scanned with the most minute and diligent attention; hence, any stranger who may happen to arrive in such a country town has, in a manner, to run the gauntlet, and is severely quizzed from every doorstep. By dint of perseverance in the methods thus indicated a quantity of droll stories may be collected; and, indeed, the people of Angers, who are of an ingenious turn, and quick at repartee, have been nicknamed "the tattlers" on these very grounds.

The largest houses of the old quarter in which the nobles once dwelt are all at the upper end of the street, and in one of these the events took place which are about to be narrated in the course of this story. As has been already said, it was a melancholy house, a venerable relic of a bygone age, built for the men and women of an older and simpler world, from which our modern France is farther and farther removed day by day. After you have followed for some distance the windings of the picturesque street, where memories of the past are called up by every detail at every turn, till at length you fall unconsciously to musing, you come upon a sufficiently gloomy recess in which a doorway is dimly visible, the door of *M. Grandet's house.* Of all the pride and glory of proprietorship conveyed to the provincial mind by those three words, it is impossible to give any idea, except by giving the biography of the owner—M. Grandet.

M. Grandet enjoyed a certain reputation in Saumur. Its causes and effects can scarcely be properly estimated by outsiders who have not lived in a country town for a longer or shorter time. There were still old people in existence who could remember former times, and called M. Grandet "Goodman Grandet," but there were not many of them left, and they were rapidly disappearing year by year.

In 1789 Grandet was a master cooper, in a very good way of business, who could read and write and cast accounts. When the French Republic, having confiscated the lands of the Church in the district of Saumur, proceeded to sell them by auction, the cooper was forty years of age, and had just married the daughter of a wealthy timber merchant. As Grandet possessed at that moment his wife's dowry as well as some considerable amount of ready money of his own, he repaired to the bureau of the *district;* and making due allowance for two hundred double louis offered by his father-in-law to that man of stern morals, the Republican who conducted the sale, the cooper acquired some of the best vineland in the neighborhood, an old abbey, and a few little farms, for an old song, to all of which property, though it might be ill-gotten, the law gave him a clear title.

There was little sympathy felt with the Revolution in Saumur. Goodman Grandet was looked upon as a bold spirit, a Republican, a patriot, an "advanced thinker," and whatnot; but all the "thinking" the cooper ever did turned simply and solely on the subject of his vines. He was nominated as a member of the administration of the district of Saumur, and exercised a pacific influence both in politics and in commerce. Politically, he befriended the ci-devants, and did all that he could to prevent the sale of their property; commercially, he contracted to supply two thousand hogsheads of white wine to the Republican armies, taking his payment for the aforesaid hogsheads in the shape of certain broad acres of rich meadow land belonging to a convent, the property of the nuns having been reserved till the last.

In the days of the Consulate, Master Grandet became mayor; acted prudently in his public capacity, and did very well for himself. Times changed, the Empire was established, and he became *Monsieur* Grandet. But M. Grandet had been looked upon as a red Republican, and Napoleon had no liking for Republicans, so the mayor was replaced by a large landowner, a man with a *de* before his name, and a prospect of one day becoming a baron of the Empire. M. Grandet turned his back upon municipal honors without a shadow of regret. He had looked well after the interests of the town during his term of office, excellent roads had been made, passing in every case by his own domains. His house and land had been assessed very moderately, the burden of the taxes did not fall too grievously upon him; since the assessment, moreover, he had given ceaseless attention and care to the cultivation of his vines, so that they had become the *tête du pays*, the technical term for those vineyards which produce wine of the finest quality. He had a fair claim to the Cross of the Legion of Honor, and he received it in 1806.

By this time M. Grandet was fifty-seven years old, and his wife about thirty-six. The one child of the marriage was a daughter, a little girl ten years of age. Providence doubtless sought to console M. Grandet for his official downfall, for in this year he succeeded to three fortunes; the total value was matter for conjecture, no certain information being forthcoming. The first fell in on the death of Mme. de la Gaudinière, Mme. Grandet's mother; the deceased lady had been a de la Bertellière, and her father, old M. de la Bertellière, soon followed her; the third in order was Mme. Gentillet, M. Grandet's grandmother on the mother's side. Old M. de la Bertellière used to call an investment "throwing money away;" the sight of his hoards of gold repaid him better than any rate of interest upon it. The town of Saumur, therefore, roughly calculated the value of the amount that the late de la Bertellière was likely to have saved out of his yearly takings; and M. Grandet received a new distinction which none of our manias for equality can efface—he paid more taxes than any one else in the country round.

He now cultivated a hundred acres of vineyard; in a good year they would yield seven or eight hundred puncheons. He had thirteen little farms, an old abbey (motives of economy had led him to wall up the windows, and so preserve the traceries and stained glass), and a hundred and twenty-seven acres of grazing land, in which three thousand poplars, planted in 1793, were growing taller and larger every year. Finally, he owned the house in which he lived.

In these visible ways his prosperity had increased. As to his capital, there were only two people in a position to make a guess at its probable amount. One of these was the notary, M. Cruchot, who transacted all the necessary business whenever M. Grandet made an investment; and the other was M. des Grassins, the wealthiest banker in the town, who did Grandet many good offices which were unknown to Saumur. Secrets of this nature, involving extensive business transactions, are usually well kept; but the discreet caution of MM. Cruchot and des Grassins did not prevent them from addressing M. Grandet in public with such profound deference that close observers might draw their own conclusions. Clearly the wealth of their late mayor must be prodigious indeed that he should receive such obsequious attention.

There was no one in Saumur who did not fully believe the
report which told how, in a secret hiding-place, M. Grandet
had a hoard of louis, and how every night he went to look at
it, and gave himself up to the inexpressible delight of gazing
at the huge heap of gold.   He was not the only money-lover
in Saumur.   Sympathetic observers looked at his eyes and
felt that the story was true, for they seemed to have the yellow
metallic glitter of the coin over which it was said they had
brooded.   Nor was this the only sign.   Certain small indefinable habits, furtive movements, slight mysterious promptings of greed did not escape the keen observation of fellow-
worshipers.   There is something vulpine about the eyes of a
man who lends money at an exorbitant rate of interest; they
gradually and surely contract like those of the gambler, the
sensualist, or the courtier; and there is, so to speak, a sort of
freemasonry among the passions, a written language of hieroglyphs and signs for those who can read them.

M. Grandet therefore inspired in all around him the respectful esteem which is but the due of a man who has never
owed any one a farthing in his life; a just and legitimate
tribute to an astute old cooper and vine-grower who knew beforehand with the certainty of an astronomer when five hundred casks would serve for the vintage, and when to have a
thousand in readiness; a man who had never lost on any
speculation, who had always a stock of empty barrels whenever casks were so dear that they fetched more than the
contents were worth; who could store his vintage in his own
cellars, and afford to bide his time, so that his puncheons
would bring him in a couple of hundred francs, while many
a little proprietor who could not wait had to be content with
half that amount.   His famous vintage in the year 1811,
discreetly held, and sold only as good opportunities offered,
had been worth two hundred and forty thousand livres to
him.

In matters financial M. Grandet might be described as

combining the characteristics of the Bengal tiger and the boa constrictor. He could lay low and wait, crouching, watching for his prey, and make his spring unerringly at last; then the jaws of his purse would unclose, a torrent of coin would be swallowed down, and, as in the case of the gorged reptile, there would be a period of inaction; like the serpent, moreover, he was cold, apathetic, methodical, keeping to his own mysterious times and seasons.

No one could see the man pass without feeling a certain kind of admiration, which was half-dread, half-respect. The tiger's clutch was like steel, his claws were sharp and swift; was there any one in Saumur who had not felt them? Such an one, for instance, wanted to borrow money to buy that piece of land which he had set his heart upon; M. Cruchot had found the money for him—at eleven per cent. And there was So-and-so yonder; M. des Grassins had discounted his bills, but it was at a ruinous rate.

There were not many days when M. Grandet's name did not come up in conversation, in familiar talk in the evenings, or in the gossip of the town. There were people who took a kind of patriotic pride in the old vine-grower's wealth. More than one innkeeper or merchant had found occasion to remark to a stranger with a certain complacency, "There are millionaires in two or three of our firms here, sir; but as for M. Grandet, he himself could hardly tell you how much he was worth!"

In 1816 the shrewdest heads in Saumur set down the value of the cooper's landed property at about four millions; but as, to strike a fair average, he must have drawn something like a hundred thousand francs (they thought) from his property between the years 1793 and 1817, the amount of money he possessed must nearly equal the value of the land. So when M. Grandet's name was mentioned over a game at boston, or a chat about the prospects of the vines, these folk would look wise and remark, "Who is that you are talking of? Old Grandet? Old Grandet must have five or six millions, there is no doubt about it."

"Then you are cleverer than I am; I have never been able to find out how much he has," M. Cruchot or M. des Grassins would put in, if they overheard the speech.

If any one from Paris mentioned the Rothschilds or M. Laffitte, the good people in Saumur would ask if any of those persons were as rich as M. Grandet? And if the Parisian should answer in the affirmative with a pitying smile, they looked at one another incredulously and flung up their heads. So great a fortune was like a golden mantle; it covered its owner and all that he did. At one time some of the eccentricities of his mode of life gave rise to laughter at his expense; but the satire and the laughter had died out, and M. Grandet still went his way, till at last even his slightest actions came to be taken as precedents, and every trifling thing he said or did carried weight. His remarks, his clothing, his gestures, the way he blinked his eyes, had all been studied with the care with which a naturalist studies the workings of instinct in some wild creature; and no one failed to discern the taciturn and profound wisdom that underlay all these manifestations.

"We shall have a hard winter," they would say; "old Grandet has put on his fur gloves, we must gather the grapes." Or, "Goodman Grandet is laying in a lot of cask staves; there will be plenty of wine this year."

M. Grandet never bought either meat or bread. Part of his rents were paid in kind, and every week his tenants brought in poultry, eggs, butter, and wheat sufficient for the needs of his household. Moreover, he owned a mill, and the miller, besides paying rent, came over to fetch a certain quantity of corn, and brought him back both the bran and the flour. Big Nanon, the one maidservant, baked all the bread once a week on Saturday mornings (though she was not so young as she had been). Others of the tenants were market gardeners, and M. Grandet had arranged that these were to keep him supplied with fresh vegetables. Of fruit there was no lack; indeed, he sold a good deal of it in the market. Firewood was gathered from his own hedges, or taken from old stumps of trees that grew by the sides of his fields. His tenants chopped up the wood, carted it into the town, and obligingly stacked his faggots for him, receiving in return—his thanks. So he seldom had occasion to spend money. His only known items of expenditure were for sacramental bread, for sittings in the church for his wife and daughter, their dress, Nanon's wages, renewals of the linings of Nanon's saucepans, repairs about the house, candles, rates and taxes, and the necessary outlays of money for improvements. He had recently acquired six hundred acres of woodland, and, being unable to look after it himself, had induced a keeper belonging to a neighbor to attend to it, promising to repay the man for his trouble. After this purchase had been made, and not before, game appeared on the Grandets' table.

Grandet's manners were distinctly homely. He did not say very much. He expressed his ideas, as a rule, in brief, sententious phrases, uttered in a low voice. Since the time of the Revolution, when for a while he had attracted some attention, the worthy man had contracted a tiresome habit of stammering as soon as he took part in a discussion or began to speak at any length. He had other peculiarities. He habitually drowned his ideas in a flood of words more or less incoherent; his singular inaptitude for reasoning logically was usually set down to a defective education; but this, like his unwelcome fluency, the trick of stammering, and various other mannerisms, was assumed, and for reasons which, in the course of the story, will be made sufficiently clear. In conversation, moreover, he had other resources: four phrases, like algebraical formulæ, which fitted every case, were always forthcoming to solve every knotty problem in business or domestic life—"I do not know," "I cannot do it," "I will have nothing to do with it," and " We shall see." He never committed himself; he never said yes or no; he never put anything down in writing. He listened with apparent indifference when he was spoken to, caressing his chin with his right hand, while the back of his left supported his elbow. When once he had formed his opinion in any matter of business, he never changed it; but he pondered long even over the smallest transactions. When in the course of deep and weighty converse he had managed to fathom the intentions of an antagonist, who meanwhile flattered himself that *he* at last knew where to have Grandet, the latter was wont to say, "I must talk it over with my wife before I can give a definite answer." In business matters the wife, whom he had reduced to the most abject submission, was unquestionably a most convenient support and screen.

He never paid visits, never dined away from home, nor asked any one to dinner; his movements were almost noiseless; he seemed to carry out his principles of economy in everything; to make no useless sound, to be chary of spending even physical energy. His respect for the rights of ownership was so habitual that he never displaced nor disturbed anything belonging to another. And yet, in spite of the low tones of his voice, in spite of his discretion and cautious bearing, the cooper's real character showed itself in his language and manners, and this was more especially the case in his own house, where he was less on his guard than elsewhere.

As to Grandet's exterior. He was a broad, square-shouldered, thick-set man, about five feet high; his legs were thin (he measured perhaps twelve inches round the calves), his knee-joints large and prominent. He had a bullet-shaped head, a sun-burned face, scarred with the smallpox, and a narrow chin; there was no trace of a curve about the lines of his mouth. He possessed a set of white teeth, eyes with the expression of stony avidity in them with which the basilisk is credited, a deeply-furrowed brow on which there were prominences not lacking in significance, hair that had once been of a sandy hue, but which was now fast turning gray; so that thoughtless youngsters, rash enough to make jokes on so serious a subject, would say that M. Grandet's very hair was "gold and silver." On his nose, which was broad and blunt at the tip, was a variegated wen; gossip affirmed, not without some appearance of truth, that spite and rancor were the cause of this affection. There was a dangerous cunning about this face, although the man, indeed, was honest according to the letter of the law; it was a selfish face; there were but two things in the world for which its owner cared—the delights of hoarding wealth, in the first place, and, in the second, the only being who counted for anything in his estimation, his daughter Eugénie, his only child, who one day should inherit that wealth. His attitude, manner, bearing, and everything about him plainly showed that he had the belief in himself which is the natural outcome of an unbroken record of successful business speculations. Pliant and smooth-spoken though he might appear to be, M. Grandet was a man of bronze. He was always dressed after the same fashion; in 1819 he looked in this respect exactly as he had looked at any time since 1791. His heavy shoes were secured by leather laces; he wore thick woolen stockings all the year round, knee breeches of chestnut brown homespun, silver buckles, a brown velvet waistcoat adorned with yellow stripes and buttoned up to the throat, a loosely-fitting coat with ample skirts, a black cravat, and a broad-brimmed Quaker-like hat. His gloves, like those of the gendarmerie, were chosen with a view to hard wear; a pair lasted him nearly two years. In order to keep them clean, he always laid them down on the same place on the brim of his hat, till the action had come to be mechanical with him. So much, and no more, Saumur knew of this her citizen.

A few fellow-townspeople, six in all, had the right of entry to Grandet's house and society. First among these in order of importance was M. Cruchot's nephew. Ever since his appointment as president of the court of first instance, this young man had added the appellation "de Bonfons" to his original name of Cruchot; in time he hoped that the Bonfons would efface the Cruchot, when he meant to drop the Cruchot altogether, and was at no little pains to compass this end. Already he styled himself C. de Bonfons. Any litigant who was so ill inspired as to address him in court as "M. Cruchot" was soon made painfully aware that he had blundered. The magistrate was about thirty-three years of age, and the owner of the estate of Bonfons (*Boni Fontis*), which brought in annually seven thousand livres. In addition to this he had prospects; he would succeed some day to the property of his uncle the notary, and there was yet another uncle besides, the Abbé Cruchot, a dignitary of the chapter of Saint Martin of Tours; both relatives were commonly reported to be men of substance. The three Cruchots, with a goodly number of kinsfolk, connected too by marriage with a score of other houses, formed a sort of party in the town, like the family of the Medicis in Florence long ago; and, like the Medicis, the Cruchots had their rivals—their Pazzi.

Mme. des Grassins, the mother of a son twenty-three years of age, came assiduously to take a hand at cards with Mme. Grandet, hoping to marry her own dear Adolphe to Mademoiselle Eugénie. She had a powerful ally in her husband the banker, who had secretly rendered the old miser many a service, and who could give opportune aid on her field of battle. The three des Grassins had likewise their host of adherents, their cousins and trusty auxiliaries.

The Abbé (the Talleyrand of the Cruchot faction), well supported by his brother the notary, closely disputed the ground with the banker's wife; they meant to carry off the wealthy heiress for their nephew the president. The struggle between the two parties for the prize of the hand of Eugénie

Grandet was an open secret; all Saumur watched it with the keenest interest. Which would Mlle. Grandet marry? Would it be M. le Président or M. Adolphe des Grassins? Some solved the problem by saying that M. Grandet would give his daughter to neither. The old cooper (said they) was consumed with an ambition to have a peer of France for his son-in-law, and he was on the lookout for a peer of France, who for the consideration of an income of three hundred thousand livres would find all the past, present, and future barrels of the Grandets no obstacle to a match. Others demurred to this, and urged that both M. and Mme. des Grassins came of a good family, that they had wealth enough for anything, that Adolphe was a very good-looking, pretty behaved young man, and that unless the Grandets had a Pope's nephew somewhere in the background, they ought to be satisfied with a match in every way so suitable; for they were nobodies after all; all Saumur had seen Grandet going about with an adze in his hands, and, moreover, he had worn the red cap of Liberty in his time.

The more astute observers remarked that M. Cruchot de Bonfons was free of the house in the High Street, while his rival only visited there on Sundays. Some maintained that Mme. des Grassins, being on more intimate terms with the women of the house, had opportunities of inculcating certain ideas which sooner or later must conduce to her success. Others retorted that the Abbé Cruchot had the most insinuating manner in the world, and that with a churchman on one side and a woman on the other the chances were about even.

"It is gown against cassock," said a local wit.

Those whose memories went farther back said that the Grandets were too prudent to let all that property go out of the family. Mlle. Eugénie Grandet of Saumur would be married one of these days to the son of the other M. Grandet of Paris, a rich wholesale wine merchant. To these both Cruchotins and Grassinistes were wont to reply as follows:

"In the first place, the brothers have not met twice in thirty years. Then M. Grandet of Paris is ambitious for that son of his. He himself is mayor of his division of the department, a deputy, a colonel of the National Guard, and a judge of the tribunal of commerce. He does not own to any relationship with the Grandets of Saumur, and is seeking to connect himself with one of Napoleon's dukes."

What will not people say of an heiress? Eugénie Grandet was a stock subject of conversation for twenty leagues round; nay, in public conveyances, even as far as Angers on the one hand and Blois on the other!

In the beginning of the year 1811 the Cruchotins gained a signal victory over the Grassinistes. The young Marquis de Froidfond being compelled to realize his capital, the estate of Froidfond, celebrated for its park and its handsome château, was for sale; together with its dependent farms, rivers, fishponds, and forest; altogether it was worth three million francs. M. Cruchot, President Cruchot, and the Abbé Cruchot by uniting their forces had managed to prevent a proposed division into small lots. The notary made an uncommonly good bargain for his client, representing to the young Marquis that the purchase money of the small lots could only be collected after endless trouble and expense, and that he would have to sue a large proportion of the purchasers for it; while here was M. Grandet, a man whose credit stood high, and who was moreover ready to pay for the land at once in hard coin, it would be better to take M. Grandet's offer. In this way the fair marquisate of Froidfond was swallowed down by M. Grandet, who, to the amazement of Saumur, paid for it in ready money (deducting discount of course) as soon as the required formalities were completed. The news of this transaction traveled far and wide; it reached Orleans, it was spoken of at Nantes.

M. Grandet went to see his château, and on this wise: a cart happened to be returning thither, so he embraced this opportunity of visiting his newly-acquired property, and took a look round in the capacity of owner. Then he returned to Saumur, well convinced that this investment would bring him in a clear five per cent., and fired with a magnificent ambition; he would add his own bits of land to the marquisate of Froidfond, and everything should lie within a ring fence. For the present he would set himself to replenish his almost exhausted coffers; he would cut down every stick of timber in his copses and forests, and fell the poplars in his meadows.

It is easy after this explanation to understand all that was conveyed by the words, "M. Grandet's house"—the cold, dreary, and silent house at the upper end of the town, under the shadow of the ruined ramparts.

Two pillars supported the arch above the doorway, and for these, as also for the building of the house itself, a porous crumbling stone peculiar to the district along the banks of the Loire had been employed, a kind of tufa so soft that at most it scarcely lasts for two hundred years. Rain and frost had gnawed numerous irregular holes in the surface, with a curious effect; the piers and the voussoirs looked as though they were composed of the vermicular stones often met with in French architecture. The doorway might have been the portal of a gaol. Above the arch there was a long sculptured bas-relief of harder stone, representing the four seasons, four forlorn figures, aged, blackened, and weather-worn. Above the bas-relief there was a projecting ledge of masonry where some chance-sown plants had taken root; yellow pellitory, bindweed, a plantain or two, and a little cherry tree, that even now had reached a fair height.

The massive door itself was of dark oak, shrunk and warped, and full of cracks; but, feeble as it looked, it was firmly held together by a series of iron nails with huge heads, driven into the wood in a symmetrical design. In the middle there was a small square grating covered with rusty iron bars, which served as an excuse for a door knocker which hung there from a ring, and struck upon the menacing head a great iron bolt. The knocker itself, oblong in shape, was of the kind that our ancestors used to call a "Jaquemart," and not unlike a huge note of admiration. If an antiquary had examined it carefully, he might have found some traces of the grotesque human head that it once represented, but the features of the typical clown had long since been effaced by constant wear. The little grating had been made in past times of civil war, so that the household might recognize their friends without before admitting them, but now it afforded to inquisitive eyes a view of a dank and gloomy archway, and a flight of broken steps leading to a not unpicturesque garden shut in by thick walls through which the damp was oozing, and a hedge of sickly-looking shrubs. The walls were part of the old fortifications, and up above on the ramparts there were yet other gardens belonging to some of the neighboring houses.

A door beneath the arch of the gateway opened into a large parlor, the principal room on the ground floor. Few people comprehend the importance of this apartment in little towns in Anjou, Berri, and Touraine. The parlor is also the hall, drawing-room, study, and boudoir all in one; it is the stage on which the drama of domestic life is played, the very heart and centre of the home. Hither the hairdresser repaired once in six months to cut M. Grandet's hair. The tenants and the curé, the sous-préfet, and the miller's lad were all alike shown into this room. There were two windows which looked out upon the street, the floor was boarded, the walls were paneled from floor to ceiling, covered with old carvings, and painted gray. The rafters were left visible, and were likewise painted gray, the plaster in intervening spaces was yellow with age.

An old brass clock-case inlaid with arabesques in tortoise-shell stood on the chimney-piece, which was of white stone, and adorned with rude carvings. Above it stood a mirror of a greenish hue, the edges were beveled in order to display the thickness of the glass, and reflected a thin streak of colored light into the room, which was caught again by the polished surface of another mirror of Damascus steel, which hung upon the wall.

Two branched sconces of gilded copper which adorned either end of the chimney-piece answered a double purpose. The branch roses which served as candle-sockets were removable, and the main stem, fitted into an antique copper contrivance on a bluish marble pedestal, did duty as a candlestick for ordinary days.

The old-fashioned chairs were covered with tapestry, on which the fables of La Fontaine were depicted; but a thorough knowledge of the author was required to make out the subjects, for the colors had faded badly, and the outlines of the figures were hardly visible through a multitude of darns. Four sideboards occupied the four corners of the room, each of these articles of furniture terminating in a tier of very dirty shelves. An old inlaid card-table with a chess-board marked out upon its surface stood in the space between the two windows, and on the wall, above the table, hung an oval barometer in a dark wooden setting, adorned by a carved bunch of ribbons; they had been gilt ribbons once upon a time, but generations of flies had wantonly obscured the gilding, till its existence had become problematical. Two portraits in pastel hung on the wall opposite the fireplace. One was believed to represent Mme. Grandet's grandfather, old M. de la Bertellière, as a lieutenant in the Guards, and the other the late Mme. Gentillet, as a shepherdess.

Crimson curtains of *gros de Tours* were hung in the windows and fastened back with silk cords and huge tassels. This luxurious upholstery, so little in harmony with the manners and customs of the Grandets, had been included in the purchase of the house, like the pier-glass, the brass timepiece, the tapestry-covered chairs, and the rosewood corner sideboards. In the further window stood a straw-bottom chair, raised on blocks of wood, so that Mme. Grandet could watch the passers-by as she sat. A work-table of cherry wood, bleached and faded by the light, filled the other window space, and close beside it Eugénie Grandet's little armchair was set.

The lives of mother and daughter had flowed on tranquilly for fifteen years. Day after day, from April to November, they sat at work in the windows; but the first day of the latter month found them beside the fire, where they took up their positions for the winter. Grandet would not allow a fire to be lighted in the room before that date, nor again after the 31st of March, let the early days of spring or of autumn be cold as they might. Big Nanon managed by stealth to fill a little brasier with glowing ashes from the kitchen fire, and in this way the chilly evenings of April and October were rendered tolerable for Mme. and Mlle. Grandet. All the household linen was kept in repair by the mother and daughter; and so conscientiously did they devote their days to this duty (no light task in truth), that if Eugénie wanted to embroider a collarette for her mother she was obliged to steal the time from her hours of slumber, and to resort to a deception to obtain from her father the candle by which she worked. For a long while past it had been the miser's wont to dole out the candles to his daughter and big Nanon in the same way that he gave out the bread and the other matters daily required by the household.

Perhaps big Nanon was the one servant in existence who could and would have endured her master's tyrannous rule. Every one in the town used to envy M. and Mme. Grandet. "Big Nanon," so called on account of her height of five feet eight inches, had been a part of the Grandet household for thirty-five years. She was held to be one of the richest servants in Saumur, and this on a yearly wage of seventy livres! The seventy livres had accumulated for thirty-five years, and quite recently Nanon had deposited four thousand livres with M. Cruchot for the purchase of an annuity. This result of a long and persevering course of thrift appealed to the imagination—it seemed tremendous. There was not a maidservant in Saumur but was envious of the poor woman, who by the time she had reached her sixtieth year would have scraped together enough to keep herself from want in her old age; but no one thought of the hard life and all the toil which had gone to the making of that little hoard.

Thirty-five years ago, when Nanon had been a homely, hard-featured girl of two-and-twenty, she had not been able to find a place because her appearance had been so much against her. Poor Nanon! it was really very hard. If her head had been set on the shoulders of a grenadier it would have been greatly admired, but there is a fitness in things, and Nanon's style of beauty was inappropriate. She had been a herdswoman on a farm for a time, till the farmhouse had been burnt down, and then it was that, full of the robust courage that shrinks from nothing, she came to seek service in Saumur.

At that time M. Grandet was thinking of marriage, and already determined to set up housekeeping. The girl, who had been rebuffed from door to door, came under his notice. He was a cooper, and therefore a good judge of physical strength; he foresaw at once how useful this feminine Hercules could be, a strongly-made woman who stood planted as firmly on her feet as an oak tree rooted in the soil where it has grown for two generations, a woman with square shoulders, large hips, and hands like a ploughman's, and whose honesty was as unquestionable as her virtue. He was not dismayed by a martial countenance, a disfiguring wart or two, a complexion like burnt clay, and a pair of sinewy arms; neither did Nanon's rags alarm the cooper, whose heart was not yet hardened against misery. He took the poor girl into his service, gave her food, clothes, shoes, and wages. Nanon found her hard life not intolerably hard. Nay, she secretly shed tears of joy at being so treated; she felt a sincere attachment for this master, who expected as much from her as ever feudal lord required of a serf.

Nanon did all the work of the house. She did the cooking and the washing, carrying all the linen down to the Loire and bringing it back on her shoulders. She rose at daybreak and went to bed late. It was she who, without any assistance, cooked for the vintagers in the autumn, and looked sharply after the market-folk. She watched over her master's property like a faithful dog, and with a blind belief in him; she obeyed his most arbitrary commands without a murmur—his whims were law to her.

After twenty years of service, in the famous year 1811, when the vintage had been gathered in after unheard-of toil and trouble, Grandet made up his mind to present Nanon with his old watch, the only gift she had ever received from him. She certainly had the reversion of his old shoes (which happened to fit her), but as a rule they were so far seen into already that they were of little use to any one else, and could not be looked upon as a present. Sheer necessity had made the poor girl so penurious that Grandet grew quite fond of her at last, and regarded her with the same sort of affection that a man gives to his dog; and as for Nanon, she cheerfully wore the collar of servitude set round with spikes that she had ceased to feel. Grandet might stint the day's allowance of bread, but she did not grumble. The fare might be scanty and poor, but Nanon's spirits did not suffer, and her health appeared to benefit; there was never any illness in that house.

And then Nanon was one of the family. She shared every mood of Grandet's, laughed when he laughed, was depressed when he was out of spirits, took her views of the weather or of the temperature from him, and worked with him and for him. This equality was an element of sweetness which made up for many hardships in her lot. Out in the vineyards her master had never said a word about the small peaches, plums, or nectarines eaten under the trees that are planted between the rows of vines.

"Come, Nanon, take as much as you like," he would say, in years when the branches were bending beneath their load, and fruit was so abundant that the farmers round about were forced to give it to the pigs.

For the peasant girl, for the outdoor farm servant, who had known nothing but harsh treatment from childhood, for the girl who had been rescued from starvation by charity, old Grandet's equivocal laughter was like a ray of sunshine. Besides, Nanon's simple nature and limited intelligence could only entertain one idea at a time ; and during those thirty-five years of service one picture was constantly present to her mind—she saw herself a barefooted girl in rags standing at the gate of M. Grandet's timber-yard, and heard the sound of the cooper's voice, saying, "What is it, lassie?" and the warmth of gratitude filled her heart to-day as it did then. Sometimes, as he watched her, the thought came up in Grandet's mind how that no syllable of praise or admiration had ever been breathed in her ears, that all the tender feelings that a woman inspires had no existence for her, and that she might well appear before God one day as chaste as the Virgin Mary herself. And such times, prompted by a sudden impulse of pity, he would exclaim, "Poor Nanon!"

The remark was always followed by an indescribable look from the old servant. The words so spoken from time to time were separate links in a long and unbroken chain of friendship. But in this pity in the miser's soul, which gave a thrill of pleasure to the lonely woman, there was something indescribably revolting ; it was a cold-blooded pity that stirred the cooper's heart ; it was a luxury that cost him nothing. But for Nanon it meant the height of happiness ! Who will not likewise say, "Poor Nanon!" God will one day know His angels by the tones of their voices and by the sorrow hidden in their hearts.

There were plenty of households in Saumur where servants were better treated, but where their employers, nevertheless, enjoyed small comfort in return. Wherefore people asked, "What have the Grandets done to that big Nanon of theirs that she should be so attached to them? She would go through fire and water to serve them!"

Her kitchen, with its barred windows that looked out into the yard, was always clean, cold and tidy, a thorough miser's kitchen, in which nothing was allowed to be wasted. When Nanon had washed her plates and dishes, put the remains of the dinner into the safe, and raked out the fire, she left her kitchen (which was only separated from the dining-room by the breadth of a passage), and sat down to spin hemp in the company of her employers, for a single candle must suffice for the whole family in the evening. The serving-maid slept in a little dark closet at the end of the passage, lit only by a borrowed light. Nanon had an iron constitution and sound health, which enabled her to sleep with impunity year after year in this hole, where she could hear the slightest sound that broke the heavy silence brooding day and night over the house; she lay like a watch-dog, with one ear open; she was never off duty, not even while she slept.

Some description of the rest of the house will be necessary in the course of the story in connection with later events; but the parlor, wherein all the splendor and luxury of the house was concentrated, has been sketched already, and the emptiness and bareness of the upper rooms can be surmised for the present.

It was in the middle of November, in the year 1819, twilight was coming on, and big Nanon was lighting a fire in the parlor for the first time. It was a festival day in the calendar of the Cruchotins and Grassinistes, wherefore the six antagonists were preparing to set forth, all armed cap-à-pie, for a contest in which each side meant to outdo the other in proofs of friendship. The Grandet's parlor was to be the scene of action. That morning Mme. and Mlle. Grandet, duly attended by Nanon, had repaired to the parish church to hear mass. All Saumur had seen them go, and every one had been put in mind of the fact that it was Eugénie's birthday. M. Cruchot, the Abbé Cruchot, and M. C. de Bonfons, therefore, having calculated the hour when dinner would be over, were eager to be first in the field, and to arrive before the Grassinistes to congratulate Mlle. Grandet. All three carried huge bunches of flowers gathered in their little garden plots, but the stalks of the magistrate's bouquet were ingeniously bound round by a white satin ribbon with a tinsel fringe at the ends.

In the morning M. Grandet had gone to Eugénie's room before she had left her bed, and had solemnly presented her with a rare gold coin. It was her father's wont to surprise her in this way twice every year—once on her birthday, once on the equally memorable day of her patron saint. Mme. Grandet usually gave her daughter a winter or a summer dress, according to circumstances. The two dresses and two gold coins, which she received on her father's birthday and on New Year's Day, altogether amounted to an annual income of nearly a hundred crowns; Grandet loved to watch the money accumulating in her hands. He did not part with his money; he felt that it was only like taking it out of one box and putting it into another; and besides, was it not, so to speak, fostering a proper regard for gold in his heiress? She was being trained in the way in which she should go. Now and then he asked for an account of her wealth (formerly swelled by gifts from the La Bertellières), and each time he did so he used to tell her, "This will be your dozen when you are married."

The *dozen* is an old-world custom which has lost none of its force, and is still religiously adhered to in several midland districts in France. In Berri or Anjou, when a daughter is married, it is incumbent upon her parents, or upon her bridegroom's family, to give her a purse containing either a dozen, or twelve dozen, or twelve hundred gold or silver coins, the amount varying with the means of the family. The poorest herd-girl would not be content without her *dozen* when she married, even if she could only bring twelve pence as a dower. They talk even yet at Issoudun of a fabulous dozen once given to a rich heiress, which consisted of a hundred and forty-four Portuguese moidores; and when Catherine de Medicis was married to Henry II., her uncle, Clement VII., gave the bride a dozen antique gold medals of priceless value.

Eugénie wore her new dress at dinner, and looked prettier than usual in it; her father was in high good-humor.

"Let us have a fire," he cried, "as it is Eugénie's birthday! It will be a good omen."

"Mademoiselle will be married within the year, that's certain," said big Nanon, as she removed the remains of a goose, that pheasant of the coopers of Saumur.

"There is no one that I know of in Saumur who would do for Eugénie," said Mme. Grandet, with a timid glance at her husband, a glance that revealed how completely her husband's tyranny had broken the poor woman's spirit.

Grandet looked at his daughter, and said merrily, "We must really begin to think about her; the little girl is twenty-three years old to-day."

Neither Eugénie nor her mother said a word, but they exchanged glances; they understood each other.

Mme. Grandet's face was thin and wrinkled and yellow as saffron; she was awkward and slow in her movements, one of those beings who seem born to be tyrannized over. She was a large-boned woman, with a large nose, large eyes, and a prominent forehead; there seemed to be, at first sight, some dim suggestion of a resemblance between her and some shriveled, spongy, dried-up fruit. The few teeth that remained to her were dark and discolored; there were deep lines fretted about her mouth, and her chin was something after the "nutcracker" pattern. She was a good sort of a woman, and a La Bertellière to the backbone. The Abbé Cruchot had more than once found occasion to tell her that she had not been so bad looking when she was young, and she did not disagree with him. An angelic sweetness of disposition, the helpless meekness of an insect in the hands of cruel children, a sincere piety, a kindly heart, and an even temper that nothing could ruffle or sour, had gained universal respect and pity for her.

Her appearance might provoke a smile, but she had brought her husband more than three hundred thousand francs, partly as her dowry, partly through bequests. Yet Grandet never gave his wife more than six francs at a time for pocket-money, and she always regarded herself as dependent upon her husband. The meek gentleness of her nature forbade any revolt against his tyranny; but so deeply did she feel the humiliation of her position that she never asked him for a sou, and when M. Cruchot demanded her signature to any document, she always gave it without a word. This foolish sensitive pride, which Grandet constantly and unwittingly hurt, this magnanimity which he was quite incapable of understanding, were Mme. Grandet's dominant characteristics.

Her dress never varied. Her gown was always of the same dull, greenish shade of laventine, and usually lasted her nearly a twelvemonth; the large handkerchief at her throat was of some kind of cotton material; she wore a straw bonnet, and was seldom seen without a black silk apron. She left the house so rarely that her walking shoes were seldom worn out; indeed, her requirements were very few, she never wanted anything for herself. Sometimes it would occur to Grandet that it was a long while since he had given the last six francs to his wife, and his conscience would prick him a little; and after the vintage, when he sold his wine, he always demanded pin-money for his wife over and above the bargain. These four or five louis out of the pockets of the Dutch or Belgian merchants were Mme. Grandet's only certain source of yearly income. But although she received her five louis, her husband would often say to her, as if they had one common purse,

"Have you a few sous that you can lend me?" and she, poor woman, glad that it was in her power to do anything for the man whom her confessor always taught her to regard as her lord and master, used to return to him more than one crown out of her little store in the course of the winter. Every month, when Grandet disbursed the five-franc piece which he allowed his daughter for needles, thread, and small expenses of dress, he remarked to his wife (after he had buttoned up his pocket), "And how about you, mother; do you want anything?" And with a mother's dignity Mme. Grandet would answer, "We will talk about that by-and-by, dear."

Her magnanimity was entirely lost upon Grandet; he considered that he did very handsomely by his wife. The philosophic mind, contemplating the Nanons, the Mme. Grandets, the Eugénies of this life, holds that the Author of the universe is a profound satirist, and who will quarrel with the conclusion of the philosophic mind? After the dinner, when the question of Eugénie's marriage had been raised for the first time, Nanon went up to M. Grandet's room to fetch a bottle of black-currant cordial, and very nearly lost her footing on the staircase as she came down.

"Great stupid! Are *you* going to take to tumbling about?" inquired her master.

"It is all along of the step, sir; it gave way. The staircase isn't safe."

"She is quite right," said Mme. Grandet. "You ought to have had it mended long ago. Eugénie all but sprained her foot on it yesterday."

"Here," said Grandet, who saw that Nanon looked very pale, "as to-day is Eugénie's birthday, and you have nearly fallen downstairs, take a drop of black-currant cordial; that will put you right again."

"I deserve it, too, upon my word," said Nanon. "Many a one would have broken the bottle in my place; I should have broken my elbow first, holding it up to save it."

"Poor Nanon!" muttered Grandet, pouring out the black-currant cordial for her.

"Did you hurt yourself?" asked Eugénie, looking at her in concern.

"No, I managed to break the fall; I came down on my side."

"Well," said Grandet, "as to-day is Eugénie's birthday, I will mend your step for you. Somehow, you women-folk cannot manage to put your foot down in the corner, where it is still solid and safe."

Grandet took up the candle, left the three women without any other illumination in the room than the bright dancing firelight, and went to the bakehouse, where tools, nails, and odd pieces of wood were kept.

"Do you want any help?" Nanon called to him, when the first blow sounded on the staircase.

"No! no! I am an old hand at it," answered the cooper.

At this very moment, while Grandet was doing the repairs himself to his worm-eaten staircase, and whistling with all his might as memories of his young days came up in his mind, the three Cruchots knocked at the house-door.

"Oh, it's you, is it, M. Cruchot?" asked Nanon, as she took a look through the small square grating.

"Yes," answered the magistrate.

Nanon opened the door, and the glow of the firelight shone on the three Cruchots, who were groping in the archway.

"Oh! you have come to help us keep her birthday," Nanon said, as the scent of flowers reached her.

"Excuse me a moment, gentlemen," cried Grandet, who recognized the voices of his acquaintances; "I am your very humble servant! There is no pride about me; I am patching up a broken stair here myself."

"Go on, go on, M. Grandet! The charcoal burner is mayor in his own house," said the magistrate sententiously.

Nobody saw the allusion, and he had his laugh all to himself. Mme. and Mlle. Grandet rose to greet them. The magistrate took advantage of the darkness to speak to Eugénie.

"Will you permit me, mademoiselle, on the anniversary of your birthday, to wish you a long succession of prosperous years, and may you for long preserve the health with which you are blessed at present."

He then offered her such a bouquet of flowers as was seldom seen in Saumur; and, taking the heiress by both arms, gave her a kiss on either side of the throat, a fervent salute which brought the color into Eugénie's face. The magistrate was tall and thin, somewhat resembling a rusty nail; this was his notion of paying court.

"Do not disturb yourselves," said Grandet, coming back into the room. "Fine doings these of yours, M. le Président, on high days and holidays!"

"With mademoiselle beside him every day would be a holiday for my nephew," answered the Abbé Cruchot, also armed with a bouquet; and with that the Abbé kissed Eugénie's hand. As for M. Cruchot, he kissed her unceremoniously on both cheeks, saying, "This sort of thing makes us feel older, eh? A whole year older every twelve months."

Grandet set down the candle in front of the brass clock on the chimney-piece; whenever a joke amused him he kept on repeating it till it was worn threadbare; he did so now.

"As to-day is Eugénie's birthday," he said, "let us have an illumination."

He carefully removed the branches from the two sconces, fitted the sockets into either pedestal, took from Nanon's hands a whole new candle wrapped in a scrap of paper, fixed it firmly in the socket, and lighted it. Then he went over to his wife and took up his position beside her, looking by turns at his daughter, his friends, and the two lighted candles.

The Abbé Cruchot was a fat, dumpy little man with a well-worn sandy peruke. His peculiar type of face might have belonged to some old lady whose life is spent at the card-table. At this moment he was stretching out his feet and displaying a very neat and strong pair of shoes with silver buckles on them.

"The des Grassins have not come round?" he asked.

"Not yet," answered Grandet.

"Are they sure to come?" put in the old notary, with various contortions of a countenance as full of holes as a colander.

"Oh! yes, I think they will come," said Mme. Grandet.

"Is the vintage over?" asked President de Bonfons, addressing Grandet; "are all your grapes gathered?"

"Yes, everywhere!" answered the old vine-grower, rising and walking up and down the length of the room; he straightened himself up as he spoke with a conscious pride that appeared in that word "everywhere."

As he passed by the door that opened into the passage, Grandet caught a glimpse of the kitchen; the fire was still alight, a candle was burning there, and big Nanon was about to begin her spinning by the hearth; she did not wish to intrude upon the birthday party.

"Nanon!" he called, stepping out into the passage. "Nanon! why ever don't you rake out the fire; put out the candle and come in here! *Pardieu!* the room is large enough to hold us all."

"But you are expecting grand visitors, sir."

"Have you any objection to them? They are all descended from Adam just as much as you are."

Grandet went back to the president.

"Have you sold your wine?" he inquired.

"Not I; I am holding it. If the wine is good now, it will be better still in two years' time. The growers, as you know, of course, are in a ring, and mean to keep prices up. The Belgians shall not have it all their own way this year. And if they go away, well and good, let them go; they will come back again."

"Yes; but we must hold firm," said Grandet in a tone that made the magistrate shudder.

"Suppose he should sell his wine behind our backs?" he thought.

At that moment another knock at the door announced the des Grassins, and interrupted a quiet talk between Mme. Grandet and the Abbé Cruchot.

Mme. des Grassins was a dumpy, lively, little person with a pink-and-white complexion, one of those women for whom the course of life in a country town has flowed on with almost claustral tranquillity, and who, thanks to this regular and virtuous existence, are still youthful at the age of forty. They are something like the late roses in autumn, which are fair and pleasant to the sight, but the almost scentless petals have a pinched look, there is a vague suggestion of coming winter about them. She dressed tolerably well, her gowns came from Paris, she was a leader of society in Saumur, and received on certain evenings. Her husband had been a quartermaster in the Imperial Guard, but he had retired from the army with a pension, after being badly wounded at Austerlitz. In spite of his consideration for Grandet, he still retained, or affected to retain, the bluff manners of a soldier.

"Good-day, Grandet," he said, holding out his hand to the cooper with that wonted air of superiority with which he eclipsed the Cruchot faction. "Mademoiselle," he added, addressing Eugénie, after a bow to Mme. Grandet, "you are always charming, ever good and fair, and what more can one wish you?"

With that he presented her with a small box, which a servant was carrying, and which contained a Cape heath, a plant only recently introduced into Europe, and very rare.

Mme. des Grassins embraced Eugénie very affectionately, squeezed her hand, and said, "I have commissioned Adolphe to give you my little birthday gift."

A tall, fair-haired young man, somewhat pallid and weakly

in appearance, came forward at this; his manners were passably good, although he seemed to be shy. He had just completed his law studies in Paris, where he had managed to spend eight or ten thousand francs over and above his allowance. He now kissed Eugénie on both cheeks, and laid a workbox with gilded silver fittings before her; it was a showy, trumpery thing enough, in spite of the little shield on the lid, on which an E. G. had been engraved in Gothic characters, a detail which gave an imposing air to the whole. Eugénie raised the lid with a little thrill of pleasure, the happiness was as complete as it was unlooked for—the happiness that brings bright color into a young girl's face and makes her tremble with delight. Her eyes turned to her father as if to ask whether she might accept the gift; M. Grandet answered the mute inquiry with a "Take it, my daughter!" in tones which would have made the reputation of an actor. The three Cruchots stood dumfounded when they saw the bright, delighted glance that Adolphe des Grassins received from the heiress, who seemed to be dazzled by such undreamed-of splendors.

M. des Grassins offered his snuff-box to Grandet, took a pinch himself, brushed off a few stray specks from his blue coat and from the ribbon of the Legion of Honor at his button-hole, and looked at the Cruchots, as though to say, "Parry that thrust if you can!" Mme. des Grassins' eyes fell on the blue glass jars in which the Cruchots' bouquets had been set. She looked at their gifts with the innocent air of pretended interest which a satirical woman knows how to assume upon occasion. It was a delicate crisis. The Abbé got up and left the others, who were forming a circle round the fire, and joined Grandet in his promenade up and down the room. When the two elders had reached the embrasure of the window at the farther end, away from the group by the fire, the priest said in the miser's ear, "Those people yonder are throwing their money out of the windows."

"What does that matter to me, so long as it comes my way?" the old vine-grower answered.

"If you had a mind to give your daughter golden scissors, you could very well afford it," said the Abbé.

"I shall give her something better than scissors," Grandet answered.

"What an idiot my nephew is!" thought the Abbé, as he looked at the magistrate, whose dark, ill-favored countenance was set off to perfection at that moment by a shock head of hair. "Why couldn't *he* have hit on some expensive piece of foolery?"

"We will take a hand at cards, Mme. Grandet," said Mme. des Grassins.

"But as we are all here, there are enough of us for two tables——"

"As to-day is Eugénie's birthday, why not all play together at loto?" said old Grandet; "these two children could join in the game."

The old cooper, who never played at any game whatever, pointed to his daughter and Adolphe.

"Here, Nanon, move the tables out."

"We will help you, Mademoiselle Nanon," said Mme. des Grassins cheerfully; she was thoroughly pleased, because she had pleased Eugénie.

"I have never seen anything so pretty anywhere," the heiress had said to her. "I have never been so happy in my life before."

"It was Adolphe who chose it," said Mme. des Grassins in the girl's ear; "he brought it from Paris."

"Go your ways, accursed scheming woman," muttered the magistrate to himself. "If you or your husband ever find yourselves in a court of law, you shall be hard put to it to gain the day."

The notary, calmly seated in his corner, watched the Abbé, and said to himself, "The des Grassins may do what they like;

my fortune and my brother's and my nephew's fortunes altogether mount up to eleven hundred thousand francs. The des Grassins, at the very utmost, have only half as much, and they have a daughter. Let them give whatever they like, all will be ours some day—the heiress and her presents too."

Two tables were in readiness by half-past eight o'clock. Mme. de Grassins, with her winning ways, had succeeded in placing her son next to Eugénie. The actors in the scene, so commonplace in appearance, so full of interest beneath the surface, each provided with slips of pasteboard of various colors and blue glass counters, seemed to be listening to the little jokes made by the old notary, who never drew a number without making some remark upon it, but they were all thinking of M. Grandet's millions. The old cooper himself eyed the group with a certain self-complacency; he looked at Mme. des Grassins with her pink feathers and her fresh toilet, at the banker's soldierly face, at Adolphe, at the magistrate, at the Abbé and the notary, and within himself he said: "They are all after my crowns; that is what they are here for. It is for my daughter that they come to be bored here. Aha! and my daughter is for none of them, and all these people are so many harpoons to be used in my fishing."

The merriment of this family party, the laughter, only sincere when it came from Eugénie or her mother, and to which the low whirring of Nanon's spinning-wheel made an accompaniment, the sordid meanness playing for high stakes, the young girl herself, like some rare bird, the innocent victim of its high value, tracked down and snared by specious pretenses of friendship; taken altogether, it was a sorry comedy that was being played in the old gray-painted parlor, by the dim light of the two candles. Was it not, however, a drama of all time, played out everywhere all over the world, but here reduced to its simplest expression? Old Grandet towered above the other actors, turning all this sham affection to his own account, and reaping a rich harvest from this simulated friendship. His face hovered above the scene like the interpretation of an evil dream. He was like the incarnation of the one god who yet finds worshipers in modern times, of money and the power of wealth.

With him the gentler and sweeter impulses of human life only occupied the second place; but they so filled three purer hearts there that there was no room in them for other thoughts—the hearts of Nanon, and of Eugénie and her mother. And yet, how much ignorance mingled with their innocent simplicity! Eugénie and her mother knew nothing of Grandet's wealth; they saw everything through a medium of dim ideas, peculiar to their own narrow world, and neither desired nor despised money, accustomed as they were to do without it. Nor were they conscious of an uncongenial atmosphere; the strength of their feelings, their inner life, made of them a strange exception in this gathering, wholly intent upon material interests. Appalling is the condition of man; there is no drop of happiness in his lot but has its source in ignorance.

Just as Mme. Grandet had won sixteen sous, the largest amount that had ever been punted beneath that roof, and big Nanon was beaming with delight at the sight of Madame pocketing that splendid sum, there was a knock at the house-door, so sudden and so loud that it startled the women for the moment.

"No one in Saumur would knock in that way!" said the notary.

"What do they thump like that for?" said Nanon. "Do they want to break our door down?"

"Who the devil is it?" cried Grandet.

Nanon took up one of the two candles and went to open the door. Grandet followed her.

"Grandet! Grandet!" cried his wife; a vague terror seized her, and she hurried to the door of the room.

The players all looked at each other.

"Suppose we go too?" said M. des Grassins. "That knock means no good, it seemed to me."

But M. des Grassins scarcely caught a glimpse of a young man's face and of a porter who was carrying two huge trunks and an assortment of carpet bags, before Grandet turned sharply on his wife and said—

"Go back to your loto, Mme. Grandet, and leave me to settle with this gentleman here."

With that he slammed the parlor door, and the loto players sat down again, but they were too much excited to go on with the game.

"Is it any one who lives in Saumur, M. des Grassins?" his wife inquired.

"No, a traveler."

"Then he must have come from Paris."

"As a matter of fact," said the notary, drawing out a heavy antique watch, a couple of fingers' breadth in thickness, and not unlike a Dutch punt in shape, " as a matter of fact, it is nine o'clock. *Peste !* the mail-coach is not often behind time."

"Is he young looking?" put in the Abbé Cruchot.

"Yes," answered M. des Grassins. " The luggage he has with him must weigh three hundred kilos at least."

"Nanon does not come back," said Eugénie.

"It must be some relation of yours," the president remarked.

"Let us put down our stakes," said Mme. Grandet gently. "M. Grandet was vexed, I could tell that by the sound of his voice, and perhaps he would be displeased if he came in and found us all discussing his affairs."

"Mademoiselle," Adolphe addressed his neighbor, "it will be your cousin Grandet no doubt, a very nice-looking young fellow whom I once met at a ball at M. de Nucingen's."

Adolphe went no further, his mother stamped on his foot

under the table. Aloud, she asked him for two sous for his stake, adding in an undertone, meant only for his ears, "Will you hold your tongue, you great silly!"

They could hear the footsteps of Nanon and the porter on the staircase, but Grandet returned to the room almost immediately, and just behind him came the traveler who had excited so much curiosity, and loomed so large in the imaginations of those assembled; indeed, his sudden descent into their midst might be compared to the arrival of a snail in a beehive, or the entrance of a peacock into some humdrum village poultry-yard.

"Take a seat near the fire," said Grandet, addressing the stranger.

The young man looked round the room and bowed very gracefully before seating himself. The men rose and bowed politely in return, the women courtesied rather ceremoniously.

"You are feeling cold, I expect, sir," said Mme. Grandet; "you have no doubt come from——"

"Just like the women!" broke in the good man, looking up from the letter which he held in his hand. "Do let the gentleman have a little peace."

"But, father, perhaps the gentleman wants something after his journey," said Eugénie.

"He has a tongue in his head," the vine-grower answered severely.

The stranger alone felt any surprise at this scene, the rest were quite used to the worthy man and his arbitrary behavior. But after the two inquiries had received the summary answers, the stranger rose and stood with his back to the fire, held out a foot to the blaze, so as to warm the soles of his boots, and said to Eugénie, "Thank you, cousin, I dined at Tours. And I do not require anything," he added, glancing at Grandet; "I am not in the least tired."

"Do you come from Paris?" (it was Mme. des Grassins who now put the inquiry).

M. Charles (for this was the name borne by the son of M. Grandet of Paris), hearing some one question him, took out an eyeglass that hung suspended from his neck by a cord, fixed it in his eye, made a deliberate survey of the objects upon the table and of the people sitting round it, eyed Mme. des Grassins very coolly, and said (when he had completed his survey), "Yes, madame. You are playing at loto, aunt," he added; "pray go on with your game, it is too amusing to be broken off——"

"I knew it was the cousin," thought Mme. des Grassins, and she gave him a side glance from time to time.

"Forty-seven," cried the old Abbé. "Keep count. Mme. des Grassins, that is your number, is it not?"

M. des Grassins put down a counter on his wife's card; the lady herself was not thinking of loto, her mind was full of melancholy forebodings, she was watching Eugénie and the cousin from Paris. She saw how the heiress now and then stole a glance at her cousin, and the banker's wife could easily discover in those glances a *crescendo* of amazement or of curiosity.

There was certainly a strange contrast between M. Charles Grandet, a handsome young man of two-and-twenty, and the worthy provincials, who, tolerably disgusted already with his aristocratic airs, were scornfully studying the stranger with a view to making game of him. This requires some explanation.

At two-and-twenty childhood is not so very far away, and youth, on the borderland, has not finally and forever put away childish things; Charles Grandet's vanity was childish, but perhaps ninety-nine young men out of a hundred would have been carried away by it and behaved exactly as he did.

Some days previously his father had bidden him to go on a visit of several months to his uncle in Saumur; perhaps M. Grandet (of Paris) had Eugénie in his mind. Charles, launched in this way into a country town for the first time in his life, had his own ideas. He would make his appearance in provincial society with all the superiority of a young man of fashion ; he would reduce the neighborhood to despair by his splendor; he would inaugurate a new epoch, and introduce all the latest and most ingenious refinement of Parisian luxury. To be brief, he meant to devote more time at Saumur than in Paris to the care of his nails, and to carry out schemes of elaborate and studied refinements in dress at his leisure ; there should be none of the not ungraceful negligence of attire which a young man of fashion sometimes affects.

So Charles took with him into the country the most charming of shooting costumes, the sweetest thing in hunting-knives and sheaths, and a perfect beauty of a rifle. He packed up a most tasteful collection of waistcoats: gray, white, black, beetle-green shot with gold, speckled and spangled; double waistcoats, waistcoats with rolled collars, stand-up collars, turned-down collars, open at the throat, buttoned up to the chin with a row of gold buttons. He took samples of all the ties and cravats in favor at that epoch. He took two of Buisson's coats. He took his finest linen, and the dressing-case with gold fittings that his mother had given him. He took all his dandy's paraphernalia, not forgetting an enchanting little writing-case, the gift of the most amiable of women (for him at least), a great lady whom he called Annette, and who at that moment was traveling with her husband in Scotland, a victim to suspicions which demanded the temporary sacrifice of her happiness.

In short, his cargo of Parisian frivolities was as complete as it was possible to make it ; nothing had been omitted, from the horsewhip, useful as a preliminary, to the pair of richly-chased and mounted pistols that terminate a duel. There was all the ploughing gear required by a young idler in the field of life.

His father had told him to travel alone and modestly, and he had obeyed. He had come in the coupé of the diligence, which he secured all to himself; and was not ill-satisfied to save wear, in this way, to a smart and comfortable traveling carriage which he had ordered, and in which he meant to go to meet his Annette, the aforesaid great lady who——etc., and whom he was to rejoin next June at Baden-Baden.

Charles expected to meet scores of people during his visit to his uncle; he expected to have some shooting on his uncle's land; he expected, in short, to find a large house on a large estate; he had not thought to find his relatives in Saumur at all; he had only found out that they lived there by asking the way to Froidfond, and even after this discovery he expected to see them in a large mansion. But whether his uncle lived in Saumur or at Froidfond, he was determined to make his first appearance properly, so he had assumed a most fascinating traveling costume, made with the simplicity that is the perfection of art, a most *adorable* creation, to use the word which in those days expressed superlative praise of the special qualities of a thing or of a man. At Tours he had summoned a hairdresser, and his handsome chestnut hair was curled afresh. He had changed his linen and put on a black satin cravat, which, in combination with a round collar, made a very becoming setting for a pale and satirical face. A long overcoat, fitting tightly at the waist, gave glimpses of a cashmere waistcoat with a rolled collar, and beneath this again a second waistcoat of some white material. His watch was carelessly thrust into a side pocket, and save in so far as a gold chain secured it to a button-hole, its continuance there appeared to be purely accidental. His gray trousers were buttoned at the sides, and the seams were adorned with designs embroidered in black silk. A pair of gray gloves had nothing to dread from contact with a gold-headed cane, which he managed to admiration. A discriminating taste was evinced throughout the costume, and shone conspicuous in the traveling cap. Only a Parisian, and a Parisian moreover from some remote and lofty sphere, could trick himself out in such attire, and bring all its absurd details into harmony by coxcombry carried to such a pitch that it ceased to be ridiculous; this young man carried it off, moreover, with a swaggering air befitting a dead shot, conscious of the possession of a handsome pair of pistols and the good graces of an Annette.

If, moreover, you wish to thoroughly understand the surprise with which the Saumurois and the young Parisian mutually regarded each other, you must behold, as did the former, the radiant vision of this elegant traveler shining in the gloomy old room, as well as the figures that composed the family picture that met the stranger's eyes. There sat the Cruchots; try to imagine them.

To begin with, all three took snuff, with utter disregard of personal cleanliness or of the black deposit with which their shirt frills were encrusted. Their limp silk handkerchiefs were twisted into a thick rope, and wound tightly about their necks. Their collars were crumpled and soiled, their linen was dingy; there was such a vast accumulation of underwear in their presses, that it was only necessary to wash twice in the year, and the linen acquired a bad color with lying by. Age and ugliness might have wrought together to produce a masterpiece in them. Their hard-featured, furrowed, and wrinkled faces were in keeping with their creased and threadbare clothing, and both they and their garments were worn, shrunken, twisted out of shape. Dwellers in country places are apt to grow more or less slovenly and careless of their appearance; they cease by degrees to dress for others; the career of a pair of gloves is indefinitely prolonged, there is a general want of freshness and a decided neglect of detail. The slovenliness of the Cruchots, therefore, was not conspicuous; they were in harmony with the rest of the company, for there was one point on which both Cruchotins and Grassinistes were agreed for the most part—they held the fashions in horror.

The Parisian assumed his eyeglass again in order to study the curious accessories of the room; his eyes traveled over the rafters in the ceiling, over the dingy panels covered with fly-spots in sufficient abundance to punctuate the whole of the "Encyclopédie méthodique" and the "Moniteur" besides. The loto players looked up at this and stared at him; if a giraffe had been in their midst they could hardly have gazed with more eager curiosity. Even M. des Grassins and his son, who had beheld a man of fashion before in the course of their lives, shared in the general amazement; perhaps they felt the indefinable influence of the general feeling about the stranger, perhaps they regarded him not unapprovingly. "You see how they dress in Paris," their satirical glances seemed to say to their neighbors.

One and all were at liberty to watch Charles at their leisure, without any fear of offending the master of the house, for by this time Grandet was deep in a long letter which he held in his hand. He had taken the only candle from the table beside him, without any regard for the convenience of his guests or for their pleasure.

It seemed to Eugénie, who had never in her life beheld such a paragon, that her cousin was some seraphic vision, some creature fallen from the skies. The perfume exhaled by those shining locks, so gracefully curled, was delightful to her. She would fain have passed her fingers over the delicate, smooth surface of those wonderful gloves. She envied Charles his little hands, his complexion, the youthful refinement of his features. In fact, the sight of her cousin gave her the same sensations of exquisite pleasure that might be aroused in a young man by the contemplation of the fanciful portraits of ladies in English "Keepsakes," portraits drawn by Westall and engraved by Finden, with a burin so skillful that you fear to breathe upon the vellum surface lest the celestial vision should disappear. And yet—how should the impression produced by a young exquisite upon an ignorant girl whose life was spent in darning stockings and mending her father's clothes, in the dirty wainscoted window embrasure whence, in an hour, she saw scarcely one passer-by in the silent street, how should her dim impressions be conveyed by such an image as this?

Charles drew from his pocket a handkerchief embroidered by the great lady who was traveling in Scotland. It was a dainty piece of work wrought by love, in hours that were lost to love; Eugénie gazed at her cousin, and wondered, was he really going to use it? Charles' manners, his way of adjusting his eyeglass, his superciliousness, his affectations, his manifest contempt for the little box which had but lately given so much pleasure to the wealthy heiress, and which in his eyes seemed to be a very absurd piece of rubbish; everything, in short, which had given offense to the Cruchots and the Grassinistes pleased Eugénie so much that she lay awake for long that night thinking about this phœnix of a cousin.

Meanwhile the numbers were drawn but languidly, and very soon the loto came to an end altogether. Big Nanon came into the room and said aloud, "Madame, you will have to give me some sheets to make the gentleman's bed."

Mme. Grandet disappeared with Nanon, and Mme. des Grassins said in a low voice, "Let us keep our sous, and give up the game."

Each player took back his coin from the chipped saucer which held the stakes. Then there was a general stir, and a wheeling movement in the direction of the fire.

"Is the game over?" inquired Grandet, still reading his letter.

"Yes, yes," answered Mme. des Grassins, seating herself next to Charles.

Eugénie left the room to help her mother and Nanon, moved by a thought that came with the vague feeling that stirred her heart for the first time. If she had been questioned by a skillful confessor, she would have no doubt admitted that her thought was neither for Nanon nor for her mother, but that she was seized with a restless and urgent desire to see that all was right in her cousin's room, to busy herself on her cousin's account, to see that nothing was forgotten, to think of everything he might require, and to make sure that it was there, to make certain that everything was as neat and pretty as might be. She alone, so Eugénie thought already, could enter into her cousin's ideas and understand his tastes.

As a matter of fact, she came just at the right moment. Her mother and Nanon were about to leave the room in the belief that it was all in readiness; Eugénie convinced them in a moment that everything was yet to do. She filled Nanon's head with these ideas: the sheets had not been aired, Nanon must bring the warming-pan, there were ashes, there was a fire downstairs. She herself covered the old table with a clean white cloth, and told Nanon to mind and be sure to change it every morning. There must be a good fire in the room; she overcame her mother's objections, she induced Nanon to put a good supply of firewood outside in the passage, and to say nothing about it to her father. She ran downstairs into the parlor, sought in one of the sideboards for an old japanned tray which had belonged to the late M. de la Bertellière, and from the same source she procured a hexagonal crystal glass, a little gilt spoon with almost all the gilding rubbed off, and an old slender-necked glass bottle with Cupids engraved upon it; these she deposited in triumph on a corner of the chimney-piece. More ideas had crowded up in her mind during that one quarter of an hour than in all the years since she had come into the world.

"Mamma," she began, "he will never be able to bear the smell of a tallow candle. Suppose that we buy a wax candle?"

She fled, lightly as a bird, to find her purse, and drew thence the five francs which she had received for the month's expenses.

"Here, Nanon, be quick."

"But what will your father say?"

This dreadful objection was raised by Mme. Grandet, when she saw her daughter with an old Sèvres china sugar-basin which Grandet had brought back with him from the château at Froidfond.

"And where is the sugar to come from?" she went on. "Are you mad?"

"Nanon can easily buy the sugar when she goes for the candle, mamma."

"But how about your father?"

"Is it a right thing that his nephew should not have a glass of *eau sucrée* to drink if he happens to want it? Besides, he will not notice it."

"Your father always notices things," said Mme. Grandet, shaking her head.

Nanon hesitated; she knew her master.

"Do go, Nanon; it is my birthday to-day, you know!"

Nanon burst out laughing in spite of herself at the first joke her young mistress had ever been known to make, and did her bidding.

While Eugénie and her mother were doing their best to adorn the room which M. Grandet had allotted to his nephew, Mme. des Grassins was bestowing her attention on Charles, and making abundant use of her eyes as she did so.

"You are very brave," she said, "to leave the pleasures of the capital in winter in order to come to stay in Saumur. But if you are not frightened away at first sight of us, you shall see that even here we can amuse ourselves." And she gave him a languishing glance, in true provincial style.

Women in the provinces are wont to affect a demure and staid demeanor, which gives a furtive and eager eloquence to their eyes, a peculiarity which may be noted in ecclesiastics, for whom every pleasure is stolen or forbidden. Charles was so thoroughly out of his element in this room, it was all so far removed from the great château and the splendid surroundings in which he had thought to find his uncle, that, on paying closer attention to Mme. des Grassins, she almost reminded him of Parisian faces half obliterated already by these strange, new impressions. He responded graciously to the advances which had been made to him, and naturally they fell into conversation.

Mme. des Grassins gradually lowered her voice to tones suited to the nature of her confidences. Both she and Charles Grandet felt a need of mutual confidence, of explanations and an understanding; so after a few minutes spent in coquettish chatter and jests that covered a serious purpose, the wily provincial dame felt free to converse without fear of being overheard, under cover of a conversation on the sale of the vintage, the one all-absorbing topic at that moment in Saumur.

"If you will honor us with a visit," she said, "you will certainly do us a pleasure; my husband and I shall be very glad to see you. Our salon is the only one in Saumur where you will meet both the wealthy merchant society and the noblesse. We ourselves belong in a manner to both; they do not mix with each other at all except at our house; they come to us because they find it amusing. My husband, I am proud to say, is very highly thought of in both circles. So we will do our best to beguile the tedium of your stay. If you are going to remain with the Grandets, what will become of you! *Bon Dieu!* Your uncle is a miser, his mind runs on nothing but his vine-cuttings; your aunt is a saint who cannot put two ideas together; and your cousin is a silly little thing, a common sort of girl, with no breeding and no money, who spends her life in mending dish-cloths."

"'Tis a very pretty woman," said Charles to himself; Mme. des Grassins' coquettish glances had not been thrown away upon him.

"It seems to me that you mean to monopolize the gentleman," said the big banker, laughing, to his wife, an unlucky observation, followed by remarks more or less spiteful from the notary and the president; but the Abbé gave them a shrewd glance, took a pinch of snuff, and handed his snuff-box to the company, while he gave expression to their thoughts, "Where could the gentleman have found any one better qualified to do the honors of Saumur?" he said.

"Come, Abbé, what do you mean by that?" asked M. des Grassins.

"It is meant, sir, in the most flattering sense for you, for madame, for the town of Saumur, and for this gentleman," added the shrewd ecclesiastic, turning towards Charles. Without appearing to pay the slightest heed to their talk, he had managed to guess the drift of it.

Adolphe des Grassins spoke at last, with what was meant to be an off-hand manner. "I do not know," he said, addressing Charles, "whether you have any recollection of me; I once had the pleasure of dancing in the same quadrille at a ball given by M. le Baron de Nucingen, and——"

"I remember it perfectly," answered Charles, surprised to find himself the object of general attention.

"Is this gentleman your son?" he asked of Mme. des Grassins.

The Abbé gave her a spiteful glance.

"Yes, I am his mother," she answered.

"You must have been very young when you came to Paris?" Charles went on, speaking to Adolphe.

"We cannot help ourselves, sir," said the Abbé. "Our babes are scarcely weaned before we send them to Babylon."

Mme. des Grassins gave the Abbé a strangely penetrating glance; she seemed to be seeking the meaning of those words.

"You must go into the country," the Abbé went on, "if you want to find women not much on the other side of thirty, with a grown-up son a licentiate of law, who look as fresh and youthful as Mme. des Grassins. It only seems like the other day when the young men and the ladies stood on chairs to see you dance, madame," the Abbé added, turning towards his fair antagonist; "your triumphs are as fresh in my memory as if they had happened yesterday."

"Oh! the old wretch!" said Mme. des Grassins to herself, "is it possible that he has guessed?"

"It looks as though I should have a great success in Saumur," thought Charles. He unbuttoned his overcoat and stood with his hands in his waistcoat pocket, gazing into space, striking the attitude which Chantrey thought fit to give to Byron in his statue of that poet.

Meanwhile Grandet's inattention, or rather his preoccupation, during the reading of his letter had escaped neither the notary nor the magistrate. Both of them tried to guess at the contents by watching the almost imperceptible changes in the worthy man's face, on which all the light of a candle was concentrated. The vine-grower was hard put to it to preserve his wonted composure. His expression must be left to the imagination, but here is the fatal letter:

"My Brother:—It is nearly twenty-three years now since we saw each other. The last time we met it was to make arrangements for my marriage, and we parted in high spirits. Little did I then think, when you were congratulating yourself on our prosperity, that one day you would be the sole hope and stay of our family. By the time that this letter reaches your hands, I shall be no more. In my position, I could not survive the disgrace of bankruptcy; I have held up my head above the surface till the last moment, hoping to weather the storm; it is all of no use, I must sink now. Just after the failure of my stockbroker came the failure of Roguin (my notary); my last resources have been swept away, and I have nothing left. It is my heavy misfortune to owe nearly four millions; my assets only amount to twenty-five per cent. of my debts. I hold heavy stocks of wine, and, owing to the abundance and good quality of your vintages, they have fallen ruinously in value. In three days' time all Paris will say, 'M. Grandet was a rogue!' and I, honest though I am, shall lie wrapped in a winding sheet of infamy. I have despoiled my own son of his mother's fortune and of the spotless name on which I have brought disgrace. He knows nothing of all this—the unhappy child whom I have idolized. Happily for him, he did not know when we bade each other good-bye, and my heart overflowed with tenderness for him, how soon it should cease to beat. Will he not curse me some day? Oh! my brother, my brother, a child's curse is an awful thing! If we curse our children, they may appeal against us, but their curses cling to us for ever! Grandet, you are my older brother, you must shield me from this; do not let Charles say bitter things of me when I am lying in my grave. Oh! my brother, if every word in this letter were written in my tears, in my blood, it would not cost me such bitter anguish, for then I should be weeping, bleeding, dying, and the agony would be ended; but now I am still suffering—I see the death before me with dry eyes. You therefore are Charles' father now! He has no relations on his mother's side for reasons which you know. Why did I not defer to social prejudices? Why did I yield to love? Why did I marry the natural daughter of a noble? Charles is the last of his family; he is alone in the world. Oh! my unhappy boy, my son!—— Listen, Grandet, I am asking nothing for myself, and you could scarcely satisfy my creditors if you would; your fortune cannot be sufficient to meet a demand of three millions; it is for my son's sake that I write. You must know, my brother, that as I think of you my petition is made with clasped hands; that this is my dying prayer to you. Grandet, I know that you will be a father to him; I know that I shall not ask in vain, and the sight of my pistols does not cause me a pang.

"And then Charles is very fond of me; I was kind to him, I never said him nay; he will not curse me! For the rest, you will see how sweet-tempered and obedient he is; he takes after his mother; he will never give you any trouble, poor boy! He is accustomed to luxurious ways; he knows nothing of the hardships that you and I experienced in the early days when we were poor—— And now he has not a penny, and he is alone in the world, for all his friends are sure to leave him, and it is I who have brought these humiliations upon him. Ah! if I had only the power to send him straight to heaven now, where his mother is! This is madness! To go back to my misfortunes and Charles' share in them. I have sent him to you so that you may break the news of my death and explain to him what his future must be. Be a father to him; ah! more than that, be an indulgent father! Do not expect him to give up his idle ways all at once; it would kill him. On my knees I beg him to renounce all claims to his mother's fortune; but I need not ask that of him, his sense of honor will prevent him from adding himself to the list of my creditors; see that he resigns his claims when the right time comes. And you must lay everything before him, Grandet—the struggle and the hardships that he will have to face in the life that I have spoiled for him; and then if he has any tenderness still left for me, tell him from me that all is not lost for him—be sure you tell him that. Work, which was our salvation, can restore the fortune which I have lost; and if he will listen to his father's voice, which would fain make itself heard yet a little while from the grave, let him leave this country and go to the Indies! And, brother, Charles is honest and energetic; you will help him with his first trading venture, I know you will; he would die sooner than not repay you; you will do as much as that for him, Grandet, or you will lay up regrets for yourself. Ah! if my boy finds no kindness and no help in you, I shall for ever pray God to punish your hard-heartedness. If I could have withheld a few payments, I might have saved a little sum for him—he surely has a right to some of his mother's fortune—but the payments at the end of the month taxed all my resources, and I could not manage it. I would fain have died with my mind at rest about his future; I wish I could have received your solemn promise, coming straight from your hand it would have brought warmth with it for me; but time presses. Even while Charles is on his way, I am compelled to file my schedule. My affairs are all in order; I am endeavoring so to arrange everything that it will be evident that my failure is due neither to carelessness nor to dishonesty, but simply to disasters which I could not help. Is it not for Charles' sake that I take these pains? Farewell, my brother. May God bless you in every way for the generosity with which you (as I cannot doubt) will accept and fulfill this trust. There will be one voice that will never cease to pray for you in the world whither we must all go sooner or later, and where I am even now.

VICTOR-ANGE-GUILLAUME GRANDET.

"So you are having a chat?" said old Grandet, folding up the letter carefully in the original creases, and putting it into his waistcoat pocket.

He looked at his nephew in a shy and embarrassed way, seeking to dissemble his feelings and his calculations.

"Do you feel warmer?"

"I am very comfortable, my dear uncle."

"Well, whatever are the women after?" his uncle went on; the fact that his nephew would sleep in the house had by that time slipped from his memory. Eugénie and Mme. Grandet came into the room as he spoke.

"Is everything ready upstairs?" the good man inquired. He had now quite recovered himself, and recollected the facts of the case.

"Yes, father."

"Very well then, nephew, if you are feeling tired, Nanon will show you to your room. Lord! there is nothing very smart about it, but you will overlook that here among poor vine-growers, who never have a penny to bless themselves with. The taxes swallow up everything we have."

"We don't want to be intrusive, Grandet," said the banker. "You and your nephew may have some things to talk over; we will wish you good-evening. Good-bye till to-morrow."

Every one rose at this, and took leave after their several fashions. The old notary went out under the archway to look for his lantern, lighted it, and offered to see the des Grassins to their house. Mme. des Grassins had not been prepared for the event which had brought the evening so early to a close, and her maid had not appeared.

"Will you honor me by taking my arm, madame?" said the Abbé Cruchot, addressing Mme. des Grassins.

"Thank you, M. l'Abbé," said the lady drily; "my son is with me."

"I am not a compromising acquaintance for a lady," the Abbé continued.

"Take M. Cruchot's arm," said her husband.

The Abbé, with the fair lady on his arm, walked on quickly for several paces, so as to put a distance between them and the rest of the party.

"That young man is very good-looking, madame," he said, with a pressure on her arm to give emphasis to the remark. "'Tis good-bye to the baskets, the vintage is over! You must give up Mlle. Grandet; Eugénie is meant for her cousin. Unless he happens to be smitten with some fair face in Paris, your son Adolphe will have yet another rival——"

"Nonsense, M. l'Abbé."

"It will not be long before the young man will find out that Eugénie is a girl who has nothing to say for herself; and she has gone off in looks. Did you notice her? She was as yellow as a quince this evening."

"Which, possibly, you have already pointed out to her cousin?"

"Indeed, I have not taken the trouble——"

"If you always sit beside Eugénie, madame," interrupted the Abbé, "you will not need to tell the young man much about his cousin; he can make his own comparisons."

"He promised me at once to come to dine with us the day after to-morrow."

"Ah! madame," said the Abbé, "if you would only——"

"Would only what, M. l'Abbé? Do you mean to put evil suggestions into my mind? I have not come to the age of thirty-nine with a spotless reputation (heaven be thanked) to compromise myself now—not for the empire of the Great Mogul! We are both of us old enough to know what that kind of talk means; and I must say that your ideas do not square very well with your sacred calling. For shame! this is worthy of 'Faublas.'"

"So you have read 'Faublas?'"

"No, M. l'Abbé; 'Les Liaisons dangereuses' is what I meant to say."

"Oh! that book is infinitely more moral," said the Abbé, laughing. "But you would make me out to be as depraved as young men are nowadays. I only meant that you——"

"Do you dare to tell me that you meant no harm? The thing is plain enough. If that young fellow (who certainly is good-looking, that I grant you) paid court to me, it would not be for the sake of my interest with that cousin of his. In Paris, I know, there are tender mothers who sacrifice themselves thus for their children's happiness and welfare, but we are not in Paris, M. l'Abbé."

"No, madame."

"And," continued she, "neither Adolphe nor I would purchase a hundred millions at such a price."

"Madame, I said nothing about a hundred millions. Perhaps such a temptation might have been too much for either of us. Still, in my opinion, an honest woman may indulge in a little harmless coquetry, in the strictest propriety; it is a part of her social duties, and——"

"Do you think so?"

"Do we not owe it to ourselves, madame, to endeavor to be as agreeable as possible to others?——Permit me to blow my nose. Take my word for it, madame," resumed the Abbé, "that he certainly regarded you with rather more admiration than he saw fit to bestow on me, but I can forgive him for honoring beauty rather than gray hairs——"

"It is perfectly clear," said the president in his thick voice, "why M. Grandet of Paris is sending his son to Saumur; he has made up his mind to make a match——"

"Then why should the cousin have dropped from the skies like this?" answered the notary.

"There is nothing in that," remarked M. des Grassins, "old Grandet is so close."

"Des Grassins," said his wife, "I have asked that young man to come and dine with us. So you must go to M. and Mme. de Larsonnière, dear, and ask them to come, and the du Hautoys; and they must bring that pretty girl of theirs, of course; I hope she will dress herself properly for once. Her mother is jealous of her, and makes her look such a figure. I hope that you gentlemen will do us the honor of coming too?" she added, stopping the procession in order to turn to the two Cruchots, who, seeing the Abbé in conversation with Mme. des Grassins, had fallen behind.

"Here we are at your door, madame," said the notary. The three Cruchots took leave of the three des Grassins, and on their way home the talent for pulling each other to pieces, which provincials possess in perfection, was fully called into play; the great event of the evening was exhaustively discussed, and all its bearings upon the respective positions of Cruchotins and Grassinistes were duly considered. Clearly it behooved both alike to prevent Eugénie from falling in love with her cousin, and to hinder Charles from thinking of Eugénie. Sly hints, plausible insinuations, faint praise, vindications undertaken with an air of candid friendliness—what resistance could the Parisian offer when the air hurtled with deceptive weapons such as these?

As soon as the four relatives were left alone in the great room, M. Grandet spoke to his nephew.

"We must go to bed. It is too late to begin to talk to-night of the business that brought you here; to-morrow will be time enough for that. We have breakfast here at eight o'clock. At noon we take a snatch of something, a little fruit, a morsel of bread, and a glass of white wine, and, like Parisians, we dine at five o'clock. That is the way of it. If you care to take a look at the town, or to go into the country round about, you are quite free to do so. You will excuse me if, for business reasons, I cannot always accompany you. Very likely you will be told hereabouts that I am rich; 'tis always M. Grandet here and M. Grandet there. I let them talk. Their babble does not injure my credit in any way. But I have not a penny to bless myself with; and, old as I am, I work like any young journeyman who has nothing in the world but his plane and a pair of stout arms. Perhaps you will find out for yourself some of these days what a lot of work it takes to earn a crown when you have to toil and moil for it yourself. Here, Nanon, bring the candles."

"I hope you will find everything you want, nephew," said Mme. Grandet; "but if anything has been forgotten, you will call Nanon."

"It would be difficult to want anything, my dear aunt, for I believe I have brought all my things with me. Permit me to wish you and my young cousin good-night."

Charles took a lighted wax-candle from Nanon; it was a commodity of local manufacture, which had grown old in the shop, very dingy, very yellow, and so like the ordinary tallow variety that M. Grandet had no suspicion of the article of luxury before him; indeed, it never entered into his head to imagine that there could be such a thing in the house.

"I will show you the way," said the good man.

One of the doors in the dining-room gave immediate access to the archway and to the staircase; but to-night, out of compliment to his guest, Grandet went by way of the passage which separated the kitchen from the dining-room. A folding-door, with a large oval pane of glass let into it, closed in the passage at the end nearest the staircase, an arrangement intended to keep out the blasts of cold air that rushed through the archway. With a like end in view, strips of list had been nailed to the doors; but in winter the east wind found its way in, and whistled none the less shrewdly about the house, and the dining-room was seldom even tolerably warm.

Nanon went out, drew the bolts on the entrance gate, fastened the door of the dining-room, went across to the stable to let loose a great wolf-dog with a cracked voice; it sounded as though the animal was suffering from laryngitis. His savage temper was well known, and Nanon was the only human being who could manage him. There was some wild strain in both these children of the fields; they understood each other.

Charles glanced round at the dingy yellow walls and smoke-begrimed ceiling, and saw how the crazy, worm-eaten stairs shook beneath his uncle's heavy tread; he was fast coming to his senses, this was sober reality indeed! The place looked like a hen-roost. He looked round questioningly at the faces of his aunt and cousin, but they were so thoroughly accustomed to the staircase and its peculiarities that it never occurred to them that it could cause any astonishment; they took his signal of distress for a simple expression of friendliness, and smiled back at him in the most amiable way. That smile was the last straw; the young man was at his wits' end.

"What the devil made my father send me here?" said he to himself.

Arrived on the first landing, he saw before him three doors

painted a dull red-brown color; there were no mouldings round any of them, so that they would have been scarcely visible in the dusty surface of the wall if it had not been for the very apparent heavy bars of iron with which they were embellished, and which terminated in a sort of rough ornamental design, as did the ends of the iron scutcheons which surrounded the keyholes. A door at the head of the stairs, which had once given entrance into the room over the kitchen, was evidently blocked up. As a matter of fact, the only entrance was through Grandet's own room, and this room over the kitchen was the vine-grower's sanctum.

Daylight was admitted into it by a single window which looked out upon the yard, and which, for greater security, was protected by a grating of massive iron bars. The master of the house allowed no one, not even Mme. Grandet, to set foot in this chamber; he kept the right of entry to himself, and sat there, undisturbed and alone, like an alchemist in the midst of his crucibles. Here, no doubt, there was some cunningly-contrived and secret hiding-place; for here he stored up the title-deeds of his estates; here, too, he kept the delicately-adjusted scales in which he weighed his gold louis; and here every night he made out receipts, wrote acknowledgments of sums received, and laid his schemes, so that other business men seeing Grandet never busy, and always prepared for every emergency, might have been excused for imagining that he had a fairy or familiar spirit at his beck and call. Here, no doubt, when Nanon's snoring shook the rafters, when the savage watch-dog bayed and prowled about the yard, when Mme. Grandet and Eugénie were fast asleep, the old cooper would come to be with his gold, and hug himself upon it, and toy with it, and fondle it, and brood over it, and so, with the intoxication of the gold upon him, at last to sleep. The walls were thick, the closed shutters kept their secret. He alone had the key of this laboratory, where, if reports spoke truly, he pored over plans on which every fruit tree belonging to him was mapped out, so that he could reckon out his crops, so much to every vine stem; and his yield of timber, to a faggot.

The door of Eugénie's room was opposite this closed-up portal, the room occupied by M. and Mme. Grandet was at the end of the landing, and consisted of the entire front of the house. It was divided within by a partition, Mme. Grandet's chamber was next to Eugénie's, with which it communicated by a glass door; the other half of the room, separated from the mysterious cabinet by a thick wall, belonged to the master of the house. Goodman Grandet had cunningly lodged his nephew on the second story, in an airy garret immediately above his own room, so that he could hear every sound and inform himself of the young man's goings and comings, if the latter should take it into his head to leave his quarters.

Eugénie and her mother, arrived on the first landing, kissed each other and said good-night; they took leave of Charles in a few formal words, spoken with an apparent indifference, which in her heart the girl was far from feeling, and went to their rooms.

"This is your room, nephew," said Grandet, addressing Charles as he opened the door. "If you should wish to go out, you will have to call Nanon; for if you don't it will be 'no more at present from your most obedient,' the dog will gobble you down before you know where you are. Goodnight, sleep well. Ha! ha! the ladies have lighted a fire in your room," he went on.

Just at that moment big Nanon appeared, armed with a warming-pan.

"Did any one ever see the like?" said M. Grandet. "Do you take my nephew for a sick woman; he is not an invalid. Just be off, Nanon! you and your hot ashes."

"But the sheets are damp, sir, and the gentleman looks as delicate as a woman."

"All right, go through with it, since you have taken it into your head," said Grandet, shrugging his shoulders, "but mind you don't set the place on fire," and the miser groped his way downstairs, muttering vaguely to himself.

Charles, breathless with astonishment, was left among his trunks. He looked round about him, at the sloping roof of the attic, at the wall-paper of a pattern peculiar to little country inns, bunches of flowers symmetrically arranged on a buff-colored background; he looked at the rough stone chimney-piece full of rifts and cracks (the mere sight of it sent a chill through him, in spite of the fire in the grate), at the ramshackle cane-seat chairs, at the open night-table large enough to hold a fair-sized sergeant-at-arms, at the strip of worn rag-carpet beside the canopied bedstead, at the curtains which shook every moment as if the whole worm-eaten structure would fall to pieces; finally, he turned his attention to big Nanon, and said earnestly—

"Look here, my good girl, am I really in M. Grandet's house? M. Grandet, formerly mayor of Saumur, and brother of M. Grandet of Paris?"

"Yes, sir, you are; and you are staying with a very kind, a very amiable and excellent gentleman. Am I to help you to unpack those trunks of yours?"

"Faith, yes, old soldier, I wish you would. Did you serve in the horse marines?"

"Oh! oh! oh!" chuckled Nanon. "What may they be? What are the horse marines? Are they old salts? Do they go to sea?"

"Here, look out my dressing-gown; it is in that portmanteau, and this is the key."

Nanon was overcome with astonishment at the sight of a green silk dressing-gown, embroidered with gold flowers after an antique pattern.

"Are you going to sleep in *that?*" she inquired.

"Yes."

"Holy Virgin! What a beautiful altar cloth it would make for the parish church! Oh, my dear young gentleman, you should give it to the church, and you will save your soul, which you are like to lose for that thing. Oh! how nice you look in it. I will go and call mademoiselle to look at you."

"Come now, Nanon, since that is your name, will you hold your tongue, and let me go to bed. I will set my things straight to-morrow, and as you have taken such a fancy to my gown, you shall have a chance to save your soul. I am too good a Christian to take it away with me when I go; you shall have it, and you can do whatever you like with it."

Nanon stood stockstill, staring at Charles; she could not bring herself to believe that he really meant what he said.

"You are going to give that grand dressing-gown to *me!*" she said, as she turned to go. "The gentleman is dreaming already. Good-night."

"Good-night, Nanon. What anyhow am I doing here?" said Charles to himself, as he dropped off to sleep. "My father is no fool; I have not been sent here for nothing. Pooh! 'Serious business to-morrow,' as some old Greek wiseacre used to say."

"*Sainte Vierge!* how nice he is!" said Eugénie to herself in the middle of her prayers, and that night they remained unfinished.

Mme. Grandet alone lay down to rest, with no thought in her quiet mind. Through the door in the thin partition she could hear her husband pacing to and fro in his room. Like all sensitive and timid women, she had thoroughly studied the character of her lord and master. Just as the sea-mew foresees the coming storm, she knew by almost imperceptible signs that a tempest was raging in Grandet's mind, and, to use her own expression, she "lay like one dead" at such seasons. Grandet's eyes turned towards his sanctum; he looked at the door, which was lined with sheet iron on the inner side (he himself had seen to that), and muttered, "What a preposterous notion this is of my brother's, to leave his child to me! A pretty legacy! I haven't twenty crowns to spare, and what would twenty crowns be to a popinjay like that, who looked at my weather-glass as if it wasn't fit to light the fire with?"

And Grandet, meditating on the probable outcome of this mournful dying request, was perhaps more perturbed in spirit than the brother who had made it.

"Shall I really have that golden gown?" Nanon said, and she fell asleep wrapped round in her altar cloth, dreaming for the first time in her life of shining embroideries and flowered brocade, just as Eugénie dreamed of love.

In a girl's innocent and uneventful life there comes a mysterious hour of joy when the sunlight spreads through the soul, and it seems to her that the flowers express the thoughts that rise within her, thoughts that are quickened by every heart-beat, only to blend in a vague feeling of longing, when the days are filled with innocent melancholy and delicious happiness. Children smile when they see the light for the first time, and when a girl dimly divines the presence of love in the world she smiles as she smiled in her babyhood. If light is the first thing that we learn to love, is not love like light in the heart? This moment had come for Eugénie; she saw the things of life clearly for the first time.

Early rising is the rule in the country, so, like most other girls, Eugénie was up betimes in the morning; this morning she rose earlier than usual, said her prayers, and began to dress; her toilet was henceforth to possess an interest unknown before. She began by brushing her chestnut hair, and wound the heavy plaits about her head, careful that no loose ends should escape from the braided coronet which made an appropriate setting for a face both frank and shy, a simple coiffure which harmonized with the girlish outlines.

As she washed her hands again and again in the cold spring

water that roughened and reddened the skin, she looked down at her pretty rounded arms and wondered what her cousin did to have hands so soft and so white, and nails so shapely. She put on a pair of new stockings, and her best shoes, and laced herself carefully, without passing over a single eyelet-hole. For the first time in her life, in fact, she wished to look her best, and felt that it was pleasant to have a pretty new dress to wear, a becoming dress which was nicely made.

The church clock struck just as she had finished dressing; she counted the strokes, and was surprised to find that it was still only seven o'clock. She had been so anxious to have plenty of time for her toilet that she had risen too early, and now there was nothing left to do. Eugénie, in her ignorance, never thought of studying the position of a tress of hair, and of altering it a dozen times to criticise its effect; she simply folded her arms, sat down by the window, and looked out upon the yard, the long strip of garden, and the terraced gardens up above upon the ramparts.

It was a somewhat dreary outlook thus shut in by the grim rock walls, but not without a charm of its own, the mysterious beauty of quiet overshaded gardens, or of wild and solitary places. Under the kitchen window there was a well with a stone coping round it; a pulley was suspended above the water from an iron bracket overgrown by a vine; the vine leaves were red and faded now that the autumn was nearly at an end, and the crooked stem was plainly visible as it wound its way to the house wall, and crept along the house till it came to an end by the wood-stack, where the faggots were arranged with as much neatness and precision as the volumes on some book-lover's shelves. The flagstones in the yard were dark with age and mosses, and dank with the stagnant air of the place; weeds grew here and there among the chinks. The massive outworks of the old fortifications were green with moss, with here and there a long dark brown streak where the water dripped, and the eight tumble-down steps, which gave access to the garden at the farther end of the yard, were almost hidden by a tall growth of plants; the general effect of the crumbling stones had a vague resemblance to some crusader's tomb erected by his widow in the days of yore and long since fallen into ruin.

Along the low mouldering stone-wall there was a fence of open lattice-work, rotten with age, and fast falling to pieces; overrun by various creeping plants that clambered over it at their own sweet will. A couple of stunted apple trees spread out their gnarled and twisted branches on either side of the wicket gate that led into the garden—three straight gravel walks with strips of border in between, and a line of box-edging on either side; and at the farther end, underneath the ramparts, a sort of arbor of lime trees, and a row of raspberry canes. A huge walnut tree grew at the end nearest to the house, and almost overshadowed the cooper's strong room with its spreading branches.

It was one of those soft bright autumn mornings peculiar to the districts along the Loire; there was not a trace of mist; the light frosty rime of the previous night was rapidly disappearing as the mild rays of the autumn sun shone on the picturesque surroundings, the old walls, the green tangled growth in the yard and garden.

All these things had been long familiar to Eugénie's eyes, but to-day it seemed to her that there was a new beauty about them. A throng of confused thoughts filled her mind as the sunbeams overflowed the world without. A vague, inexplicable new happiness stirred within her, and enveloped her soul, as a bright cloud might cling about some object in the material world. The quaint garden, the old walls, every detail in her little world seemed to be living through this new experience with her; the nature without her was in harmony with her inmost thoughts. The sunlight crept along the wall till it reached a maiden-hair fern; the changing hues of a pigeon's breast shone from the thick fronds and glossy stems, and all

Eugénie's future grew bright with radiant hopes. Henceforward the bit of wall, its pale flowers, its blue harebells and bleached grasses, was a pleasant sight for her; it called up associations which had all the charm of the memories of childhood.

The rustling sound made by the leaves as they fell to the earth, the echoes that came up from the court, seemed like answers to the girl's secret questionings as she sat and mused; she might have stayed there by the window all day and never have noticed how the hours went by, but other thoughts surged up within her soul. Again and again she rose and stood before the glass, and looked at herself, as a conscientious writer scrutinizes his work, criticises it, and says hard things about it to himself.

"I am not pretty enough for him!"

This was what Eugénie thought, in her humility, and the thought was fertile in suffering. The poor child did not do herself justice; but humility, or, more truly, fear, is born with love. Eugénie's beauty was of a robust type often found among the lower middle classes, a type which may seem somewhat wanting in refinement, but in her the beauty of the Venus of Milo was ennobled and purified by the beauty of Christian sentiment, which invests woman with a dignity unknown to ancient sculptors. Her head was very large; the masculine but delicate outlines of her forehead recalled the Jupiter of Phidias; all the radiance of her pure life seemed to shine from the clear gray eyes. An attack of smallpox, so mild that it had left no scars on the oval face or features, had yet somewhat blurred their fresh fair coloring, and coarsened the smooth and delicate surface, still so fine and soft that her mother's gentle kiss left a passing trace of faint red on her cheek. Perhaps her nose was a little too large, but it did not contradict the kindly and affectionate expression of the mouth, and the red lips covered with finely-etched lines. Her throat was daintily rounded. There was something that attracted attention and stirred the imagination in the curving lines of her figure, covered to the throat by her high-necked dress; no doubt she possessed little of the grace that is due to the toilet, and her tall frame was strong rather than lissome, but this was not without its charm for judges of beauty.

For Eugénie was both tall and strongly built. She had nothing of the prettiness that ordinary people admire; but her beauty was unmistakable, and of a kind in which artists alone delight. A painter in quest of an exalted and spiritual type, searching women's faces for the beauty which Raphael dreamed of and conjured into being, the eyes full of proud humility, the pure outlines, often due to some chance inspiration of the artist, but which a virtuous and Christian life can alone acquire or preserve—a painter haunted by this ideal would have seen at once in Eugénie Grandet's face her unconscious and innate nobility of soul, a world of love behind the quiet brow, and in the way she had with her eyelids and in her eyes that divine something which baffles description. There was a serene tranquillity about her features, unspoiled and unwearied by the expression of pleasure; it was as if you watched, across some placid lake, the shadowy outlines of hills far off against the sky. The beauty of Eugénie's face, so quiet and so softly colored, was like that of some fair, half-opened flower about which the light seems to hover; in its quality of restfulness, its subtle revelation of a beautiful nature, lay the charm that attracted beholders. Eugénie was still on the daisied brink of life, where illusions blossom and joys are gathered which are not known in later days. So she looked in the glass, and with no thought of love as yet in her mind, she said, "He will not give me a thought; I am too ugly!"

Then she opened her door, went out on to the landing, and bent over the staircase to hear the sounds in the house.

"He is not getting up yet," she thought. She heard Nanon's morning cough as the good woman went to and fro, swept out.

the dining-room, lit the kitchen fire, chained up the dog, and talked to her friends the brutes in the stable.

Eugénie fled down the staircase, and ran over to Nanon, who was milking the cow.

"Nanon," she cried, "do let us have some cream for my cousin's coffee, there's a dear."

"But, mademoiselle, you can't have cream off this morning's milk," said Nanon, as she burst out laughing. "I can't make cream for you. Your cousin is as charming as charming can be, that he is! You haven't seen him in that silk night rail of his, all flowers and gold! I did though! The linen he wears is every bit as fine as M. le Curé's surplice."

"Nanon, make some cake for us."

"And who is to find the wood to heat the oven and the flour and the butter?" asked Nanon, who in her capacity of Grandet's prime minister was a person of immense importance in Eugénie's eyes, and even in Eugénie's mother's. "Is *he* to be robbed to make a feast for your cousin? Ask for the butter and the flour and the firewood; he is your father, go and ask him, he may give them to *you*. There! there he is, just coming downstairs to see after the provisions——"

But Eugénie had escaped into the garden; the sound of her father's footstep on the creaking staircase terrified her. She was conscious of a happiness that shrank from the observation of others, a happiness which, as we are apt to think, and perhaps not without reason, shines from our eyes, and is written at large upon our foreheads. And not only so, she was conscious of other thoughts. The bleak discomfort of her father's house had struck her for the first time, and, with a dim feeling of vexation, the poor child wished that she could alter it all, and bring it more into harmony with her cousin's elegance. She felt a passionate longing to do something for him, without the slightest idea what that something should be. The womanly instinct awakened in her at the first sight of her cousin was only the stronger because she had reached her three-and-twentieth year, and mind and heart were fully developed; and she was so natural and simple that she acted on the promptings of her angelic nature without submitting herself, her impressions, or her feelings to any introspective process.

For the first time in her life the sight of her father struck a sort of terror into her heart; she felt that he was the master of her fate, and that she was guiltily hiding some of her thoughts from him. She began to walk hurriedly up and down, wondering how it was that the air was so fresh; there was a reviving force in the sunlight, it seemed to be within her as well as without, it was as if a new life had begun.

While she was still thinking how to gain her end concerning the cake, a quarrel came to pass between Nanon and Grandet, a thing as rare as a winter swallow. The good man had just taken his keys, and was about to dole out the provisions required for the day.

"Is there any bread left over from yesterday!" he asked of Nanon.

"Not a crumb, sir."

Grandet took up a large loaf, round in form and close in consistence, shaped in one of the flat baskets which they use for baking in Anjou, and was about to cut it, when Nanon broke in upon him with—

"There are five of us to-day, sir."

"True," answered Grandet; "but these loaves of yours weigh six pounds apiece; there will be some left over. Besides, these young fellows from Paris never touch bread, as you will soon see."

"Then do they eat *kitchen?*" asked Nanon.

This word *kitchen* in the Angevin dictionary signifies anything which is spread upon bread; from butter, the commonest variety, to preserved peaches, the most distinguished of all *kitchens;* and those who, as small children, have nibbled off the *kitchen* and left the bread, will readily understand the bearing of Nanon's remark.

"No," replied Grandet, with much gravity, "they eat neither bread nor *kitchen;* they are like a girl in love, as you may say."

Having at length cut down the day's rations to the lowest possible point, the miser was about to go to his fruit-loft, first carefully locking up the cupboards of his storeroom, when Nanon stopped him.

"Just give me some flour and butter, sir," she said, "and I will make a cake for the children."

"Are you going to turn the house upside down because my nephew is here?"

"Your nephew was no more in my mind than your dog, no more than he was in yours—— There now! you have only put out six lumps of sugar, and I want eight."

"Come, come, Nanon; I have never seen you like this before. What has come over you? Are you mistress here? You will have six lumps of sugar and no more."

"Oh, very well; and what is your nephew to sweeten his coffee with?"

"He can have two lumps; I shall go without it myself."

"*You* go without sugar! and at your age! I would sooner pay for it out of my own pocket."

"Mind your own business."

In spite of the low price of sugar, it was, in Grandet's eyes, the most precious of all colonial products. For him it was always something to be used sparingly; it was still worth six francs a pound, as in the time of the Empire, and this pet economy had become an inveterate habit with him. But every woman, no matter how simple she may be, can devise some shift to gain her ends; and Nanon allowed the question of the sugar to drop, in order to have her way about the cake.

"Mademoiselle," she called through the window, "wouldn't you like some cake?"

"No, no," answered Eugénie.

"Stay, Nanon," said Grandet as he heard his daughter's voice; "there!"

He opened the flour-bin, measured out some flour, and added a few ounces of butter to the piece which he had already cut.

"And firewood; I shall want firewood to heat the oven," said the inexorable Nanon.

"Ah! well, you can take what you want," he answered ruefully; "but you will make a fruit tart at the same time, and you must bake the dinner in the oven, that will save lighting another fire."

"Why!" cried Nanon; there is no need to tell me that!"

Grandet gave his trusty prime minister a glance that was almost paternal.

"Mademoiselle," cried Nanon, "we are going to have a cake."

Grandet came back again with the fruit, and began by setting down a plateful on the kitchen table.

"Just look here, sir," said Nanon, "what lovely boots your nephew has! What leather, how nice it smells! What are they to be cleaned with? Am I to put your egg blacking on them?"

"No, Nanon," said Eugénie; "I expect the egg would spoil the leather. You had better tell him that you have no idea how to clean black morocco—— Yes, it is morocco, and he himself will buy you something in Saumur to clean his boots with. I have heard it said that they put sugar into their blacking, and that is what makes it so shiny."

"Then is it good to eat?" asked Nanon, as she picked up the boots and smelt them. "Why, why! they smell of madame's eau-de-Cologne! Oh, how funny!"

"*Funny!*" said her master; "people spend more money on their boots than they are worth that stand in them, and you think it funny!" He had just returned from a second and final expedition to the fruit-loft, carefully locking the door after him.

"You will have soup once or twice a week while your nephew is here, sir, will you not?"

"Yes."

"Shall I go round to the butcher's?"

"You will do nothing of the kind. You can make some chicken-broth; the tenants will keep you going. But I shall tell Cornoiller to kill some ravens for me. That kind of game makes the best broth in the world."

"Is it true, sir, that they live on dead things?"

"You are a fool, Nanon! They live, like everybody else, on anything that they can pick up. Don't we all live on dead things? What about legacies? And the good man Grandet, having no further order to give, drew out his watch, and finding that there was yet half an hour to spare before breakfast, took up his hat, gave his daughter a kiss, and said, "Would you like to take a walk along the Loire? I have something to see after in the meadows down there."

Eugénie put on her straw hat lined with rose-colored silk; and then father and daughter went down the crooked street towards the market-place.

"Where are you off to so early this morning?" said the notary Cruchot, as he met the Grandets.

"We are going to take a look at something," responded his friend, in nowise deceived by this early move on the notary's part.

Whenever Grandet was about to "take a look at something," the notary knew by experience that there was something to be gained by going with him. With him, therefore, he went.

"Come along, Cruchot," said Grandet, addressing the notary. "You are one of my friends; I am going to show you what a piece of folly it is to plant poplars in good soil——"

"Then the sixty thousand francs that you fingered for those poplars of yours in the meadows by the Loire are a mere trifle to you?" said Cruchot, opening his eyes wide in his bewilderment. "And such luck as you had too! —— Felling your timber just when there was no white wood to be had in Nantes, so that every trunk fetched thirty francs!"

Eugénie heard and did not hear, utterly unconscious that the most critical moment of her life was rapidly approaching, that a paternal and sovereign decree was about to be pronounced, and that the old notary was to bring all this about. Grandet had reached the magnificent meadow-land by the Loire, which had come into his hands in his Republican days. Some thirty laborers were busy digging out the roots of the poplars that once stood there, filling up the holes that were left, and leveling the ground.

"Now, M. Cruchot, see how much space a poplar takes up," said he, addressing the notary. "Jean," he called to a workman, m—m—measure r—round the sides with your rule."

"Eight feet four times over," said the workman when he had finished.

"Thirty-two feet of loss," said Grandet to Cruchot. "Now along that line there were three hundred poplars, weren't there? Well, then, three hundred t—t—times thirty-two f—feet will eat up five hundredweight of hay, allow twice as much again for the space on either side, and you get fifteen hundredweight; then there is the intervening space— say a thousand t—t—trusses of hay altogether."

"Well," said Cruchot, helping his friend out, "and a thousand trusses of that hay would fetch something like six hundred francs."

"S—s—say t—twelve hundred, because the s—second crop is worth three or four hundred francs. Good, then reckon up what t—t—twelve hundred francs per annum d—d—during f—forty years comes to, at compound interest, of course."

"Sixty thousand francs, or thereabouts," said the notary.

"That is what I make it! Sixty thousand f—f—francs. Well," the vine-grower went on without stammering, "two thousand poplars will not bring in fifty thousand francs in forty years. So you lose on them. That *I* found out," said Grandet, who was vastly pleased with himself. "Jean," he continued, turning to the laborer, "fill up all the holes except those along the riverside, where you can plant those poplar saplings that I bought. If you set them along by the Loire, they will grow there finely at the expense of the government," he added, and as he looked round at Cruchot the wen on his nose twitched slightly, the most sardonic smile could not have said more.

"Yes, it is clear enough, poplars should only be planted in poor soil," said Cruchot, quite overcome with amazement at Grandet's astuteness.

"Y—e—s, sir," said the cooper ironically.

Eugénie was looking out over the glorious landscape and along the Loire, without heeding her father's arithmetic; but Cruchot's talk with his client took another turn, and her attention was suddenly aroused.

"So you have a son-in-law come from Paris; they are talking about nothing but your nephew in all Saumur. I shall soon have settlements to draw up; eh, père Grandet?"

"Did you come out early to t—t—tell me that?" inquired Grandet, and again the wen twitched. "Very well, you are an old crony of mine; I will be p—plain with you, and t—t—tell you what you w—want to know. I would rather fling my d—d—daughter into the Loire, look you, than g—give her to her cousin. You can give that out. But, no; l—l— let people gossip."

Everything swam before Eugénie's eyes. Her vague hopes of distant happiness had suddenly taken definite shape, had sprung up and blossomed, and then her harvest of flowers had been as suddenly cut down and lay on the earth. Since yesterday she had woven the bonds of happiness that unite two souls, and henceforward sorrow, it seemed, was to strengthen them. Is it not written in the noble destiny of woman that the grandeur of sorrow should touch her more closely than all the pomp and splendor of fortune?

How came it that a father's feelings had been extinguished (as it seemed) in her father's heart? What crime could be laid at Charles' door? Mysterious questions! Mysterious and sad forebodings already surrounded her growing love, that mystery within her soul. When they turned to go home again, she trembled in every limb; and as they went up the shady street, along which she had lately gone so joyously, the shadows looked gloomy, the air she breathed seemed full of the melancholy of autumn, everything about her was sad. Love, that had brought these keener perceptions, was quick to interpret every boding sign. As they neared home, she walked on ahead of her father, knocked at the house-door, and stood waiting beside it. But Grandet, seeing that the notary carried a newspaper still in its wrapper, asked, "How are consols?"

"I know you will not take my advice, Grandet," Cruchot replied. "You should buy at once; the chance of making twenty per cent. on them in two years is still open to you, and they pay a very fair rate of interest besides, five thousand livres is not a bad return on eighty thousand francs. You can buy now at eighty francs fifty centimes."

"We shall see," remarked Grandet pensively, rubbing his chin.

"*Mon Dieu!*" exclaimed the notary, who by this time had unfolded his newspaper.

"Well, what is it?" cried Grandet as Cruchot put the paper in his hands and said—

"Read that paragraph."

"M. Grandet, one of the most highly-respected merchants

in Paris, shot himself through the head yesterday afternoon, after putting in an appearance on 'Change as usual. He had previously sent in his resignation to the President of the Chamber of Deputies, resigning his position as Judge of the Tribunal of Commerce at the same time. His affairs had become involved through the failures of his stockbroker and notary, MM. Roguin and Souchet. M. Grandet, whose character was greatly esteemed, and whose credit stood high, would no doubt have found temporary assistance on the market which would have enabled him to tide over his difficulties. It is to be regretted that a man of such high character should have given way to the first impulse of despair"—and so forth, and so forth.

"I knew it," the old vine-grower said.

Phlegmatic though Cruchot was, he felt a horrible shudder run through him at the words; perhaps Grandet of Paris had stretched imploring hands in vain to the millions of Grandet of Saumur; the blood ran cold in his veins.

"And his son?" he asked presently; "he was in such spirits yesterday evening."

"His son knows nothing as yet," Grandet answered, imperturbable as ever.

"Good-morning, M. Grandet," said Cruchot. He understood the position now, and went to reassure the President de Bonfons.

Grandet found breakfast ready. Mme. Grandet was already seated in her chair, mounted on the wooden blocks, and was knitting woolen cuffs for the winter. Eugénie ran to her mother and put her arms about her, with the eager hunger for affection that comes of a hidden trouble.

"You can get your breakfast," said Nanon, bustling downstairs in a hurry; "he is sleeping like a cherub. He looks so nice with his eyes shut! I went in and called him, but it was all one, he never heard me."

"Let him sleep," said Grandet; "he will wake soon enough to hear bad news, in any case."

"What is the matter?" asked Eugénie. She was putting into her cup the two smallest lumps of sugar, weighing goodness knows how many grains; her worthy parent was wont to amuse himself by cutting up sugar whenever he had nothing better to do.

Mme. Grandet, who had not dared to put the question herself, looked at her husband.

"His father has blown his brains out."

"*My uncle?*" said Eugénie.

"Oh! that poor boy!" cried Mme. Grandet.

"Poor indeed!" said Grandet; "he has not a penny."

"Ah! well, he is sleeping as if he were the king of all the world," said Nanon pityingly.

Eugénie could not eat. Her heart was wrung as a woman's heart can be when for the first time her whole soul is filled with sorrow and compassion for the sorrow of one she loves. She burst into tears.

"You did not know your uncle, so what is there to cry about?" said her father with a glance like a hungry tiger; just such a glance as he would give, no doubt, to his heaps of gold.

"But who wouldn't feel sorry for the poor young man, sir?" said the serving-maid; "sleeping there like a log, and knowing nothing of his fate."

"I did not speak to you, Nanon! Hold your tongue."

In that moment Eugénie learned that a woman who loves must dissemble her feelings. She was silent.

"Until I come back, Mme. Grandet, you will say nothing about this to him, I hope," the old cooper continued. "They are making a ditch in my meadows along the road, and I must go and see after it. I shall come back for the second breakfast at noon, and then my nephew and I will have a talk about his affairs. As for you, Mademoiselle Eugénie, if you are crying over that popinjay, let us have no more of it, child. He will be off post-haste to the Indies directly, and you will never set eyes on *him* any more."

Her father took up his gloves, which were lying on the rim of his hat, put them on in his cool, deliberate way, inserting the fingers of one hand between those of the other, dovetail fashion, so as to thrust them down well into the tips of the gloves, and then he went out.

"Oh! mamma, I can scarcely breathe!" cried Eugénie, when she was alone with her mother; "I have never suffered like this!"

Mme. Grandet, seeing her daughter's white face, opened the window and let fresh air into the room.

"I feel better now," said Eugénie after a little while.

This nervous excitement in one who was usually so quiet and self-possessed produced an effect on Mme. Grandet. She looked at her daughter, and her mother's love and sympathetic instinct told her everything. But, in truth, the celebrated Hungarian twin-sisters, united to each other by one of nature's errors, could scarcely have lived in closer sympathy than Eugénie and her mother. Were they not always together: together in the window where they sat the livelong day, together at church; did they not breathe the same air even when they slept?

"My poor little girl!" said Mme. Grandet, drawing Eugénie's head down till it rested upon her bosom.

Her daughter lifted her face, and gave her mother a questioning look which seemed to read her inmost thoughts.

"Why must he be sent to the Indies?" said the girl. "If he is in trouble, ought he not to stay here with us? Is he not our nearest relation?"

"Yes, dear child, that would only be natural; but your father has reasons for what he does, and we must respect them."

Mother and daughter sat in silence; the one on her chair mounted on the wooden blocks, the other in her little armchair. Both women took up their needlework. Eugénie felt that her mother understood her, and her heart was full of gratitude for such tender sympathy.

"How kind you are, dear mamma!" she said as she took her mother's hand and kissed it.

The worn, patient face, aged with many sorrows, lighted up at the words.

"Do you like him?" asked Eugénie.

For all answer, Mme. Grandet smiled. Then after a moment's pause she murmured, "You cannot surely love him already? That would be a pity."

"Why would it be a pity?" asked Eugénie. "You like him, Nanon likes him, why should I not like him too? Now then, mamma, let us set the table for his breakfast."

She threw down her work, and her mother followed her example, saying as she did so, "You are a mad girl!"

But none the less did she sanction her daughter's freak by assisting in it.

Eugénie called Nanon.

"Haven't you all you want yet, mamselle?"

"Nanon, surely you will have some cream by twelve o'clock?"

"By twelve o'clock? Oh! yes," answered the old servant.

"Very well, then, let the coffee be very strong. I have heard M. des Grassins say that they drink their coffee very strong in Paris. Put in plenty."

"And where is it to come from?"

"You must buy some."

"And suppose the master meets me?"

"He is down by the river."

"I will just slip out then. But M. Fessard asked me when I went about the candle if the Three Holy Kings were paying us a visit. Our goings on will be all over the town."

"Your father would be quite capable of beating us," said Mme. Grandet, "if he suspected anything of all this."

"Oh! well, then, never mind; he will beat us, we will take the beating on our knees."

At this Mme. Grandet raised her eyes to heaven, and said no more. Nanon put on her sun-bonnet and went out. Eugénie spread a clean linen tablecloth, then she went upstairs in quest of some bunches of grapes which she had amused herself by hanging from some strings up in the attic. She tripped lightly along the corridor, so as not to disturb her cousin, and could not resist the temptation to stop a moment before the door to listen to his even breathing.

"Trouble wakes while he is sleeping," she said to herself.

She arranged her grapes on the few last green vine-leaves as daintily as any experienced *chef d'office*, and set them on the table in triumph. She levied contributions on the pears which her father had counted out, and piled them up pyramid-fashion, with autumn leaves among them. She came and went, and danced in and out. She might have ransacked the house; the will was in nowise lacking, but her father kept everything under lock and key, and the keys were in his pocket. Nanon came back with two new-laid eggs. Eugénie could have flung her arms round the girl's neck.

"The farmer from La Lande had eggs in his basket; I asked him for some, and to please me he let me have these, the nice man."

After two hours of industrious application, Eugénie succeeded in preparing a very simple meal; it cost but little, it is true, but it was a terrible infringement of the immemorial laws and customs of the house. No one sat down to the midday meal, which consisted of a little bread, some fruit or butter, and a glass of wine. Twenty times in those two hours Eugénie had left her work to watch the coffee boil, or to listen for any sound announcing that her cousin was getting up; now looking round on the table drawn up to the fire, with one of the armchairs set beside it for her cousin, on the two plates of fruit, the egg-cups, the bottle of white wine, the bread, and the little pyramid of white sugar in a saucer; Eugénie trembled from head to foot at the mere thought of the glance her father would give her if he should happen to come in at that moment. Often, therefore, did she look at the clock, to see if there was yet time for her cousin to finish his breakfast before her parent's return.

"Never mind, Eugénie, if your father comes in, I will take all the blame," said Mme. Grandet.

Eugénie could not keep back the tears. "Oh! my kind mother," she cried; "I have not loved you enough!"

Charles, after making innumerable pirouettes round his room, came down at last, singing gay little snatches of song. Luckily it was only eleven o'clock after all. He had taken as much pains with his appearance (the Parisian!) as if he had been staying in the château belonging to the high-born fair one who was traveling in Scotland; and now he came in with that gracious air of condescension which sits not ill on youth, and which gave Eugénie a melancholy pleasure. He had come to regard the collapse of his castles in Anjou as a very good joke, and went up to his aunt quite gaily.

"I hope you slept well, dear aunt? And you too, cousin?"

"Very well, sir; how did you sleep?"

"Soundly."

"Cousin, you must be hungry," said Eugénie; "sit down."

"Oh! I never breakfast before twelve o'clock, just after I rise. But I have fared so badly on my journey, that I will yield to persuasion. Besides——" he drew out the daintiest little watch that ever issued from Bréguet's workshop. "Dear me, it is only eleven o'clock; I have been up betimes."

"Up betimes?" asked Mme. Grandet.

"Yes, but I wanted to set my things straight. Well, I am quite ready for something, something not very substantial, a fowl or a partridge."

"Holy Virgin!" exclaimed Nanon, hearing these words.

"A partridge," said Eugénie to herself. She would willingly have given all she had for one.

"Come and take your seat," said Mme. Grandet, addressing her nephew.

The dandy sank into the armchair in a graceful attitude, much as a pretty woman might recline on her sofa. Eugénie and her mother drew their chairs to the fire and sat near him.

"Do you always live here?" Charles inquired, thinking that the room looked even more hideous by daylight than by candlelight.

"Always," Eugénie answered, watching him as she spoke. "Always, except during the vintage. Then we go to help Nanon, and we all stay at the Abbey at Noyers."

"Do you ever take a walk?"

"Sometimes, on Sundays after vespers, when it is fine, we walk down as far as the bridge," said Mme. Grandet, "or we sometimes go to see them cutting the hay."

"Have you a theatre here?"

"Go to the play!" cried Mme. Grandet; "go to see play-actors! Why, sir, do you not know that that is a mortal sin?"

"There, sir," said Nanon, bringing in the eggs, "we will give you chickens in the shell."

"Oh! new-laid eggs," said Charles, who, after the manner of those accustomed to luxury, had quite forgotten all about his partridge. "Delicious! Do you happen to have any butter, eh, my good girl?"

"Butter? If you have butter now, you will have no cake by-and-by," said Nanon.

"Yes, of course, Nanon; bring some butter," cried Eugénie.

The young girl watched her cousin while he cut his bread and butter into strips and felt happy. The most romantic shopgirl in Paris could not more thoroughly enjoy the spectacle of innocence triumphant in a melodrama. It must be conceded that Charles, who had been brought up by a graceful and charming mother, and had received his "finishing education" from an accomplished woman of the world, was as dainty, neat, and elegant in his ways as any coxcomb of the gentler sex. The girl's quiet sympathy produced an almost magnetic effect. Charles, finding himself thus waited upon by his cousin and aunt, could not resist the influence of their overflowing kindness. He was radiant with good-humor, and the look he gave Eugénie was almost a smile. As he looked more closely at her he noticed her pure, regular features, her unconscious attitude, the wonderful clearness of her eyes, in which love sparkled, though she as yet knew nothing of love but its pain and a wistful longing.

"Really, my dear cousin," he said, "if you were in a box at the opera and in evening dress, and I would answer for it, my aunt's remark about deadly sin would be fully justified, all the men would become envious and all the women jealous."

Eugénie's heart beat fast with joy at this compliment, though it conveyed no meaning whatever to her mind.

"You are laughing at a poor little country cousin," she said.

"If you knew me better, cousin, you would know that I detest banter; it sears the heart and deadens the feelings." And he swallowed down a strip of bread and butter with perfect satisfaction.

"No," he continued, "I never make fun of others, very likely because I have not wit enough, a defect which puts me at a great disadvantage. They have a deadly trick in Paris of saying, 'He is *so* good-natured,' which, being interpreted, means—'the poor youth is as stupid as a rhinoceros.' But as I happen to be rich, and it is known that I can hit the bull's eye straight off at thirty paces with any kind of pistol anywhere, these witticisms are not leveled at me."

"It is evident from what you say, nephew," said Mme. Grandet gravely, "that you have a kind heart."

"That is a very pretty ring of yours," said Eugénie; "is there any harm in asking to see it?"

Charles took off the ring and held it out; Eugénie reddened as her cousin's rose-pink nails came in contact with her finger-tips.

"Mother, only see how fine the work is!"

"Oh, what a lot of gold there is in it," said Nanon, who brought in the coffee.

"What is that?" asked Charles, laughing, as he pointed to an oval pipkin, made of glazed brown earthenware, ornamented without by a circular fringe of ashes. It was full of a brown boiling liquid, in which coffee grounds were visible as they rose to the surface and fell again.

"Coffee; boiling hot!" answered Nanon.

"Oh! my dear aunt, I must at least leave some beneficent trace of my stay here. You are a long way behind the times! I will show you how to make decent coffee in a *cafetière à la Chaptal.*" Forthwith he endeavored to explain the principles on which this utensil is constructed, and how the coffee should be prepared.

"Bless me! if there is all that to-do about it," said Nanon, "you would have to give your whole time to it. I'll never make coffee that way, I know. Who is to cut the grass for our cow while I am looking after the coffee-pot?"

"I would do it," said Eugénie.

"*Child!*" said Mme. Grandet, with a look at her daughter; and at the word came a swift recollection of the misery about to overwhelm the unconscious young man, and the three women were suddenly silent, and gazed pityingly at him. He could not understand it.

"What is it, cousin?" he asked Eugénie.

"Hush!" said Mme. Grandet, seeing that the girl was about to reply. "You know that your father means to speak to the gentleman——"

"Say 'Charles,'" said young Grandet.

"Oh, is your name Charles?" said Eugénie. "It is a nice name."

Evil forebodings are seldom vain.

Just at that moment Mme. Grandet, Eugénie, and Nanon, who could not think of the cooper's return without shuddering, heard the familiar knock at the door.

"That is papa!" cried Eugénie.

She took away the saucer full of sugar, leaving one or two lumps on the tablecloth. Nanon hurried away with the egg-cups. Mme. Grandet started up like a frightened fawn. There was a sudden panic of terror, which amazed Charles, who was quite at a loss to account for it.

"Why, what is the matter?" he asked.

"My father is coming in," explained Eugénie.

"Well, and what then?"

M. Grandet entered the room, gave one sharp glance at the table, and another at Charles. He saw how it was at once.

"Aha! you are making a fête for your nephew. Good, very good, oh! very good, indeed!" he said, without stammering. "When the cat is away, the mice may play."

"Fête?" thought Charles, who had not the remotest conception of the state of affairs in the Grandet household.

"Bring me my glass, Nanon," said the good man.

Eugénie went for the glass. Grandet drew from his waistcoat pocket a large clasp-knife with a stag's horn handle, cut a slice of bread, buttered it slowly and sparingly, and began to eat as he stood. Just then Charles put some sugar into his coffee; this called Grandet's attention to the pieces of sugar on the table; he looked hard at his wife, who turned pale, and came a step or two towards him; he bent down and said in the poor woman's ear—

"Where did all that sugar come from?"

"Nanon went out to Fessard's for some; there was none in the house."

It is impossible to describe the painful interest that this

dumb show possessed for the three women; Nanon had left her kitchen, and was looking into the dining-room to see how things went there. Charles meanwhile tasted his coffee, found it rather strong, and looked round for another piece of sugar, but Grandet had already pounced upon it and taken it away.

"What do you want, nephew?" the old man inquired.

"The sugar."

"Pour in some more milk if your coffee is too strong," answered the master of the house.

Eugénie took up the saucer, of which Grandet had previously taken possession, and set it on the table, looking quietly at her father the while. Truly, the fair Parisian who exerts all the strength of her weak arms to help her lover to escape by a ladder of silken cords, displays less courage than Eugénie showed when she put the sugar upon the table. The Parisian will have her reward. She will proudly exhibit the bruises on a round white arm, her lover will bathe them with tears and cover them with kisses, and pain will be extinguished in bliss; but Charles had not the remotest conception of what his cousin endured for him, or of the horrible dismay that filled her heart as she met her father's angry eyes; he would never even know of her sacrifice.

"You are eating nothing, wife!"

The poor bond-slave went to the table, cut a piece of bread in fear and trembling, and took a pear. Eugénie, grown reckless, offered the grapes to her father, saying as she did so—

"Just try some of my fruit, papa! You will take some, will you not, cousin? I brought those pretty grapes down on purpose for you."

"Oh! if they could have their way, they would turn Saumur upside down for you, nephew! As soon as you have finished we will take a turn in the garden together; I have some things to tell you that would take a deal of sugar to sweeten them."

Eugénie and her mother both gave Charles a look, which the young man could not mistake.

"What do you mean by that, uncle? Since my mother died——" (here his voice softened a little) "there is no misfortune possible for me——"

"Who can know what afflictions God may send to make trial of us, nephew?" said his aunt.

"Tut, tut, tut," muttered Grandet, "here you are beginning with your folly already! I am sorry to see that you have such white hands, nephew."

He displayed the fists, like shoulders of mutton, with which nature had terminated his own arms.

"That is the sort of hand to rake the crowns together! You put the kind of leather on your feet that we used to make pocket-books of to keep bills in. That is the way you have been brought up. That's bad! that's bad!"

"What do you mean, uncle? I'll be hanged if I understand one word of this."

"Come along," said Grandet.

The miser shut his knife with a snap, drained his glass, and opened the door.

"Oh! keep up your courage, cousin!"

Something in the girl's voice sent a sudden chill through Charles; he followed his formidable relative with dreadful misgivings. Eugénie and her mother and Nanon went into the kitchen; an uncontrollable anxiety led them to watch the two actors in the scene which was about to take place in the damp little garden.

Uncle and nephew walked together in silence at first. Grandet felt the situation to be a somewhat awkward one; not that he shrank at all from telling Charles of his father's death, but he felt a kind of pity for a young man left in this way without a penny in the world, and he cast about for phrases that should break this cruel news as gently as might be.

"You have lost your father!" he could say that; there was

nothing in that; fathers usually predecease their children. But, "You have not a penny!" All the woes of the world were summed up in those words, so for the third time the worthy man walked the whole length of the path in the centre of the garden, crunching the gravel beneath his heavy boots, and no word was said.

At all great crises in our lives, any sudden joy or great sorrow, there comes a vivid consciousness of our surroundings that stamps them on the memory forever; and Charles, with every faculty strained and intent, saw the box-edging to the borders, the falling autumn leaves, the mouldering walls, the gnarled and twisted boughs of the fruit-trees, and till his dying day every picturesque detail of the little garden came back with the memory of the supreme hour of that early sorrow.

"It is very fine, very warm," said Grandet, drawing in a deep breath of air.

"Yes, uncle, but why——"

"Well, my boy," his uncle resumed, "I have some bad news for you. Your father is very ill——"

"What am I doing here?" cried Charles. "Nanon!" he shouted, "order post-horses! I shall be sure to find a carriage of some sort in the place, I suppose," he added, turning to his uncle, who had not stirred from where he stood.

"Horses and carriage are of no use," Grandet answered, looking at Charles, who immediately stared straight before him in silence. "Yes, my poor boy, you guess what has happened; he is dead. But that is nothing; there is something worse; he has shot himself through the head——"

"*My father?*"

"Yes, but that is nothing either. The newspapers are discussing it, as if it were any business of theirs. There, read for yourself."

Grandet had borrowed Cruchot's paper, and now he laid

the fatal paragraph before Charles. The poor young fellow—he was only a lad as yet—made no attempt to hide his emotion, and burst into tears.

"Come, that is better," said Grandet to himself. "That look in his eyes frightened me. He is crying; he will pull through. Never mind, my poor nephew," Grandet resumed aloud, not knowing whether Charles heard him or no, "that is nothing, you will get over it, but——"

"Never! never! My father! my father!"

"He has ruined you; you are penniless."

"What is that to me. Where is my father?——my father!" The sound of his sobbing filled the little garden, reverberated in ghastly echoes from the walls. Tears are as infectious as laughter; the three women wept with pity for him. Charles broke from his uncle without waiting to hear more, and sprang into the yard, found the staircase, and fled to his own room, where he flung himself across the bed and buried his face in the bedclothes, that he might give way to his grief in solitude as far as possible from these relations.

"Let him alone till the first shower is over," said Grandet, going back to the parlor. Eugénie and her mother had hastily returned to their places, had dried their eyes, and were sewing with cold trembling fingers.

"But that fellow is good for nothing," went on Grandet; "he is so taken up with dead folk that he doesn't even think about the money."

Eugénie shuddered to hear the most sacred of sorrows spoken of in such a way; from that moment she began to criticise her father. Charles' sobs, smothered though they were, rang through that house of echoes; the sounds seemed to come from under the earth, a heartrending wail that grew fainter towards the end of the day, and only ceased as night drew on.

"Poor boy!" said Mme. Grandet.

It was an unfortunate remark! M. Grandet looked at his

wife, then at Eugénie, then at the sugar basin; he recollected the sumptuous breakfast prepared that morning for their unhappy kinsman, and planted himself in the middle of the room.

"Oh! by-the-by," he said, in his usual cool, deliberate way, "I hope you will not carry your extravagance any farther, Mme. Grandet; I do not give you MY money for you to squander it on sugar for that young rogue."

"Mother had nothing whatever to do with it," said Eugénie. "It was I——"

"Because you are come of age," Grandet interrupted his daughter, "you think you can set yourself to thwart me, I suppose. Mind what you are about, Eugénie——"

"But, father, your own brother's son ought not to have to go without sugar in your house."

"Tut, tut, tut, tut!" came from the cooper in a cadence of four semitones. "'Tis 'my nephew' here, and 'my brother's son' there; Charles is nothing to us; he has not a brass farthing. His father is a bankrupt, and when the young sprig has cried as much as he wishes, he shall clear out of this; I will not have my house turned topsy-turvy for him."

"What is a bankrupt, father?" asked Eugénie.

"A bankrupt," replied her father, "is guilty of the most dishonorable action that can dishonor a man."

"It must be a very great sin," said Mme. Grandet, "and our brother will perhaps be eternally lost."

"There you are with your preachments," her husband retorted, shrugging his shoulders. "A bankrupt, Eugénie," her father continued, "is a thief whom the law unfortunately takes under its protection. People trusted Guillaume Grandet with their goods, confiding in his character for fair-dealing and honesty; he has taken all they have, and left them nothing but the eyes in their heads to cry over their losses with. A bankrupt is worse than a highwayman; a highwayman sets upon you, and you have a chance to defend yourself; he risks his life besides, while the other——Charles is disgraced, in fact."

The words filled the poor girl's heart; they weighed upon her with all their weight; she herself was so scrupulously conscientious; no flower in the depths of a forest had grown more delicately free from spot or stain; she knew none of the maxims of worldly wisdom, and nothing of its quibbles and its sophistries. So she accepted her father's cruel definition and sweeping statements as to bankrupts; he drew no distinction between a fraudulent bankruptcy and a failure from unavoidable causes, and how should she?

"But, father, could you not have prevented this misfortune?"

"My brother did not ask my advice; besides, his liabilities amount to four millions."

"How much is a million, father?" asked Eugénie, with the simplicity of a child who would fain have its wish fulfilled at once.

"A million?" queried Grandet. "Why, it is a million francs, four hundred thousand five-franc pieces; there are twenty sous in a franc, and it takes five francs of twenty sous each to make a five-franc piece."

"*Mon Dieu! Mon Dieu!*" cried Eugénie, "how came my uncle to have four millions of his own? Is there really anybody in France who has so many millions as that?"

Grandet stroked his daughter's chin and smiled. The wen seemed to grow larger.

"What will become of cousin Charles?"

"He will set out for the East Indies, and try to make a fortune. That is his father's wish."

"But has he any money to go with?"

"I shall pay his passage out as far as——yes——as far as Nantes."

Eugénie sprang up and flung her arms about her father's neck.

"Oh! father," she said, "you are good!"

Her warm embrace embarrassed Grandet somewhat, perhaps, too, his conscience was not quite at ease.

"Does it take a long while to make a million?" she asked.

"Lord! yes," said the cooper; "you know what a Napoleon is; well, then, it takes fifty thousand of them to make a million."

"Mamma, we will have a *neuvaine* said for him."

"That was what I was thinking," her mother replied.

"Just like you! always thinking how to spend money. Really, one might suppose that we had any amount of money to throw away!"

As he spoke, a sound of low hoarse sobbing, more ominous than any which had preceded it, came from the garret. Eugénie and her mother shuddered.

"Nanon," called Grandet, "go up and see that he is not killing himself."

"Look here! you two," he continued, turning to his wife and daughter, whose cheeks grew white at his tones, "there is to be no nonsense, mind! I am leaving the house. I am going round to see the Dutchmen who are going to-day. Then I shall go to Cruchot and have a talk with him about all this."

He went out. As soon as the door closed upon Grandet, Eugénie and her mother breathed more freely. The girl had never felt constraint in her father's presence until that morning; but a few hours had wrought rapid changes in her ideas and feelings.

"Mamma, how many louis is a hogshead of wine worth?"

"Your father gets something between a hundred and a hundred and fifty francs for his; sometimes two hundred, I believe, from what I have heard him say."

"And would there be fourteen hundred hogsheads in a vintage?"

"I don't know how many there are, child, upon my word; your father never talks about business to me."

"But, anyhow, papa must be rich."

"May be. But M. Cruchot told me that your father bought Froidfond two years ago. That would be a heavy pull on him."

Eugénie, now at a loss as to her father's wealth, went no farther with her arithmetic.

"He did not even so much as see me, the poor dear!" said Nanon on her return. "He is lying there on his bed like a calf, crying like a Magdalen; you never saw the like! Poor young man, what can be the matter with him?"

"Let us go up at once and comfort him, mamma; if we hear a knock, we will come downstairs."

There was something in the musical tones of her daughter's voice which Mme. Grandet could not resist. Eugénie was sublime; she was a girl no longer, she was a woman. With beating hearts they climbed the stairs and went together to Charles' room. The door was open. The young man saw nothing, and heard nothing; he was absorbed in his grief, an inarticulate cry broke from him now and again.

"How he loves his father!" said Eugénie in a low voice, and in her tone there was an unmistakable accent which betrayed the passion in her heart, and hopes of which she herself was unaware. Mme. Grandet, with the quick instinct of a mother's love, glanced at her daughter and spoke in a low voice in her ear.

"Take care," she said, "or you may love him."

"Love him!" said Eugénie. "Ah! if you only knew what my father said."

Charles moved slightly as he lay, and saw his aunt and cousin.

"I have lost my father," he cried; "my poor father! If he had only trusted me and told me about his losses, we might have worked together to repair them. *Mon Dieu!*

my kind father! I was so sure that I should see him again, and I said good-bye so carelessly, I am afraid, never thinking——"

His words were interrupted by sobs.

"We will surely pray for him," said Mme. Grandet. "Submit yourself to the will of God."

"Take courage, cousin," said Eugénie gently; "nothing can give your father back to you; you must now think how to save your honor——"

A woman always has her wits about her, even in her capacity of comforter, and with instinctive tact Eugénie sought to divert her cousin's mind from his sorrow by leading him to think about himself.

"My honor?" cried the young man, hastily pushing back the hair from his eyes. He sat upright upon the bed, and folded his arms. "Ah! true. My uncle said that my father had failed."

He hid his face in his hands with a heartrending cry of pain.

"Leave me! leave me! cousin Eugénie," he entreated. "Oh! God, forgive my father, for he must have been terribly unhappy!"

There was something in the sight of this young sorrow, this utter abandonment of grief, that was horribly engaging. It was a sorrow that shrank from the gaze of others, and Charles' gesture of entreaty that they should leave him to himself was understood by Eugénie and her mother. They went silently downstairs again, took their places by the great window, and sewed on for nearly an hour without a word to each other.

Eugénie had looked round the room; it was a stolen glance. In one of those hasty surveys by which a girl sees everything in a moment, she had noticed the pretty trifles on the toilet-table—the scissors, the razors mounted with gold. The gleams of splendor and luxury, seen amidst all this misery, made Charles still more interesting in her eyes, perhaps by the very force of the contrast. Their life had been so lonely and so quiet; such an event as this, with its painful interest, had never broken the monotony of their lives, little had occurred to stir their imagination, and now this tragical drama was being enacted under their eyes.

"Mamma," said Eugénie, "shall we wear mourning?"

"Your father will decide that," replied Mme. Grandet, and once more they sewed in silence. Eugénie's needle moved with a mechanical regularity, which betrayed her preoccupation of mind. The first wish of this adorable girl was to share her cousin's mourning. About four o'clock a sharp knock at the door sent a sudden thrill of terror through Mme. Grandet.

"What can have brought your father back?" she said to her daughter.

The vine-grower came in in high good-humor. He rubbed his hands so energetically that nothing but a skin like leather could have borne it, and indeed his hands were tanned like Russia leather, though the fragrant pine-rosin and incense had been omitted in the process. For a time he walked up and down and looked at the weather, but at last his secret escaped him.

"I have hooked them, wife," he said, without stammering; "I have them safe. Our wine is sold! The Dutchmen and Belgians were setting out this morning; I hung about in the market-place in front of their inn, looking as simple as I could. What's-his-name—you know the man—came up to me. All the best growers are hanging off and holding their vintages; they wanted to wait, and so they can, I have not hindered them. Our Belgian was at his wits' end, I saw that. So the bargain was struck; he is taking the whole of our vintage at two hundred francs the hogshead, half of it paid down at once in gold, and I have promissory notes for the rest. There are six louis for you. In three months' time prices will go down."

The last words came out quietly enough, but there was something so sardonic in the tone that if the little knots of growers, then standing in the twilight in the market-place of Saumur, in dismay at the news of Grandet's sale, had heard him speak, they would have shuddered; there would have been a panic on the market—wines would have fallen fifty per cent.

"You have a thousand hogsheads this year, father, have you not?" asked Eugénie.

"Yes, little girl."

These words indicated that the cooper's joy had indeed reached high-water mark.

"That will mean two hundred thousand francs?"

"Yes, Mademoiselle Grandet."

"Well, then, father, you can easily help Charles."

The surprise, the wrath, and bewilderment with which Belshazzar beheld *Mene, Mene, Tekel, Upharsin,* written upon his palace wall were as nothing compared with Grandet's cold fury; he had forgotten all about Charles, and now he found that all his daughter's inmost thoughts were of his nephew, and that this arithmetic of hers referred to him. It was exasperating.

"Look here!" he thundered; "ever since that scapegrace set foot in *my* house everything has gone askew. You take it upon yourselves to buy sugar-plums, and make a great set-out for him. I will not have these doings. I should think, at my age, I ought to know what is right and proper to do. At any rate, I have no need to take lessons from my daughter, nor from any one else. I shall do for my nephew whatever it is right and proper for me to do; it is no business of yours, you need not meddle in it. And now, as for you, Eugénie," he added, turning towards her, "if you say another word about it, I will send you and Nanon off to the Abbey at Noyers, see if I don't. Where is that boy? has he come downstairs yet?"

"No, dear," answered Mme. Grandet.

"Why, what is he doing then?"

"He is crying for his father," Eugénie said.

Grandet looked at his daughter, and found nothing to say. There was some touch of the father even in him. He took one or two turns up and down, and then went straight to his strong-room to think over possible investments. He had thoughts of buying consols. Those two thousand acres of woodland had brought him in six hundred thousand francs; then there was the money from the sale of the poplars, there was last year's income from various sources, and this year's savings, to say nothing of the bargain which he had just concluded; so that, leaving those two hundred thousand francs out of the question, he possessed a lump sum of nine hundred thousand livres. That twenty per cent., to be made in so short a time upon his outlay, tempted him. Consols stood at seventy. He jotted down his calculations on the margin of the paper that had brought the news of his brother's death; the moans of his nephew sounded in his ears the while, but he did not hear them; he went on with his work until Nanon thumped vigorously on the thick wall to summon her master to dinner. On the last step of the staircase beneath the archway, Grandet paused and thought.

"There is the interest beside the eight per cent.—I will do it. Fifteen hundred thousand francs in two years' time, in gold from Paris too, full weight. Well, what has become of my nephew?"

"He said he did not want anything," replied Nanon. "He ought to eat, or he will fall ill."

"It is so much saved," was her master's comment.

"Lord! yes," she replied.

"Pooh! he will not keep on crying for ever. Hunger drives the wolf from the woods."

Dinner was a strangely silent meal. When the cloth had been removed, Mme. Grandet spoke to her husband:

"We ought to go into mourning, dear."

"Really, Mme. Grandet, you must be hard up for ways of getting rid of money. Mourning is in the heart; it is not put on with clothes."

"But for a brother mourning is indispensable, and the Church bids us——"

"Then buy mourning out of your six louis; a band of crape will do for me; you can get me a band of crape."

Eugénie said nothing, and raised her eyes to heaven. Her generous instincts, so long repressed and dormant, had been suddenly awakened, and every kindly thought had been harshly checked as it had arisen. Outwardly this evening passed just as thousands of others had passed in their monotonous lives, but for the two women it was the most painful that they had ever spent. Eugénie sewed without raising her head; she took no notice of the workbox which Charles had looked at so scornfully yesterday evening. Mme. Grandet knitted away at her cuffs. Grandet sat twirling his thumbs, absorbed in schemes which should one day bring about results that would startle Saumur. Four hours went by. Nobody dropped in to see them. As a matter of fact, the whole town was ringing with the news of Grandet's sharp practice, following on the news of his brother's failure and his nephew's arrival. So imperatively did Saumur feel the need to thrash these matters thoroughly out, that all the vine-growers, great or small, were assembled beneath the des Grassins' roof, and frightful were the imprecations which were launched at the head of their late mayor.

Nanon was spinning; the whirr of her wheel was the only sound in the great room beneath the gray-painted rafters.

"Our tongues don't go very fast," she said, showing her large teeth, white as blanched almonds.

"There is no call for them to go," answered Grandet, roused from his calculations.

He beheld a vision of the future—he saw eight millions in

three years' time—he had set forth on a long voyage upon a golden sea.

"Let us go to bed. I will go up and wish my nephew a good-night from you all, and see if he wants anything."

Mme. Grandet stayed on the landing outside her room-door to hear what her worthy husband might say to Charles. Eugénie, bolder than her mother, went a step or two up the second flight.

"Well, nephew, you are feeling unhappy? Yes, cry, it is only natural, a father is a father. But we must bear our troubles patiently. Whilst you have been crying, I have been thinking for you; I am a kind uncle, you see. Come, don't lose heart. Will you take a little wine? Wine costs nothing at Saumur; it is common here; they offer it as they might offer you a cup of tea in the Indies. But you are all in the dark," Grandet went on. "That's bad, that's bad; one ought to see what one is doing."

Grandet went to the chimney-piece.

"What!" he cried, "a wax-candle! Where the devil have they fished that from? I believe the wenches would pull up the floor of my house to cook eggs for that boy."

Mother and daughter, hearing these words, fled to their rooms, and crept into their beds like frightened mice.

"Mme. Grandet, you have a lot of money somewhere, it seems," said the vine-grower, walking into his wife's rooms.

"I am saying my prayers, dear; wait a little," faltered the poor mother.

"The devil take your pious notions!" growled Grandet.

Misers have no belief in a life to come, the present is all in all to them. But if this thought gives an insight into the miser's springs of action, it possesses a wider application, it throws a pitiless light upon our own era—for money is the one all-powerful force, ours is pre-eminently the epoch when money is the lawgiver, socially and politically. Books and institutions, theories and practice, all alike combine to weaken the belief in a future life, the foundation on which the social edifice has been slowly reared for eighteen hundred years. The grave has almost lost its terrors for us. That future which awaited us beyond the *requiem* has been transported into the present, and one hope and one ambition possesses us all—to pass *per fas et nefas* into this earthly paradise of luxury, vanity, and pleasure, to deaden the soul and mortify the body for a brief possession of this promised land, just as in other days men were found willing to lay down their lives and to suffer martyrdom for the hope of eternal bliss. This thought can be read at large; it is stamped upon our age, which asks of the voter—the man who makes the laws—not "What do you think?" but "What can you pay?" And what will become of us when this doctrine has been handed down from the bourgeoisie to the people?

"Mme. Grandet, have you finished?" asked the cooper.

"I am praying for you, dear."

"Very well, good-night. To-morrow morning I shall have something to say to you."

Poor woman! she betook herself to sleep like a school-boy who has not learned his lessons, and sees before him the angry face of the master when he wakes. Sheer terror led her to wrap the sheets about her head to shut out all sounds, but just at that moment she felt a kiss on her forehead; it was Eugénie who had slipped into the room in the darkness, and stood there barefooted in her nightdress.

"Oh! mother, my kind mother," she said, "I shall tell him to-morrow morning that it was all my doing."

"No, don't; if you do, he will send you away to Noyers. Let me manage it; he will not eat me, after all."

"Oh! mamma, do you hear?"

"What?"

"*He* is crying still."

"Go back to bed, dear. The floor is damp, it will strike cold to your feet."

So ended the solemn day, which had brought for the poor wealthy heiress a lifelong burden of sorrow; never again would Eugénie Grandet sleep as soundly or as lightly as heretofore. It not seldom happens that at some time in their lives this or that human being will act literally "unlike himself," and yet in very truth in accordance with his nature. Is it not rather that we form our hasty conclusions of him without the aid of such light as psychology affords, without attempting to trace the mysterious birth and growth of the causes which led to these unforeseen results? And this passion, which had its roots in the depths of Eugénie's nature, should perhaps be studied as if it were the delicate fibre of some living organism to discover the secret of its growth. It was a passion that would influence her whole life, so that one day it would be sneeringly called a malady. Plenty of people would prefer to consider a catastrophe improbable rather than undertake the task of tracing the sequence of the events that led to it, to discovering how the links of the chain were forged one by one in the mind of the actor. In this case, Eugénie's past life will suffice to keen observers of human nature; her artless impulsiveness, her sudden outburst of tenderness will be no surprise to them. Womanly pity, that treacherous feeling, had filled her soul but the more completely because her life had been so uneventful that it had never been so called forth before.

So the trouble and excitement of the day disturbed her rest; she woke again and again to listen for any sound from her cousin's room, thinking that she still heard the moans that all day long had vibrated through her heart. Sometimes she seemed to see him lying up there, dying of grief; sometimes she dreamed that he was being starved to death. Towards morning she distinctly heard a terrible cry. She dressed herself at once, and in the dim light of the dawn fled noiselessly up the stairs to her cousin's room. The door stood open, the wax-candle had burned itself down to the socket.

Nature had asserted herself; Charles, still dressed, was sleeping in the armchair, with his head fallen forward on the bed; he had been dreaming as famished people dream. Eugénie admired the fair young face. It was flushed and tear-stained; the eyelids were swollen with weeping; he seemed to be still crying in his sleep, and Eugénie's own tears fell fast. Some dim feeling that his cousin was present awakened Charles; he opened his eyes, and saw her distress.

"Pardon me, cousin," he said dreamily. Evidently he had lost all reckoning of time, and did not know where he was.

"There are hearts here that feel for you, cousin, and *we* thought that you might perhaps want something. You should go to bed; you will tire yourself out if you sleep like that."

"Yes," he said, "that is true."

"Good-bye," she said, and fled, half in confusion, half-glad that she had come. Innocence alone dares to be thus bold, and virtue armed with knowledge weighs its actions as carefully as vice.

Eugénie had not trembled in her cousin's presence, but when she reached her own room again she could scarcely stand. Her ignorant life had suddenly come to an end; she remonstrated with herself, and blamed herself again and again. "What will he think of me? He will believe that I love him." Yet she knew that this was exactly what she wished him to believe. Love spoke plainly within her, knowing by instinct how love calls forth love. The moment when she stole into her cousin's room became a memorable event in the girl's lonely life. Are there not thoughts and deeds which, in love, are for some souls like a solemn betrothal?

An hour later she went to her mother's room, to help her to dress, as she always did. Then the two women went downstairs and took their places by the window, and waited for Grandet's coming in the anxiety which freezes or burns. Some natures cower, and others grow reckless, when a scene or painful agitation is in prospect; the feeling of dread is so widely felt that domestic animals will cry out when the slightest pain is inflicted on them as a punishment, while the same creature if hurt inadvertently will not utter a sound.

The cooper came downstairs, spoke in an absent-minded way to his wife, kissed Eugénie, and sat down to table. He seemed to have forgotten last night's threats.

"What has become of my nephew? The child is not much in the way."

"He is asleep, sir," said Nanon.

"So much the better, he won't want a wax-candle for that," said Grandet facetiously.

His extraordinary mildness and satirical humor puzzled Mme. Grandet; she looked earnestly at her husband. The good man—here, perhaps, it may be observed that in Touraine, Anjou, Poitou, and Brittany the designation *good man (bonhomme)*, which has been so often applied to Grandet, conveys no idea of merit; it is allowed to people of the worst temper as well as to good-natured idiots, and is applied without distinction to any man of a certain age—the good man, therefore, took up his hat and gloves with the remark—

"I am going to have a look round in the market-place; I want to meet the Cruchots."

"Eugénie, your father certainly has something on his mind."

As a matter of fact, Grandet always slept but little, and was wont to spend half the night in revolving and maturing schemes, a process by which his views, observations, and plans gained amazingly in clearness and precision; indeed, this was the secret of that constant success which was the admiration of Saumur. Time and patience combined will effect most things, and the man who accomplishes much is the man with the strong will who can wait. The miser's life is a constant exercise of every human faculty in the service of a personality. He believes in self-love and interest, and in no other motives of action, but interest is in some sort another form of self-love, to wit, a practical form dealing with the tangible and the concrete, and both forms are comprised in one master-passion, for self-love and interest are but two manifestations of egoism. Hence, perhaps, the prodigious interest which a miser excites when cleverly put upon the stage. What man is utterly without ambition? And what social ambition can be obtained without money? Every one has something in common with this being; he is a personification of humanity, and yet is revolting to all the feelings of humanity.

Grandet really "had something on his mind," as his wife used to say. In Grandet, as in every miser, there was a keen relish for the game, a constant craving to play men off one against another for his own benefit, to mulct them of their crowns without breaking the law. And did not every victim who fell into his clutches renew his sense of power, his just contempt for the weak of the earth who let themselves fall such an easy prey? Ah! who has understood the meaning of the lamb that lies in peace at the feet of God, that most touching symbol of meek victims who are doomed to suffer here below, and of the future that awaits them hereafter, of weakness and suffering glorified at last? But here on earth it is quite otherwise; the lamb is the miser's legitimate prey, and by him (when it is fat enough) it is contemptuously penned, killed, cooked, and eaten. On money and on this feeling of contemptuous superiority, we may say, the miser thrives.

During the night this excellent man's ideas had taken an entirely new turn; hence his unusual mildness. He had been weaving a web to entangle them in Paris; he would envelop them in its toils, they should be as clay in his hands; they should hope and tremble, come and go, toil and sweat, and all for his amusement, all for the old cooper in the dingy room at the head of the worm-eaten staircase in the old house at Saumur; it tickled his sense of humor.

He had been thinking about his nephew. He wanted to save his dead brother's name from dishonor in a way that should not cost a penny either to his nephew or to himself. He was about to invest his money for three years, his mind was quite at leisure from his own affairs; he really needed some outlet for his malicious energy, and here was an opportunity supplied by his brother's failure. The claws were idle, he had nothing to squeeze between them, so he would pound the Parisians for Charles' benefit, and exhibit himself in the light of an excellent brother at a very cheap rate. As a matter of fact, the honor of the family name counted for very little with him in this matter; he looked at it from the purely impersonal point of view of the gambler, who likes to see a game well played, although it is no affair of his. The Cruchots were necessary to him, but he did not mean to go in search of them; they should come to him. That very evening the comedy should begin, the main outlines were decided upon already, to-morrow he would be held up as an object of admiration all over the town, and his generosity should not cost him a farthing!

Eugénie, in her father's absence, was free to busy herself openly for her cousin, to feel the pleasure of pouring out for him in many ways the wealth of pity that filled her heart; for in pity alone women are content that we should feel their superiority, and the sublimity of devotion is the one height which they can pardon us for leaving to them.

Three or four times Eugénie went to listen to her cousin's breathing, that she might know whether he was awake or still sleeping; and when she was sure that he was rising, she turned her attention to his breakfast, and cream, coffee, fruit, eggs, plates, and glasses were all in turn the objects of her especial care. She softly climbed the rickety stairs to listen again. Was he dressing? Was he still sobbing? She went to the door at last and spoke—

"Cousin!"

"Yes, cousin."

"Would you rather have breakfast downstairs or up here in your room?"

"Whichever you please."

"How do you feel?"

"I am ashamed to say that I am hungry."

This talk through the closed door was like an episode in a romance for Eugénie.

"Very well then, we will bring your breakfast up to your room, so that my father may not be vexed about it."

She sprang downstairs, and ran into the kitchen with the swiftness of a bird.

"Nanon, just go and set his room straight."

The familiar staircase which she had gone up and down so often, and which echoed with every sound, seemed no longer old in Eugénie's eyes; it was radiant with light, it seemed to speak a language which she understood, it was young again as she herself was, young like the love in her heart. And the mother, the kind, indulgent mother, was ready to lend herself to her daughter's whims, and as soon as Charles' room was ready they both went thither to sit with him. Does not Christian charity bid us comfort the mourner? Little religious sophistries were not wanting by which the women justified themselves.

Charles Grandet received the most tender and affectionate care. Such delicate tact and sweet kindness touched him very closely in his desolation; and for these two souls, they found a moment's freedom from the restraint under which they lived; they were at home in an atmosphere of sorrow; they could give him the quick sympathy of fellowship in misfortune. Eugénie could avail herself of the privilege of relationship to set his linen in order, and to arrange the trifles that lay on the dressing-table; she could admire the wonderful knickknacks at her leisure; all the paraphernalia of luxury, the delicately-wrought gold and silver passed through her hands, her fingers dwelt lingeringly on them under the pretext of looking closely at the workmanship.

Charles was deeply touched by the generous interest which his aunt and cousin took in him. He knew Parisian life quite sufficiently to know that under these circumstances his old acquaintances and friends would have grown cold and distant at once. But his trouble had brought out all the peculiar beauty of Eugénie's character, and he began to admire the simplicity of manner which had provoked his amusement but yesterday. So when Eugénie waited on her cousin with such frank good-will, taking from Nanon the earthenware bowl full of coffee and cream to set it before him herself, the Parisian's eyes filled with tears; and when he met her kind glance, he impulsively took her hand in his and fervently kissed it.

"Well, what is the matter now?" she asked.

"Oh! they are tears of gratitude," he answered.

Eugénie turned hastily away, took the candles from the chimney-piece and held them out to Nanon.

"Here," she said, "take these away."

When she could look at her cousin again, the flush was still on her face, but her eyes at least did not betray her, and gave no sign of the excess of joy that flooded her heart; yet the same thought was dawning in both their souls, and could be read in the eyes of either, and they knew that the future was theirs. This thrill of happiness was all the sweeter to Charles in his great sorrow, because it was so little expected.

There was a knock at the door, and both the women hurried down to their places by the window. It was lucky for them that their flight downstairs was sufficiently precipitate, and that they were at their work when Grandet came in, for if he had met them beneath the archway, all his suspicions would be aroused at once. After the mid-day meal, which he took standing, the keeper, who had not yet received his promised reward, appeared from Froidfond, bringing with him a hare, some partridges shot in the park, a few eels, and a couple of pike sent by him from the miller's.

"Aha! so here is old Cornoiller; you come just when you are wanted, like salt fish in Lent. Is all that fit to eat?"

"Yes, sir; all killed the day before yesterday."

"Come, Nanon, look alive! Just take this, it will do for dinner to-day; the two Cruchots are coming."

Nanon opened her eyes with amazement, and stared first at one and then at another.

"Oh! indeed," she said, "and where are the herbs and the bacon to come from?"

"Wife," said Grandet, "let Nanon have six francs, and remind me to go down into the cellar to look out a bottle of good wine."

"Well, then, M. Grandet," the gamekeeper began (he wished to see the question of his salary properly settled, and was duly primed with a speech), "M. Grandet——"

"Tut, tut, tut," said Grandet, "I know what you are going to say; you are a good fellow, we will see about that to-morrow, I am very busy to-day. Give him five francs, wife," he added, looking at Mme. Grandet, and with that he beat a retreat. The poor woman was only too happy to purchase peace at the price of eleven francs. She knew by experience that Grandet usually kept quiet for a fortnight after he had made her disburse coin by coin the money which he had given her.

"There, Cornoiller," she said, as she slipped ten francs into his hand; "we will repay you for your services one of these days."

Cornoiller had no answer ready, so he went.

"Madame," said Nanon, who had by this time put on her black bonnet and had a basket on her arm, "three francs will be quite enough; keep the rest. I shall manage just as well with three."

"Let us have a good dinner, Nanon; my cousin is coming downstairs," said Eugénie.

"There is something very extraordinary going on, I am sure," said Mme. Grandet. "This makes the third time since we were married that your father has asked any one here to dinner."

It was nearly four o'clock in the afternoon; Eugénie and her mother had laid the cloth and set the table for six persons, and the master of the house had brought up two or three bottles of the exquisite wines, which are jealously hoarded in the cellars of the vine-growing district.

Charles came into the dining-room looking white and sad; there was a pathetic charm about his gestures, his face, his looks, the tones of his voice; his sorrow had given him the interesting look that women like so well, and Eugénie only loved him the more because his features were worn with pain. Perhaps, too, this trouble had brought them nearer in other ways. Charles was no longer the rich and handsome young man who lived in a sphere far beyond her ken; he was a kinsman in deep and terrible distress, and sorrow is a great leveler. Woman has this in common with the angels—all suffering creatures are under her protection.

Charles and Eugénie understood each other without a word being spoken on either side. The poor dandy of yesterday, fallen from his high estate, to-day was an orphan, who sat in a corner of the room, quiet, composed, and proud; but from time to time he met his cousin's eyes, her kind and affectionate glance rested on him, and compelled him to shake off his dark and sombre broodings, and to look forward with her to a future full of hope, in which she loved to think that she might share.

The news of Grandet's dinner-party caused even greater excitement in Saumur than the sale of his vintage, although this latter proceeding had been a crime of the blackest dye, an act of high treason against the vine-growing interest. If Grandet's banquet to the Cruchots has been prompted by the same idea which on a memorable occasion cost Alcibiades' dog its tail, history might perhaps have heard of the miser; but he felt himself to be above public opinion in this town which he exploited; he held Saumur too cheap.

It was not long before the des Grassins heard of Guillaume Grandet's violent end and impending bankruptcy. They determined to pay a visit to their client·that evening, to condole with him in his affliction, and to show a friendly interest; while they endeavored to discover the motives which could have led Grandet to invite the Cruchots to dinner at such a time.

Precisely at five o'clock President C. de Bonfons and his uncle the notary arrived, dressed up to the nines this time. The guests seated themselves at table, and began by attacking their dinner with remarkably good appetites. Grandet was solemn, Charles was silent, Eugénie was dumb, and Mme. Grandet said no more than usual; if it had been a funeral repast, it could not well have been less lively. When they rose from the table, Charles addressed his aunt and uncle—

"Will you permit me to withdraw? I have some long and difficult letters to write."

"By all means, nephew."

When Charles had left the room, and his amiable relative could fairly assume that he was out of earshot and deep in his correspondence, Grandet gave his wife a sinister glance.

"Mme. Grandet, what we are going to say will be Greek to you; it is half-past seven o'clock, you ought to be off to bed by this time. Good-night, my daughter." He kissed Eugénie, and mother and daughter left the room.

Then the drama began. Now, if ever in his life, Grandet displayed all the shrewdness which he had acquired in the course of his long experience of men and business, and all the cunning which had gained him the nickname of "old fox" among those who had felt his teeth a little too sharply. Had the ambition of the late mayor of Saumur soared a little higher; if he had had the luck to rise to a higher social sphere, and destiny had sent him to mingle in some congress in which the fate of nations is at stake, the genius which he was now devoting to his own narrow ends would doubtless have done France glorious service. And yet, after all, the probability is that once away from Saumur the worthy cooper would have cut but a poor figure, and that minds, like certain plants and animals, are sterile when removed to a distant climate and an alien soil.

"M-m-monsieur le P-p-président, you were s-s-saying that b-b-bankruptcy——"

Here the trick of stammering which it had pleased the vine-grower to assume so long ago that every one believed it to be natural to him (like the deafness of which he was wont to complain in rainy weather), grew so unbearably tedious for the Cruchot pair, that as they strove to catch the syllables, they made unconscious grimaces, moving their lips as if they would fain finish the words in which the cooper entangled both himself and them at his pleasure.

And here, perhaps, is the fitting place to record the history of Grandet's deafness and the impediment in his speech. No one in Anjou had better hearing or could speak Angevin French more clearly and distinctly than the wily vine-grower—when he chose. Once upon a time, in spite of all his shrewdness, a Jew had gotten the better of him. In the course of their discussion the Israelite had applied his hand to his ear, in the manner of an ear-trumpet, the better to catch what was said, and had gibbered to such purpose in his search for a word, that Grandet, a victim to his own humanity, felt constrained to suggest to that crafty Hebrew the words and ideas of which the Israelite appeared to be in search, to finish himself the reasonings of the said Hebrew, to say for that accursed alien all that he ought to have said for himself, till Grandet ended by fairly changing places with the Jew.

From this curious contest of wits the vine-grower did not emerge triumphant; indeed, for the first and last time in his business career he made a bad bargain. But loser though he was from a money point of view, he had received a great practical lesson, and later on he reaped the fruits of it. Wherefore in the end he blessed the Jew who had shown him how to wear out the patience of an opponent, and to keep him so closely employed in expressing his adversary's ideas that he completely lost sight of his own. The present business required more deafness, more stammering, more of the mazy circumlocutions in which Grandet was wont to involve himself, than any previous transaction in his life; for, in the first place, he wished to throw the responsibility of his ideas on some one else; some one else was to suggest his own schemes to him, while he was to keep himself to himself, and leave every one in the dark as to his real intentions.

"Mon-sieur de B-B-Bonfons." (This was the second time in three years that he had called the younger Cruchot "M. de Bonfons," and the president might well consider that this was almost tantamount to being acknowledged as the crafty cooper's son-in-law.)

"You were s-s-s-saying that in certain cases, p-p-p-proceedings in b-b-bankruptcy might be s-s-s-stopped b-b-by—— "

"At the instance of a Tribunal of Commerce. That is done every day of the year," said M. C. de Bonfons, guessing, as he thought, at old Grandet's idea, and running away with it. "Listen!" he said, and in the most amiable way he prepared to explain himself.

"I am l-listening," replied the older man meekly, and his face assumed a demure expression; he looked like some small boy who is laughing in his sleeve at the schoolmaster while appearing to pay the most respectful attention to every word.

"When anybody who is in a large way of business and is much looked up to, like your late brother in Paris, for instance—— "

"My b-b-brother, yes."

"When any one in that position is likely to find himself insolvent——"

"Ins-s-solvent, do they call it?"

"Yes. When his failure is imminent, the Tribunal of Commerce, to which he is amenable (do you follow me?) has power by a judgment to appoint liquidators to wind up the business. Liquidation is not bankruptcy, do you understand? It is a disgraceful thing to be a bankrupt, but a *liquidation* reflects no discredit on a man."

"It is quite a d-d-d-different thing, if only it d-d-does not cost any more," said Grandet.

"Yes. But a liquidation can be privately arranged without having recourse to the Tribunal of Commerce," said the president as he took a pinch of snuff. "How is a man declared bankrupt!"

"Yes, how?" inquired Grandet. "I have n-n-never thought about it."

"In the first place, he may himself file a petition and leave his schedule with the clerk of the court, the debtor himself draws it up or authorizes some one else to do so, and it is duly registered. Or, in the second place, his creditors may make him a bankrupt. But supposing the debtor does not file a petition, and none of his creditors make application to the court for a judgment declaring him bankrupt; now let us see what happens then!"

"Yes, let us s-s-see."

"In that case, the family of the deceased, or his representatives, or his residuary legatee, or the man himself (if he is not dead), or his friends for him (if he has absconded), liquidate his affairs. Now, possibly, *you* may intend to do this in your brother's case?" inquired the president.

"Oh! Grandet," exclaimed the notary, "that would be acting very handsomely. We in the provinces have our notions of honor. If you saved your name from dishonor, for it is your name, you would be——"

"Sublime!" cried the president, interrupting his uncle.

"Of course, my b-b-brother's n-n-name was Grandet, th-that is certain sure, I d-d-don't deny it, and anyhow this l-l-l-l-liquidation would be a very g-good thing for my n-n-nephew in every way, and I am very f-f-fond of him. But we shall see. I know n-n-nothing of those sharpers in Paris, and their t-tricks. And here am I at S-Saumur, you see! There are my vine-cuttings, m-my d-d-draining; in sh-sh-short, there are my own af-f-fairs, to s-s-see after. *I* have n-n-never accepted a bill. What is a bill? I have t-t-taken many a one, b-b-but I have n-n-never put my n-n-name to a piece of p-paper. You t-t-take 'em and you can d-d-d-discount 'em, and that is all I know. I have heard s-s-say that you can b-b-b-buy them——"

"Yes," assented the president. "You can buy bills on the market, less so much per cent. Do you understand?"

Grandet held his hand to his ear, and the president repeated his remark.

"But it s-s-seems there are t-t-two s-sides to all this?" replied the vine-grower. "At my age, I know n-n-nothing about this s-s-sort of thing. I must st-top here to l-look after the g-g-grapes, the vines d-d-don't stand still, and the g-g-grapes have to p-pay for everything. The vintage m-must be l-l-looked after before anything else. Then I have a g-great d-d-deal on my hands at Froidfond that I can't p-p-possibly l-l-l-leave to any one else. I don't underst-t-tand a word of all this; it is a p-p-pretty kettle of fish, confound it; I can't l-l-leave home to s-see after it. You s-s-s-say that to bring about a l-l-liquidation I ought to be in Paris. Now you can't be in t-t-two p-places at once unless you are a b-b-bird."

"*I* see what you mean," cried the notary. "Well, my old friend, you have friends, friends of long standing ready to do a great deal for you."

"Come, now!" said the vine-grower to himself, "so you are making up your minds, are you?"

"And if some one were to go to Paris, and find up your brother Guillaume's largest creditor, and say to him——"

"Here, just l-l-listen to me a moment," the cooper struck in. "Say to him——what? S-s-something like this: 'M. Grandet of Saumur th-this, M. Grandet of Saumur th-th-that. He l-l-loves his brother, he has a r-r-regard for his n-nephew; Grandet thinks a l-l-lot of his f-family, he means to d-do well by them. He has just s-s-sold his vintage uncommonly well. Don't drive the thing into b-b-b-bankruptcy, call a meeting of the creditors, and ap-p-point l-l-liquidators. Then s-see what Grandet will do. You will do a great d-deal b-b-better for yourselves by coming to an arrangement than by l-l-letting the l-l-lawyers poke their noses into it.' That is how it is, eh?"

"Quite so!" said the president.

"Because, look you here, Monsieur de Bon-Bon-Bonfons, you must l-l-look before you l-l-l-leap. And you can't d-do more than you can. A big af-f-fair like this wants l-l-looking into, or you may ru-ru-ruin yourself. That is so, isn't it, eh?"

"Certainly," said the president, "I myself am of the opinion that in a few months' time you could buy up the debts for a fixed sum and pay by installments. Aha! you can trail a dog a long way with a bit of bacon. When a man has not been declared bankrupt, as soon as the bills are in your hands, you will be as white as snow."

"As s-s-s-snow?" said Grandet, holding his hand to his ear. "S-s-s-snow. I don't underst-t-tand."

"Why, then, just listen to me!" cried the president.

"I am l-l-listening——"

"A bill of exchange is a commodity subject to fluctuations in value. This is a deduction from Jeremy Bentham's theory of interest. He was a publicist who showed conclusively that the prejudices entertained against money-lenders were irrational."

"Bless me!" put in Grandet.

"And seeing that, according to Bentham, money itself is a commodity, and that which money represents is no less a commodity," the president went on; "and since it is obvious that the commodity called a bill of exchange is subject to the same laws of supply and demand that control production of all kinds, a bill of exchange bearing this or that signature, like this or that article of commerce, is scarce or plentiful in the market, commands a high premium or is worth nothing at all. Wherefore the decision of this court—— There! how stupid I am, I beg your pardon; I mean I am of the opinion that you could easily buy up your brother's debts for twenty-five per cent of their value."

"You m-m-m-mentioned Je-je-je-jeremy Ben——"

"Bentham, an Englishman."

"That is a Jeremiah who will save us many lamentations in business matters," said the notary, laughing.

"The English s-s-sometimes have s-s-s-sensible notions," said Grandet. "Then, according to B-Bentham, how if my b-b-brother's b-bills are worth n-n-n-nothing? If I am right, it looks to me as if——the creditors would——n-no, they wouldn't——I underst-t-tand."

"Let me explain all this to you," said the president. "In law, if you hold all the outstanding bills of the firm of Grandet, your brother, his heirs and assigns, would owe no one a penny. So far, so good."

"Good," echoed Grandet.

"And in equity; suppose that your brother's bills were negotiated upon the market (negotiated, do you understand the meaning of that term?) at a loss of so much per cent.; and suppose one of your friends happened to be passing, and bought up the bills; there would have been no physical force brought to bear upon the creditors, they gave them up of their own free-will, and the estate of the late Grandet of Paris would be clear in the eye of the law."

"True," stuttered the cooper, "b-b-business is business.

So that is s-s-s-settled. But, for all that, you understand that it is a d-d-difficult matter. I have not the m-m-money, nor have I the t-t-t-time, nor——"

"Yes, yes; you cannot be at the trouble. Well, now, I will go to Paris for you if you like (you must stand the expenses of the journey, that is a mere trifle). I will see the creditors, and talk to them, and put them off; it can all be arranged; you will be prepared to add something to the amount realized by the liquidation so as to get the bills into your hands."

"We shall s-see about that; I cannot and *will* not under-t-t-take anything unless I know——You can't d-d-do more than you can, you know."

"Quite so, quite so."

"And I am quite bewildered with all these head-splitting ideas that you have sp-prung upon me. Th-this is the f-f-f-first t-time in my l-l-life that I have had to th-th-think about such th——"

"Yes, yes, you are not a consulting barrister."

"I am a p-p-poor vine-grower, and I know n-n-nothing about what you have just t-t-t-told me; I m-m-must th-think it all out."

"Well! then," began the president, as if he meant to reopen the discussion.

"Nephew!" interrupted the notary reproachfully.

"Well, uncle?" answered the president.

"Let M. Grandet explain what he means to do. It is a very important question, and you are to receive his instructions. Our dear friend might now very pertinently state——"

A knock at the door announced the arrival of the des Grassins; their coming and exchange of greetings prevented Cruchot senior from finishing his sentence. Nor was he ill-pleased with this diversion; Grandet was looking askance at him already, and there was that about the wen on the cooper's face which indicated that a storm was brewing within. And on sober reflection it seemed to the cautious notary that a president of a court of first instance was not exactly the person to dispatch to Paris, there to open negotiations with creditors, and to lend himself to a more than dubious transaction which, however you looked at it, hardly squared with notions of strict honesty; and not only so, but he had particularly noticed that M. Grandet had shown not the slightest inclination to disburse anything whatever, and he trembled instinctively at the thought of his nephew becoming involved in such a business. He took advantage of the entrance of the des Grassins, took his nephew by the arm, and drew him into the embrasure of the window.

"You have gone quite as far as there is any need," he said, "that is quite enough of such zeal; you are overreaching yourself in your eagerness to marry the girl. The devil! You should not rush into a thing open-mouthed, like a crow at a walnut. Leave the steering of the ship to me for a bit, and just shift your sails according to the wind. Now, is it a part you ought to play, compromising your dignity as magistrate in such a——"

He broke off suddenly, for he heard M. des Grassins saying to the old cooper, as he held out his hand—

"Grandet, we have heard of the dreadful misfortunes which have befallen your family—the ruin of the firm of Guillaume Grandet and your brother's death; we have come to express our sympathy and to offer you our consolation in this sad calamity."

"There is only one misfortune," the notary interrupted at this point, "the death of the younger M. Grandet; and if he had thought to ask his brother for assistance, he would not have taken his own life. Our old friend here, who is a man of honor to his finger-tips, is prepared to discharge the debts contracted by the firm of Grandet in Paris. In order to spare our friend the worry of what is, after all, a piece of lawyer's business, my nephew the president offers to start immediately for Paris, so as to arrange with the creditors, and duly satisfy their claims."

The three des Grassins were thoroughly taken aback by these words; Grandet appeared to acquiesce in what had been said, for he was pensively stroking his chin. On their way to the house the family had commented very freely upon Grandet's niggardliness, and indeed had almost gone so far as to accuse him of fratricide.

"Ah! just what I expected!" cried the banker, looking at his wife. "What was I saying to you only just now as we came along, Mme. des Grassins? Grandet, I said, is a man who will never swerve a hair's-breadth from the strict course of honor; he will not endure the thought of the slightest spot on his name! Money without honor is a disease. Oh! we have a keen sense of honor in the provinces! This is noble—really noble of you, Grandet. I am an old soldier, and I do not mince matters, I say what I think straight out; and *mille tonnerres!* this is sublime!"

"Then the s-s-sub-sublime costs a great d-d-deal," stuttered the cooper, as the banker shook him warmly by the hand.

"But this, my good Grandet (no offense to you, M. le Président), is simply a matter of business," des Grassins went on, "and requires an experienced man of business to deal with it. There will have to be accounts kept of sales and outgoing expenses; you ought to have tables of interest at your finger-ends. I must go to Paris on business of my own, and I could undertake——"

"Then we must s-s-see about it, and t-t-t-try to arrange between us to p-p-provide for anything that m-may t-t-turn up, but I d-d-don't want to be d-d-drawn into anything that I would rather not d-d-d-do," continued Grandet, "because, you see, M. le Président naturally wants me to pay his expenses." The good man did not stammer over these last words.

"Eh?" said Mme. des Grassins. "Why, it is a pleasure

to stay in Paris! For my part, I should be glad to go there at my own expense."

She made a sign to her husband, urging him to seize this opportunity of discomfiting their enemies and cheat them of their mission. Then she flung a withering glance at the now crestfallen and miserable Cruchots. Grandet seized the banker by the button-hole and drew him aside.

"I should feel far more confidence in you than in the president," he remarked; "and besides that," he added (and the wen twitched a little), "there are other fish to fry. I want to make an investment. I have several thousand francs to put into consols, and I don't mean to pay more than eighty for them. Now, from all I can hear, that machine always runs down at the end of the month. You know all about these things, I expect?"

"*Pardieu!* I should think I did. Well, then, I shall have to buy several thousand livres worth of consols for you."

"Just by way of a beginning. But mum, I want to play at this game without letting any one know about it. You will buy them for me at the end of the month, and say nothing to the Cruchots; it would only annoy them. Since you are going to Paris, we might as well see at the same time what trumps are for my poor nephew's sake."

"That is an understood thing. I shall travel post to Paris to-morrow," said des Grassins aloud, "and I will come round to take your final instructions at—when shall we say?"

"At five o'clock, before dinner," said the vine-grower, rubbing his hands.

The two factions for a little while remained facing each other. Des Grassins broke the silence again, clapping Grandet on the shoulder, and saying—

"It is a fine thing to have a good uncle like——"

"Yes, yes," returned Grandet, falling into the stammer again, "without m-making any p-p-parade about it; I am a good uncle; I l-l-loved my brother; I will give p-p-p-proof of it, if-if-if it d-doesn't cost——"

Luckily the banker interrupted him at this point.

"We must go, Grandet. If I am to set out sooner than I intended, I shall have to see after some business at once before I go."

"Right, quite right. I myself, in connection with you know what, must p-p-put on my cons-s-sidering cap, as P-President Cruchot s-s-says."

"Plague take it! I am no longer M. de Bonfons," thought the magistrate moodily, and his face fell; he looked like a judge who is bored by the cause before him.

The heads of the rival clans went out together. Both had completely forgotten Grandet's treacherous crime of that morning; his disloyal behavior had faded from their minds. They sounded each other, but to no purpose, as to Grandet's real intentions (if intentions he had) in this new turn that matters had taken.

"Are you coming with us to Mme. Dorsonval's?" des Grassins asked the notary.

"We are going there later on," replied the president. "With my uncle's permission, we will go first to see Mlle. de Gribeaucourt; I promised just to look in on her to say goodnight."

"We shall meet again, then," smiled Mme. des Grassins.

But when the des Grassins were at some distance from the two Cruchots, Adolphe said to his father, "They are in a pretty stew, eh?"

"Hush!" returned his mother, "they can very likely hear what we are saying, and, besides, that remark of yours was not in good taste; it sounds like one of your law school phrases."

"Well, uncle!" cried the magistrate, when he saw the des Grassins were out of earshot, "I began by being President de Bonfons and ended as plain Cruchot."

"I saw myself that you were rather put out about it; and the des Grassins took the wind out of our sails. How stupid you are, for all your sharpness! Let *them* set sail, on the strength of a 'We shall see' from Grandet; be easy, my boy, Eugénie shall marry you for all that."

A few moments later and the news of Grandet's magnanimity was set circulating in three houses at once; the whole town talked of nothing but Grandet's devotion to his brother. The sale of his vintage in utter disregard of the agreement made among the vine-growers was forgotten; every one fell to praising his scrupulous integrity and to lauding his generosity, a quality which no one had suspected him of possessing. There is that in the French character which is readily excited to fury or to passionate enthusiasm by any meteor that appears above their horizon, that is captivated by the bravery of a blatant fact. Can it be that collectively men have no memories?

As soon as Grandet had bolted the house-door he called to Nanon:

"Don't go to bed," he said, "and don't unchain the dog; there is something to be done, and we must do it together. Cornoiller will be round with the carriage from Froidfond at eleven o'clock. You must sit up for him, and let him in quietly; don't let him rap at the door, and tell him not to make a noise. You get into trouble with the police if you raise a racket at night. And, besides, there is no need to let all the quarter know that I am going out."

Having thus delivered himself, Grandet went up to his laboratory, and Nanon heard him stirring about, rummaging, going and coming, all with great caution. Clearly he had no wish to waken his wife or daughter, and above all things he desired in nowise to excite any suspicion in the mind of his nephew; he had seen that a light was burning in the young man's room, and had cursed his relative forthwith.

In the middle of the night Eugénie heard a sound like the

groan of a dying man; her cousin was always in her thoughts, and for her the dying man was Charles. How white and despairing he had looked when he wished her good-night; perhaps he had killed himself. She hastily wrapped herself in her capuchine, a sort of long cloak with a hood to it, and determined to go to see for herself. Some rays of bright light streaming through the cracks of her door frightened her not a little at first, perhaps the house was on fire; but she was soon reassured. She could hear Nanon's heavy footsteps outside, and the sounds of the old servant's voice mingled with the neighing of several horses.

"Can my father be taking Charles away?" she asked herself, as she set her door ajar, cautiously for fear the hinges should creak, so that she could watch all that was going on in the corridor.

All at once her eyes met those of her father, and, absent and indifferent as they looked, a cold shudder ran through her. The cooper and Nanon were coming along carrying something which hung by a chain from a stout cudgel, one end of which rested on the right shoulder of either; the something was a little barrel such as Grandet sometimes amused himself by making in the bakehouse, when he had nothing better to do.

"Holy Virgin! how heavy it is, sir!" said Nanon in a whisper.

"What a pity it is only full of pence!" replied the cooper. "Lookout! or you will knock down the candlestick."

The scene was lighted by a single candle set between two balusters.

"Cornoiller," said Grandet to his gamekeeper *in partibus*, "have you your pistols with you?"

"No, sir. Lord, love you! What can there be to fear for a keg of coppers?"

"Oh! nothing, nothing," said M. Grandet.

"Besides, we shall get over the ground quickly," the keeper

went on; "your tenants have picked out their best horses for you."

"Well, well. You did not let them know where I was going?"

"I did not know that myself."

"Right. Is the carriage strongly built?"

"That's all right, master. Why, what is the weight of a few paltry barrels like those of yours? It would carry two or three thousand like them."

"Well," said Nanon, "I know there's pretty nigh eighteen hundredweight *there*, that there is!"

"Will you hold you tongue, Nanon! You tell my wife that I have gone into the country, and that I shall be back to dinner. Hurry up, Cornoiller; we must be in Angers before nine o'clock."

The carriage started. Nanon bolted the gateway, let the dog loose, and lay down and slept in spite of her bruised shoulder; and no one in the quarter had any suspicion of Grandet's journey or of its object. The worthy man was a miracle of circumspection. Nobody ever saw a penny lying about in that house full of gold. He had learned that morning from the gossip on the quay that some vessels were being fitted out at Nantes, and that in consequence gold was so scarce there that it was worth double its ordinary value, and speculators were buying it in Angers. The old cooper, by the simple device of borrowing his tenants' horses, was prepared to sell his gold at Angers, receiving in return an order upon the Treasury from the Receiver-General for the sum destined for the purchase of his consols, and an addition in the shape of the premium paid on his gold.

"My father is going out," said Eugénie to herself. She had heard all that had passed from the head of the staircase.

Silence reigned once more in the house. The rattle of the wheels in the streets of sleeping Saumur grew more and more distant, and at last died away. Then it was that a sound

THE DOOR STOOD AJAR; SHE THRUST IT OPEN.

seemed to reach Eugénie's heart before it fell on her ears, a wailing sound that rang through the thin walls above—it came from her cousin's room. There was a thin line of light, scarcely wider than a knife edge, beneath his door; the rays slanted through the darkness and left a bright gleaming bar along the balusters of the crazy staircase.

"He is unhappy," she said, as she went up a little farther.

A second moan brought her to the landing above. The door stood ajar; she thrust it open. Charles was sleeping in the rickety old armchair, his head drooped over to one side, his hand hung down and nearly touched the floor, the pen that he had let fall lay beneath his fingers. Lying in this position, his breath came in quick, sharp jerks that startled Eugénie. She entered hastily.

"He must be very tired," she said to herself, as she saw a dozen sealed letters lying on the table. She read the addresses —*MM. Farry, Breilman and Co., carriage builders; M. Buisson, tailor;* and so forth.

"Of course, he has been settling his affairs, so that he may leave France as soon as possible," she thought.

Her eyes fell upon two unsealed letters. One of them began—"My dear Annette "—— She felt dazed, and could see nothing for a moment. Her heart beat fast, her feet seemed glued to the floor.

"*His dear Annette!* He loves, he is beloved!—— Then there is no more hope!—— What does he say to her?" These thoughts flashed through her heart and brain. She read the words everywhere: on the walls, on the very floor, in letters of fire.

"Must I give him up already? No, I will not read the letter. I ought not to stay—— And yet, even if I did read it?"

She looked at Charles, gently took his head in her hands, and propped it against the back of the chair. He submitted like a child, who even while he is sleeping knows that it is his mother who is bending over him, and, without waking, feels his mother's kisses. Like a mother, Eugénie raised the drooping hand, and, like a mother, laid a soft kiss on his hair. "*Dear Annette!*" A mocking voice shrieked the words in her ear.

"I know that perhaps I may be doing wrong, but I will read that letter," she said.

Eugénie turned her eyes away; her high sense of honor reproached her. For the first time in her life there was a struggle between good and evil in her soul. Hitherto she had never done anything for which she needed to blush. Love and curiosity silenced her scruples. Her heart swelled higher with every phrase as she read; her quickened pulses seemed to send a sharp, tingling glow through her veins, and to heighten the vivid emotions of her first love.

"MY DEAR ANNETTE: — Nothing should have power to separate us save this overwhelming calamity that has befallen me, a calamity that no human foresight could have predicted. My father has died by his own hand; his fortune and mine are both irretrievably lost. I am left an orphan at an age when, with the kind of education I have received, I am almost a child; and, nevertheless, I must now endeavor to show myself a man, and to rise from the dark depths into which I have been hurled. I have been spending part of my time to-night in revolving plans for my future. If I am to leave France as an honest man, as of course I mean to do, I have not a hundred francs that I can call my own with which to tempt fate in the Indies or in America. Yes, my poor Anna, I am going in quest of fortune to the most deadly foreign climes. Beneath such skies, they say, fortunes are rapidly and surely made. As for living on in Paris, I could not bring myself to do it. I could not face the coldness, the contempt, and the affronts that a ruined man, the son of a bankrupt, is sure

to receive. Great heaven! to owe two millions!——
I should fall in a duel before a week had passed. So I
shall not return to Paris. Your love—the tenderest, the
most devoted love that ever ennobled the heart of man—
would not seek to draw me back. Alas! my darling, I
have not money enough to take me to you, that I might give
and receive one last kiss, a kiss that should put strength into
me for the task that lies before me——"

"Poor Charles, I did well to read this. I have money,
and he shall have it," said Eugénie. She went on with the
letter when her tears permitted her to see.

"I have not even begun to think of the hardships of poverty. Supposing that I find I have the hundred louis to pay
for my passage out, I have not a sou to lay out on a trading
venture. Yet, no; I shall not have a hundred louis, nor yet
a hundred sous; I have no idea whether anything will be left
when I have settled all my debts in Paris. If there is nothing,
I shall simply go to Nantes and work my passage out. I will
begin at the bottom of the ladder, like many another man of
energy who has gone out to the Indies as a penniless youth,
to return thence a rich man. This morning I began to look
my future steadily in the face. It is far harder for me than
for others; I have been the petted child of a mother who
idolized me, indulged by the best and kindest of fathers; and
at my very entrance into the world I met with the love of an
Anna. As yet I have only known the primrose paths of life;
such happiness could not last. Yet, dear Annette, I have
more fortitude than could be looked for from a thoughtless
youth; above all, from a young man thus lapped round in
happiness from the cradle, spoiled and flattered by the most
delightful woman in Paris, the darling of fortune, whose
wishes were as law to a father who—— Oh! my father! He
is dead, Annette! Well, I have thought seriously over my

position, and I have likewise thought over yours. I have grown much older in the last twenty-four hours. Dear Anna, even if, to keep me beside you, you were to give up all the luxuries that you enjoy, your box at the opera, and your toilet, we should not have nearly sufficient for the necessary expenses of the extravagant life that I am accustomed to; and, besides, I could not think of allowing you to make such sacrifices for me. To-day, therefore, we part forever."

"Then this is to take leave of her! Holy Virgin! what happiness!"

Eugénie started and trembled for joy. Charles stirred in his chair, and Eugénie felt a chill of dread. Luckily, however, he did not awaken. She went on reading.

"When shall I come back? I cannot tell. Europeans grow old before their time in those tropical countries, especially Europeans who work hard. Let us look forward and try to see ourselves in ten years' time. In ten years from now your little girl will be eighteen years old; she will be your constant companion; that is, she will be a spy upon you. If the world will judge you very harshly, your daughter will probably judge more harshly still; such ingratitude on a young girl's part is common enough, and we know how the world regards these things. Let us take warning and be wise. Only keep the memory of those four years of happiness in the depths of your soul, as I shall keep them buried in mine; and be faithful, if you can, to your poor friend. I shall not be too exacting, dear Annette; for, as you can see, I must submit to my altered lot; I am compelled to look at life in a business-like way, and to base my calculations on dull, prosaic fact. So I ought to think of marriage as a necessary step in my new existence; and I will confess to you that here, in my uncle's house in Saumur, there is a cousin whose manners, face, character, and heart you would approve; and who, moreover, has, it appears——"

"How tired he must have been to break off like this when he was writing to *her!*" said Eugénie to herself, as the letter ended abruptly in the middle of a sentence. She was ready with excuses for him.

How was it possible that an inexperienced girl should discover the coldness and selfishness of this letter? For young girls, religiously brought up as she had been, are innocent and unsuspecting, and can see nothing but love when they have set foot in love's enchanted kingdom. It is as if a light from heaven shone in their own souls, shedding its beams upon their path; their lover shines transfigured before them in reflected glory, radiant with fair colors from love's magic fires, and endowed with noble thoughts which perhaps in truth are none of his. Women's errors spring, for the most part, from a belief in goodness, and a confidence in truth. In Eugénie's heart the words, "My dear Annette—my beloved," echoed like the fairest language of love; they stirred her soul like organ music—like the divine notes of the *Venite adoremus* falling upon her ears in childhood.

Surely the tears, not dry even yet upon her cousin's eyelids, betokened the innate nobility of nature that never fails to attract a young girl. How could she know that Charles' love and grief for his father, albeit genuine, was due rather to the fact that his father had loved him than to a deeply-rooted affection on his own part for his father? M. and Mme. Guillaume Grandet had indulged their son's every whim; every pleasure that wealth could bestow had been his; and thus it followed that he had never been tempted to make the hideous calculations that are only too common among the younger members of a family in Paris, when they see around them all the delights of Parisian life, and reflect with disgust that, so long as their parents are alive, all these enjoyments are not for them. The strange result of the father's lavish kindness had been a strong affection on the part of his son, an affection unalloyed by any after-thought. But, for all that, Charles was a thorough child of Paris, with the Parisian's habit of mind; Annette herself had impressed upon him the importance of thinking out all the consequences of every step; he was not youthful, despite the mask of youth.

He had received the detestable education of a world in which more crimes (in thought and word at least) are committed in one evening than come before a court of justice in the course of a whole session; a world in which great ideas perish, done to death by a witticism, and where it is reckoned a weakness not to see things as they are. To see things as they are—that means, believe in nothing, put faith in nothing and in no man, for there is no such thing as sincerity in opinion or affection; mistrust events, for even events at times have been known to be manufactured. To see things as they are you must weigh your friend's purse morning by morning; you must know by instinct the right moment to interfere for your own profit in every matter that turns up; you must keep your judgment rigorously suspended, be in no hurry to admire a work of art or a noble deed, and give every one credit for interested motives on every possible occasion.

After many follies, the great lady, the fair Annette, compelled Charles to think seriously; she talked to him of his future, passing a fragrant hand through his hair, and imparted counsel to him on the art of getting on in the world, while she twisted a stray curl about her fingers. She had made him effeminate, and now she set herself to make a materialist of him, a twofold work of demoralization, a corruption none the less deadly because it never offended against the canons of good society, good manners, and good taste.

"You are a simpleton, Charles," she would say; "I see that it will be no easy task to teach you the ways of the world. You were very naughty about M. des Lupeaulx. Oh! he is not over-fastidious, I grant you, but you should wait until he falls from power, and then you may despise him as much as you like. Do you know what Mme. Campan used to say to us? 'My children, so long as a man is a Minister, adore him; if he falls, help to drag him to the shambles. He is a kind of deity so long as he is in power, but after he is fallen and ruined he is viler than Marat himself, for he is still alive, while Marat is dead and out of sight. Life is nothing but a series of combinations, which must be studied and followed very carefully if a good position is to be successfully maintained.'"

Charles had no very exalted aims; he was too much of a worldling; he had been too much spoiled by his father and mother, too much flattered by the society in which he moved, to be stirred by any lofty enthusiasm. In the clay of his nature there was a grain of gold, due to his mother's teaching; but it had been passed through the Parisian draw-plate, and beaten out into a thin surface gilding which must soon be worn away by contact with the world.

At this time Charles, however, was only one-and-twenty, and it is taken for granted that freshness of heart accompanies the freshness of youth; it seems so unlikely that the mind within should be at variance with the young face, and the young voice, and the candid glance. Even the hardest judge, the most sceptical attorney, the flintiest-hearted money-lender will hesitate to believe that a wizened heart and a warped and corrupted nature can dwell beneath a young exterior, when the forehead is smooth and tears come so readily to the eyes. Hitherto Charles had never had occasion to put his Parisian maxims in practice; his character had not been tried, and consequently had not been found wanting; but, all unknown to him, egoism had taken deep root in his nature. The seeds of this baneful political economy had been sown in his heart; it was only a question of time, they would spring up and flower so soon as the soil was stirred, as soon as he ceased to be an idle spectator and became an actor in the drama of real life.

A young girl is nearly always ready to believe unquestioningly in the promise of a fair exterior; but even if Eugénie had been as keenly observant and as cautious as girls in the provinces sometimes are, how could she have brought herself to mistrust her cousin, when all he did and said, and everything about him, seemed to be the spontaneous outcome of a noble nature? This was the last outburst of real feeling, the last reproachful sigh of conscience in Charles' life; fate had thrown them together at that moment, and, unfortunately for her, all her sympathies had been aroused for him.

So she laid down the letter that seemed to her so full of love, and gave herself up to the pleasure of watching her sleeping cousin; the dreams and hopes of youth seemed to hover over his face, and then and there she vowed to herself that she would love him always. She glanced over the other letter; there could be no harm in reading it, she thought; she should only receive fresh proofs of the noble qualities with which, womanlike, she had invested the man whom she had idealized.

"MY DEAR ALPHONSE," so it began, "by the time this letter is in your hands I shall have no friends left; but I will confess that though I put no faith in the worldly-minded people who use the word so freely, I have no doubts of your friendship for me. So I am commissioning you to settle some matters of business. I look to you to do the best you can for me in this, for all I have in the world is involved in it. By this time you must know how I am situated. I have nothing, and have made up my mind to go out to the Indies. I have just written to all the people to whom any money is owing, and the enclosed list is as accurate as I can make it from memory. I think the sale of my books, furniture, carriages, horses, and so forth ought to bring in sufficient to pay my debts. I only mean to keep back a few trinkets of little value, which will go some way towards a trading venture. I will send you a power of attorney in due form for this sale, my dear Alphonse, in case any difficulty should arise. You might send my guns and everything of that sort to me here. And you must take 'Briton;' no one would ever give me anything like as much as the splendid animal is worth; I would rather give him to you, you must regard him as the mourning ring which a dying man leaves in his will to his executor. Farry, Breilman and Co. have been building a very comfortable traveling carriage for me, but they have not sent it home yet; get them to keep it if you can, and if they decline to have it left on their hands, make the best arrangement you can for me, and do all you can to save my honor in the position in which I am placed. I lost six louis at play to that fellow from the British Isles, mind that he is——"

"Dear cousin," murmured Eugénie, letting the sheet fall, and, seizing one of the lighted candles, she hastened on tiptoe to her own room.

Once there, it was not without a keen feeling of pleasure that she opened one of the drawers in an old oak chest—a most beautiful specimen of the skill of the craftsmen of the Renaissance, you could still make out the half-effaced royal salamander upon it. From this drawer she took a large red velvet money-bag, with gold tassels, and the remains of a golden fringe about it, a bit of faded splendor that had belonged to her grandmother. In the pride of her heart she felt its weight, and joyously set to work to reckon up the value of her little hoard, sorting out the different coins. *Imprimis*, twenty Portuguese moidores, as new and fresh as when they were struck in 1725, in the reign of John V.; each was nominally worth five lisbonines, or a hundred and sixty-five francs, but actually they were worth a hundred and eighty francs (so her father used to tell her), a fancy value on account of the rarity and beauty of the aforesaid coins, which shone like the sun. *Item*, five genovines, rare Genoese coins of a hundred livres each, their current value was perhaps about eighty francs, but collectors would give a hundred for them. These had come to her from old M. de la Bertellière. *Item*, three Spanish quadruples of the time of Philip V., bearing the date 1729. Mme. Gentillet had given them to her, one by one, always with the same little speech: "There's a little yellow bird, there's a buttercup for you, worth ninety-eight livres! Take great care of it, darling; it will be the flower of your flock." *Item* (and those were the coins that her father thought most of, for the gold was a fraction over the twenty-three carats), a hundred Dutch ducats, struck at the Hague in 1756, and each worth about thirteen francs. *Item*, a great curiosity!—— a few coins dear to a miser's heart, three rupees bearing the sign of the Balance, and five with the sign of the Virgin stamped upon them, all pure gold of twenty-four carats—the magnificent coins of the Great Mogul. The weight of metal in them alone was worth thirty-seven francs forty centimes, but amateurs who love to finger gold would give fifty francs for such coins as those. *Item*, the double napoleon that had been given to her the day before, and which she had carelessly slipped into the red velvet bag.

There were new gold-pieces fresh from the mint among her treasures, real works of art, which old Grandet liked to look at from time to time, so that he might count them over and tell his daughter of their intrinsic value, expatiating also upon the beauty of the bordering, the sparkling field, the ornate lettering with its sharp, clean, flawless outlines. But now she gave not a thought to their beauty and rarity; her father's mania and the risks she ran by despoiling herself of a hoard so precious in his eyes were all forgotten. She thought of nothing but her cousin, and managed at last to discover, after many mistakes in calculation, that she was the owner of eighteen hundred francs all told, or of nearly two thousand francs if the coins were sold for their actual value as curiosities.

She clapped her hands in exultation at the sight of her riches, like a child who is compelled to find some outlet for his overflowing glee and dances for joy. Father and daughter had both counted their wealth that night; he in order to sell his gold, she that she might cast it abroad on the waters of love. She put the money back into the old purse, took it up, and went upstairs with it without a moment's hesitation. Her cousin's distress was the one thought in her mind; she did not even remember that it was night, conventionalities were utterly forgotten; her conscience did not reproach her, she was strong in her happiness and her love.

As she stood upon the threshold with the candle in one hand and the velvet bag in the other, Charles awoke, saw his cousin, and was struck dumb with astonishment. Eugénie came forward, set the light on the table, and said with an unsteady voice:

"Cousin Charles, I have to ask your forgiveness for something I have done; it was very wrong, but if you will overlook it, God will forgive me."

"What can it be?" asked Charles, rubbing his eyes.

"I have been reading those two letters."

Charles reddened.

"Do you ask how I came to do it?" she went on, "and why I came up here? Indeed, I do not know now; and I am almost tempted to feel glad that I read the letters, for through reading them I have come to know your heart, your soul, and——"

"And what?" asked Charles.

"And your plans—the difficulty that you are in for want of money——"

"My *dear* cousin——"

"Hush! hush! do not speak so loud, do not let us wake anybody. Here are the savings of a poor girl who has no wants," she went on, opening the purse. "You must take them, Charles. This morning I did not know what money was; you have taught me that it is simply a means to an end, that is all. A cousin is almost a brother; surely you may borrow from your sister."

Eugénie, almost as much a woman as a girl, had not foreseen a refusal, but her cousin was silent.

"Why, are you going to refuse me?" asked Eugénie. The silence was so deep that the beating of her heart was audible. Her pride was wounded by her cousin's hesitation, but the thought of his dire need came vividly before her, and she fell on her knees.

"I will not rise," she said, "until you have taken that money. Oh! cousin, say something, for pity's sake!——so that I may know that you respect me, that you are generous, that——"

This cry, wrung from her by a noble despair, brought tears to Charles' eyes; he would not let her kneel, she felt his hot tears on her hands, and sprang to her purse, which she emptied out upon the table.

"Well, then, it is 'Yes,' is it not?" she said, crying for joy. "Do not scruple to take it, cousin; you will be quite rich. That gold will bring you luck, you know. Some day you shall pay it back to me, or, if you like, we will be partners; I will submit to any conditions that you may impose. But you ought not to make so much of this gift."

Charles found words at last.

"Yes, Eugénie, I should have a little soul indeed if I would not take it. But nothing for nothing, confidence for confidence."

"What do you mean?" she asked, startled.

"Listen, dear cousin, I have there——"

He interrupted himself for a moment to show her a square box in a leather case, which stood on the chest of drawers.

"There is something there that is dearer to me than life. That box was a present from my mother. Since this morning I have thought that if she could rise from her tomb she herself would sell the gold that in her tenderness she lavished on this dressing-case, but I cannot do it—it would seem like sacrilege."

Eugénie grasped her cousin's hand tightly in hers at these last words.

"No," he went on after a brief pause, during which they looked at each other with tearful eyes, "I do not want to pull it to pieces, nor to risk taking it with me on my wanderings. I will leave it in your keeping, dear Eugénie. Never did one friend confide a more sacred trust to another; but you shall judge for yourself."

He drew the box from its leather case, opened it, and displayed before his cousin's astonished eyes a dressing-case resplendent with gold—the curious skill of the craftsman had only added to the value of the metal.

"All that you are admiring is nothing," he said, pressing the spring of a secret drawer. "There is something which is worth more than all the world to me," he added sadly.

He took out two portraits, two of Mme. de Mirbel's masterpieces, handsomely set in pearls.

"How lovely she is! Is not this the lady to whom you were writing?"

"No," he said, with a little smile; that is my mother, and this is my father—your aunt and uncle. Eugénie, I could beg and pray of you on my knees to keep this treasure safe for me. If I should die, and lose your little fortune, the gold will make good your loss; and to you alone can I leave those two portraits, for you alone are worthy to take charge of them, but do not let them pass into any other hands, rather destroy them——"

Eugénie was silent.

"Well, 'it is *Yes*, is it not?'" he said, and there was a winning charm in his manner.

As the last words were spoken, she gave him for the first time such a glance as a loving woman can, a bright glance that reveals a depth of feeling within her. He took her hand and kissed it.

"Angel of purity! what is money henceforward between

us two? It is nothing, is it not? but the feeling, which alone gave it worth, will be everything."

"You are like your mother. Was her voice as musical as yours, I wonder?"

"Oh! far more sweet——"

"Yes, for you," she said, lowering her eyelids. "Come, Charles, you must go to bed; I wish it. You are very tired. Good-night."

Her cousin had caught her hand in both of his; she drew it gently away, and went down to her room, her cousin lighting the way. In the doorway of her room they both paused.

"Oh! why am I a ruined man?" he said.

"Pshaw! my father is rich, I believe," she returned.

"My poor child," said Charles, as he set one foot in her room, and propped himself against the wall by the doorway, "if your father had been rich, he would not have left my father die, and you would not be lodged in such a poor place as this; he would live altogether in quite a different style."

"But he has Froidfond."

"And what may Froidfond be worth?"

"I do not know; but there is Noyers too."

"Some miserable farmhouse!"

"He has vineyards and meadows——"

"They are not worth talking about," said Charles scornfully. "If your father had even twenty-four thousand livres a year, do you suppose that you would sleep in a bare, cold room like this?" he added, as he made a step forward with his left foot. "That is where my treasures will be," he went on, nodding towards the old chest, a device by which he tried to conceal his thoughts from her.

"Go," she said, "and try to sleep," and she barred his entrance into an untidy room. Charles drew back; and the cousins bade each other a smiling good-night.

They fell asleep, to dream the same dream; and from that time forward Charles found that there were still roses to be gathered in the world in spite of his mourning. The next morning Mme. Grandet saw her daughter walking with Charles before breakfast. He was still sad and subdued; how, indeed, should he be otherwise than sad? He had been brought very low in his distress; he was gradually finding out how deep the abyss was into which he had fallen, and the thought of the future weighed heavily upon him.

"My father will not be back before dinner," said Eugénie, in reply to an anxious look in her mother's eyes.

The tones of Eugénie's voice had grown strangely sweet; it was easy to see from her face and manner that the cousins had some thought in common. Their souls had rushed together, while perhaps as yet they scarcely knew the power or the nature of this force which was binding them to each other.

Charles sat in the dining-room; no one intruded upon his sorrow. Indeed, the three women had plenty to do. Grandet had gone without any warning, and his work-people were at a standstill. The slater came, the plumber, the bricklayer, and the carpenter followed; so did laborers, tenants, and vine-dressers, some came to pay their dues, and others to receive them, and yet others to make bargains for the repairs which were being done. Mme. Grandet and Eugénie, therefore, were continually going and coming; they had to listen to interminable histories from laborers and country people.

Everything that came into the house Nanon promptly and securely stowed away in her kitchen. She always waited for her master's instructions as to what should be kept, and what should be sold in the market. The worthy cooper, like many little country squires, was wont to drink his worst wine, and to reserve his spoiled or wind-fallen orchard fruit for home consumption.

Towards five o'clock that evening Grandet came back from Angers. He had made fourteen thousand francs on his gold, and carried a government certificate bearing interest until the day when it should be transferred into *rentes*. He had left

Cornoiller also in Angers to look after the horses, which had been nearly foundered by the night journey, and had given instructions to bring them back leisurely after they had had a thorough rest.

"I have been to Angers, wife," he said; "and I am hungry."

"Have you had nothing to eat since yesterday?" called Nanon from her kitchen.

"Nothing whatever," said the worthy man.

Nanon brought in the soup. Des Grassins came to take his client's instructions just as the family were sitting down to dinner. Grandet had not so much as seen his nephew all this time.

"Go on with your dinner, Grandet," said the banker. "We can have a little chat. Have you heard what gold is fetching in Angers, and that people from Nantes are buying it there? I am going to send some over."

"You need not trouble yourself," answered his worthy client; "they have quite enough there by this time. I don't like you to lose your labor when I can prevent it; we are too good friends for that."

"But gold is at thirteen francs fifty centimes premium."

"Say *was* at a premium."

"How the deuce did you get to know that?"

"I went over to Angers myself last night," Grandet told him in a low voice.

The banker started, and a whispered conversation followed; both des Grassins and Grandet looked at Charles from time to time, and once more a gesture of surprise escaped the banker, doubtless at the point when the old cooper commissioned him to purchase *rentes* to bring in a hundred thousand livres.

"M. Grandet," said des Grassins, addressing Charles, "I am going to Paris, and if there is anything I can do for you——"

"Thank you, sir, there is nothing," Charles replied.

"You must thank him more heartily than that, nephew. This gentleman is going to wind up your father's business and settle with his creditors."

"Then is there any hope of coming to an arrangement?" asked Charles.

"Why, are you not my nephew?" cried the cooper, with a fine assumption of pride. "Our honor is involved; is not your name Grandet?"

Charles rose from his chair, impulsively flung his arms about his uncle, turned pale, and left the room. Eugénie looked at her father with affection and pride in her eyes.

"Well, let us say good-bye, my good friend," said Grandet. "I am very much at your service. Try to get round those fellows over yonder."

The two diplomatists shook hands, and the cooper went to the door with his neighbor; he came back to the room again when he had closed the door on des Grassins, flung himself down in his easy-chair, and said to Nanon: "Bring me some cordial."

But he was too much excited to keep still; he rose and looked at old M. de la Bertellière's portrait, and began to "dance a jig," in Nanon's phrase, singing to himself—

> "Once in the *Gardes françaises*
> I had a grandpapa——"

Nanon, Mme. Grandet, and Eugénie all looked at each other in silent dismay. The vine-grower's ecstasies never boded any good.

The evening was soon over. Old Grandet went off early to bed, and no one was allowed to stay up after that; when he slept, every one else must likewise sleep, much as in Poland, in the days of Augustus the Strong, whenever the king drank all his subjects were loyally tipsy. Wherefore, Nanon, Charles, and Eugénie were no less tired than the master of the house; and as for Mme. Grandet, she slept or woke, ate or drank, as her husband bade her. Yet during the two hours allotted to the digestion of his dinner the cooper was more facetious than he had ever been in his life before, and uttered not a few of his favorite aphorisms; one example will serve to plumb the depths of the cooper's mind. When he had finished his cordial, he looked pensively at the glass, and thus delivered himself—

"You have no sooner set your lips to a glass than it is empty! Such is life. You cannot have your cake and eat it too, and you can't turn over your money and keep it in your purse; if you could only do that, life would be too glorious."

He was not only jocose, he was good-natured, so that when Nanon came in with her spinning-wheel—"You must be tired," he said; "let the hemp alone."

"And if I did," the servant answered," why, I should have to sit with my hands before me."

"Poor Nanon! would you like some cordial?"

"Cordial? Oh! I don't say no. Madame makes it much better than the apothecaries do. The stuff they sell is like physic."

"They spoil the flavor with putting too much sugar in it," said the good man.

The next morning, at the eight o'clock breakfast, the party seemed, for the first time, almost like one family. Mme. Grandet, Eugénie, and Charles had been drawn together by these troubles, and Nanon herself unconsciously felt with them. As for the old vine-grower, he scarcely noticed his nephew's presence in the house, his greed for gold had been satisfied, and he was very shortly to be quit of this young sprig by the cheap and easy expedient of paying his nephew's traveling expenses as far as Nantes.

Charles and Eugénie meanwhile were free to do what seemed to them good. They were under Mme. Grandet's eyes, and

Grandet reposed complete faith in his wife in all matters of conduct and religion. Moreover, he had other things to think of; his meadows were to be drained, and a row of poplars was to be planted along the Loire, and there was all the ordinary winter work at Froidfond and elsewhere; in fact, he was exceedingly busy.

And now began the springtime of love for Eugénie. Since that hour in the night when she had given her gold to her cousin, her heart had followed the gift. They shared a secret between them; they were conscious of this understanding whenever they looked at each other; and this knowledge, that brought them more and more closely together, drew them in a manner out of the current of every-day life. And did not relationship justify a certain tenderness in the voice and kindness in the eyes? Eugénie therefore quietly set herself to work to make her cousin forget his grief in the childish joys of growing love.

For the beginnings of love and the beginnings of life are not unlike. Is not the child soothed by smiles and cradle-songs, and fairy tales of a golden future that lies before him? Above him, too, the bright wings of hope are always spread, and does he not shed tears of joy or of sorrow, wax petulant over trifles and quarrelsome over the pebbles with which he builds a tottering palace, or the flowers that are no sooner gathered than forgotten? Is he not also eager to outstrip time, and to live in the future? Love is the soul's second transformation.

Love and childhood were almost the same thing for Charles and Eugénie; the dawn of love and its childish beginnings were all the sweeter because their hearts were full of gloom; and this love, that from its birth had been enveloped in crape, was in keeping with their homely surroundings in the melancholy old house. As the cousins interchanged a few words by the well in the silent courtyard, or sat out in the little garden towards sunset time, wholly absorbed by the momentous nothings that each said to each, or wrapped in the stillness that always brooded over the space between the ramparts and the house, Charles learned to think of love as something sacred. Hitherto, with his great lady, his "dear Annette," he had experienced little but its perils and storms; but that episode in Paris was over, with its coquetry and passion, its vanity and emptiness, and he turned to this love in its purity and truth.

He came to feel a certain fondness for the old house, and their way of life no longer seemed absurd to him. He would come downstairs early in the morning so as to snatch a few words with Eugénie before her father gave out the stores; and when the sound of Grandet's heavy footstep echoed on the staircase, he fled into the garden. Even Eugénie's mother did not know of this morning tryst of theirs, and Nanon made as though she did not see it; it was a small piece of audacity that gave the keen relish of a stolen pleasure to their innocent love. Then when breakfast was over, and the elder Grandet had gone to see after his business and his improvements, Charles sat in the gray parlor between the mother and daughter, finding a pleasure unknown before in holding skeins of thread for them to wind, in listening to their talk, and watching them sew. There was something that appealed to him strongly in the almost monastic simplicity of the life, which had led him to discover the nobleness of the natures of these two unworldly women. He had not believed that such lives as these were possible in France; in Germany he admitted that old-world manners lingered still, but in France they were only to be found in fiction and in Auguste Lafontaine's novels. It was not long before Eugénie became an embodiment of his ideal, Goethe's Marguerite without her error.

Day after day, in short, the poor girl hung on his words and looks, and drifted farther along the stream of love. He snatched at every happiness as some swimmer might catch at an overhanging willow branch, that so he might reach the bank and rest there for a little while.

Was not the time of parting very near now? The shadow of that parting seemed to fall across the brightest hours of those days that fled so fast; and not one of them went by but something happened to remind her how soon it would be upon them.

For instance, three days after des Grassins had started for Paris, Grandet had taken Charles before a magistrate with the funereal solemnity with which such acts are performed by provincials, and in the presence of that functionary the young man had had to sign a declaration that he renounced all claim to his father's property. Dreadful repudiation! An impiety amounting to apostasy! He went to M. Cruchot to procure two powers of attorney, one for des Grassins, the other for the friend who was commissioned to sell his own personal effects. There were also some necessary formalities in connection with his passport; and finally, on the arrival of the plain suit of mourning which Charles had ordered from Paris, he sent for a clothier in Saumur, and disposed of his now useless wardrobe. This transaction was peculiarly pleasing to old Grandet.

"Ah! *Now* you look like a man who is ready to set out, and means to make his way in the world," he said, as he saw his nephew in a plain, black overcoat of rough cloth. "Good, very good!"

"I beg you to believe, sir," Charles replied, "that I shall face my position with proper spirit."

"What does this mean?" asked his worthy relative; there was an eager look in the good man's eyes at the sight of a handful of gold which Charles held out to him.

"I have gathered together my studs and rings and everything of any value that I have; I am not likely to want them now; but I know of nobody in Saumur, and this morning I thought I would ask you——"

"To buy it?" Grandet broke in upon him.

"No, uncle, to give me the name of some honest man who——"

"Give it to me, nephew; I will take it up stairs and find out what it is worth, and let you know the value to a centime. Jeweler's gold," he commented, after an examination of a long chain, "jeweler's gold, eighteen to nineteen carats, I should say."

The worthy soul held out his huge hand for it, and carried off the whole collection.

"Cousin Eugénie," said Charles, "permit me to offer you these two clasps; you might use them to fasten ribbons round your wrists, that sort of bracelet is all the rage just now."

"I do not hesitate to take it; cousin," she said, with a look of intelligence.

"And, aunt, this is my mother's thimble; I have treasured it up till now in my dressing-case," and he gave a pretty gold thimble to Mme. Grandet, who for the past ten years had longed for one.

"It is impossible to thank you in words, dear nephew," said the old mother, as her eyes filled with tears. "But morning and evening I shall repeat the prayer for travelers, and pray most fervently for you. If anything should happen to me, Eugénie shall take care of it for you."

"It is worth nine hundred and eighty-nine francs seventy-five centimes, nephew," said Grandet, as he came in at the door. "But to save you the trouble of selling it, I will let you have the money in livres."

This expression "in livres" means, in the districts along the Loire, that a crown of six livres is to be considered worth six francs, without deduction.

"I did not venture to suggest such a thing," Charles answered, "but I shrank from hawking my trinkets about in the town where you are living. Dirty linen ought not to be washed in public, as Napoleon used to say. Thank you for obliging me."

Grandet scratched his ear, and there was a moment's silence in the room.

"And, dear uncle," Charles went on, somewhat nervously, and as though he feared to wound his uncle's susceptibilities, "my cousin and aunt have consented to receive trifling mementoes from me; will you not in your turn accept these sleeve-links, which are useless to me now; they may perhaps recall to your memory a poor boy, in a far-off country, whose thoughts will certainly often turn to those who are all that remain to him now of his family."

"Oh! my boy, my boy, you must not strip yourself like that for us——"

"What have you there, wife?" said the cooper, turning eagerly towards her. "Ah! a gold thimble? And you, little girl? Diamond clasps; what next! Come, I will accept your studs, my boy," he continued, squeezing Charles' hand. "But——you must let me pay——your——yes, your passage out to the Indies. Yes, I mean to pay your passage. Besides, my boy, when I estimated your jewelry I only took it at its value as metal, you see, without reckoning the workmanship, and it may be worth a trifle more on that account. So that is settled. I will pay you fifteen hundred francs—— in livres; Cruchot will lend it me, for I have not a brass farthing in the house; unless Perrotet, who is getting behindhand with his dues, will pay me in coin. There! there! I will go and see about it," and he took up his hat, put on his gloves, and went forthwith.

"Then you are going?" said Eugénie, with sad, admiring eyes.

"I cannot help myself," he answered, with his head bent down.

For several days Charles looked, spoke, and behaved like a man who is in deep trouble, but who feels the weight of such heavy obligations, that his misfortunes only brace him for greater effort. He had ceased to pity himself; he had become a man. Never had Eugénie augured better of her cousin's character than she did on the day when she watched him come downstairs in his plain, black mourning suit, which set off his pale, sad face to such advantage. The two women had also gone into mourning, and went with Charles to the *requiem* mass celebrated in the parish church for the soul of the late Guillaume Grandet.

Charles received letters from Paris as they took the midday meal; he opened and read them.

"Well, cousin," said Eugénie, in a low voice, "are your affairs going on satisfactorily?"

"Never put questions of that sort, my girl," remarked Grandet. "I never talk to you about my affairs, and why the devil should you meddle in your cousin's? Just let the boy alone."

"Oh! my dear uncle, I have no secrets of any sort," said Charles.

"Tut, tut, tut. You will find out that you must bridle your tongue in business, nephew."

When the two lovers were alone in the garden, Charles drew Eugénie to the old bench under the walnut tree where they so often sat of late.

"I felt sure of Alphonse, and I was right," he said; "he has done wonders, and has settled my affairs prudently and loyally. All my debts in Paris are paid, my furniture sold well, and he tells me that he has acted on the advice of an old sea captain who had made the voyage to the Indies, and has invested the surplus money in ornaments and odds and ends for which there is a great demand out there. He has sent my packages to Nantes, where an East Indiaman is taking freight for Java, and so, Eugénie, in five days we must bid each other farewell, for a long while at any rate, and perhaps forever. My trading venture and the ten thousand francs which two of my friends have sent me are a very poor start; I cannot expect to return for many years. Dear cousin, let us not consider ourselves bound in any way; I may die, and very likely some good opportunity for settling yourself——"

"You love me?" she asked.

"Oh! yes, indeed," he replied, with an earnestness of manner that betokened a like earnestness in his feelings.

"Then I will wait for you, Charles. *Dieu!* my father is looking out of his window," she exclaimed, evading her cousin, who had drawn closer to embrace her.

She fled to the archway; and seeing that Charles followed her thither, she retreated farther, flung back the folding door at the foot of the staircase, and with no very clear idea, save that of flight, she rushed towards the darkest corner of the passage, outside Nanon's sleeping hole; and there Charles, who was close beside her, grasped both hands in his and pressed her to his heart; his arms went round her waist, Eugénie resisted no longer, and leaning against her lover she received and gave the purest, sweetest, and most perfect of all kisses.

"Dear Eugénie, a cousin is better than a brother; he can marry you," said Charles.

"Amen, so be it!" cried Nanon, opening the door behind them, and emerging from her den. Her voice startled the two lovers, who fled into the dining-room, where Eugénie took up her sewing, and Charles seized on Mme. Grandet's prayer book, opened it at the litanies of the Virgin, and began to read industriously.

"Why!" said Nanon, "so we are all saying our prayers!"

As soon as Charles fixed the day for his departure, Grandet bustled about and affected to take the greatest interest in the whole matter. He was liberal with advice, and with anything else that cost him nothing, first seeking out a packer for Charles, and then, saying that the man wanted too much for his cases, setting to work with all his might to make them himself, using odd planks for the purpose. He was up betimes every morning planing, fitting, nailing deal boards together, squaring and shaping; and, in fact, he made some strong cases, packed all Charles' property in them, and undertook to send them by steamer down the Loire to Nantes in time to go by the merchant ship, and to insure them during the voyage.

Since that kiss given and taken in the passage, the hours sped with terrible rapidity for Eugénie. At times she thought of following her cousin; for of all ties that bind one human being to another, this passion of love is the closest and strongest, and those who know this, and know how every day shortens love's allotted span, and how not time alone but age and mortal sickness and all the untoward accidents of life combine to menace it—these will know the agony that Eugénie suffered. She shed many tears as she walked up and down the little garden; it had grown so narrow for her now; the courtyard, the old house, and the town had all grown narrow, and her thoughts fared forth already across vast spaces of sea.

It was the day before the day of departure. That morning, while Grandet and Nanon were out of the house, the precious casket that held the two portraits was solemnly deposited in Eugénie's chest, beside the now empty velvet bag in the only drawer that could be locked, an installation which was not affected without many tears and kisses. When Eugénie locked the drawer and hid the key in her bosom, she had not the courage to forbid the kiss by which Charles sealed the act.

"The key shall always stay there, dear."

"Ah! well, my heart will always be there with it too."

"Oh! Charles, you should not say that," she said a little reproachfully.

"Are we not married?" he replied. "I have your word; take mine."

"Thine forever!" they said together, and repeated it a second time. No holier vow was ever made on earth; for

Charles' love had received a moment's consecration in the presence of Eugénie's simple sincerity.

It was a melancholy group round the breakfast-table next morning. Even Nanon herself, in spite of Charles' gift of a new gown and a gilt cross, had a tear in her eye; but she was free to express her feelings, and did so.

"Oh! that poor, delicate young gentleman who is going to sea," was the burden of her discourse.

At half-past ten the whole family left the house to see Charles start for Nantes in the diligence. Nanon had let the dog loose and locked the door, and meant to carry Charles' handbag. Every shopkeeper in the ancient street was in the doorway to watch the little procession pass. M. Cruchot joined them in the market-place.

"Eugénie," whispered her mother, "mind you do not cry!"

They reached the gateway of the inn, and there Grandet kissed Charles on both cheeks. "Well! nephew," he said, "set out poor and come back rich; you leave your father's honor in safe-keeping. I—Grandet—will answer to you for that; you will only have to do your part——"

"Oh! uncle, this sweetens the bitterness of parting. Is not this the greatest gift you could possibly give me?"

Charles had broken in upon the old cooper's remarks before he quite understood their drift; he put his arms round his uncle's neck, and let fall tears of gratitude on the vine-grower's sunburned cheeks; Eugénie clasped her cousin's hand in one of hers and her father's in the other, and held them tightly. Only the notary smiled to himself; he alone understood the worthy man, and he could not help admiring his astute cunning. The four Saumurois and a little group of onlookers hung about the diligence till the last moment; and looked after it until it disappeared across the bridge, and the sound of the wheels grew faint and distant.

"A good riddance!" said the cooper.

Luckily, no one but M. Cruchot heard this ejaculation;

Eugénie and her mother had walked along the quay to a point of view whence they could still see the diligence, and stood there waving their handkerchiefs and watching Charles' answering signal till he was out of sight; then Eugénie turned.

"Oh! mother, mother, if I had God's power for one moment," she said.

To save farther interruption to the course of the story, it is necessary to glance a little ahead, and give a brief account of the course of events in Paris, of Grandet's calculations, and the action taken by his worthy lieutenant the banker in the matter of Guillaume Grandet's affairs. A month after des Grassins had gone, Grandet received a certificate for a hundred thousand livres per annum of *rentes*, purchased at eighty francs. No information was ever forthcoming as to how and when the actual coin had been paid, or the receipt taken, which in due course had been exchanged for the certificate. The inventory and statement of his affairs which the miser left at his death threw no light upon the mystery, and Cruchot fancied that in some way or other Nanon must have been the unconscious instrument employed; for about that time the faithful serving-maid was away from home for four or five days, ostensibly to see after matters at Froidfond, as if its worthy owner were likely to forget anything there that required looking after! As for Guillaume Grandet's creditors, everything had happened as the cooper had intended and foreseen.

At the Bank of France (as everybody knows) they keep accurate lists of all the great fortunes in Paris or in the departments. The names of des Grassins and of Felix Grandet of Saumur were duly to be found inscribed therein; indeed, they shone conspicuous there as well-known names in the business world, as men who were not only financially sound, but owners of broad acres unencumbered by mortgages. And now it was said that des Grassins of Saumur had come to

Paris with intent to call a meeting of the creditors of the firm of Guillaume Grandet; the shade of the wine merchant was to be spared the disgrace of protested bills. The seals were broken in the presence of the creditors, and the family notary proceeded to make out an inventory in due form.

Before very long, in fact, des Grassins called a meeting of the creditors, who with one voice appointed the banker of Saumur as trustee conjointly with François Keller, the head of a large business house, and one of the principal creditors, empowering them to take such measures as they thought fit, in order to save the family name (and the bills) from being dishonored. The fact that des Grassins was acting as his agent produced a hopeful tone in the meeting, and things went smoothly from the first; the banker did not find a single dissentient voice. No one thought of passing his bill to his profit and loss account, and each one said to himself—

"Grandet of Saumur is going to pay!"

Six months went by. The Parisian merchants had withdrawn the bills from circulation, and had consigned them to the depths of their portfolios. The cooper had gained his first point. Nine months after the first meeting the two trustees paid the creditors a dividend of forty-seven per cent. This sum had been raised by the sale of the late Guillaume Grandet's property, goods, chattels and general effects; the most scrupulous integrity characterized these proceedings; indeed, the whole affair was conducted with the most conscientious honesty, and the delighted creditors fell to admiring Grandet's wonderful, indubitable, and high-minded probity. When these praises had duly circulated for a sufficient length of time, the creditors began to ask themselves when the remainder of their money would be forthcoming, and bethought them of collectively writing a letter to Grandet.

"Here we are!" was the old cooper's comment, as he flung the letter in the fire. "Patience, patience, my dear friends."

By way of a reply to the propositions contained in the letter, Grandet of Saumur required them to deposit with a notary all the bills and claims against the estate of his deceased brother, accompanying each with receipts for the payments already made. The accounts were to be audited, and the exact condition of affairs was to be ascertained. Innumerable difficulties were cleared away by this notion of the deposit.

A creditor, generally speaking, is a sort of maniac; there is no saying what a creditor will do. One day he is in a hurry to bring the thing to an end, the next he is all for fire and sword, a little later and he is sweetness and benignity itself. To-day, very probably, his wife is in a good humor, his youngest hope has just cut a tooth, everything is going on comfortably at home, he has no mind to abate his claims one jot; but to-morrow comes and it rains, and he cannot go out; he feels low in his mind, and agrees hastily to anything and everything that is likely to settle the affair; the next morning brings counsel; he requires a guarantee, and by the end of the month he talks about an execution, the inhuman, bloodthirsty wretch! The creditor is not unlike that common or house sparrow on whose tail small children are encouraged to try to put a grain of salt—a pleasing simile which a creditor may twist to his own uses, and apply to his bills, from which he fondly hopes to derive some benefit at last. Grandet had observed these atmospheric variations among creditors; and his forecasts in the present case were correct, his brother's creditors were behaving in every respect exactly as he wished. Some waxed wroth, and flatly declined to have anything to do with the deposit, or to give up the vouchers.

"Good!" said Grandet; "that is all right!" He rubbed his hands as he read the letters which des Grassins wrote to him on the subject.

Yet others refused to consent to the aforesaid deposit unless their position was clearly defined in the first place; it was to be made without prejudice, and they reserved the right to declare the estate bankrupt should they deem it advisable. This opened a fresh correspondence, and occasioned a farther delay, after which Grandet finally agreed to all the conditions, and as a consequence the more tractable creditors brought the recalcitrant to hear reason, and the deposit was made, not, however, without some grumbling.

"That old fellow is laughing in his sleeve at you and us too," said they to des Grassins.

Twenty-three months after Guillaume Grandet's death, many of the merchants had forgotten all about their claims in the course of events in a business life in Paris, or they only thought of them to say to themselves—

"It begins to look as though the forty-seven per cent. is about all I shall get out of that business."

The cooper had reckoned on the aid of time, who, as he was wont to say, is a good fellow. By the end of the third year des Grassins wrote to Grandet saying that he had induced most of the creditors to give up their bills, and that the amount now owing was only about ten per cent. of the outstanding two million four hundred thousand francs. Grandet replied that there yet remained the notary and the stockbroker, whose failures had been the death of his brother; *they* were still alive. They might be solvent again by this time, and proceedings ought to be taken against them; something might be recovered in this way which would still farther reduce the sum-total of the deficit.

When the fourth year drew to a close the deficit had been duly brought down to the sum of twelve hundred thousand francs; the limit appeared to have been reached. Six months farther were spent in parleyings between the trustees and the creditors, and between Grandet and the trustees. In short, strong pressure being brought to bear upon Grandet of Saumur, he announced, somewhere about the ninth month of the same year, that his nephew, who had made a fortune in the East

Indies, had signified his intention of settling in full all claims on his father's estate; and that meantime he could not take it upon himself to act, nor to defraud the creditors by winding up the affair before he had consulted his nephew; he added that he had written to him, and was now awaiting an answer.

The middle of the fifth year had been reached, and still the creditors were held in check by the magic words *in full*, let fall judiciously from time to time by the sublime cooper, who was laughing at them in his sleeve; "those PARISIANS," he would say to himself, with a mild oath, and a cunning smile would steal across his features.

In fact, a martyrdom unknown to the calendars of commerce was in store for the creditors. When next they appear in the course of this story, they will be found in exactly the same position that they were in now when Grandet had done with them. Consols went up to a hundred and fifteen, old Grandet sold out, and received from Paris about two million four hundred thousand francs in gold, which went into his wooden kegs to keep company with the six hundred thousand francs of interest which his investment had brought in.

Des Grassins stayed on in Paris, and for the following reasons. In the first place, he had been appointed a deputy; and in the second, he, the father of a family, bored by the exceeding dulness of existence in Saumur, was smitten with the charms of Mlle. Florine, one of the prettiest actresses of the Théâtre de Madame, and there was a recrudescence of the quartermaster in the banker. It is useless to discuss his conduct; at Saumur it was pronounced to be profoundly immoral. It was very lucky for his wife that she had brains enough to carry on the concern at Saumur in her own name, and could extricate the remains of her fortune, which had suffered not a little from M. des Grassins' extravagance and folly. But the quasi-widow was in a false position, and the Cruchotins did all that in them lay to make matters worse; she had to give up all hope of a match between her son and Eugénie Grandet, and married her daughter very badly. Adolphe des Grassins went to join his father in Paris, and there acquired, so it was said, an unenviable reputation. The triumph of the Cruchotins was complete.

"Your husband has taken leave of his senses," Grandet took occasion to remark as he accommodated Mme. des Grassins with a loan (on good security). "I am very sorry for you; you are a nice little woman."

"Ah!" sighed the poor lady, "who could have believed that day when he set out for Paris to see after that business of yours that he was hurrying to his own ruin?"

"Heaven is my witness, madame, that to the very last I did all I could to prevent him, and M. le Président was dying to go; but we know now why your husband was so set upon it."

Clearly, therefore, Grandet lay under no obligation to des Grassins.

In every situation a woman is bound to suffer in many ways that a man does not, and to feel her troubles more acutely than he can; for a man's vigor and energy are constantly brought into play; he acts and thinks, comes and goes, busies himself in the present, and looks to the future for consolation. This was what Charles was doing. But a woman cannot help herself—hers is a passive part; she is left face to face with her trouble, and has nothing to divert her mind from it; she sounds the depths of the abyss of sorrow, and its dark places are filled with her prayers and tears. So it was with Eugénie. She was beginning to understand that the web of a woman's life will always be woven of love and sorrow and hope and fear and self-sacrifice; hers was to be a woman's lot in all things without a woman's consolations, and her moments of happiness (to make use of Bossuet's wonderful illustration) were to be like the scattered nails driven into the wall, when all collected together they scarcely filled the hollow of the hand. Troubles seldom keep us waiting for them, and for Eugénie they were gathering thick and fast.

The day after Charles had gone, the Grandet household fell back into the old ways of life; there was no difference for any one but Eugénie—for her the house had grown very empty all of a sudden. Charles' room should remain just as he had left it; Mme. Grandet and Nanon lent themselves to this whim of hers, willingly maintained the *statu quo,* and said nothing to her father.

"Who knows?" Eugénie said. "He may come back to us sooner than we think."

"Ah! I wish I could see him here again," replied Nanon. "I could get on with him well enough! He was very nice, and an excellent gentleman; and he was pretty-like, his hair curled over his head just like a girl's."

Eugénie gazed at Nanon.

"Holy Virgin! mademoiselle, with such eyes, you are like to lose your soul. You shouldn't look at people in that way."

From that day Mlle. Grandet's beauty took a new character. The grave thoughts of love that slowly enveloped her soul, the dignity of a woman who is beloved, gave to her face the sort of radiance that early painters expressed by the aureole. Before her cousin came into her life, Eugénie might have been compared to the Virgin as yet unconscious of her destiny; and now that he had passed out of it, she seemed like the Virgin Mother; she, too, bore love in her heart. Spanish art has depicted these two Marys, so different one from the other —Christianity, with its many symbols, knows no more glorious types than these.

The day after Charles had left them, Eugénie went to mass (as she had resolved to do daily), and on her way back bought a map of the world from the only bookseller in the town. This she pinned to the wall beside her glass, so that she might follow the course of her cousin's voyage to the Indies; and night and morning might be beside him for a little while on that far-off vessel, and see him and ask all the endless questions she longed to ask.

"Are you well? Are you not sad? Am I in your thoughts when you see the star that you told me about? You made me see how beautiful it was."

In the morning she used to sit like one in a dream under the great walnut tree, on the old gray, lichen-covered, worm-eaten bench where they had talked so kindly and so foolishly, where they had built such fair castles in the air in which to live. She thought of the future as she watched the little strip of sky shut in by the high walls on every side, then her eyes wandered over the old buttressed wall and the roof—Charles' room lay beneath it. In short, this solitary persistent love mingling with all her thoughts became the substance, or, as our forefathers would have said, the "staff" of her life.

If Grandet's self-styled friends came in of an evening, she would seem to be in high spirits, but the liveliness was only assumed; she used to talk about Charles with her mother and Nanon the whole morning through, and Nanon—who was of the opinion that without faltering in her duty to her master she might yet feel for her young mistress' troubles—Nanon spoke on this wise—

"If I had had a sweetheart, I would have——I would have gone with him to hell. I would have——well, then, I would just have laid down my life for him, but——no such chance! I shall die without knowing what it is to love. Would you believe it, mamselle, there is that old Cornoiller, who is a good man all the same, dangling about after my savings, just like the others who come here paying court to you and sniffing after the master's money. I see through it; I may be as big as a haystack, but I am as sharp as a needle yet. Well! and yet do you know, mamselle, it may not be love, but I rather like it."

In this way two months went by. The secret that bound the three women so closely together had brought a new interest into the household life hitherto so monotonous. For them Charles still dwelt in the house, and came and went beneath the old gray rafters of the parlor. Every morning and evening Eugénie opened the dressing-case and looked at her aunt's portrait. Her mother, suddenly coming into her room one Sunday morning, found her absorbed in tracing out a likeness to Charles in the lady of the miniature, and Mme. Grandet learned for the first time a terrible secret, how that Eugénie had parted with her treasures and had taken the case in exchange.

"You have let him have it all!" cried the terrified mother. "What will you say to your father on New Year's Day when he asks to see your gold?"

Eugénie's eyes were set in a fixed stare; the horror of this thought so filled the women that half the morning went by, and they were distressed to find themselves too late for high mass, and were only in time for the military mass. The year 1819 was almost over; there were only three more days left. In three days a terrible drama would begin, a drama undignified by poison, dagger, or bloodshed, but fate dealt scarcely more cruelly with the princely house of Atreus than with the actors in this bourgeois tragedy.

"What is to become of us?" said Mme. Grandet, laying down her knitting on her knee.

Poor mother! all the events of the past two months had sadly hindered the knitting, the woolen cuffs for winter wear were not finished yet, a homely and apparently insignificant fact which was to work trouble enough for her. For want of the warm cuffs she caught a chill after a violent perspiration brought on by one of her husband's fearful outbursts of rage.

"My poor child, I have been thinking that if you had only told me about this, we should have had time to write to M. des Grassins in Paris. He might have managed to send us some gold-pieces like those of yours; and although Grandet knows the look of them so well, still perhaps——"

"But where could we have found so much money?"

"I would have raised it on my property. Besides, M. des Grassins would have befriended us——"

"There is not time enough now," faltered Eugénie in a smothered voice. "To-morrow morning we shall have to go to his room to wish him a happy New Year, shall we not?"

"Oh! Eugénie, why not go and see the Cruchots about it?"

"No, no, that would be putting ourselves in their power; I should be entirely in their hands then. Besides, I have made up my mind. I have acted quite rightly, and I repent of nothing; God will protect me. May His holy will be done! Ah! if you had read that letter, mother, you would have thought of nothing but him."

The next morning, January 1, 1820, the mother and daughter were in an agony of distress that they could not hide; sheer terror suggested the simple expedient of omitting the solemn visit to Grandet's room. The bitter weather served as an excuse; the winter of 1819-20 was the coldest that had been known for years, and snow lay deep on the roofs.

Mme. Grandet called to her husband as soon as she heard him stirring, "Grandet, just let Nanon light a bit of fire in here for me, the air is so sharp that I am shivering under the bedclothes, and at my time of life I must take care of myself. And then," she went on after a little pause, "Eugénie shall come in here to dress. The poor girl may do herself a mischief if she dresses in her own room in such cold. We will come downstairs into the sitting-room and wish you a happy New Year there by the fire."

"Tut, tut, tut, what a tongue! What a way to begin the year, Mme. Grandet! You have never said so much in your life before. You have not had a sop of bread in wine, I suppose?"

There was a moment's pause. Doubtless his wife's proposal suited his notions, for he said, "Very well, I will do as you wish, Mme. Grandet. You really are a good sort of woman, it would be a pity for you to expire before you are due, though, as a rule, the La Bertellières make old bones, don't they, hey?" he cried, after a pause. "Well, their money has fallen in at last; I forgive them," and he coughed.

"You are in spirits this morning," said the poor wife.

"I always am in spirits."

> Hey! hey! cooper gay,
> Mend your tub and take your pay.

He had quite finished dressing, and came into his wife's room. "Yes, *nom d'un petit bon-homme!* it is a mighty hard frost, all the same. We shall have a good breakfast to-day, wife. Des Grassins has sent me a pâté de foies gras, truffled! I am going round to the coach office to see after it. He should have sent a double napoleon for Eugénie along with it," said the cooper, coming closer, and lowering his voice. "I have no gold, I certainly had a few old coins still left, I may tell you that in confidence, but I had to let them go in the course of business," and by way of celebrating the first day of the year he kissed his wife on the forehead.

"Eugénie," cried the kind mother, as soon as Grandet had gone, "I don't know which side of the bed your father got out on, but he is in a good humor this morning. Pshaw! we shall pull through."

"What can have come over the master?" cried Nanon as she came into the room to light the fire. "First of all, he says, 'Good-morning, great stupid, a happy New Year! Go upstairs and light a fire in my wife's room; she is feeling cold.' I thought I must be off my head when I saw him holding out his hand with a six-franc piece in it that hadn't been clipped a bit! There! madame, only look at it! Oh! he is a worthy man, all the same—he is a good man, he is.

There are some as get harder-hearted the older they grow; but he turns sweeter, like your cordial that improves with keeping. He is a very good and a very excellent man——"

Grandet's speculation had been completely successful; this was the cause of his high spirits. M. des Grassins—after deducting various amounts which the cooper owed him, partly for discounting Dutch bills to the amount of a hundred and fifty thousand francs, and partly for advances of money for the purchase of a hundred thousand livres worth of consols— M. des Grassins was sending him, by diligence, thirty thousand francs in crowns, the remainder (after the aforesaid deductions had been made) of the cooper's half-yearly dividends, and informed Grandet that consols were steadily rising. They stood at eighty-nine at the present moment, and well-known capitalists were buying for the next account at the end of January at ninety-two. In two months Grandet had made twelve per cent. on his capital; he had straightened his accounts; and henceforward he would receive fifty thousand francs every half-year, clear of taxes or any outgoing expenses. In short, he had grasped the theory of consols (a class of investment of which the provincial mind is exceedingly shy), and, looking ahead, he beheld himself the master of six millions of francs in five years' time—six millions, which would go on accumulating with scarcely any trouble on his part—six millions of francs! And there was the value of his landed property to add to this; he saw himself in a fair way to build up a colossal fortune. The six francs given to Nanon were perhaps in reality the payment for an immense service which the girl had unwittingly done her master.

"Oho! what can M. Grandet be after? He is running as if there were a fire somewhere," the shopkeepers said to each other as they took down their shutters that New Year's morning.

A little later when they saw him coming back from the

quay followed by a porter from the coach office, who was wheeling a barrow piled up with little bags full of something——

"Ah!" said they, "water always makes for the river, the old boy was hurrying after his crowns."

"They flow in on him from Paris, and Froidfond, and Holland," said one.

"He will buy Saumur before he has done," cried another.

"He does not care a rap for the cold; he is always looking after his business," said a woman to her husband.

"Hi! M. Grandet! if you have more of that than you know what to do with, I can help you to get rid of some of it."

"Eh! they are only coppers," said the vine-grower.

"Silver, he means," said the porter in a low voice.

"Keep a still tongue in your head, if you want me to bear you in mind," said M. Grandet as he opened the door.

"Oh! the old fox, I thought he was deaf," said the porter to himself, "but it looks as though he could hear well enough in cold weather."

"Here is a franc for a New Year's gift, and keep quiet about this. Off with you! Nanon will bring back the barrow. Nanon!" cried Grandet, "are the women-folk gone to mass?"

"Yes, sir."

"Come, look sharp, and lend a hand here, then," he cried, and loaded her with the bags. In another minute the crowns were safely transferred to his room, where he locked himself in.

"Thump on the wall when breakfast is ready," he called through the door, and take the wheelbarrow back to the coach office."

It was ten o'clock before the family breakfasted.

"Your father will not ask to see your gold now," said

Mme. Grandet as they came back from mass; and if he does, you can shiver and say it is too cold to go up stairs for it. We shall have time to make up the money again before your birthday——"

Grandet came down the stairs with his head full of schemes for transforming the five-franc pieces just received from Paris into gold coin, which should be neither clipped nor light weight. He thought of his admirably timed investment in government stock, and made up his mind that he would continue to put his money into consols until they rose to a hundred francs. Such meditations as these boded ill for Eugénie. As soon as he came in the two women wished him a prosperous New Year, each in her own way; Mme. Grandet was grave and ceremonious, but his daughter put her arms round his neck and kissed him. "Aha! child," he said, kissing her on both cheeks, "I am thinking and working for you, you see!——I want you to be happy, and if you are to be happy, you must have money; for you won't get anything without it. Look! here is a brand new napoleon, I sent to Paris on purpose for it. *Nom d'un petit bon-homme!* there is not a speck of gold in the house, except yours, you are the one who has the gold. Let me see your gold, little girl."

"Bah!" it is too cold, let us have breakfast," Eugénie answered.

"Well, then, after breakfast we will have a look at it, eh? It will be good for our digestions. That great des Grassins sent us this, all the same," he went on, "so get your breakfast, children, for it costs us nothing. Des Grassins is going on nicely; I am pleased with him; the old fish is doing Charles a service, and all free gratis. Really, he is managing poor dear Grandet's affairs very cleverly. Ououh! ououh!" he cried, with his mouth full, "this is good! Eat away, wife, there is enough here to last us for two days at least."

"I am not hungry. I am very poorly, you know that very well."

"Oh! Ah! but you have a sound constitution; you are a La Bertellière, and you can put away a great deal without any fear of damaging yourself. You may be a trifle sallow, but I have a liking for yellow myself."

The prisoner shrinking from a public and ignominious death could not well await his doom with a more sickening dread than Mme. Grandet and Eugénie felt as they foresaw the end of breakfast and the inevitable sequel. The more boisterously the cooper talked and ate, the lower sank their spirits; but to the girl, in this crisis, a certain support was not lacking, love was strong within her. "I would die a thousand deaths," she thought, "for him, for him!"

She looked at her mother, and courage and defiance shone in her eyes.

By eleven o'clock they had finished breakfast. "Clear everything away," Grandet told Nanon, "but leave us the table. We can look over your little treasure more comfortably so," he said with his eyes on Eugénie. "*Little*, said I? 'Tis not so small, though, upon my word. Your coins altogether are actually worth five thousand nine hundred and fifty-nine francs, then with forty more this morning, that makes six thousand francs all but one. Well, I will give you another franc to make up the sum, because, you see, little girl—— Well! now, why are you listening to us! Just take yourself off, Nanon, and set about your work!"

Nanon vanished.

"Listen, Eugénie, you must let me have your gold. You will not refuse to let your papa have it? Eh, little daughter?"

Neither of the women spoke.

"I myself have no gold left. I had some once, but I have none now. I will give you six thousand francs in silver for it, and you shall invest it; I will show you how. There is really no need to think of a *dozen*. When you are married (which will be before very long) I will find a husband for you who will give you the handsomest *dozen* that has ever been heard of hereabouts. There is a splendid opportunity just now; you can invest your six thousand francs in government stock, and every six months, when dividends are due, you will have about two hundred francs coming in, all clear of taxes, and no repairs to pay for, and no frosts nor hail nor bad seasons, none of all the tiresome drawbacks you have to lay your account with if you put your money into land. You don't like to part with your gold, eh? Is that it, little girl? Never mind, let me have it all the same. I will look out for gold coins for you, ducats from Holland, and genovines and Portuguese moidores and rupees, the Mogul's rupees; and what with the coins I shall give you on your birthday and so forth, you will have half your little hoard again in three years time, beside the six thousand francs in the funds. What do you say, little girl? Look up, child! There! there! bring it here, my pet. You owe me a good kiss for telling you business secrets and mysteries of the life and death of five-franc pieces. Five-franc pieces! Yes, indeed, the coins live and gad about just like men do; they go and come and sweat and multiply."

Eugénie rose and made a few steps towards the door; then she turned abruptly, looked her father full in the face, and said—

"All *my* gold is gone; I have none left."

"All your gold is gone!" echoed Grandet, starting up, as a horse might rear when the cannon thunders not ten paces from him.

"Yes, it is all gone."

"Eugénie! you are dreaming!"

"No."

"By my father's pruning-hook!" Whenever the cooper swore in this fashion, the floors and ceilings trembled.

"Lord have mercy!" cried Nanon; "how white the mistress is!"

"Grandet! you will kill me with your angry fits," said the poor wife.

"Tut, tut, tut; none of your family ever die. Now, Eugénie! what have you done with your money?" he burst out as he turned upon her.

The girl was on her knees beside Mme. Grandet.

"Look! sir," she said, "my mother is very ill——do not kill her."

Grandet was alarmed; his wife's dark, sallow complexion had grown so white.

"Nanon, come and help me up to bed," she said in a feeble voice. "This is killing me——"

Nanon gave an arm to her mistress, and Eugénie supported her on the other side; but it was only with the greatest difficulty that they reached her room, for the poor mother's strength completely failed her, and she stumbled at every step. Grandet was left alone in the parlor. After a while, however, he came part of the way upstairs, and called out—

"Eugénie! Come down again as soon as your mother is in bed."

"Yes, father."

In no long time she returned to him, after comforting her mother as best she could.

"Now, my daughter," Grandet addressed her, "you will tell me where your money is."

"If I am not perfectly free to do as I like with your presents, father, please take them back again," said Eugénie coldly. She went to the chimney-piece for the napoleon, and gave it to her father.

Grandet pounced upon it, and slipped it into his waistcoat pocket.

"I will never give you anything again, I know," he said, pointing his thumb at her. "You look down on your father, do you? You have no confidence in him? Do you know what a father is? If he is not everything to you, he is nothing. *Now;* where is your gold?"

"I do respect you and love you, father, in spite of your

anger; but I would very humbly point out to you that I am twenty-one years old. You have told me that I am of age often enough for me to know it. I have done as I liked with my money, and rest assured that it is in good hands——"

"Whose?"

"That is an inviolable secret," she said. "Have you not your secrets?"

"Am I not the head of my family? May I not be allowed to have my own business affairs?"

"This is my own affair."

"It must be something very unsatisfactory, Mlle. Grandet, if you cannot tell your own father about it."

"It is perfectly satisfactory, and I cannot tell my father about it."

"Tell me, at any rate, when you parted with your gold."

Eugénie shook her head.

"You still had it on your birthday, hadn't you, eh?"

But if greed had made her father crafty, love had taught Eugénie to be wary; she shook her head again.

"Did any one ever hear of such obstinacy, or of such a robbery?" cried Grandet, in a voice which gradually rose till it rang through the house. "What! *here*, in my house, in my own house, some one has taken your gold! Taken all the gold that there was in the place! And I am not to know who it was? Gold is a precious thing. The best of girls go wrong and throw themselves away one way or another; that happens among great folk, and even among decent citizens; but think of throwing gold away! For you gave it to somebody, I suppose, eh?"

Eugénie gave no sign.

"Did any one ever see such a daughter! Can you be a child of mine? If you have parted with your money, you must have a receipt for it——"

"Was I free to do as I wished with it—Yes or no? Was it mine?"

"Why, you are a child."

"I am of age."

At first Grandet was struck dumb by his daughter daring to argue with him, and in this way! He turned pale, stamped, swore, and finding words at last, he shouted—

"Accursed serpent! Miserable girl! Oh! you know well that I love you, and you take advantage of it! You ungrateful child! She would rob and murder her own father! *Pardieu!* you would have thrown all we have at the feet of that vagabond with the morocco boots. By my father's pruning-hook, I cannot disinherit you, but *nom d'un tonneau,* I can curse you; you and your cousin and your children. Nothing good can come out of this; do you hear? If it was to Charles that—— But, no, that is impossible. What if that miserable puppy should have robbed me?"

He glared at his daughter, who was still silent and unmoved.

"She does not stir! She does not flinch! She is more of a Grandet than I am. You did not give your gold away for nothing, anyhow. Come, now; tell me about it?"

Eugénie looked up at her father; her satirical glance exasperated him.

"Eugénie, this is my house; so long as you are under your father's roof you must do as your father bids you. The priests command you to obey me."

Eugénie bent her head again.

"You are wounding all my tenderest feelings," he went on. "Get out of my sight until you are ready to obey me. Go to your room and stay there until I give you leave to come out of it. Nanon will bring you bread and water. Do you hear what I say? Go!"

Eugénie burst into tears, and fled away to her mother. Grandet took several turns in his garden without heeding the snow or the cold; then, suspecting that his daughter would be in his wife's room, and delighted with the idea of catching them in flagrant disobedience to orders, he climbed the stairs

"Do you hear what I say? Go!"

as stealthy as a cat, and suddenly appeared in Mme. Grandet's room. He was right; she was stroking Eugénie's hair, and the girl lay with her face hidden in her mother's breast.

"Poor child! Never mind, your father will relent."

"She has no longer a father!" said the cooper. "Is it really possible, Mme. Grandet, that we have brought such a disobedient daughter into the world? A pretty bringing up; and pious, too, above all things! Well! how is it you are not in your room? Come, off to prison with you; to prison, miss."

"Do you mean to take my daughter away from me, sir?" said Mme. Grandet, as she raised a flushed face and bright, feverish eyes.

"If you want to keep her, take her along with you, and the house will be rid of you both at once—— *Tonnerre!* Where is the gold? What has become of the gold?"

Eugénie rose to her feet, looked proudly at her father, and went into her room; he turned the key in the door.

"Nanon!" he shouted, "you can rake out the fire in the parlor; then he came back and sat down in an easy-chair that stood between the fire and his wife's bedside, saying as he did so, "Of course she gave her gold to that miserable seducer, Charles, who only cared for our money."

Mme. Grandet's love for her daughter gave her courage in the face of this danger; to all appearance she was deaf, dumb, and blind to all that was implied by this speech. She turned on her bed so as to avoid the angry glitter of her husband's eyes.

"I knew nothing about all this," she said. "Your anger makes me so ill, that if my forebodings come true I shall only leave this room when they carry me out feet foremost. I think you might have spared me this scene, sir. I, at all events, have never caused you any vexation. Your daughter loves you, and I am sure she is as innocent as a newborn babe; so do not make her miserable, and take back your word. This cold is terribly sharp; it might make her seriously ill."

"I shall neither see her nor speak to her. She shall stop in her room on bread and water until she has done as her father bids her. What the devil! the head of a family ought to know when gold goes out of his house, and where it goes. She had the only rupees that there are in France, for aught I know; then there were genovines besides, and Dutch ducats——"

"Eugénie is our only child, and even if she had flung them into the water——"

"Into the water!" shouted the worthy cooper. "*Into the water!* Mme. Grandet, you are raving! When I say a thing I mean it, as you well know. If you want to have peace in the house, get her to confess to you, and worm this secret out of her. Women understand each other, and are cleverer at this sort of thing than we are. Whatever she may have done, I certainly shall not eat her. Is she afraid of me? If she had covered her cousin with gold from head to foot, he is safe on the high-seas by this time, hein! We cannot run after him——"

"Really, sir——" his wife began.

But Mme. Grandet's nature had developed during her daughter's trouble; she felt more keenly, and perhaps her thoughts moved more quickly, or it may be that excitement and the strain upon her overwrought nerves had sharpened her mental faculties. She saw the wen on her husband's face twitch ominously even as she began to speak, and changed her purpose without changing her voice.

"Really, sir, have I any more authority over her than you have? She has never said a word about it to me. She takes after you."

"Goodness! your tongue is hung in the middle this morning! Tut, tut, tut; you are going to fly in my face, I suppose? Perhaps you and she are both in it."

He glared at his wife.

"Really, M. Grandet, if you want to kill me, you have

only to keep on as you are doing. I tell you, sir, and if it were to cost me my life, I would say it again—you are too hard on your daughter; she is a great deal more sensible than you are. The money belonged to her; she could only have made a good use of it, and our good works ought to be known to God alone. Sir, I implore you, take Eugénie back into favor. It will lessen the effect of the shock your anger gave me, and perhaps will save my life. My daughter, sir; give me back my daughter!"

"I am off," he said. "It is unbearable here in my house, when a mother and daughter talk and argue as if——Brooouh! Pouah! You have given me bitter New Year's gifts, Eugénie!" he called. "Yes, yes, cry away! You shall repent it, do you hear? What is the good of taking the sacrament six times a quarter if you give your father's gold away on the sly to an idle rascal who will break your heart when you have nothing else left to give him? You will find out what he is, that Charles of yours, with his morocco boots and his stand-off airs. He can have no heart and no conscience either, when he dares to carry off a poor girl's money without the consent of her parents."

As soon as the street-door was shut, Eugénie stole out of her room and came to her mother's bedside.

"You were very brave for your daughter's sake," she said.

"You see where crooked ways lead us, child!——You have made me tell a lie."

"Oh! mother, I will pray to God to let all the punishment fall on me."

"Is it true?" asked Nanon, coming upstairs in dismay, "that mademoiselle here is to be put on bread and water for the rest of her life?"

"What does it matter, Nanon?" asked Eugénie calmly.

"Why, before I would eat 'kitchen' while the daughter of the house is eating dry bread, I would——no, no, it won't do."

"Don't say a word about it, Nanon," Eugénie warned her.

"It would stick in my throat; but you shall see."

Grandet dined alone, for the first time in twenty-four years.

"So you are a widower, sir," said Nanon. "It is a very dismal thing to be a widower when you have a wife and daughter in the house."

"I did not speak to you, did I? Keep a still tongue in your head, or you will have to go. What have you in that saucepan that I can hear boiling away on the stove?"

"Some dripping that I am melting down——"

"There will be some people here this evening; light the fire."

The Cruchots and their friends, Mme. des Grassins and her son, all came in about eight o'clock, and to their amazement saw neither Mme. Grandet nor her daughter.

"My wife is not very well to-day, and Eugénie is upstairs with her," replied the old cooper, without a trace of perturbation on his face.

After an hour spent, in more or less trivial talk, Mme. des Grassins, who had gone upstairs to see Mme. Grandet, came down again to the dining-room, and was met with a general inquiry of "How is Mme. Grandet?"

"She is very far from well," the lady said gravely. "Her health seems to me to be in a very precarious state. At her time of life you ought to take great care of her, papa Grandet."

"We shall see," said the vine-grower abstractedly, and the whole party took leave of him. As soon as the Cruchots were out in the street and the door was shut behind them, Mme. des Grassins turned to them and said, "Something has happened among the Grandets. The mother is very ill; she herself has no idea how ill she is, and the girl's eyes are red, as if she had been crying for a long while. Are they wanting to marry her against her will?"

That night, when the cooper had gone to bed, Nanon, in list slippers, stole up to Eugénie's room, and displayed a raised pie, which she had managed to bake in a saucepan.

"Here, mademoiselle," said the kind soul, "Cornoiller brought a hare for me. You eat so little that the pie will last you for quite a week, and there is no fear of its spoiling in this frost. You shall not live on dry bread, at any rate; it is not at all good for you."

"Poor Nanon!" said Eugénie, as she pressed the girl's hand.

"I have made it very dainty and nice, and *he* never found out about it. I paid for the lard and the bay-leaves out of my six francs; I can surely do as I like with my own money," and the old servant fled, thinking that she heard Grandet stirring.

Several months went by. The cooper went to see his wife at various times in the day, and never mentioned his daughter's name—never saw her, nor made the slightest allusion to her. Mme. Grandet's health grew worse and worse; she had not once left her room since that terrible January morning. But nothing shook the old cooper's determination; he was hard, cold, and unyielding as a block of granite. He came and went, his manner of life was in nowise altered; but he did not stammer now, and he talked less; perhaps, too, in matters of business, people found him harder than before, but errors crept into his book-keeping.

Something had certainly happened in the Grandet family, both Cruchotins and Grassinistes were agreed on that head; and "What can be the matter with the Grandets?" became a stock question which people asked each other at every social gathering in Saumur.

Eugénie went regularly to church, escorted by Nanon. If Mme. des Grassins spoke to her in the porch as she came out, the girl would answer evasively, and the lady's curiosity remained ungratified. But after two months spent in this fashion it was almost impossible to hide the real state of affairs from Mme. des Grassins or from the Cruchots; a time came when all pretexts were exhausted, and Eugénie's constant absence still demanded an explanation. A little later, though no one could say how or when the secret leaked out, it became common property, and the whole town knew that ever since New Year's Day Mlle. Grandet had been locked up in her room by her father's orders, and that there she lived on bread and water in solitary confinement, and without a fire. Nanon, it was reported, cooked dainties for her, and brought food secretly to her room at night. Further particulars were given. It was even said that only when Grandet was out of the house could the young girl nurse her mother, or indeed see her at all.

People blamed Grandet severely. He was regarded as an outlaw, as it were, by the whole town; all his hardness, his bad faith was remembered against him, and every one shunned him. They whispered and pointed at him as he went by; and as his daughter passed along the crooked street on her way to mass or to vespers, with Nanon at her side, people would hurry to their windows and look curiously at the wealthy heiress' face—a face so sad and so divinely sweet.

The town gossip reached her ears as slowly as it reached her father's. Her imprisonment and her father's displeasure were as nothing to her; had she not her map of the world? And from her window could she not see the little bench, the old wall, and the garden walks? Was not the sweetness of those past kisses still upon her lips? So, sustained by love and by the consciousness of her innocence in the sight of God, she could patiently endure her solitary life and her father's anger; but there was another sorrow, so deep and so overwhelming that Eugénie could not find a refuge from it. The gentle, patient mother was gradually passing away; it seemed as if the beauty of her soul shone out more and more brightly in those dark days as she drew nearer to the tomb. Eugénie often bitterly blamed herself for this illness, telling herself that she had been the innocent cause of the painful malady that was slowly consuming her mother's life; and, in spite of all her mother said to comfort her, this remorseful feeling made her cling more closely to the love she was to lose so soon. Every morning, as soon as her father had left the house, she went to sit at her mother's bedside. Nanon used to bring her breakfast to her there. But for poor Eugénie in her sadness, this suffering was almost more than she could bear; she looked at her mother's face, and then at Nanon, with tears in her eyes, and was dumb; she did not dare to speak of her cousin now. It was always Mme. Grandet who began to talk of him; it was she who was forced to say, "Where is *he*? Why does *he* not write?"

Neither mother nor daughter had any idea of the distance.

"Let us think of him without talking about him, mother," Eugénie would answer. "You are suffering; you come before every one;" and when she said "every one," Eugénie meant *him*.

"I have no wish to live any longer, child," Mme. Grandet used to say. "God in His protecting care has led me to look forward joyfully to death as the end of my sorrows."

Everything that she said was full of Christian piety. For the first few months of the year her husband breakfasted in her room, and always, as he walked restlessly about, he heard the same words from her, uttered with angelic gentleness, but with firmness; the near approach of death had given her the courage which she had lacked all her life.

"Thank you, sir, for the interest which you take in my health," she said in response to the merest formality of an inquiry; "but if you really wish to sweeten the bitterness of my last moments, and to alleviate my sufferings, forgive our daughter, and act like a Christian, a husband, and a father."

At these words Grandet would come and sit down by the bed, much as a man who is threatened by a shower betakes himself resignedly to the nearest sheltering archway. He would say nothing, and his wife might say what she liked. To the most pathetic, loving, and fervent prayers, he would reply, "My poor wife, you are looking a bit pale to-day."

His daughter seemed to have passed entirely out of his mind; the mention of her name brought no change over his stony face and hard-set mouth. He always gave the same vague answers to her pleadings, couched in almost the same words, and did not heed his wife's white face, nor the tears that flowed down her cheeks.

"May God forgive you, as I do, sir," she said. "You will have need of mercy some day."

Since his wife's illness had began he had not ventured to make use of his formidable "Tut, tut, tut," but his tyranny was not relaxed one whit by his wife's angelic gentleness.

Her plain face was growing almost beautiful now as a beautiful nature showed itself more and more, and her soul grew absolute. It seemed as if the spirit of prayer had purified and refined the homely features—as if they were lit up by some inner light. Which of us has not known such faces as this, and seen their final transfiguration—the triumph of a soul that has dwelt for so long among pure and lofty thoughts that they set their seal unmistakably upon the roughest lineaments at last? The sight of this transformation wrought by the physical suffering which stripped the soul of the rags of humanity that hid it, had a certain effect, however feeble, upon that man of bronze—the old cooper. A stubborn habit of silence had succeeded to his old contemptuous ways, a wish to keep up his dignity as a father of a family was apparently the motive for this course.

The faithful Nanon no sooner showed herself in the market-place than people began to rail at her master and to make jokes at his expense; but however loudly public opinion condemned old Grandet, the maidservant, jealous for the honor of the family, stoutly defended him.

"Well, now," she would say to those who spoke ill of her

master, "don't we all grow harder as we grow older? And would you have him different from other people? Just hold your lying tongues. Mademoiselle lives like a queen. She is all by herself no doubt, but she likes it; and my master and mistress have their very good reasons for what they do."

At last, one evening towards the end of spring, Mme. Grandet, feeling that this trouble, even more than her illness, was shortening her days, and that any farther attempt on her part to obtain forgiveness for Eugénie was hopeless, confided her troubles to the Cruchots.

"To put a girl of twenty-two on a diet of bread and water!——" cried the President de Bonfons, "and without just and sufficient cause! Why, that constitutes legal cruelty; she might lodge a complaint; *in as much as*——"

"Come, nephew," said the notary, "that is enough of your law court jargon. Be easy, madame; I will bring this imprisonment to an end to-morrow."

Eugénie heard, and came out of her room.

"Gentlemen," she said, impelled by a certain pride, "do nothing in this matter, I beg of you. My father is master in his own house, and so long as I live under his roof I ought to obey him. No one has any right to criticise his conduct; he is answerable to God, and to God alone. If you have any friendly feeling for me, I entreat you to say nothing whatever about this. If you expose my father to censure, you would lower us all in the eyes of the world. I am very thankful to you, gentlemen, for the interest you have taken in me, and you will oblige me still farther if you will put a stop to the gossip that is going on in the town. I only heard of it by accident."

"She is right," said Mme. Grandet.

"Mademoiselle, the best possible way to stop people's talk would be to set you at liberty," said the old notary respectfully; he was struck with the beauty which solitude and love and sadness had brought into Eugénie's face.

"Well, Eugénie, leave it in M. Cruchot's hands, as he seems to think success is certain. He knows your father, and he knows, too, how to put the matter before him. You and your father must be reconciled at all costs, if you want me to be happy during the little time I have yet to live."

The next morning Grandet went out to take a certain number of turns round the little garden, a habit that he had fallen into during Eugénie's incarceration. He chose to take the air while Eugénie was dressing; and when he had reached the great walnut tree, he stood behind it for a few moments and looked at her window. He watched her as she brushed her long hair, and there was a sharp struggle doubtless between his natural stubborn will and a longing to take his daughter in his arms and kiss her.

He would often go to sit on the little worm-eaten bench where Charles and Eugénie had vowed to love each other for ever; and she, his daughter, also watched her father furtively, or looked into her glass and saw him reflected there, and the garden and the bench. If he rose and began to walk again, she went to sit in the window. It was pleasant to her to be there. She studied the bit of old wall, the delicate sprays of wild flowers that grew in its crevices, the maidenhair fern, the morning glories, and a little plant with thick leaves and white or yellow flowers, a sort of stone-crop that grows everywhere among the vines at Saumur and Tours.

Old M. Cruchot came early on a bright June morning and found the vine-grower sitting on the little bench with his back against the wall, absorbed in watching his daughter.

"What can I do for you, M. Cruchot?" he asked, as he became aware of the notary's presence.

"I have come about a matter of business."

"Aha! Have you some gold to exchange for crowns?"

"No, no. It is not a question of money this time, but of your daughter Eugénie. Everybody is talking about you and her."

"What business is it of theirs? A man's house is his castle."

"Just so; and a man can kill himself if he has a mind to, or he can do worse, he can throw his money out of the windows."

"What?"

"Eh! but your wife is very ill, my friend. You ought even to call in M. Bergerin, her life is in danger. If she were to die for want of proper care, you would hear of it, I am sure."

"Tut, tut, tut!" you know what is the matter with her, and when once one of these doctors sets foot in your house, they will come five or six times a day."

"After all, Grandet, you will do as you think best. We are old friends; there is no one in all Saumur who has your interests more at heart than I, so it was only my duty to let you know this. Whatever happens, you are responsible, and you understand your own business, so there it is. Besides, that was not what I came to speak about. There is something else more serious for you, perhaps; for, after all, you do not wish to kill your wife, she is too useful to you. Just think what your position would be if anything happened to Mme. Grandet; you would have your daughter to face. You would have to give an account to Eugénie of her mother's share of your joint estate; and if she chose, your daughter might demand her mother's fortune, for she, and not you, will succeed to it; and in that case you might have to sell Froidfond."

Cruchot's words were like a bolt from the blue; for much as the worthy cooper knew about business, he knew very little law. The idea of a forced sale had never occurred to him.

"So I should strongly recommend you to treat her kindly," the notary concluded.

"But do you know what she has done, Cruchot?"

"No. What was it?" asked the notary; he felt curious to

know the reason of the quarrel, and a confidence from old Grandet was an interesting novelty.

"She has given away her gold."

"Oh! well, it belonged to her, didn't it?"

"That is what they all say!" said Grandet, letting his arms fall with a tragic gesture.

"And for a trifle like that you would shut yourself out from all hope of any concessions which you will want her to make if her mother dies?"

"Ah! do you call six thousand francs in gold a trifle?"

"Eh! my old friend, have you any idea what it will cost you to have your property valued and divided if Eugénie should compel you to do so?"

"What would it cost?"

"Two, three, or even four thousand francs. How could you know what it was worth unless you put it up to public auction? While if you come to an understanding——"

"By my father's pruning hook!" cried the vine-grower, sinking back, and turning quite pale. "We will see about this, Cruchot."

After a moment of agony or of dumb bewilderment, Grandet spoke, with his eyes fixed on his neighbor's face. "Life is very hard," he said. "It is full of troubles. Cruchot," he went on, earnestly, "you are incapable of deceiving me; give me your word of honor that this ditty of yours has a solid foundation. Let me look at the Code; I want to see the Code!"

"My poor friend," said the notary, "I ought to understand my own profession."

"Then it is really true? I shall be plundered, cheated, robbed, and murdered by my own daughter!"

"She is her mother's heiress."

"Then what is the good of having children? Oh! my wife, I love my wife; luckily, she has a sound constitution; she is a La Bertellière."

"She has not a month to live."

The cooper struck his forehead, took a few paces, and then came back again.

"What is to be done?" he demanded of Cruchot, with a tragic expression on his face.

"Well, perhaps Eugénie might simply give up her claims to her mother's property. You do not mean to disinherit her, do you? But do not treat her harshly if you want her to make a concession of that kind. I am speaking against my own interests, my friend. How do I make a living but by drawing up inventories and conveyances and deeds of arrangement and by winding up estates?"

"We shall see, we shall see. Let us say no more about this now, Cruchot. You have wrung my very soul. Have you taken any gold lately?"

"No; but I have some old louis, nine or ten perhaps, which you can have. Look here, my good friend, make it up with Eugénie; all Saumur is pointing a finger at you."

"The rogues!"

"Well, consols have risen to ninety-nine, so you should be satisfied for once in your life."

"At ninety-nine, Cruchot?"

"Yes."

"Hey! hey! ninety-nine!" the old man said, as he went with the notary to the street-door. He felt too much agitated by what he had just heard to stay quietly at home; so he went up to his wife's room.

"Come, mother, you may spend the day with your daughter, I am going to Froidfond. Be good, both of you, while I am away. This is our wedding-day, dear wife. Stay! here are ten crowns for you, for the Fête-Dieu procession; you have wanted to give it for long enough. Take a holiday! have some fun, keep up your spirits and get well. *Vive la joie!*"

He threw down ten crowns of six francs each upon the bed, took her face in his hands, and kissed her on the forehead.

"You are feeling better, dear wife, are you not?"

"But how can you think of receiving God, who forgives, into your house, when you have shut your heart against your daughter?" she said, with deep feeling in her voice.

"Tut, tut, tut!" said the father soothingly; "we will see about that."

"Merciful heaven! Eugénie!" called the mother, her face flushed with joy; "Eugénie, come and give your father a kiss, you are forgiven!" But her worthy father had vanished. He fled with all his might in the direction of his vineyards, where he set himself to the task of constructing his new world out of this chaos of strange ideas.

Grandet had just entered upon his sixty-seventh year. Avarice had gained a stronger hold upon him during the past two years of his life; indeed, all lasting passions grow with man's growth; and it had come to pass with him, as with all men whose lives are ruled by one master-idea, that he clung with all the force of his imagination to the symbol which represented that idea for him. Gold—to have gold, that he might see and touch it, had become with him a perfect monomania. His disposition to tyrannize had also grown with his love of money, and it seemed to him to be monstrous that he should be called upon to give up the least portion of his property on the death of his wife. Was he to render an account of her fortune, and to have an inventory drawn up of everything he possessed—personalty and real estate, and put it all up to auction?

"That would be stark ruin," he said aloud to himself, as he stood among his vines and examined their stems.

He made up his mind at last, and came back to Saumur at dinner-time fully determined on his course. He would humor Eugénie, and coax and cajole her so that he might die royally, keeping the control of his millions in his hands until his latest sigh. It happened that he let himself in with his master key; he crept noiselessly as a wolf up the stairs to his wife's room, which he entered just as Eugénie was setting the dressing-case, in all its golden glory, upon her mother's bed. The two women had stolen a pleasure in Grandet's absence; they were looking at the portraits and tracing out Charles' features in his mother's likeness.

"It is just his forehead and his mouth!" Eugénie was saying, as the vine-grower opened the door.

Mme. Grandet saw how her husband's eyes darted upon the gold. "Oh! God, have pity upon us!" she cried.

The vine-grower seized upon the dressing-case as a tiger might spring upon a sleeping child.

"What may this be?" he said, carrying off the treasure to the window, where he ensconced himself with it. "Gold! solid gold!" he cried, "and plenty of it too; there is a couple of pounds' weight here. Aha! so this was what Charles gave you in exchange for your pretty gold-pieces? Why did you not tell me? It was a good stroke of business, little girl. You are your father's own daughter, I see. (Eugénie trembled from head to foot.) This belongs to Charles, doesn't it?" the good man went on.

"Yes, father; it is not mine. That case is a sacred trust."

"Tut, tut, tut! he has gone off with your money; you ought to make good the loss of your little treasure."

"Oh! father!——"

The old man had taken out his pocket-knife, with a view to wrenching away a plate of the precious metal, and for the moment had been obliged to lay the case on a chair beside him. Eugénie sprang forward to secure her treasure; but the cooper, who had kept an eye upon his daughter as well as upon the casket, put out his arm to prevent this, and thrust her back so roughly that she fell on to the bed.

"Sir! sir!" cried the mother, rising and sitting upright.

Grandet had drawn out his knife, and was about to insert the blade beneath the plate.

"Father!" cried Eugénie, going down on her knees and dragging herself nearer to him as she knelt; "father, in the name of all the saints, and the Holy Virgin, for the sake of Christ who died on the cross, for your own soul's salvation, father, if you have any regard for my life, do not touch it! The case is not yours, and it is not mine. It belongs to an unhappy kinsman, who gave it into my keeping, and I ought to give it back to him untouched."

"What do you look at it for if it is a deposit? Looking at it is worse than touching it."

"Do not pull it to pieces, father! You will bring dishonor upon me. Father! do you hear me?"

"For pity's sake, sir!" entreated the mother.

"Father!"

The shrill cry rang through the house and brought the frightened Nanon upstairs. Eugénie caught up a knife that lay within her reach.

"Well?" said Grandet, calmly, with a cold smile on his lips.

"Sir! you are killing me!" said the mother.

"Father, if you cut away a single scrap of gold, I shall stab myself with this knife. It is your doing that my mother is dying, and now my death will also be laid at your door. It shall be wound for wound."

Grandet held his knife suspended above the case, looked at his daughter, and hesitated.

"Would you really do it, Eugénie?" he asked.

"Yes, sir!" said the mother.

"She would do as she says," cried Nanon. "Do be sensible, sir, for once in your life."

The cooper wavered for a moment, looking first at the gold and then at his daughter.

Mme. Grandet fainted.

"There! sir, you see, the mistress is dying," cried Nanon.

"There! there! child, do not let us fall out about a box.

Just take it back!" cried the cooper hastily, throwing the case on to the bed. "And, Nanon, go for M. Bergerin. Come! come! mother," he said, and he kissed his wife's hand; "never mind, there! there! we have made it up, haven't we, little girl? No more dry bread; you shall eat whatever you like—— Ah! she is opening her eyes. Well, now, little mother, dear little mother, don't take on so! Look! I am going to kiss Eugénie! She loves her cousin, does she? She shall marry him if she likes; she shall keep his little case for him. But you must live for a long while yet, my poor wife! Come! turn your head a little. Listen! you shall have the finest altar at the Fête-Dieu that has ever been seen in Saumur."

"Oh! *mon Dieu!* how can you treat your wife and daughter in this way!" moaned Mme. Grandet.

"I will never do so again, never again!" cried the cooper. "You shall see, my poor wife."

He went to his strong room and returned with a handful of louis d'or, which he scattered on the coverlet.

"There! Eugénie, there! wife, those are for you," he said, fingering the gold coins as they lay. "Come! cheer up, and get well, you shall want for nothing, neither you nor Eugénie. There are a hundred louis for her. You will not give them away, will you, eh, Eugénie?"

Mme. Grandet and her daughter gazed at each other in amazement.

"Take back the money, father; we want nothing, nothing but your love."

"Oh! well, just as you like," he said, as he pocketed the louis, "let us live together like good friends. Let us all go down to the dining-room and have dinner, and play loto every evening, and put our two sous into the pool, and be as merry as the maids. Eh! my wife?"

"Alas! how I wish that I could, if you would like it," said the dying woman, "but I am not strong enough to get up."

"Poor mother!" said the cooper, "you do not know how much I love you; and you too, child!"

He drew his daughter to him and embraced her with fervor.

"Oh! how pleasant it is to kiss one's daughter after a squabble, my little girl! There! mother, do you see? We are quite at one again now. Just go and lock that away," he said to Eugénie, as he pointed to the case. "There! there! don't be frightened; I will never say another word to you about it."

M. Bergerin, who was regarded as the cleverest doctor in Saumur, came before very long. He told Grandet plainly after the interview that the patient was very seriously ill; that any excitement might be fatal to her; that with a light diet, perfect tranquillity, and the most constant care, her life might possibly be prolonged until the end of the autumn.

"Will it be an expensive illness?" asked Grandet. "Will she want a lot of physic?"

"Not much physic, but very careful nursing," answered the doctor, who could not help smiling.

"After all, M. Bergerin, you are a man of honor," said Grandet uneasily. "I can depend upon you, can I not? Come and see my wife whenever and as often as you think it really necessary. Preserve her life. My good wife—I am very fond of her, you see, though I may not show it; it is all shut up inside me, and I am one that takes things terribly to heart; I am in trouble too. It all began with my brother's death; I am spending, oh!—heaps of money in Paris for him—the very eyes out of my head, in fact, and it seems as if there were no end to it. Good-day, sir. If you can save my wife, save her, even if it takes a hundred or two hundred francs."

In spite of Grandet's fervent wishes that his wife might be restored to health, for this question of the inheritance was like a foretaste of death for him; in spite of his readiness to fulfill the least wishes of the astonished mother and daughter in every possible way; in spite of Eugénie's tenderest and most devoted care, it was evident that Mme. Grandet's life was rapidly drawing to a close. Day by day she grew weaker, and, as often happens at her time of life, she had no strength to resist the disease that was wasting her away. She seemed to have no more vitality than the autumn leaves; and as the sunlight shining through the leaves turns them to gold, so she seemed to be transformed by the light of heaven. Her death was a fitting close to her life, a death wholly Christian; is not that saying that it was sublime? Her love for her daughter, her meek virtues, her angelic patience, had never shone more brightly than in that month of October, 1822, when she passed away. All through her illness she had never uttered the slightest complaint, and her spotless soul left earth for heaven with but one regret—for the daughter whose sweet companionship had been the solace of her dreary life, and for whom her dying eyes foresaw troubles and sorrows manifold. She trembled at the thought of this lamb, spotless as she herself was, left alone in the world among selfish beings who sought to despoil her of her fleece, her treasure.

"There is no happiness save in heaven," she said just before she died; "you will know that one day, my child."

On the morrow after her mother's death, it seemed to Eugénie that she had yet one more reason for clinging fondly to the old house where she had been born, and where she had found life so hard of late—it became for her the place where her mother had died. She could not see the old chair set on little blocks of wood, the place by the window where her mother used to sit, without shedding tears. Her father showed her such tenderness, and took such care of her, that she began to think that she had never understood his nature; he used to come to her room and take her down to breakfast on his arm, and sit looking at her for whole hours with something almost like kindness in his eyes, with the same brooding look that he gave his gold. Indeed, the old cooper almost trembled before his daughter, and was altogether so unlike himself, that Nanon and the Cruchotins wondered at these signs of weakness, and set it down to his advanced age; they began to fear that the old man's mind was giving way. But when the day came on which the family began to wear their mourning, M. Cruchot, who alone was in his client's confidence, was invited to dinner, and these mysteries were explained. Grandet waited till the table had been cleared, and the doors carefully shut.

Then he began: "My dear child you are your mother's heiress, and there are some little matters of business that we must settle between us. Is that not so, eh, Cruchot?"

"Yes."

"Is it really pressing; must it be settled to-day, father?"

"Yes, yes, little girl. I could not endure this suspense any longer, and I am sure you would not make things hard for me."

"Oh! father——"

"Well, then, everything must be decided to-night."

"Then what do you want me to do?"

"Well, little girl, it is not for me to tell you. You tell her, Cruchot."

"Mademoiselle, your father wants neither to divide nor to sell his property, nor to pay a heavy succession duty upon the ready money he may happen to have just now. So if these complications are to be avoided, there must be no inventory made out, and all the property must remain undivided for the present——"

"Cruchot, are you quite sure of what you are saying that you talk in this way before a child?"

"Let me say what I have to say, Grandet."

"Yes, yes, my friend. Neither you nor my daughter would plunder me. You would not plunder me, would you, little girl?"

"But what am I to do, M. Cruchot?" asked Eugénie, losing patience.

"Well," said the notary, "you must sign this deed, by which you renounce your claims to your mother's property; the property would be secured to you, but your father would have the use of it for his life, and there would be no need to make a division now."

"I understand nothing of all this that you are saying," Eugénie answered; "give me the deed, and show me where I am to sign my name."

Grandet looked from the document to his daughter, and again from his daughter to the document. His agitation was so great that he actually wiped several drops of perspiration from his forehead.

"I would much rather you simply waived all claim to your poor dear mother's property, little girl," he broke in, "instead of signing that deed. It will cost a lot to register it. I would rather you renounced your claims and trusted to me for the future. I would allow you a good round sum, say a hundred francs every month. You could pay for masses then, you see; you could have masses said for any one that——Eh? A hundred francs (in livres) every month?"

"I will do just as you like, father."

"Mademoiselle," said the notary, "it is my duty to point out to you that you are robbing yourself without guarantee——"

"*Eh! mon Dieu!*" she answered. "What does that matter to me?"

"Do be quiet, Cruchot. So it is settled, quite settled!" cried Grandet, taking his daughter's hand and striking his own into it. "You will not go back from your word, Eugénie? You are a good girl, hein!"

"Oh! father——"

In his joy he embraced his daughter, almost suffocating her as he did so.

"There! child, you have given fresh life to your father; but you are only giving him what he gave you, so we are quits. This is how business ought to be conducted, and life is a business transaction. Bless you! You are a good girl, and one that really loves her old father. You can do as you like now. Then good-bye till to-morrow, Cruchot," he added, turning to the horrified notary. "You will see that the deed of renunciation is properly drawn up for the clerk of the court."

By noon next day the declaration was drawn up, and Eugénie herself signed away all her rights to her heritage. Yet a year slipped by, and the cooper had not kept his promise, and Eugénie had not received a sou of the monthly income which was to have been hers; when Eugénie spoke to him about it, half-laughingly, he could not help blushing; he hurried up to his room, and when he came down again he handed her about a third of the jewelry which he had purchased of his nephew.

"There! child," he said, with a certain sarcastic ring in his voice; "will you take these for your twelve hundred francs?"

"Oh! father, really? Will you really give them to me?"

"You shall have as much next year again," said he, flinging it into her lap; "and so, before very long, you will have all his trinkets," he added, rubbing his hands. He had made a very good bargain, thanks to his daughter's sentiment about the jewelry, and was in high good-humor.

Yet, although the old man was still hale and vigorous, he began to see that he must take his daughter into his confidence, and that she must learn to manage his concerns. So with this end in view he required her to be present while he gave out the daily stores, and for two years he made her receive the portion of the rent which was paid in kind. Gradually she came to know the names of the vineyards and farms; he took her with him when he visited his tenants. By the end of the third year he considered the initiation was complete; and, in truth, she had fallen into his ways unquestioningly, till it had become a matter of habit with her to do as her father had done before her. He had no further doubts, gave over the keys of the storeroom into her keeping, and installed her as mistress of the house.

Five years went by in this way, and no event disturbed their monotonous existence. Eugénie and her father lived a life of methodical routine with the same regularity of movement that characterized the old clock; doing the same things at the same hour day after day, year after year. Every one knew that there had been a profound sorrow in Mlle. Grandet's life; every circle in Saumur had its theories of this secret trouble, and its suspicions as to the state of the heiress' heart, but she never let fall a word that could enlighten any one on either point.

She saw no one but the three Cruchots and a few of their friends, who had gradually been admitted as visitors to the house. Under their instructions she had mastered the game of whist, and they dropped in nearly every evening for a rubber. In the year 1827 her father began to feel the infirmities of age, and was obliged to take her still farther into his confidence; she learned the full extent of his landed possessions, and was recommended in all cases of difficulty to refer to the notary Cruchot, whose integrity could be depended upon. Grandet reached the age of eighty-two, and towards the end of the year had a paralytic seizure, from which he never rallied. M. Bergerin gave him up, and Eugénie realized that very shortly she would be quite alone in the world; the thought drew her more closely to her father; she clung to this last link of affection that bound her to another soul. Love was all the world for her, as it is for all women who love; and Charles had gone out of her world. She nursed her father with sublime devotion; the old man's intellect had grown feeble, but the greed of gold had become an instinct which survived his faculties.

Grandet died as he had lived. Every morning during that slow death he had himself wheeled across his room to a place beside the fire, whence he could keep the door of his cabinet in view; on the other side of the door, no doubt, lay his hoarded treasures of gold. He sat there, passive and motionless; but if any one entered the room, he would glance uneasily at the newcomer, and then at the door with its sheathing of iron plates. He would ask the meaning of every sound, however faint, and, to the notary's amazement, the old man heard the dog bark in the yard at the back of the house. He roused from this apparent stupor at the proper hour on the days for receiving his rents and dues, for settling accounts with his vine-dressers, and giving receipts. Then he shifted his armchair round on its casters, until he faced the door of his cabinet, and his daughter was called upon to open it, and to put away the little bags of money in neat piles, one upon the other. He would watch her until it was all over and the door was locked again; and as soon as she had returned the precious key to him, he would turn round noiselessly and take up his old position, putting the key in his waistcoat pocket, where he felt for it from time to time.

His old friend the notary felt sure that it was only a question of time, and that Eugénie must of necessity marry his nephew the magistrate, unless, indeed, Charles Grandet returned; so he redoubled his attentions. He came every day to take Grandet's instructions, went at his bidding to Froidfond, to farm and meadow and vineyard; sold vintages, and exchanged all moneys received for gold, which was secretly sent to join the piles of bags stored up in the cabinet.

Then death came up close at last, and the vine-grower's strong frame wrestled with the Destroyer. Even in those days he would sit as usual by the fire, facing the door of his cabinet. He used to drag off the blankets that they wrapped round him, and try to fold them, and say to Nanon, "Lock that up; lock that up, or they will rob me."

So long as he could open his eyes, where the last spark of life seemed to linger, they used to turn at once to the door of the room where all his treasures lay, and he would say

HE WOULD SIT FOR WHOLE HOURS WITH HIS EYES FIXED ON THE LOUIS.

to his daughter, in tones that seemed to thrill with a panic of fear—

"*Are they there still?*"

"Yes, father."

"Keep watch over the gold!——Let me see the gold," her father would say.

Then Eugénie used to spread out the louis on a table before him, and he would sit for whole hours with his eyes fixed on the louis in an unseeing stare, like that of a child who begins to see for the first time; and sometimes a weak imbecile smile, painful to see, would steal across his features.

"That warms me!" he muttered more than once, and his face expressed a perfect content.

When the curé came to administer the sacrament, all the life seemed to have died out of the miser's eyes, but they lit up for the first time for many hours at the sight of the silver crucifix, the candlesticks, and holy water vessel, all of silver; he fixed his gaze on the precious metal, and the wen twitched for the last time.

As the priest held the gilded crucifix above him that the image of Christ might be laid to his lips, he made a frightful effort to clutch it—a last effort which cost him his life. He called to Eugénie, who saw nothing; she was kneeling beside him, bathing in tears the hand that was growing cold already. "Give me your blessing, father," she entreated. "Be very careful!" the last words came from him; "one day you will render an account to me of everything here below." Which utterance clearly shows that a miser should adopt Christianity as his religion.

So Eugénie Grandet was now alone in the world, and her house was left to her desolate. There was no one but Nanon with whom she could talk over her troubles; she could look into no other eyes and find a response to them; big Nanon was the only human being who loved her for herself.

For Eugénie, Nanon was a providence; she was no longer a servant, she was an humble friend.

M. Cruchot informed Eugénie that she had three hundred thousand livres a year, derived from landed property in and around Saumur, besides six millions in the three per cents. (invested when the funds were at sixty francs, whereas they now stood at seventy-seven), and in ready money two millions in gold, and a hundred thousand francs in silver, without counting any arrears that were due. Altogether her property amounted to about seventeen million francs.

"Where can my cousin be?" she said to herself.

On the day when M. Cruchot laid these facts before his new client, together with the information that the estate was now clear and free from all outstanding liabilities, Eugénie and Nanon sat on either side of the hearth, in the parlor, now so empty and so full of memories; everything recalled past days, from her mother's chair set on its wooden blocks to the glass tumbler out of which her cousin once drank.

"Nanon, we are alone, you and I."

"Yes, mamselle; if I only knew where he was, the charming young gentleman, I would set off on foot to find him."

"The sea lies between us," said Eugénie.

While the poor lonely heiress, with her faithful old servant for company, was shedding tears in the cold, dark house, which was all the world she knew, men talked from Orleans to Nantes of nothing but Mlle. Grandet and her seventeen millions. One of her first acts was to settle a pension of twelve hundred francs on Nanon, who, possessing already an income of six hundred francs of her own, at once became a great match. In less than a month she exchanged her condition of spinster for that of wife, at the instance and through the persuasion of Antoine Cornoiller, who was promoted to the position of bailiff and keeper to Mlle. Grandet. Mme.

Cornoiller had an immense advantage over her contemporaries; her large features had stood the test of time better than those of many a comelier woman. She might be fifty-nine years of age, but she did not look more than forty; thanks to an almost monastic regimen, she possessed rugged health and a high color, time seemed to have no effect on her, and perhaps she had never looked so well in her life as she did on her wedding-day. She had the compensating qualities of her style of ugliness; she was tall, stout, and strong; her face wore an indestructible expression of good-humor, and Cornoiller's lot seemed an enviable one to many beholders.

"Fast color," said the draper.

"She might have a family yet," said the dry-salter; "she is as well preserved as if she had been kept in brine, asking your pardon."

"She is rich; that fellow Cornoiller has done a good day's work," said another neighbor.

When Nanon left the old house and went down the crooked street on her way to the parish church, she met with nothing but congratulations and good-wishes. Nanon was very popular with her neighbors. Eugénie gave her three dozen spoons and forks as a wedding present. Cornoiller, quite overcome with such munificence, spoke of his mistress with tears in his eyes; he would have let himself be cut in pieces for her. Mme. Cornoiller became Eugénie's confidential servant; she was not only married, and had a husband of her own, her dignity was yet further increased, her happiness was doubled. *She* had at last a storeroom and a bunch of keys; *she* too gave out provisions just as her late master used to do. Then she had two subordinates—a cook and a waiting-woman, who took charge of the house linen and made Mlle. Grandet's dresses. As for Cornoiller, he combined the functions of forester and steward. It is needless to say that the cook and waiting-woman of Nanon's choosing were real domestic *treasures*. The tenants scarcely noticed the death of their late landlord; they were thoroughly broken in to a severe discipline, and M. and Mme. Cornoiller's reign was no whit less rigorous than that of the old régime.

Eugénie was a woman of thirty, and as yet had known none of the happiness of life. All through her joyless, monotonous childhood she had had but one companion, a broken-spirited mother, whose sensitive nature had found little but suffering in a hard life. That mother had joyfully taken leave of existence, pitying the daughter who must still live on in the world. Eugénie would never lose the sense of her loss, but little of the bitterness of self-reproach mingled with her memories of her mother. She felt that she had always done a daughter's duty to her mother.

Love, her first and only love, had been a fresh source of suffering for Eugénie. For a few brief days she had seen her lover; she had given her heart to him between two stolen kisses; then he had left her, and had set the lands and seas of the world between them. Her father had cursed her for this love; it had nearly cost her her mother's life; it had brought her pain and sorrow and a few faint hopes. She had striven towards her happiness till her own forces had failed her, and another had not come to her aid.

Our souls live by giving and receiving; we have need of another soul; whatever it gives us we make our own, and give back again in overflowing measure. This is as vitally necessary for our inner life as breathing is for our corporeal existence. Without that wonderful physical process we perish; the heart suffers from lack of air, and ceases to beat. Eugénie was beginning to suffer.

She found no solace in her wealth; it could do nothing for her; her love, her religion, her faith in the future made up all her life. Love was teaching her what eternity meant. Her own heart and the Gospel each spoke to her of a life to come; life was everlasting, and love no less eternal. Night and day she dwelt with these two infinite thoughts, perhaps for her they were but one. She withdrew more and more into herself; she loved, and believed that she was loved.

For seven years her passion had wholly engrossed her.

Her treasures were not those millions left to her by her father, the money that went on accumulating year after year; but the two portraits which hung above her bed, Charles' leather case, the jewels which she had bought back from her father, and which were now proudly set forth on a layer of cotton wool inside the drawer in the old chest, and her aunt's thimble which Mme. Grandet had used; every day Eugénie took up a piece of embroidery, a sort of Penelope's web, which she had only begun that she might wear the golden thimble, endeared to her by so many memories.

It seemed hardly probable that Mlle. Grandet would marry while she still wore mourning. Her sincere piety was well known. So the Cruchot family, counseled by the astute old Abbé, was fain to be content with surrounding the heiress with the most affectionate attentions. Her dining-room was filled every evening with the warmest and most devoted Cruchotins, who endeavored to surpass each other in singing the praises of the mistress of the house in every key. She had her physician-in-ordinary, her grand almoner, her chamberlain, her mistress of the robes, her prime minister, and last, but by no means least, her chancellor—a chancellor whose aim it was to keep her informed of everything. If the heiress had expressed any wish for a train-bearer, they would have found one for her. She was a queen, in fact, and never was queen so adroitly flattered. A great soul never stoops to flattery; it is the resource of little natures, who succeed in making themselves smaller still, that they may the better creep into the hearts of those about whom they circle. Flattery, by its very nature, implies an interested motive. So the people who filled Mlle. Grandet's sitting-room every evening (they addressed her and spoke of her among themselves as Mlle. de Froidfond now) heaped their praises upon their hostess in a manner truly marvelous. This chorus of praise embarrassed Eugénie at first; but however gross the flattery might be, she became accustomed to hear her beauty extolled, and if some newcomer had considered her to be plain, she certainly would have winced more under the criticism than she might have done eight years ago. She came at last to welcome their homage, which in her secret heart she laid at the feet of her idol. So also, by degrees, she accepted the position, and allowed herself to be treated as a queen, and saw her little court full every evening.

M. le Président de Bonfons was the hero of the circle; they lauded his talents, his personal appearance, his learning, his amiability; he was an inexhaustible subject of admiring comment. Such an one would call attention to the fact that in seven years the magistrate had largely increased his fortune; Bonfons had at least ten thousand francs a year; and his property, like the lands of all the Cruchots in fact, lay within the compass of the heiress' vast estates.

"Do you know, mademoiselle," another courtier would remark, "that the Cruchots have forty thousand livres a year among them!"

"And they are putting money by," said Mlle. de Gribeaucourt, an old and trusty Cruchotine. "Quite lately a gentleman came from Paris on purpose to offer M. Cruchot two hundred thousand francs for his professional connection. If he could gain an appointment as justice of the peace, he ought to take the offer."

"He means to succeed M. de Bonfons as President, and is taking steps to that end," said Mme. d'Orsonval, "for M. le Président will be a councilor, and then a president of a court; he is so gifted that he is sure to succeed."

"Yes," said another, "he is a very remarkable man. Do you not think so, mademoiselle?"

"M. le Président" had striven to act up to the part he wanted to play. He was forty years old, his countenance was dark and ill-favored, he had, moreover, the wizened look which is frequently seen in men of his profession; but he affected the airs of youth, sported a malacca cane, refrained from taking snuff in Mlle. Grandet's house, and went thither arrayed in a white cravat and a shirt with huge frills, which gave him a quaint family resemblance to a turkey-gobbler. He called the fair heiress "our dear Eugénie," and spoke as if he were an intimate friend of the family. In fact, but for the number of those assembled, and the substitution of whist for loto, and the absence of M. and Mme. Grandet, the scene was scarcely changed; it might almost have been that first evening on which this story began.

The pack was still in pursuit of Eugénie's millions; it was a more numerous pack now; they gave tongue together, and hunted down their prey more systematically.

If Charles had come back from the far-off Indies, he would have found the same motives at work and almost the same people. Mme. des Grassins, for whom Eugénie had nothing but kindness and pity, still remained to vex the Cruchots. Eugénie's face still shone out against the dark background, and Charles (though invisible) reigned there supreme as in other days.

Yet some advance had been made. Eugénie's birthday bouquet was never forgotten by the magistrate. Indeed, it had become an institution; every evening he brought the heiress a huge and wonderful bouquet. Mme. Cornoiller ostentatiously placed these offerings in a vase, and promptly flung them into a corner of the yard as soon as the visitors had departed.

In the early spring Mme. des Grassins made a move, and sought to trouble the felicity of the Cruchotins by talking to Eugénie of the Marquis de Froidfond, whose ruined fortunes might be retrieved if the heiress would return his estate to him by a marriage contract. Mme. des Grassins lauded the Marquis and his title to the skies; and, taking Eugénie's quiet smile for consent, she went about saying that M. le Président Cruchot's marriage was not such a settled thing as *some* people imagined.

"M. de Froidfond may be fifty years old," she said, "but he looks no older than M. Cruchot; he is a widower, and has a family, it is true; but he is a marquis, he will be a peer of France one of these days, it is not such a bad match as times go. I know of my own certain knowledge that when old Grandet added his own property to the Froidfond estate he meant to graft his family into the Froidfonds. He often told me as much. Oh! he was a shrewd old man, this old man Grandet."

"Ah! Nanon," Eugénie said one evening, as she went to bed, "why has he not once written to me in seven years!——"

While these events were taking place in Saumur, Charles was making his fortune in the East. His first venture was very successful. He had promptly realized the sum of six thousand dollars. Crossing the line had cured him of many early prejudices; he soon saw very clearly that the best and quickest way of making money was the same in the tropics as in Europe—by buying and selling men. He made a descent on the African coasts and bargained for negroes and other goods in demand in various markets. He threw himself heart and soul into his business, and thought of nothing else. He set one clear aim before him, to reappear in Paris, and to dazzle the world there with his wealth, to attain a position even higher than the one from which he had fallen.

By dint of rubbing shoulders with many men, traveling in many lands, coming in contact with various customs and religions, his code had been relaxed, and he had grown sceptical. His notions of right and wrong became less rigid when he found that what was looked upon as a crime in one country was held up to admiration in another. He saw that every one was working for himself, that disinterestedness was rarely to be met with, and grew selfish and suspicious ; the hereditary failings of the Grandets came out in him—the hardness, the shiftiness, and the greed of gain. He sold Chinese coolies, negro slaves, swallow-nests, children, artists, and anything and everything that brought in money. He became a moneylender on a large scale. Long practice in cheating the custom authorities had made him unscrupulous in other ways. He would make the voyage to St. Thomas, buy booty of the pirates there for a low price, and sell the merchandise in the dearest market.

During his first voyage Eugénie's pure and noble face had been with him, like the image of the Virgin which Spanish sailors set on the prows of their vessels ; he had attributed his first success to a kind of magical efficacy possessed by her prayers and vows ; but as time went on, the women of other countries, negresses, mulattoes, white skins, and yellow skins, orgies and adventures in many lands, completely effaced all recollection of his cousin, of Saumur, of the old house, of the bench, and of the kiss that he had snatched in the passage. He remembered nothing but the little garden shut in by its crumbling walls where he had learned the fate that lay in store for him ; but he rejected all connection with the family. His uncle was an old fox who had filched his jewels. Eugénie had no place in his heart, he never gave her a thought ; but she occupied a page in his ledger as a creditor for six thousand francs.

Such conduct and such ideas explained Charles Grandet's silence. In the East Indies, at St. Thomas, on the coast of Africa, at Lisbon, in the United States, Charles Grandet the adventurer was known as Carl Sepherd, a pseudonym which he assumed so as not to compromise his real name. Carl Sepherd could be indefatigable, brazen, and greedy of gain ; could conduct himself, in short, like a man who resolves to make a fortune *quibuscumque viis*, and makes haste to have done with villainy as soon as possible, in order to live respected for the rest of his days.

With such methods his career of prosperity was rapid and brilliant, and in 1827 he returned to Bordeaux on board the *Marie Caroline*, a fine brig belonging to a Royalist firm. He had nineteen hundred thousand francs with him in gold dust, carefully secreted in three strong casks; he hoped to sell it to the Paris mint, and to make eight per cent. on the transaction. There was also on board the brig a gentleman-in-ordinary to his majesty Charles X., a M. d'Aubrion, a worthy old man who had been rash enough to marry a woman of fashion whose money came from estates in the West India Islands. Mme. d'Aubrion's reckless extravagance had obliged him to go out to the Indies to sell her property. M. and Mme. d'Aubrion, of the house of d'Aubrion de Buch, which had lost its *captal* or chieftain just before the Revolution, were now in straitened circumstances. They had a bare twenty thousand francs of income and a daughter, a very plain girl, whom her mother made up her mind to marry without a dowry; for life in Paris is expensive, and, as has been seen, their means were reduced. It was an enterprise the success of which might have seemed somewhat problematical to a man of the world, in spite of the cleverness with which a woman of fashion is generally credited. Perhaps even Mme. d'Aubrion herself, when she looked at her daughter, was almost ready to despair of getting rid of her to any one, even to the most besotted worshiper of rank and titles.

Mlle. d'Aubrion was a tall, spare demoiselle, somewhat like her namesake the insect; she had a disdainful mouth, overshadowed by a long nose, thick at the tip, sallow in its normal condition, but very red after a meal, an organic change which was all the more unpleasant by reason of contrast with a pallid, insipid countenance. From some points of view she was all that a worldly mother, who was thirty-eight years of age, and had still some pretensions to beauty, could desire.

But by way of compensating advantages, the Marquise d'Aubrion's distinguished air had been inherited by her daughter, and that young lady had been submitted to a Spartan regimen, which for the time being subdued the offending hue in her feature to a reasonable flesh-tint. Her mother had taught her how to dress herself. Under the same instructor she had acquired a charming manner, and had learned to assume that pensive expression which interests a man and leads him to imagine that here, surely, is the angel for whom he has hitherto sought in vain. She was carefully drilled in a certain manœuvre with her foot—to let it peep forth from beneath her petticoat, and so call attention to its small size—whenever her nose became unseasonably red; indeed, the mother had made the very best of her daughter. By means of large sleeves, stiff skirts, puffs, padding, and high-pressure corsets she had produced a highly curious and interesting result, a specimen of femininity which ought to have been put into a museum for the edification of mothers generally.

Charles became very intimate with Mme. d'Aubrion; the lady had her own reasons for encouraging him. People said that during the time on board she left no stone unturned to secure such a prize for a son-in-law. It is at any rate certain that when they landed at Bordeaux Charles stayed in the same hotel with M., Mme., and Mlle. d'Aubrion, and they all traveled together to Paris. The hôtel d'Aubrion was hampered with mortgages, and Charles was intended to come to the rescue. The mother had gone so far as to say that it would give her great pleasure to establish a son-in-law on the ground floor. She did not share M. d'Aubrion's aristocratic prejudices, and promised Charles Grandet to obtain letters patent from that easy-tempered monarch, Charles X., which should authorize him, Grandet, to bear the name and assume the arms of the d'Aubrions, and (by purchasing the entail) to succeed to the property of Aubrion, which was worth about thirty-six thousand livres a year, to say nothing of the titles of Captal de Buch and Marquis d'Aubrion. They could be very useful to each other, in short; and what with this arrangement of a joint establishment, and one or two posts about the Court, the hôtel d'Aubrion might count upon an income of a hundred thousand francs and more.

"And when a man has a hundred thousand francs a year, a name, a family, and a position at Court—for I shall procure an appointment for you as gentleman-of-the-bedchamber—the rest is easy. You can be anything you choose" (so she instructed Charles), "Master of Requests in the Council of State, Prefect, Secretary to an Embassy, the Ambassador himself if you like. Charles X. is much attached to d'Aubrion; they have known each other from childhood."

She fairly turned his head with these ambitious schemes, and during the voyage Charles began to cherish the hopes and ideas which had been so cleverly insinuated in the form of tender confidences. He never doubted but that his uncle had paid his father's creditors; he had been suddenly launched into the society of the Faubourg St. Germain, at that time the goal of social ambition; and beneath the shadow of Mlle. Mathilde's purple nose, he was shortly to appear as the Comte d'Aubrion, very much as the Dreux shone forth transformed into Brézés. He was dazzled by the apparent prosperity of the restored dynasty, which had seemed to be tottering to its fall when he left France; his head was full of wild ambitious dreams; which began on the voyage, and did not leave him in Paris. He resolved to strain every nerve to reach those pinnacles of glory which his egotistical would-be mother-in-law had pointed out to him. His cousin was only a dim speck in the remote past; she had no place in this brilliant future, no part in his dreams, but he went to see Annette. That experienced woman of the world gave counsel to her old friend; he must by no means let slip such an opportunity for an alliance; she promised to aid him in all his schemes of advancement. In her heart she was delighted to see Charles thus secured to such a plain and uninteresting girl. He had grown very attractive during his stay in the Indies; his complexion had grown darker, he had gained in manliness and self-possession; he spoke in the firm, decided tones of a man who is used to command and to success. Ever since Charles Grandet had discovered that there was a definite part for him to play in Paris, he was himself at once.

Des Grassins, hearing of his return, his approaching marriage, and his large fortune, came to see him, and spoke of the three hundred thousand francs still owing to his father's creditors. He found Charles closeted with a goldsmith, from whom he had ordered jewels for Mlle. d'Aubrion's *corbeille*, and who was submitting designs. Charles himself had brought magnificent diamonds from the Indies; but the cost of setting them, together with the silver plate and jewelry of the new establishment, amounted to more than two hundred thousand francs. He did not recognize des Grassins at first, and treated him with the cool insolence of a young man of fashion who is conscious that he has killed four men in as many duels in the Indies. As M. des Grassins had already called three or four times, Charles vouchsafed to hear him, but it was with bare politeness, and he did not pay the slightest attention to what the banker said.

"My father's debts are not mine," he said coolly. "I am obliged to you, sir, for the trouble you have been good enough to take, but I am none the better for it that I can see. I have not scraped together a couple of millions, earned with the sweat of my brow, to fling it to my father's creditors at this late day."

"But suppose that your father were to be declared bankrupt in a few days' time?"

"In a few days' time I shall be the Comte d'Aubrion, sir; so you can see that it is a matter of entire indifference to me. Besides, you know even better than I do that when a man has a hundred thousand livres a year, his father never has been a bankrupt," and he politely edged the deputy des Grassins to the door.

In the early days of the month of August, in that same year, Eugénie was sitting on the little bench in the garden where her cousin had sworn eternal love, and where she often took breakfast in summer mornings. The poor girl was almost happy for a few brief moments; she went over all the great and little events of her love before those catastrophes that followed. The morning was fresh and bright, and the garden was full of sunlight; her eyes wandered over the wall with its moss and flowers; it was full of cracks now, and all but in ruins, but no one was allowed to touch it, though Cornoiller was always prophesying to his wife that the whole thing would come down and crush somebody or other one of these days. The postman knocked at the door, and gave a letter into the hands of Mme. Cornoiller, who hurried into the garden, crying, "Mademoiselle! A letter! Is it *the* letter?" she added, as she handed it to her mistress.

The words rang through Eugénie's heart as the spoken sounds rang from the ramparts and the old garden wall.

"Paris!——It is his writing! Then he has come back."

Eugénie's face grew white; for several seconds she kept the seal unbroken, for her heart beat so fast that she could neither move nor see. Big Nanon stood and waited with both hands on her hips; joy seemed to puff like smoke from every wrinkle in her brown face.

"Do read it, mademoiselle!"

"Oh! why does he come back by way of Paris, Nanon, when he went by way of Saumur?"

"Read it; the letter will tell you why."

Eugénie's fingers trembled as she opened the envelope; a check on the firm of "Mme. des Grassins et Corret, Saumur," fell out of it and fluttered down. Nanon picked it up.

"My dear Cousin——"

("I am not 'Eugénie' now," she thought, and her heart stood still.) "You——"

"He used to say *thou!*" She folded her arms and dreaded to read any further; great tears gathered in her eyes.

"What is it? Is he dead?" asked Nanon.

"If he were, he could not write," said Eugénie, and she read the letter through. It ran as follows:

"My dear Cousin:—You will, I am sure, hear with pleasure of the success of my enterprise. You brought me luck; I have come back to France a wealthy man, as my uncle advised. I have just heard of his death, together with that of my aunt, from M. des Grassins. Our parents must die in the course of nature, and we ourselves must follow them. I hope that by this time you are consoled for your loss; time cures all trouble, as I know by experience. Yes, my dear cousin, the day of illusions has gone by for me. I am sorry, but it cannot be helped. I have knocked about the world so much, and seen so much, that I have been led to reflect on life. I was a child when I went away; I have come back a man, and I have many things to think about now which I did not even dream of then. You are free, my cousin, and I too am free still; there is apparently nothing to hinder the realization of our youthful hopes, but I am too straightforward to hide my present situation from you. I have not for a moment forgotten that I am bound to you; through all my wanderings I have always remembered the little wooden bench——"

Eugénie started up as if she were sitting on burning coals, and sat down on one of the broken stone steps in the yard.

—"the little wooden bench where we vowed to love each other for ever; the passage, the gray parlor, my attic room, the night when in your thoughtfulness and tact you made my future easier to me. Yes, these memories have been my support; I have said in my heart that you were always thinking of me when I thought of you at the hour we had agreed upon. Did you not look out into the darkness at nine o'clock? Yes, I am sure you did. I would not prove false to so sacred a friendship; I cannot deal insincerely with you.

"A marriage has been proposed to me, which is in every way satisfactory to my mind. Love in a marriage is romantic nonsense. Experience has clearly shown me that in marrying we must obey social laws and conform to conventional ideas. There is some difference of age between you and me, which would perhaps be more likely to affect your future than mine, and there are other differences of which I need not speak; your bringing up, your ways of life, and your tastes have not fitted you for Parisian life, nor would they harmonize with the future which I have marked out for myself. For instance, it is a part of my plan to maintain a great household, and to see a good deal of society; and you, I am sure, from my recollections of you, would prefer a quiet, domestic life and home-keeping ways. No, I will be open with you; I will abide by your decision; but I must first, however, lay all the facts of the case before you, that you may the better judge.

"I possess at the time of writing an income of eighty thousand livres. With this fortune I am able to marry into the d'Aubrion family; I should take their name on my marriage with their only daughter, a girl of nineteen, and secure at the same time a very brilliant position in society, and the post of gentleman-of-the-bedchamber. I will assure you at once, my dear cousin, that I have not the slightest affection for Mlle. d'Aubrion, but by this marriage I shall secure for my children a social rank which will be of inestimable value in the future. Monarchical principles are daily gaining ground. A few years hence my son, the Marquis d'Aubrion, would have an entailed estate and a yearly rental of forty thousand livres; with such advantages there would be no position to which he might not aspire. We ought to live for our children.

"You see, my cousin, how candidly I am laying the state of my heart, my hopes, and my fortunes before you. Perhaps after seven years of separation you may yourself have forgotten our childish love affair, but I have never forgotten your goodness or my promise. A less conscientious, a less upright man, with a heart less youthful than mine, might scarcely feel himself bound by it; but for me a promise, however lightly given, is sacred. When I tell you plainly that my marriage is solely a marriage of suitability, and that I have not forgotten the love of our youthful days, am I not putting myself entirely into your hands, and making you the arbitress of my fate?' Is it not implied that if I must renounce my social ambitions, I shall willingly content myself with the simple and pure happiness which is always called up by the thought of you——'"

"Tra-la-la-tan-ta-ti!" sang Charles Grandet to the air of *Non più andrai*, as he signed himself,

"Your devoted cousin,

"CHARLES."

"By Jove! that is acting handsomely," he said to himself. He looked about him for the cheque, slipped it in, and added a postscript.

"*P.S.*—I enclose a cheque on Mme. des Grassins for eight thousand francs, payable in gold to your order, comprising the capital and interest of the sum you were so kind to advance me. I am expecting a case from Bordeaux which contains a few things which you must allow me to send you as a token of my unceasing gratitude. You can send my dressing-case by the diligence to the Hôtel d'Aubrion, Rue Hillerin-Bertin."

"By the diligence!" cried Eugénie, "when I would have given my life for it a thousand times!"

Terrible and complete shipwreck of hope; the vessel had gone down, there was not a spar, not a plank in the vast ocean. There are women who when their lover forsakes them will drag him from a rival's arms and murder her, and fly for refuge to the ends of the earth, to the scaffold, or the grave. There is a certain grandeur in this no doubt; there is something so sublime in the passion of indignation which prompts the crime, that man's justice is awed into silence; but there are other women who suffer and bow their heads. They go on their way, submissive and broken-hearted, weeping and forgiving, praying till their last sigh for him whom they never forget. And this no less is love, love such as the angels know, love that bears itself proudly in anguish, that lives by the secret pain of which it dies at last. This was to be Eugénie's love now that she had read that horrible letter.

She raised her eyes to the sky and thought of her mother's prophetic words, uttered in the moment of clear vision that is sometimes given to dying eyes; and as she thought of her mother's life and death, it seemed to her that she was looking out over her own future. There was nothing left to her now but to live prayerfully till the day of her deliverance should come and the soul spread its wings for heaven.

"My mother was right," she said, weeping. "Suffer—and die."

She went slowly from the garden into the house, avoiding the passage; but when she came into the old gray parlor, it was full of memories of her cousin. On the chimney-piece there stood a certain china saucer, which she used every morning, and the old Sèvres sugar basin.

It was to be a memorable and eventful day for Eugénie. Nanon announced the curé of the parish church. He was related to the Cruchots, and therefore in the interests of the President de Bonfons. For some days past the Abbé had urged the curé to speak seriously to Mlle. Grandet about the duty of marriage from a religious point of view for a woman in her position. Eugénie, seeing her pastor, fancied that he had come for the thousand francs which she gave him every month for the poor of his parish, and sent Nanon for the money; but the curate began with a smile, "To-day, mademoiselle, I have come to take counsel with you about a poor girl in whom all Saumur takes an interest, and who, through lack of charity to herself, is not living as a Christian should."

"*Mon Dieu!* M. le Curé, just now I can think of nobody but myself. I am very miserable, my only refuge is in the Church; her heart is large enough to hold all human sorrows, her love so inexhaustible that we need never fear to drain it dry."

"Well, mademoiselle, when we speak of this girl, we shall speak of you. Listen! If you would fain work out your salvation, there are but two ways open to you: you must either leave the world or live in the world and submit to its laws —you must choose between the earthly and the heavenly vocation."

"Ah! your voice speaks to me when I need to hear a voice. Yes, God has sent you to me. I will bid the world farewell, and live for God alone, in silence and seclusion."

"But, my daughter, you should think long and prayerfully before taking so strong a measure. Marriage is life; the veil and the convent is death."

"Yes, death. Ah! if death would only come quickly, M. le Curé," she said, with dreadful eagerness.

"Death? But you have great obligations to fulfill towards society, mademoiselle. There is your family of poor, to whom you give clothes and firing in winter and work in summer. Your great fortune is a loan, of which you must give account one day. You have always looked on it as a sacred trust. It would be selfish to bury yourself in a convent, and you ought not to live alone in the world. In the first place, how can you endure the burden of your vast fortune alone? You might lose it. You will be involved in endless litigation; you will find yourself in difficulties from which you will not be able to extricate yourself. Take your pastor's word, a husband is useful; you ought not to lose what God has given into your charge. I speak to you as to a cherished lamb of my flock. You love God too sincerely to find hindrances to your salvation in the world; you are one of its fairest ornaments, and should remain in it as an example of holiness."

At this point Mme. des Grassins was announced. The banker's wife was smarting under a grievous disappointment, and thirsted for revenge.

"Mademoiselle——" she began. "Oh! M. le Curé is here——I will say no more then. I came to speak about some matters of business, but I see you are deep in something else."

"Madame," said the curé, "I leave the field to you."

"Oh! M. le Curé, pray come back again; I stand in great need of your help just now."

"Yes, indeed, my poor child!" said Mme. des Grassins.

"What do you mean?" asked Eugénie and the curé both together.

"Do you suppose that I haven't heard that your cousin has come back, and is going to marry Mlle. d'Aubrion? A woman doesn't go about with her wits in her pocket."

Eugénie was silent, there was a red flush on her face, but she made up her mind at once that henceforward no one should learn anything from her, and looked as impenetrable as her father used to do.

"Well, madame," she said, with a tinge of bitterness in her tones, "it seems that I, at any rate, carry my wits in my pocket, for I am quite at a loss to understand you. Speak out and explain yourself; you can speak freely before M. le Curé, he is my director, as you know."

"Well, then, mademoiselle, see for yourself what des Grassins says. Here is the letter."

Eugénie read:

"MY DEAR WIFE:—Charles Grandet has returned from the Indies, and has been in Paris these two months——"

"Two months!" said Eugénie to herself, and her hand fell to her side. After a moment she went on reading:

"I had to dance attendance on him, and called twice before the future Comte d'Aubrion would condescend to see me. All Paris is talking about his marriage, and the banns are published——"

"And he wrote to me after that?" Eugénie said to herself. She did not round off the sentence as a Parisienne would have done, with "Wretch that he is!" but her scorn was not one whit the less because it was unexpressed.

—"but it will be a good while yet before he marries; it is not likely that the Marquis d'Aubrion will give his daughter to the son of a bankrupt wine merchant. I called and told him of all the trouble we had been at, his uncle and I, in the matter of his father's failure, and of our clever dodges that had kept the creditors quiet so far. The insolent puppy had the effrontery to say to me—to *me*, who for five years have toiled day and night in his interest and to save his credit—that *his father's affairs were not his!* A solicitor would have wanted thirty or forty thousand francs of him in fees at the rate of one per cent. on the total of the debt! But, patience! There is something that he does owe, however, and that the law shall make him pay, that is to say, twelve hundred thousand francs to his father's creditors, and I shall declare his father bankrupt. I mixed myself up in this affair on the word of that old crocodile of a Grandet, and I have given promises in the name of the family. M. le Comte d'Aubrion may not care for his honor, but I care a good deal for mine! So I shall just explain my position to the creditors. Still, I have too much respect for Mlle. Eugénie (with whom, in happier days, we hoped to be more closely connected) to take any steps before you have spoken to her——"

There Eugénie paused, and quietly returned the letter.

"I am obliged to you," she said to Mme. des Grassins. "*We shall see*——"

"Your voice was exactly like your father's just then," exclaimed Mme. des Grassins.

"Madame," put in Nanon, producing Charles' cheque, "you have eight thousand francs to pay us."

"True. Be so good as to come with me, Mme. Cornoiller."

"M. le Curé," said Eugénie, with a noble composure that came of the thought which prompted her, "would it be a sin to remain in a state of virginity after marriage?"

"It is a case of conscience which I cannot solve. If you care to know what the celebrated Sanchez says in his great work, *De Matrimonio*, I could inform you to-morrow."

The curé took leave. Mlle. Grandet went up to her father's room and spent the day there by herself; she would not even come down to dinner, though Nanon begged and scolded. She appeared in the evening at the hour when the usual company began to arrive. The gray parlor in the Grandet's house had never been so well filled as it was that night. Every soul in the town knew by that time of Charles' return, and of his faithlessness and ingratitude; but their inquisitive curiosity was not to be gratified. Eugénie was a little late, but no one saw any traces of the cruel agitation through which she had passed; she could smile benignly in reply to the compassionate looks and words which some of the group thought fit to bestow on her; she bore her pain behind a mask of politeness.

About nine o'clock the card-players drew away from the

tables, paid their losses, and criticised the game and the various points that had been made. Just as there was a general move in the direction of the door, an unexpected development took place; the news of it rang through Saumur and four prefectures round about for days after.

"Please stay, M. le Président."

There was not a person in the room who did not thrill with excitement at the words; M. de Bonfons, who was about to take his cane, turned quite white, and sat down again.

"The President takes the millions," said Mlle. de Gribeaucourt.

"It is quite clear that President de Bonfons is going to marry Mlle. Grandet," cried Mme. d'Orsonval.

"The best trick of the game!" commented the Abbé.

"A very pretty *slam*," said the notary.

Every one said his say and cut his joke, every one thought of the heiress mounted upon her millions as if she were on a pedestal. Here was the catastrophe of the drama, begun nine years ago, taking place under their eyes. To tell the President in the face of all Saumur to "stay" was as good as announcing at once that she meant to take the magistrate for her husband. Social conventionalities are rigidly observed in little country towns, and such an infraction as this was looked upon as a binding promise.

"M. le Président," Eugénie began in an unsteady voice, as soon as they were alone, "I know what you care about in me. Swear to leave me free till the end of my life, to claim none of the rights which marriage will give you over me, and my hand is yours. Oh!" she said, seeing him about to fall on his knees, "I have not finished yet. I must tell you frankly that there are memories in my heart which can never be effaced; that friendship is all that I can give my husband; I wish neither to affront him nor to be disloyal to my own heart. But you shall only have my hand and fortune at the price of an immense service which I want you to do me."

"Anything, I will do anything," said the president.

"Here are fifteen hundred thousand francs, M. le Président," she said, drawing from her bodice a certificate for a hundred shares in the Bank of France; "will you set out for Paris? You must not even wait till the morning, but go at once, to-night. You must go straight to M. des Grassins, ask him for a list of my uncle's creditors, call them together, and discharge all outstanding claims upon Guillaume Grandet's estate. Let the creditors have capital and interest at five per cent. from the day the debts were contracted to the present time; and see that in every case a receipt in full is given, and that it is made out in proper form. You are a magistrate, you are the only person whom I feel that I can trust in such a case. You are a gentleman and a man of honor; you have given me your word, and, protected by your name, I will make the perilous voyage of life. We shall know how to make allowances for each other, for we have been acquainted for so long that it is almost as if we were related, and I am sure you would not wish to make me unhappy."

The president fell on his knees at the feet of the rich heiress in a paroxysm of joy.

"I will be your slave!" he said.

"When all the receipts are in your possession, sir," she went on, looking quietly at him, "you must take them, together with the bills, to my cousin Grandet, and give them to him with this letter. When you come back, I will keep my word."

The president understood the state of affairs perfectly well. "She is accepting me out of pique," he thought, and he hastened to do Mlle. Grandet's bidding with all possible speed, for fear some chance might bring about a reconciliation between the lovers.

As soon as M. de Bonfons left her, Eugénie sank into her chair and burst into tears. All was over, and *this* was the end.

The president traveled post-haste to Paris and reached his journey's end on the following evening. The next morning he went to des Grassins, and arranged for a meeting of the creditors in the office of the notary with whom the bills had been deposited. Every man of them appeared, every man of them was punctual to a moment—one should give even creditors their dues.

M. de Bonfons, in Mlle. Grandet's name, paid down the money in full, both capital and interest. They were paid interest! It was an amazing portent, a nine days' wonder in the business world of Paris. After the whole affair had been wound up, and when, by Eugénie's desire, des Grassins had received fifty thousand francs for his services, the president betook himself to the Hôtel d'Aubrion, and was lucky enough to find Charles at home, and in disgrace with his future father-in-law. The old Marquis had just informed that gentleman that until Guillaume Grandet's creditors were satisfied, a marriage with his daughter was not to be thought of.

To Charles, thus despondent, the president delivered the following letter:

"DEAR COUSIN:—M. le Président de Bonfons has undertaken to hand you a discharge of all claims against my uncle's estate, and to deliver it in person, together with this letter, so that I may know that it is safely in your hands. I heard rumors of bankruptcy, and it occurred to me that difficulties might possibly arise as a consequence in the matter of your marriage with Mlle. d'Aubrion. Yes, cousin, you are quite right about my tastes and manners; I have lived, as you say, so entirely out of the world that I know nothing of its ways or its calculations, and my companionship could never make up to you for the loss of the pleasures that you look to find in society. I hope that you will be happy according to the social conventions to which you have sacrificed our early love. The only thing in my power to give you to complete your happiness is your father's good name. Farewell; you will always find a faithful friend in your cousin,   Eugénie."

In spite of himself an exclamation broke from the man of social ambitions when his eyes fell on the discharge and receipts. The president smiled.

"We can each announce our marriage," said he.

"Oh! you are to marry Eugénie, are you? Well, I am glad to hear it; she is a kind-hearted girl. Why!" struck with a sudden luminous idea, "she must be rich?"

"Four days ago she had about nineteen millions," the president said, with a malicious twinkle in his eyes; "to-day she has only seventeen."

Charles was dumfounded; he stared at the president.

"Seventeen mil——"

"Seventeen millions. Yes, sir; when we are married, Mlle. Grandet and I shall muster seven hundred and fifty thousand livres a year between us."

"My dear cousin," said Charles, with some return of assurance, "we shall be able to push each other's fortunes."

"Certainly," said the president. "There is something else here," he added, "a little case that I was to give only in your hands," and he set down a box containing the dressing-case upon the table.

The door opened, and in came Mme. la Marquise d'Aubrion; the great lady seemed to be unaware of Cruchot's existence. "Look here! dear," she said, "never mind what that absurd M. d'Aubrion has been saying to you; the Duchesse de Chaulieu has quite turned his head. I repeat it, there is nothing to prevent your marriage——"

"Nothing, madame," answered Charles. "The three millions which my father owed were paid yesterday."

"In money?" she asked.

"In full, capital and interest; I mean to rehabilitate his memory."

"What nonsense!" cried Mme. la Marquise d'Aubrion. "Who is this person?" she asked in Charles' ear, as she saw Cruchot for the first time.

"My man of business," he answered in a low voice. The Marquise gave M. de Bonfons a disdainful bow, and left the room.

"We are beginning to push each other's fortunes already," said the president dryly, as he took up his hat. "Good-day, cousin."

"The old cockatoo from Saumur is laughing at me; I have a great mind to make him swallow six inches of cold steel," thought Charles.

But the president had departed.

Three days later M. de Bonfons was back in Saumur again, and announced his marriage with Eugénie. After about six months he received his appointment as Councilor to the Court-Royal at Angers, and they went thither. But before Eugénie left Saumur she melted down the trinkets that had long been so sacred and so dear a trust, and gave them, together with the eight thousand francs which her cousin had returned to her, to make a recredos for the altar in the parish church whither she had gone so often to pray to God for him. Henceforward her life was spent partly at Angers, partly at Saumur. Her husband's devotion to the government at a political crisis was rewarded; he was made President of the Chamber, and finally First President. Then he awaited a general election with impatience; he had visions of a place in the government; he had dreams of a peerage; and then, and then——

"Then he would call cousins with the king, I suppose?" said Nanon, big Nanon, Mme. Cornoiller, wife of a burgess of Saumur, when her mistress told her of these lofty ambitions and high destinies.

Yet, after all, none of these ambitious dreams were to be realized, and the name of M. de Bonfons (he had finally dropped the patronymic Cruchot) was to undergo no further transformation. He died only eight days after his appointment as deputy of Saumur. God, who sees all hearts, and who never strikes without cause, punished him, doubtless, for his presumptuous schemes, and for the lawyer's cunning with which, *accurante Cruchot*, he drafted his own marriage contract; in which husband and wife, *in case there was no issue of the marriage, bequeathed to each other all their property, both real estate and personalty, without exception or reservation, dispensing even with the formality of an inventory, provided that the omission of the said inventory should not injure their heirs and assigns, it being understood that this deed of gift, etc., etc.*, a clause which may throw some light on the profound respect with which the president constantly showed for his wife's desire to live apart. Women cited M. le Premier Président as one of the most delicately considerate of men, and pitied him, and often went so far as to blame Eugénie for clinging to her passion and her sorrow; mingling, according to their wont, cruel insinuations with their criticisms of the president's wife.

"If Mme. de Bonfons lives apart from her husband, she must be in very bad health, poor thing. Is she likely to recover? What can be the matter with her? Is it cancer or gastritis, or what is it? Why does she not go to Paris and see some specialist? She has looked very sallow for a long time past. How can she not wish to have a child? They say she is very fond of her husband; why not give him an heir in his position? Do you know, it is really dreadful! If it is only some notion which she has taken into her head, it is unpardonable. Poor president!"

There is a certain keen insight and quick apprehensiveness that is the gift of a lonely and meditative life—and loneliness, and sorrow, and the discipline of the last few years had given Eugénie this clairvoyance of the narrow lot. She knew within herself that the president was anxious for her death that he might be the sole possessor of the colossal fortune, now still further increased by the deaths of the Abbé and the notary, whom Providence had lately seen fit to promote from works to rewards. The poor solitary woman understood and pitied the president. Unworthy hopes and selfish calculations were his strongest motives for respecting Eugénie's hopeless passion. To give life to a child would be death to the egoistical dreams and ambitions that the president hugged within himself; was it for all these things that his career was cut short? while she must remain in her prison house, and the coveted gold for which she cared so little was to be heaped upon her. It was she who was to live, with the thought of heaven always before her, and holy thoughts for her companions, to give help and comfort secretly to those who were in distress. Mme. de Bonfons was left a widow three years after her marriage, with an income of eight hundred thousand livres.

She is beautiful still, with the beauty of a woman who is nearly forty years of age. Her face is very pale and quiet now, and there is a tinge of sadness in the low tones of her voice. She has simple manners, all the dignity of one who has passed through great sorrows, and the saintliness of a soul unspotted by the world; and, no less, the rigidness of an old maid, the little penurious ways and narrow ideas of a dull country town.

Although she has eight hundred thousand livres a year, she lives just as she used to do in the days of stinted allowances of fuel and food while she was still Eugénie Grandet; the fire is never lighted in the parlor before or after the dates fixed by her father, all the regulations in force in the days of her girlhood are still adhered to. She dresses as her mother did. That cold, sunless, dreary house, always overshadowed by the dark ramparts, is like her own life.

She looks carefully after her affairs; her wealth accumulates from year to year; perhaps she might even be called parsimonious, if it were not for the noble use she makes of her fortune. Various pious and charitable institutions, almshouses, and orphan asylums, a richly endowed public library, and donations to various churches in Saumur, are a sufficient answer to the charge of avarice which some few people have brought against her.

They sometimes speak of her in joke as *mademoiselle*, but, in fact, people stand somewhat in awe of Mme. de Bonfons. It was as if she, whose heart went out so readily to others, was always to be the victim of their interested calculations, and to be cut off from them by a barrier of distrust; as if for all warmth and brightness in her life she was to find only the pale glitter of metal.

"No one loves me but you," she would sometimes say to Nanon.

Yet her hands are always ready to bind the wounds that other eyes do not see, in any house; and her way to heaven is one long succession of kindness and good deeds. The real greatness of her soul has risen above the cramping influences of her early life. And this is the life-history of a woman who dwells in the world, yet is not of it; a woman so grandly fitted to be a wife and mother, but who has neither husband nor children nor kindred.

Of late the good folk of Saumur have begun to talk of a second marriage for her. Rumor is busy with her name and that of the Marquis de Froidfond; indeed, his family have begun to surround the rich widow, just as the Cruchots once flocked about Eugénie Grandet. Nanon and Cornoiller, so it is said, are in the interest of the Marquis, but nothing could be more false; for big Nanon and Cornoiller have neither of them wit enough to understand the corruptions of the world.

THE MARANAS.

(*Les Marana.*)

To Madame la Comtesse Merlin.

IN spite of the discipline enforced by Marshal Suchet in the division he commanded in the Peninsular War, all his efforts could not restrain an outbreak of license and tumult at the taking of Taragona. Indeed, according to trustworthy military authorities, the intoxication of victory resulted in something very like a sack of the town. Pillage was promptly put down by the marshal; and as soon as order was restored, a commandant appointed, the military administrators appeared upon the scene, and the town began to wear a nondescript aspect—the organization was French, but the Spanish population was left free to follow *in petto* its own national customs. It would be a task of no little difficulty to determine the exact duration of the pillage, but its cause (like that of most sublunary events) is sufficiently easy to discover.

In the marshal's division of the army there was a regiment composed almost entirely of Italians, commanded by a certain Colonel Eugène, a man of extraordinary valor, a second Murat, who, having come to the trade of war too late, had gained no Grand Duchy of Berg, no Kingdom of Naples, nor a ball through the heart at Pizzo. But if he had received no crown, his chances of receiving bullets were admirably good; and it would have been in no wise astonishing if he had had more than one of them. This regiment was made up from the wrecks of the Italian Legion, which is in Italy very much what the colonial battalions are in France. Stationed on the isle of Elba, it had provided an honorable way out of the difficulty experienced by families with regard to the future of unmanageable sons, as well as a career for those great men spoiled in the making, whom society is too ready to brand as *mauvais sujets*. All of them were men misunderstood, for the most part—men who may become heroes if a woman's smile raises them out of the beaten track of glory; or terrible after an orgy, when some ugly suggestion, dropped by a boon companion, has gained possession of their minds.

Napoleon had enrolled these men of energy in the Sixth Regiment of the line, hoping to metamorphose them into generals, with due allowance for the gaps to be made in their ranks by bullets; but the Emperor's estimate of the ravages of death proved more correct than the rest of his calculations. It was often decimated, but its character remained the same; and the Sixth acquired a name for splendid bravery in the field, and the very worst reputation in private life.

These Italians had lost their captain during the siege of Taragona. He was the famous Bianchi who had laid a wager during the campaign that he would eat a Spanish sentinel's heart—and won his bet. The story of this pleasantry of the camp is told elsewhere in the "Scènes de la Vie Parisienne;" therein will be found certain details which corroborate what has been said here concerning the legion. Bianchi, the prince of those fiends incarnate who had earned the double reputation of the regiment, possessed the chivalrous sense of honor which in the army covers a multitude of the wildest excesses. In a word, had he lived a few centuries earlier, he would have made a gallant buccaneer. Only a few days before he fell, he had distinguished himself by such conspicuous courage in action, that the marshal sought to recognize it. Bianchi had refused promotion, pension, or a fresh decoration, and asked as a favor to be allowed to mount the first scaling-ladder at the assault of Taragona as his sole reward. The marshal granted the request, and forgot his promise; but Bianchi himself put him in mind of it and of Bianchi, for the berserker captain was the first to plant the flag of France upon the wall; and there he fell, killed by a monk.

This historical digression is necessary to explain how it came to pass that the Sixth Regiment of the line was the first to enter Taragona, and how the tumult, sufficiently natural after a town has been carried by storm, degenerated so quickly into an attempt to sack it. Moreover, among these men of iron, there were two officers, otherwise but little remarkable, who were destined by force of circumstances to play an important part in this story.

The first of these, a captain on the clothing establishment— half-civilian, half-officer—was generally said, in soldierly language, to "take good care of number one."

Outside of his regiment he was wont to swagger and brag of his connection with it; he would curl his mustache and look a terrible fellow, but his mess had no great opinion of him. His money was the secret of his valorous discretion. For a double reason, moreover, he had been nicknamed "Captain of the Ravens;" because, in the first place, he scented the powder a league away; and, in the second, scurried out of range like a bird on the wing; the nickname was likewise a harmless soldier's joke, a personality of which another might have been proud. Captain Montefiore, of the illustrious family of the Montefiori of Milan (though by the law of the kingdom of Italy he might not bear his title), was one of the prettiest fellows in the army. Possibly his beauty may secretly have been additional cause of his prudence on the field of battle. A wound in the face by spoiling his profile, scarring his forehead, or seaming his cheeks, would have spoiled one of the finest heads in Italy, and destroyed the delicate proportions of a countenance such as no woman ever pictured in dreams. In Girodet's picture of the "Revolt of Cairo" there is a young dying Turk who has the same type of face, the same melancholy expression, of which women are nearly always the dupes. The Marchese di Montefiore had property of his own, but it was entailed, and he had anticipated his income for several years in order to pay for escapades peculiarly Italian and inconceivable in Paris. He had ruined himself by running a theatre in Milan for the special purpose of foisting upon the public a cantatrice who could not sing, but who loved him (so he said) to distraction.

So Montefiore the captain had good prospects, and was in no hurry to risk them for a paltry scrap of red ribbon. If he was no hero, he was at any rate a philosopher; besides, precedents (if it is allowable to make use of parliamentary expressions in this connection), precedents are forthcoming. Did not Philip II. swear during the battle of Saint-Quentin that he would never go under fire again, nor near it, save the faggots of the Inquisition? Did not the Duke of Alva approve the notion that thé involuntary exchange of a crown for a cannon-ball was the worst kind of trade in the world? Montefiore, therefore, as a marquis, was of Philip II.'s way of thinking; he was a Philippist in his quality of gay young bachelor, and in other respects quite as astute a politician as Philip II. himself. He comforted himself for his nickname, and for the slight esteem in which he was held by his regiment, with the thought that his comrades were sorry scamps; and even if they should survive this war of extermination, their opinion of him was not likely to gain much credence hereafter. Was not his face as good as a certificate of merit? He saw himself a colonel through some accident of feminine favor; or, by a skillfully effected transition, the captain on the clothing establishment would become an orderly, and the orderly would in turn become the aide-de-camp of some good-natured marshal. The bravery of the uniform and the bravery of the man were all as one to the captain on the clothing establishment. So some broad sheet would one day or other call him "the brave Colonel Montefiore," and so forth. *Then* he would have a hundred thousand scudi a year, he would marry the daughter of a noble house, and no one would dare to breathe a word against his courage nor to seek to verify his wounds. Finally, it should be stated that Captain Montefiore had a friend in the person of the quartermaster, a Provençal, born in the Nice district, Diard by name.

A friend, be it in the convict's prison or in an artist's garret, is a compensation for many troubles; and Montefiore and Diard, being a pair of philosphers, found compensations for their hard life in companionship in vice, much as two artists will lull the consciousness of their hardships to sleep by hopes of future fame. Both looked at war as a means to an end, and not as an end in itself, and frankly called those who fell, fools for their pains. Chance had made soldiers of both, when they should have been by rights deliberating in a congress round a table covered with a green cloth. Nature had cast Montefiore in the mould of Rizzio, and Diard in the crucible whence she turns out diplomatists. Both possessed the excitable, nervous, half-feminine temperament, which is always energetic, be it in good or evil; always at the mercy of the caprices of the moment, and swayed by an impulse equally unaccountable to commit a crime or to do a generous deed, to act as a hero or as a craven coward. The fate of such natures as these depends at every moment of their lives upon the intensity of the impressions produced upon the nervous system by vehement and short-lived passions.

Diard was a very fair accountant, but not one of the men would have trusted him with his purse, or made him his executor, possibly by reason of the suspicion that the soldier feels of officialdom. The quartermaster's character was not wanting in dash, nor in a certain boyish enthusiasm, which is apt to wear off as a man grows older and reasons and makes forecasts. And for the rest, his humor was variable as the beauty of a blonde can sometimes be. He was a great talker on every subject. He called himself an artist; and, in imitation of two celebrated generals, collected works of art, simply, he asserted, to secure them for posterity. His comrades would have been hard put to it to say what they really thought of him. Many of them, who were wont to borrow of him at need, fancied that he was rich; but he was a gambler, and a gambler's property cannot be called his own. He played heavily, so did Montefiore, and all the officers played with them; for to man's shame, be it said, plenty of men will meet on terms of equality round a gaming table with others whom they do not respect and will not recognize if they meet them elsewhere. It was Montefiore who had made that bet with Bianchi about the Spaniard's heart.

Montefiore and Diard were among the last to advance to the assault of the place, but they were the first to go forward into the town itself when it was taken. Such things happen in a *mêlée*, and the two friends were old hands. Mutually supported, therefore, they plunged boldly into a labyrinth of narrow dark little streets, each bent upon his own private affairs; the one in search of Madonnas on canvas, and the other of living originals.

In some quarter of Taragona, Diard espied a piece of ecclesiastical architecture, saw that it was the porch of a convent, and that the doors had been forced, and rushed in to restrain the fury of the soldiery. He was not a moment too soon. Two Parisians were about to riddle one of Albani's Virgins with shot, and of these light infantrymen he bought the picture, undismayed by the mustaches with which the zealous iconoclasts had adorned it.

Montefiore, left outside, contemplated the front of a cloth merchant's house opposite the convent. He was looking it up and down, when a corner of a blind was raised, a girl's head peered forth, a glance like a lightning flash answered his, and—a shot was fired at him from the building. Taragona carried by assault, Taragona roused to fury, firing from every window, Taragona outraged, disheveled, and half-naked, with French soldiers pouring through her blazing streets, slaying there and being slain, was surely worth a glance from fearless

Spanish eyes. What was it but a bull-fight on a grander scale? Montefiore forgot the pillaging soldiers, and for a moment heard neither the shrieks, nor the rattle of musketry, nor the dull thunder of the cannon. He, the Italian libertine, tired of Italian beauties, weary of all women, dreaming of an impossible woman because the possible had ceased to have any attraction for him, had never beheld so exquisitely lovely a profile as that of this Spanish girl. The jaded voluptuary, who had squandered his fortune on follies innumerable and on the gratification of a young man's endless desires; the most abominable monstrosity that our society can produce, could still tremble. The bright idea of setting fire to the house instantly flashed through his mind, suggested, doubtless, by the shot from the patriotic cloth merchant's window; but he was alone, and the means of doing it were to seek, fighting was going forward in the market-place, where a few desperate men still defended themselves.

He thought better of it. Diard came out of the convent, Montefiore kept his discovery to himself, and the pair made several excursions through the town together; but on the morrow the Italian was quartered in the cloth merchant's house, a very appropriate arrangement for a captain on the clothing establishment. It promised him the fulfillment of his desire to again see the Spanish girl.

The first floor of the worthy Spaniard's abode consisted of a vast dimly-lighted shop; protected in front, as the old houses in the Rue des Lombards in Paris used to be, by heavy iron bars. Behind the shop lay the parlor, lighted by windows that looked out into an inner yard. It was a large room, redolent of the spirit of the middle ages, with its old dark pictures, old tapestry, and antique *brazero*. A broad-plumed hat hung from a nail upon the wall above a matchlock used in guerilla warfare, and a heavy brigand's cloak.' The kitchen lay immediately beyond this parlor, or living-room, where meals were served and cigars smoked; and Spaniards, talking round the smouldering brasier, would nurse hot wrath and hatred of the French in their hearts.

Silver jugs and valuable plate stood on the antique buffet, but the room was fitfully and scantily illuminated, so that the daylight scarcely did more than bring out faint sparkles from the brightest objects in the room ; all the rest of it, and even the faces of its occupants, were as dark as a Dutch interior. Between the shop itself and this apartment, with its rich subdued tones and old-world aspect, a sufficiently ill-lit staircase led to a warehouse, where it was possible to examine the stuffs by the light from some ingeniously contrived windows. The merchant and his wife occupied the floor above this warehouse, and the apprentice and the maidservant were lodged still higher in the attics immediately beneath the roof. This highest story overhung the street, and was supported by brackets, which gave a quaint look to the house front. On the coming of the officer, the merchant and his wife resigned their rooms to him and went up to these attics, doubtless to avoid friction.

Montefiore gave himself out to be a Spanish subject by birth, a victim to the tyranny of Napoleon, whom he was forced to serve against his will. These half-lies produced the intended effect. He was asked to join the family at meals, as befitted his birth and rank and the name he bore. He had his private reasons for wishing to conciliate the merchant's family. He felt the presence of his madonna, much as the ogre in the fairy tale smelt the tender flesh of little Thumbkin and his brothers; but though he succeeded in winning his host's confidence, the latter kept the secret of the madonna so well that the captain not only saw no sign of the girl's existence during the first day spent beneath the honest Spaniard's roof, but heard no sound that could betray her presence in any part of the dwelling. The old house was, however, almost entirely built of wood ; every noise above or below could be heard through the walls and ceilings, and Montefiore hoped during the silence of the early hours of night to guess the young girl's whereabouts. She was the only daughter of his host and hostess, he thought; probably they had shut her up in the attics, whither they themselves had retired during the military occupation of the town. No indications, however, betrayed the hiding-place of the treasure. The officer might stand with his face glued to the small leaded diamond-shaped panes of the window, looking out into the darkness of the yard below and the grim walls that rose up around it, but no light gleaned from any window save from those of the room overhead, where he could hear the old merchant and his wife talking, coughing, coming, and going. There was not so much even as a shadow of the girl to be seen.

Montefiore was too cunning to risk the future of his passion by prowling about the house of a night, by knocking softly at all the doors, or by other hazardous expedients. His host was a hot patriot, a Spanish father, and an owner of bales of cloth; bound, therefore, in each character to be suspicious. Discovery would be utter ruin, so Montefiore resolved to bide his time patiently, hoping everything from the carelessness of human nature; for if rogues, with the best of reasons for being cautious, will forget themselves in the long run, so still more will honest men.

Next day he discovered a kind of hammock slung in the kitchen—evidently the servant slept there. The apprentice, it seemed, spent the night on the counter in the shop.

At supper-time, on the second day, Montefiore cursed Napoleon till he saw his host's sombre face relax somewhat. The man was a typical, swarthy Spaniard, with a head such as used to be carved on the head of a rebeck. A smile of gleeful hatred lurked among the wrinkles about his wife's mouth. The lamplight and fitful gleams from the brasier filled the stately room with capricious answering reflections. The hostess was just offering a cigarette to their semi-com-patriot, when Montefiore heard the rustle of a dress, and a chair was overturned behind the tapestry hangings.

"There!" cried the merchant's wife, turning pale, "may all the saints send that no misfortune has befallen us!"

"So you have some one in there, have you?" asked the Italian, who betrayed no sign of emotion.

The merchant let fall some injurious remarks as to girls. His wife, in alarm, opened a secret door, and brought in the Italian's madonna, half-dead with fear. The delighted lover scarcely seemed to notice the girl; but, lest he might overdo the affectation of indifference, he glanced at her, and turning to his host, asked in his mother tongue:

"Is she your daughter, señor?"

Perez de Lagounia (for that was the merchant's name) had had extensive business connections in Genoa, Florence, and Leghorn; he knew Italian, and replied in that language.

"No. If she had been my own daughter, I should have taken fewer precautions, but the child was put into our charge, and I would die sooner than allow the slightest harm to befall her. But what sense can you expect of a girl of eighteen?"

"She is very beautiful," Montefiore said carelessly. He did not look at her again.

"The mother is sufficiently famous for her beauty," answered the merchant. And they continued to smoke and to watch each other.

Montefiore had imposed upon himself the hard task of avoiding the least look that might compromise his attitude of indifference; but as Perez turned his head aside to spit, the Italian stole a glance at the girl, and again those sparkling eyes met his. In that one glance, with the experienced vision that gives to a voluptuary or a sculptor the power of discerning the outlines of the form beneath the draperies, he beheld a masterpiece created to know all the happiness of love. He saw a delicately fair face, which the sun of Spain had slightly tinged with a warm brown, that added to a

seraphically calm expression a flush of pride, a suffused glow
beneath the translucent fairness, due, perhaps, to the pure
Moorish blood that brought animation and color into it.
Her hair, knotted on the crown of her head, fell in thick
curls about transparent ears like a child's, surrounding them
with dark shadows that made a framework for the white
throat with its faint blue veins, in strong contrast with the
fiery eyes and the red finely-curved mouth. The *basquina* of
her country displayed the curving outlines of a figure as pliant
as a branch of willow. This was no "Madonna" of Italian
painters, but "The Madonna" of Spanish art, the Virgin of
Murillo, the only artist daring enough to depict the rapture
of the Conception, a delirious flight of the fervid imagination
of the boldest and most sensuous of painters. Three qualities
were blended in this young girl; any one of them would have
sufficed to exalt a woman into a divinity—the purity of the
pearl in the depths of the sea, the sublime exaltation of a
Saint Theresa, and a voluptuous charm of which she was herself unconscious. Her presence had the power of a talisman.
Everything in the ancient room seemed to have grown young
to Montefiore's eyes since she entered it. But if the apparition was exquisite, the stay was brief; she was taken back to
her mysterious abiding-place, and thither, shortly afterwards,
the servant took a light and her supper, without any attempt
at concealment.

"You do very wisely to keep her out of sight," said
Montefiore in Italian. "I will keep your secret. The
deuce! some of our generals would be quite capable of carrying her off by force."

Montefiore, in his intoxication, went so far as to think of
marrying the fair unknown. With this idea in his mind, he
put some questions to his host. Perez willingly told him the
strange chance that had given him his ward; indeed, the
prudent Spaniard, knowing Montefiore's rank and name, of
which he had heard in Italy, was anxious to confide the story

to his guest, to show how strong were the barriers raised between the young girl and seduction. Although in the good man's talk there was a certain homely eloquence and force in keeping with his simple manner of life, and with that carbine shot at Montefiore from the window, his story will be better given in an abbreviated form.

When the French Republic revolutionized the manners of the inhabitants of the countries which served as the theatre of its wars, a *fille-de-joie*, driven from Venice after the fall of Venice, came to Taragona. Her life had been a tissue of romantic adventure and strange vicissitudes. On no woman belonging to her class had gold been showered so often; so often the caprice of some great lord, struck with her extraordinary beauty, had heaped jewels upon her, and all the luxuries of wealth, for a time. For her this meant flowers and carriages, pages and tire-women, palaces and pictures, insolent pride, journeys like a progress of Catherine II., the life of an absolute queen, in fact, whose caprices were law, and whose whims were more than obeyed; and then—suddenly the gold would utterly vanish—how, neither she nor any one else, man of science, physicist, or chemist could tell, and she was returned again to the streets and to poverty, with nothing in the world save her all-powerful beauty. Yet through it all she lived without taking any thought for the past, the present, or the future. Thrown upon the world, and maintained in her extremity by some poor officer, a gambler, adored for his mustache, she would attach herself to him like a dog to his master, and console him for the hardships of a soldier's life, in all of which she shared, sleeping as lightly under the roof of a garret as beneath the richest of silk canopies. Whether she was in Spain or Italy, she punctually adhered to religious observances. More than once she had bidden love "return to-morrow, to-day I am God's."

But this clay in which gold and spices were mingled, this utter recklessness, these storms of passion, the religious faith lying in the heart like a diamond in the mud, the life begun and ended in the hospital, the continual game of hazard played with the soul and body as its stake; this Alchemy of Life, in short, with vice fanning the flame beneath the crucible in which great careers and fair inheritances and fortune and the honor of illustrious names were melted away; all these were the products of a peculiar genius, faithfully transmitted from mother to daughter from the times of the middle ages. The woman was called *La Marana*. In her family, whose descent since the thirteenth century was reckoned exclusively on the spindle side—the idea, person, authority, nay, the very name of a father, had been absolutely unknown. The name of *Marana* was for her what the dignity of *Stuart* was to the illustrious race of kings of Scotland, a title of honor substituted for the patronymic, when the office became hereditary in their family.

In former times, when France, Spain, and Italy possessed common interests, which at times bound them closely together, and at least as frequently embroiled all three in wars, the word *Marana*, in its widest acceptation, meant a courtesan. In those ages these women had a definite status of which no memory now exists. In France, Ninon de Lenclos and Marion Delorme alone played such a part as the Imperias, the Catalinas, and Maranas who in the preceding centuries exercised the powers of the cassock, the robe, and the sword. There is a church somewhere in Rome built by an Imperia in a fit of penitence, as Rhodope of old once built a pyramid in Egypt. The epithet by which this family of outcasts once was branded became at last their name in earnest, and even something like a patent of nobility for vice, by establishing its antiquity beyond cavil.

But for the La Marana of the nineteenth century there came a day, whether it was a day of splendor or of misery, no man knows, for the problem is a secret between her soul and God; but it was surely in an hour of melancholy, when religion made its voice heard, that with her head in the skies she became conscious of the slough in which her feet were set. Then she cursed the blood in her veins; she cursed herself; she trembled to think that she should bear a daughter; and vowed, as these women vow, with the honor and resolution of the convict, that is to say, with the strongest resolution, the most scrupulous honor to be found under the sun ; making her vow, therefore, before an altar, and consecrating it thereby, that her daughter should lead a virtuous and holy life, that of this long race of lost and sinful women there should come at last one angel who should appear for them in heaven. That vow made, the blood of the Marana regained its sway, and again the courtesan plunged into her life of adventure, with one more thought in her heart. At length she loved, with the violent love of the prostitute, as Henrietta Wilson loved Lord Ponsonby, as Mademoiselle Dupuis loved Bolingbroke, as the Marchesa di Pescara loved her husband; nay, she did not love, she adored a fair-haired half-feminine creature, investing him with all the virtues that she had not, and taking all his vices upon herself. Of this mad union with a weakling, a union blessed neither of God nor man, only to be excused by the happiness it brings, but never absolved by happiness; a union for which the most brazen front must one day blush, a daughter was born, a daughter to be saved, a daughter for whom La Marana desired a stainless life, and, above all things, the instincts of womanliness which she herself had not. Thenceforward, in poverty or prosperity, La Marana bore within her heart a pure affection, the fairest of all human sentiments, because it is the least selfish. Love has its own tinge of egoism, but there is no trace of it in a mother's affection.

And La Marana's motherhoood meant more to her than to other women. It was perhaps her hope of salvation, a plank to cling to in the shipwreck of her eternity. Was she not accomplishing part of her sacred task on earth by sending one more angel to heaven? Was not this a better thing than a tardy repentance? Was there any other way now left to her of sending up prayers from a pure heart to God?

When her daughter was given to her, her Maria-Juana-Pepita (the little one should have had the whole calendar for patron saints if the mother could have had her will), then La Marana set before herself so high an ideal of the dignity of motherhood that she sought a truce from her life of sin. She would live virtuously and alone. There should be no more midnight revels nor wanton days. All her fortunes, all her happiness lay in the child's fragile cradle. The sound of the little voice made an oasis for her amid the burning sands of her life. How should this love be compared with any other? Were not all human affections blended in it with every hope of heaven?

La Marana determined that no stain should rest upon her daughter's life, save that of the original sin of her birth, which she strove to cleanse by a baptism in all social virtues; so she asked of the child's young father a sufficient fortune, and the name he bore. The child was no longer Juana Marana, but Juana dei Mancini.

At last, after seven years of joy and kisses, of rapture and bliss, the poor Marana must part with her darling, lest she also should be branded with her hereditary shame. The mother had force of soul sufficient to give up her child for her child's sake; and sought out, not without dreadful pangs, another mother for her, a family whose manners she might learn, where good examples would be set before her. A mother's abdication is an act either atrocious or sublime; in this case, was it not sublime?

At Taragona, therefore, a lucky accident brought the Lagounias in her way, and in a manner that brought out all the honorable integrity of the Spaniard and the nobleness of his wife. For these two, La Marana appeared like an angel that unlocks the doors of a prison. The merchant's fortune and honor were in peril at the moment, and he needed prompt and secret help; La Marana handed over to him the sum of money intended for Juana's dowry, asking neither for gratitude nor for interest. According to her peculiar notions of jurisprudence, a contract was a matter of the heart, a stiletto the remedy in the hands of the weak, and God the supreme Court of Appeal.

She told Doña Lagounia the story of her miserable situation, and confided her child and her child's fortune to the honor of old Spain, and the untarnished integrity that pervaded the old house. Doña Lagounia had no children of her own, and was delighted to have an adopted daughter to bring up. The courtesan took leave of her darling, feeling that the child's future was secure, and that she had found a mother for Juana, a mother who would train her up to be a Mancini, and not a Marana.

Poor Marana, poor bereaved mother, she went away from the merchant's quiet and humble home, the abode of domestic and family virtue; and felt comforted in her grief as she pictured Juana growing up in that atmosphere of religion, piety, and honor, a maiden, a wife, and a mother, a happy mother, not for a few brief years, but all through a long lifetime. The tears that fell upon the threshold were tears that angels bear to heaven. Since that day of mourning and of hope La Marana had thrice returned to see her daughter, an irresistible presentiment each time bringing her back. The first time Juana had fallen dangerously ill.

"I knew it!" she said to Perez, as she entered his house.

Far away, and as she slept, she had dreamed that Juana was dying.

She watched over her daughter and tended her, and then one morning, when the danger was over, she kissed the sleeping girl's forehead, and went away without revealing herself. The mother within her bade the courtesan depart.

A second time La Marana came—this time to the church

where Juana dei Mancini made her first communion. The exiled mother, very plainly dressed, stood in the shadow behind a pillar, and saw her past self in her daughter, saw a divinely fair face like an angel's, pure as the newly-fallen snow on the heights of the hills. Even in La Marana's love for her child there was a trace of the courtesan; a feeling of jealousy stronger than all love that she had known awoke in her heart, and she left the church; she could no longer control a wild desire to stab Doña Lagounia, who stood there with that look of happiness upon her face, too really a mother to her child.

The last meeting between the two had taken place at Milan, whither the merchant and his wife had gone. La Marana, sweeping along the Corso in almost queenly state, flashed like lightning upon her daughter's sight, and was not recognized. Her anguish was terrible. This Marana on whom kisses were showered must hunger for one kiss in vain, one for which she would have given all the others, the girlish glad caress a daughter gives her mother, her honored mother, her mother in whom all womanly virtues shine. Juana as long as she lived was dead for her.

"What is it, love?" asked the Duc de Lina, and at the words a thought revived the courtesan's failing heart, a thought that gave her delicious happiness—Juana was safe henceforward! She might perhaps be one of the humblest of women, but not a shameless courtesan to whom any man might say, "What is it, love?"

Indeed, the merchant and his wife had done their duty with scrupulous fidelity. Juana's fortune in their hands had been doubled. Perez de Lagounia had become the richest merchant in the province, and in his feeling towards the young girl there was a trace of superstition. Her coming had saved the old house from ruin and dishonor, and had not the presence of this angel brought unlooked-for prosperity? His wife, a soul of gold, a refined and gentle nature, had brought up her charge devoutly; the girl was as pure as she was beautiful. Juana was equally fitted to be the wife of a rich merchant or of a noble; she had every qualification for a brilliant destiny. But for the war that had broken out, Perez, who dreamed of living in Madrid, would ere now have given her in marriage to some Spanish grandee.

"I do not know where La Marana is at this moment," he concluded; "but wherever she may be, if she hears that our province is occupied by your armies, and that Taragona has been besieged, she is sure to be on her way hither to watch over her daughter."

This story wrought a change in the captain's intentions; he no longer thought of making a Marchesa di Montefiore of Juana dei Mancini. He recognized the Marana blood in that swift glance the girl had exchanged with him from her shelter behind the blind, in the stratagem by which she had satisfied her curiosity, in that last look she had given him; and the libertine meant to marry a virtuous wife.

This would be a dangerous escapade, no doubt, but the perils were ;of the kind that never sink the courage of the most pusillanimous, for love and its pleasures would reward them. There were obstacles everywhere; there was the apprentice who slept on the counter, and the servant-maid on the makeshift couch in the kitchen; Perez and his wife, who kept a dragon's watch by day, were old, and doubtless slept lightly; every sound echoed through the house, everything seemed to put the adventure beyond the range of possibilities. But as a set-off against these things, Montefiore had an ally— the blood of the Marana, which throbbed feverishly in the heart of the lovely Italian girl brought up as a Spaniard, the maiden athirst for love. Passion, the girl's nature, and Montefiore were a combination that might defy the whole world.

Prompted quite as strongly by the instincts of a chartered libertine as by the vague inexplicable hopes to which we give the name of presentiments, a word that describes them with such startling aptness—Montefiore took up his stand at his window, and spent the early hours of the night there, looking down in the presumed direction of the secret hiding-place, where the old couple had enshrined their darling, the joy of their old age.

The warehouse on the *entresol* (to make use of a French word that will perhaps make the disposition of the house clearer to the reader) separated the two young people, so it was idle for the captain to try to convey a message by means of tapping upon the floor, a shift for speech that all lovers can devise under such circumstances. Chance, however, came to his assistance, or was it the young girl herself? Just as he took his stand at the window he saw a circle of light that fell upon the grim opposite wall of the yard, and in the midst of it a dark silhouette, the form of Juana. Everything that she did was shadowed there; from her attitude and the movement of her arms, she seemed to be arranging her hair for the night.

"Is she alone?" Montefiore asked himself. "If I weight a letter with a few coins, will it be safe to dangle it by a thread against the round window that no doubt lights her cell?"

He wrote a note forthwith, a note characteristic of the officer, of the soldier sent for reasons of family expediency to the isle of Elba, of the former dilettante Marquis, fallen from his high estate, and become a captain on the clothing establishment. He wrapped some coins in the note, devised a string out of various odds and ends, tied up the packet and let it down, without a sound, into the very centre of that round brightness.

"If her mother or the servant is with her," Montefiore thought, "I shall see the shadows on the wall; and if she is not alone, I will draw up the cord at once."

But when, after pains innumerable, which can readily be imagined, the weighted packet tapped at the glass, only one shadow appeared, and it was the slender figure of Juana that flitted across the wall. Noiselessly the young girl opened the circular window, saw the packet, took it in, and stood for a while reading it.

Montefiore had written in his own name and entreated an interview. He offered, in the style of old romances, his heart and hand to Juana dei Mancini—a base and commonplace stratagem that nearly always succeeds! At Juana's age, is not nobility of soul an added danger? A poet of our own days has gracefully said that "only in her strength does woman yield." Let a lover, when he is most beloved, feign doubts of the love that he inspires, and in her pride and her trust in him, a girl would invent sacrifices for his sake, knowing neither the world nor man's nature well enough to retain her self-command when passion stirs within her, and to overwhelm with her scorn the lover who can accept a whole life offered to him to turn away a groundless reproach.

In our sublimely constituted society a young girl is placed in a painful dilemma between the forecasts of prudent virtue on the one hand, and the consequences of error upon the other. If she resists, it not seldom happens that she loses a lover and the first love, that is the most attractive of all; and if she is imprudent, she loses a marriage. Cast an eye over the vicissitudes of social life in Paris, and it is impossible to doubt the necessity of a religion that shall ensure that there are no more young girls seduced daily. And Paris is situated in the forty-eighth-degree of latitude, while Taragona lies below the forty-first. The old question of climate is still useful to the novelist seeking an excuse for the suddenness of his catastrophe, and is made to explain the imprudence or the dilatoriness of a pair of lovers.

Montefiore's eyes were fixed meanwhile on the charming silhouette in the midst of the bright circle. Neither he nor Juana could see each other; an unlucky archway above her casement, with perverse malignity, cut off all chances of communication by signs, such as two lovers can contrive by leaning out of their windows. So the captain concentrated his whole mind and attention upon the round patch on the wall. Perhaps all unwittingly the girl's movements might betray her thoughts. Here again he was foiled. Juana's strange proceedings gave Montefiore no room for the faintest hope; she was amusing herself by cutting up the billet.

It often happens that virtue and discretion, in distrust, adopt shifts familiar to the jealous Bartholos of comedy. Juana, having neither paper, pen, nor ink, was scratching an answer with the point of a pair of scissors. In another moment she tied the scrap of paper to the string, the officer drew it in, opened it, held it up against the lamp, and read the perforated characters—" Come," it said.

" 'Come?'" said he to himself. " Poison, and carbine, and Perez' dagger! And how about the apprentice hardly asleep on the counter by this time, and the servant in her hammock, and the house booming like a bass viol with every sound? why, I can hear old Perez snoring away upstairs! 'Come!'——Then, has she nothing to lose?"

Acute reflection! Libertines alone can reason thus logically, and punish a woman for her devotion. The imagination of man has created Satan and Lovelace, but a maiden is an angelic being to whom he can lend nothing but his vices; so lofty, so fair is she, that he cannot set her higher nor add to her beauty; he has but the fatal power of blighting this creation by dragging it down to his miry level.

Montefiore waited till the drowsiest hour of the night, then in spite of his sober second thoughts, he crept downstairs. He had taken off his shoes, and carried his pistols with him, and now he groped his way step by step, stopping to listen in the silence; trying each separate stair, straining his eyes till he almost saw in the darkness, and ready to turn back at any moment if the least thing befell him. He wore his handsomest uniform; he had perfumed his dark hair, and taken pains with the toilet that set off his natural good looks. On occasions like these, most men are as much a woman as any woman.

Montefiore managed to reach the door of the girl's secret hiding-place without difficulty. It was a little cabinet contrived in a corner which projected into another dwelling, a not unusual freak of the builder where ground-rents are high, and houses in consequence packed very tightly together. Here Juana lived alone, day and night, out of sight of all eyes. Hitherto she had slept near her adopted mother; but when Perez and his wife removed to the top of the house, the arrangements of the attics did not permit of their taking their ward thither also. So Doña Lagounia had left the girl to the guardianship of the lock of the secret door, to the protection of religious ideas, but so much the more powerful because they had become superstitions; and with the further safeguards of a natural pride, and the shrinking delicacy of the sensitive plant, which made Juana an exception among her sex, for to the most pathetic innocence Juana Mancini united no less the most passionate aspirations. It had needed a retired life and devout training to quiet and to cool the hot blood of the Maranas that glowed in her veins, the impulses that her adopted mother called temptations of the Evil one.

A faint gleam of light beneath the door in the panels discovered its whereabouts for Montefiore. He tapped softly with the tips of his finger-nails, and Juana let him in. Quivering from head to foot with excitement, he met the young girl's look of *naïve* curiosity, and read the most complete ignorance of her peril, and a sort of childlike admiration in her eyes. He stood, awed for a moment by the picture of the sanctuary before him.

The walls were hung with gray tapestry, covered with violet flowers. A small ebony chest, an antique mirror, a huge old-fashioned armchair, also made of ebony, and covered with tapestry; another chair beside the spindle-legged table, a pretty carpet on the floor—that was all. But there were flowers on the table beside some embroidery work, and at the other end of the room stood the little narrow bed on which Juana dreamed; three pictures hung on the wall above it, and at the head stood a crucifix above a little holy water stoup, and a prayer framed and illuminated in gold. The room was full of the faint perfume of the flowers, of the soft light of the tapers; it all seemed so quiet, pure, and sacred. The subtle charm of Juana's dreamy fancies, nay of Juana herself, seemed to pervade everything; her soul was revealed by her surroundings; the pearl lay there in its shell.

Juana, clad in white, with no ornament save her own loveliness, letting fall her rosary to call on the name of Love, would have inspired even Montefiore with reverence if it had not been for the night about them and the silence, if Juana had welcomed love less eagerly, if the little white bed had not displayed the turned-down coverlet—the pillow, confidante of innumerable vague longings. Montefiore stood there for long, intoxicated by joy hitherto unknown; such joy as Satan, it may be, would know at a glimpse of paradise if the cloud-veil that envelops heaven was rent away for a moment.

"I loved you the first moment that I saw you," he said, speaking pure Tuscan in the tones of his musical Italian voice. " In you my soul and my life are set; if you so will it, they shall be yours forever."

To Juana listening, the air she breathed seemed to vibrate with the words grown magical upon her lover's tongue.

"Poor little girl! how have you breathed the atmosphere of this gloomy place so long, and lived? You meant to reign like a queen in the world, to dwell in the palace of a prince, to pass from festival to festival, to feel in your own heart the joys that you create, to see the world at your feet, to make the fairest splendors pale before the glorious beauty that shall never be rivaled—*you* have lived here in seclusion with this old tradesman and his wife!"

There was a purpose in his exclamation; he wanted to find out whether or no Juana had ever had a lover.

"Yes," she answered. "But who can have told you my inmost thoughts? For these twelve months past I have been weary to death of it. Yes, I would die rather than stay any longer in this house. Do you see this embroidery? I have set countless dreadful thoughts into every stitch of it. How often I have longed to run away and fling myself into the sea! Do you ask why? I have forgotten already——Childish troubles, but very keenly felt in spite of their childishness—— Often at night when I kissed my mother, I have given her such a kiss as one gives for a last farewell, saying in my heart, I will kill myself to-morrow. After all, I did not die. Suicides go to hell, and I was so much afraid of that, that I made up my mind to endure my life, to get up and go to bed, and do the same things hour after hour of every day. My life was not irksome, it was painful. And yet, my father and mother worship me. Oh! I am wicked! indeed, I tell my confessor so."

"Then have you always lived here without amusements, without pleasures?"

"Oh! I have not always felt like this. Until I was fifteen years old, I enjoyed seeing the festivals of the Church; I loved the singing and the music. I was so happy, because I felt that, like the angels, I was sinless, so glad that I might take the sacrament every week; in short, I loved God then. But in these three years I have changed utterly, day by day. It began when I wanted flowers here in the house, and they gave me very beautiful ones; then I wanted—— But now I want nothing any longer," she added, after a pause, and she smiled at Montefiore.

"Did you not tell me just now in your letter that you would love me for ever?"

"Yes, my Juana," murmured Montefiore. He put his arm round the waist of this adorable girl and pressed her closely to his heart. "Yes. But let me speak to you as you pray to God. Are you not fairer than Our Lady in heaven? Hear me," and he set a kiss in her hair, "for me that forehead of yours is the fairest altar on earth; I swear to worship you, my idol, to pour out all the wealth of the world upon you. My carriages are yours, my palace in Milan is yours, yours all the jewels and the diamonds, the heirlooms of my ancient house; new ornaments and dresses every day, and all the countless pleasures and delights of the world."

"Yes," she said, "I should like it all very much; but in my soul I feel that I should love my dear husband more than all things else in the world."

Mio caro sposo! Italian was Juana's native speech, and it is impossible to put into two words of another language the wonderful tenderness, the winning grace with which that brief delicious phrase is invested by the accents of an Italian tongue. "I shall find," she said, and the purity of a seraph shone in her eyes, "I shall find my beloved religion again in *him*. His and God's, God's and his!—— But you are he, are you not?" she cried, after a pause. "Surely, surely you are he! Ah! come and see the picture that my father brought me from Italy."

She took up a candle, beckoned to Montefiore, and showed him a picture that hung at the foot of the bed—Saint Michael trampling Satan under foot.

"Look!" she cried, "has he not your eyes? That made me think, as soon as I saw you in the street, that in the meeting I saw the finger of heaven. So often I have lain awake in the morning before my mother came to call me to prayer, thinking about that picture, looking at the angel, until at last I came to think that he was my husband. *Mon Dieu!* I am talking as I think to myself. What wild nonsense it must seem to you! but if you only knew how a poor recluse longs to pour out the thoughts that oppress her! I used to talk to these flowers and the woven garlands on the tapestry when I was alone; they understood me better, I think, than my father and mother—always so serious——"

"Juana," said Montefiore, as he took her hands and kissed them, passion shone in his eyes and overflowed in his gestures and in the sound of his voice, "talk to me as if I were your husband, talk to me as you talk to yourself. I have suffered all that you have suffered. Few words will be needed, when we talk together, to bring back the whole past of either life before we met; but there are not words enough in language to tell of the bliss that lies before us. Lay your hand on my heart. Do you feel how it beats? Let us vow, before God, who sees and hears us, to be faithful to each other all our lives. Stay, take this ring. Give me yours."

"Give away my ring?" she cried, startled.

"Why not?" asked Montefiore, dismayed by so much simplicity.

"Why, it came to me from our Holy Father the Pope. When I was a little girl a beautiful lady set it on my finger; she took care of me, and brought me here, and she told me to keep it always."

"Then you do not love me, Juana?"

"Ah! here it is," she cried. "Are you not more myself than I?"

She held out the ring, trembling as she did so, keeping her fingers tightly clasped upon it as she looked at Montefiore with clear, questioning eyes. That ring meant her whole self: she gave it to him.

"Oh! my Juana!" said Montefiore as he held her closely in his arms, "only a monster could be false to you. I will love you for ever."

Juana grew dreamy. Montefiore, thinking within himself that in his first interview, he must not run the slightest risk of startling a girl so innocent, whose imprudence sprang rather from virtue than from desire, was fain to content himself with thinking of the future of her beauty now that he had known its power, and of the innocent marriage of the ring, that most sublime of betrothals, the simplest and most binding of all ceremonies, the betrothal of the heart.

For the rest of the night, and all day long on the morrow Juana's imagination would surely become the accomplice of his desires. So he put constraint upon himself, and tried to be as respectful as he was tender. With these thoughts present in his mind, prompted by his passion, and yet more by the desires that Juana inspired in him, his words were insinuating and fervent. He led the innocent child to plan out the new life before them, painted the world for her in the most glowing colors, dwelt on the household details that possess such a delightful interest for young girls, and made with her the compacts over which lovers dispute, the agreements that give rights and reality to love. Then, when they had decided the hour for their nightly tryst, he went, leaving a happy but a changed Juana. The simple and innocent Juana no longer existed, already there was more passion than a girl should reveal in the last glance that she gave him, in the charming way that she held up her forehead for the touch of her lover's lips. It was all the result of solitude and irksome tasks upon this nature; if she was to be prudent and virtuous, the knowledge of the world should either have come to her gradually or have been hidden from her for ever.

"How slowly the day will go to-morrow!" she said, as another kiss, still respectfully given, was pressed upon her forehead.

"But you will sit in the dining-room, will you not? and raise your voice a little when you talk, so that I may hear you, and the sound may fill my heart."

Montefiore, beginning to understand the life that Juana led, was but the better pleased that he had managed to restrain his desires that he might the better secure his end. He returned to his room without mishap.

Ten days went by, and nothing occurred to disturb the

peace and quiet of the house. Montefiore, with the persuasive manners of an Italian, had gained the good graces of old Perez and Doña Lagounia; indeed, he was popular with the whole household—with the apprentice and the maidservant; but in spite of the confidence that he had succeeded in inspiring in them, he never attempted to take advantage of it to ask to see Juana, or to open the door of that little sealed paradise. The Italian girl, in her longing to see her lover, had often besought him to do this, but from motives of prudence he had always refused. On the contrary, he had used the character he had gained and all his skill to lull the suspicions of the old couple; he had accustomed them to his habit of never rising till mid-day, soldier as he was. The captain gave out that his health was bad. So the two lovers only lived at night when all the household was asleep.

If Montefiore had not been a libertine to whom a long experience of pleasure had given presence of mind under all conditions, they would have been lost half a score of times in those ten days. A young lover, with the single-heartedness of first love, would have been tempted in his rapture into imprudences that were very hard to resist; but the Italian was proof even against Juana, against her pouting lips, her wild spirits, against a Juana who wound the long plaits of her hair about his throat to keep him by her side. The keenest observer would have been sorely puzzled to detect those midnight meetings. It may well be believed that the Italian, sure of his ultimate success, enjoyed prolonging the ineffable pleasure of this intrigue in which he made progress step by step, in fanning the flame that gradually waxed hotter, till everything must yield to it at last.

On the eleventh day, as they sat at dinner, he deemed it expedient to confide to Perez (under the seal of secrecy) the history of the disgrace into which he had fallen among his family. It was a mésalliance, he said.

There was something revolting in this lie, told as a confidence, while that midnight drama was in progress beneath the old man's roof. Montefiore, an experienced actor, was leading up to a catastrophe planned by himself; and, like an artist who loves his art, he enjoyed the thought of it. He meant very shortly to take leave of the house and of his lady-love without regret. And when Juana, risking her life it might be to ask the question, should inquire of Perez what had become of their guest, Perez would tell her, all unwittingly, that "the Marchese di Montefiore has been reconciled with his family; they have consented to receive his wife, and he has taken her to them."

And Juana?—— The Italian never inquired of himself what would become of her; he had had ample opportunity of knowing her nobleness, her innocence, and her goodness, and felt sure that Juana would keep silence.

He obtained a message to carry for some general or other. Three days afterwards, on the night before he must start, Montefiore went straight to Juana's room instead of going first to his own. The same instinct that bids the tiger leave no morsel of his prey prompted the Italian to lengthen the night of farewells. Juana, the true daughter of two southern lands, with the passion of Spain and of Italy in her heart, was enraptured by the boldness that brought her lover to her and revealed the ardor of his love. To know the delicious torment of an illicit passion under the sanction of marriage, to conceal her husband behind the bed-curtains, half deceiving the adopted father and mother, to whom she could say in case of discovery, "I am the Marchesa di Montefiore," was not this a festival for the young and romantic girl who, for three years past, had dreamed of love—love always beset with perils? The curtains of the door fell, drawing about their madness and happiness a veil which it is useless to raise.

It was nearly nine o'clock, the merchant and his wife were reading the evening prayer, when suddenly the sound of a carriage, drawn by several horses, came from the narrow street without. Some one knocked hastily and loudly at the door of the shop. The servant ran to open it, and in a moment a woman sprang into the quaint old room—a woman magnificently dressed, though her traveling carriage was besplashed by the mire of many roads, for she had crossed Italy and France and Spain. It was La Marana! La Marana, in spite of her thirty-six years and her riotous life, in the full pride of her *bellà folgorante*, to record the superb epithet invented for her in Milan by her enraptured adorers. La Marana, the openly avowed mistress of a king, had left Naples and its festivals and sunny skies, at the very height and summit of her strange career—had left gold and madrigals and silks and perfumes, and her royal lover, when she learned from him what was passing in Spain, and how that Taragona was besieged.

"Taragona!" she cried, "and before the city is taken! I must be in Taragona in ten days!" And without another thought for courts or crowned heads, she had reached Taragona, provided with a passport that gave her something like the powers of an empress, and with gold that enabled her to cross the French empire with the speed and splendor of a rocket. There is no such thing as distance for a mother; she who is a mother, indeed, sees her child, and knows by instinct how it fares though they are as far apart as the poles.

"My daughter! my daughter!" cried La Marana.

At that cry, at this swift invasion of their house, and apparition of a queen traveling *incognito*, Perez and his wife let the prayer-book fall; that voice rang in their ears like a thunder-clap, and La Marana's eyes flashed lightnings.

"She is in there," the merchant answered quietly, after a brief pause, during which they recovered from the shock of surprise caused by La Marana's sudden appearance, and by her look and tone. "She is in there," he said again, indicating the little hiding-place.

"Yes, but has she not been ill? Is she quite——"

"Perfectly well," said Doña Lagounia.

"Oh, God!" cried La Marana, "plunge me now in hell for all eternity, if it be Thy pleasure," and she sank down utterly exhausted into a chair.

The flush that anxiety had brought to her face faded suddenly; her cheeks grew white; she who had borne up bravely under the strain, had no strength left when it was over. The joy was too intolerable, a joy more intense than her previous distress, for she was still vibrating with dread, when bliss keen as anguish came upon her.

"But how have you done!" she asked. "Taragona was taken by assault."

"Yes," answered Perez. "But when you saw that I was alive, how could you ask such a question? How should any one reach Juana but over my dead body?"

The courtesan grasped Perez' horny hand on receiving this answer; tears gathered in her eyes and fell upon his fingers as she kissed them—the costliest of all things under the sun for her, who never wept.

"Brave Perez!" she said at last; "but surely there are soldiers billeted upon you, are there not?"

"Only one," answered the Spaniard. "Luckily, we have one of the most honorable of men, an Italian by nationality, a Spaniard by birth, a hater of Bonaparte, a married man, a steady character. He rises late, and goes to bed early. He is in bad health, too, just now."

"An Italian! What is his name?"

"Captain Montefiore, he——"

"Why, he is not the Marchese di Montefiore, is he?"

"Yes, señora, the very same."

"Has he seen Juana?"

"No," said Doña Lagounia.

"You are mistaken, wife," said Perez. "The Marquis must have seen Juana once, only for a moment, it is true, but I think he must have seen her that day when she came in at supper-time."

"Ah! I should like to see my daughter."

"Nothing is easier," said Perez. "She is asleep. Though if she has left the key in the lock, we shall have to wake her."

As the merchant rose to take down the duplicate key from its place, he happened to glance up through the tall window. The light from the large round pane-opening of Juana's cell fell upon the dark wall on the opposite side of the yard, tracing a gleaming circle there, and in the midst of the lighted space he saw two shadowy figures such as no sculptor till the time of the gifted Canova could have dreamed of. The Spaniard turned to the room again.

"I do not know," he said to La Marana, "where we have put the key——"

"You look very pale!" she exclaimed.

"I will soon tell you why," he answered, as he sprang towards his dagger, caught it up, and beat violently on the door in the paneling. "Open the door!" he shouted. "Juana! open the door!"

There was an appalling despair in his tones that struck terror into the two women who heard him.

Juana did not open, because there was some delay in hiding Montefiore. She knew nothing of what had passed in the room without. The tapestry hangings on either side of the door deadened all sounds.

"Madame," said Perez, turning to La Marana, "I told you just now that I did not know where the key was. That was a lie. Here it is," and he took it from the sideboard, "but it is useless. Juana's key is in the lock, and her door is barricaded. We are deceived, wife! There is a man in Juana's room."

"By my hopes of salvation, the thing is impossible!" said Doña Lagounia.

"Do not perjure yourself, Doña Lagounia. Our honor is slain; and *she*" (he turned to La Marana, who had risen to her feet, and stood motionless as if thunderstruck by his words), "she may well scorn us. She saved our lives, our fortune, and our honor, and we have barely guarded her money for her— Juana, open the door!" he shouted, "or I will break it down!"

The whole house rang with the cry; his voice grew louder and angrier; but he was cool and self-possessed. He held Montefiore's life in his hands, in another moment he would wash away his remorse in every drop of the Italian's blood.

"Go out! go out! go out! all of you!" cried La Marana, and springing for the dagger like a tigress, she snatched it from the hand of the astonished Perez. "Go out of this room, Perez," she went on, speaking quite quietly now. "Go out, you and your wife, and the maid and the apprentice. There will be a murder here directly, and you might all be shot down by the French for it. Do not you mix yourself up in it, it is my affair entirely. When my daughter and I meet, God alone should be present. As for the man, he is mine. The whole world should not snatch him out of my hands. There, there, go! I forgive you. I see it all. The girl is a Marana. My blood flows in her veins, and you, your religion, and your honor have been powerless against it."

Her groan was dreadful to hear. She turned dry eyes upon them. She had lost everything, but she was accustomed to suffering; she was a courtesan. The door opened. La Marana henceforth heeded nothing else, and Perez, making a sign to his wife, could remain at his post. The old Spaniard, implacable where honor was concerned, determined to assist the wronged mother's vengeance. Juana, in her white draperies, stood quietly there in her room in the soft lamplight. "What do you want with me?" she asked.

In spite of herself, a light shudder ran through La Marana.

"Perez," she asked, "is there any other way out of this closet?"

Perez shook his head; and on that the courtesan went into the room.

"Juana," she said, "I am your mother, your judge—you have put yourself in the one situation in which I can reveal myself to you. You have come to my level, you whom I had thought to raise to heaven. Oh! you have fallen very low!—— You have a lover in your room."

"Madame, no one but my husband should or could be there," she answered. "I am the Marchesa di Montefiore."

"Then are there two of them?" asked old Perez sternly. "He told me that he was married."

"Montefiore! my love!" cried the girl, rending the curtains, and discovering the officer; "come forward, these people are slandering you."

The Italian's face was haggard and pale; he saw the dagger in La Marana's hand, and he knew La Marana. At one bound he sprang out of the chamber, and with a voice of thunder shouted, "Help! help! murder! they are killing a Frenchman! Soldiers of the Sixth of the line, run for Captain Diard!—— Help!"

Perez had secured the Marquis, and was about to gag him by putting his large hand over the soldier's mouth, when the courtesan stopped him.

"Hold him fast," she said, "but let him call. Throw open the doors, and leave them open; and now go out, all of you, I tell you! As for you," she continued, addressing Montefiore, "shout, and call for help—— As soon as there is a sound of your men's footsteps, this blade will be in your heart—— Are you married? Answer me."

Montefiore, lying across the threshold of the door, two paces from Juana, heard nothing, and saw nothing, for the blinding gleam of the dagger blade.

"Then he meant to deceive me;" the words came slowly from Juana. "He told me that he was free."

"He told me that he was a married man," said Perez, in the same stern tones as before.

"Holy Virgin!" exclaimed Doña Lagounia. La Marana

stooped to mutter in the ear of the Marquis, "Answer me, will you, soul of mud?"

"Your daughter——" Montefiore began.

"The daughter I once had is dead, or she soon will be," said La Marana. "I have no daughter now. Do not use that word again. Answer me, are you married?"

"No, madame," Montefiore said at last (he wished to gain time); "I mean to marry your daughter."

"My noble Montefiore!" cried Juana, with a deep breath.

"Then what made you fly and call for help!" demanded Perez.

Terrible perspicacity!

Juana said nothing, but she wrung her hands, went over to her armchair, and sat down. Even at that moment there was an uproar in the street, and in the deep silence that fell upon the parlor it was sufficiently easy to catch the sounds. A private soldier of the Sixth, who had chanced to pass along the street when Montefiore cried out for help, had gone to call up Diard. Luckily, the quartermaster was in his lodging, and came at once with several comrades.

"Why did I fly?" repeated Montefiore, who heard the sound of his friend's voice. "Because I had told you the truth. Diard! Diard!" he shrieked aloud.

But at a word from Perez, who meant that all in his house should share in the murder, the apprentice made the door fast, and the men were obliged to force it open. La Marana, therefore, could stab the guilty creature at her feet before they made an entrance; but her hand shook with pent-up wrath, and the blade slipped aside upon Montefiore's epaulette. Yet so heavy had been the blow, that the Italian rolled over almost at Juana's feet. The girl did not see him, but La Marana sprang upon her prey, and, lest she should fail this time, she held his throat in an iron grasp, and pointed the dagger at his heart.

"I am free!" he gasped. "I will marry her! I swear it

by God! by my mother! by all that is most sacred in this world. I am not married! I will marry her! Upon my word of honor, I will!" and he set his teeth in the courtesan's arm.

"That is enough, mother." said Juana; "kill him! I would not have such a coward for my husband if he were ten times more beautiful."

"Ah! that is my daughter!" cried La Marana.

"What is going on here?" asked the quartermaster, looking about him.

"This," shouted Montefiore; "they are murdering me on that girl's account; she says that I am her lover; she trapped me, and now they want to force me to marry her against my will——"

"Against your will?" cried Diard, struck with the sublime beauty that indignation, scorn, and hate had lent to Juana's face, already so fair. "You are very hard to please! If she must have a husband, here am I. Put up your dagger."

La Marana grasped the Italian, pulled him to his feet, brought him to the bedside, and said in his ear—

"If I spare your life, you may thank that last speech of yours for it. But keep it in mind. If you say a word against my daughter, we shall see each other again. What will her dowry amount to?" she asked of Perez.

"Two hundred thousand piastres down——"

"That will not be all, monsieur," said the courtesan, addressing Diard. "Who are you? You can go," she added, turning to Montefiore.

But when the Marquis heard mention of two hundred thousand piastres down, he came forward, saying, "I am really quite free——"

"You are really quite free to go," said La Marana, and the Italian went.

"Alas! monsieur," the girl spoke, addressing Diard; "I thank you, and I admire you. But my bridegroom is in heaven; I shall be the bride of Christ. To-morrow I shall enter the convent of——."

"Oh, hush! hush! Juana, my Juana!" cried her mother, holding the girl tightly in her arms. Then she whispered, "You must take another bridegroom."

Juana turned pale.

"Who are you, monsieur?" asked the mother of the Provençal.

"I am nothing as yet but a quartermaster in the Sixth Regiment of the line," said he; "but for such a wife, a man would feel that it lay in him to be a marshal of France some day. My name is Pierre-François Diard. My father was a guild magistrate, so I am not a——"

"Eh! you are an honest man, are you not?" cried La Marana. "If the Signorina Juana dei Mancini cares for you, you may both be happy. Juana," she went on gravely, "when you are the wife of a good and worthy man, remember that you will be a mother. I have sworn that you shall set a kiss upon your child's forehead without a blush—— (Here her tone changed somewhat.) I have sworn that you shall be a virtuous wife. So in this life, though many troubles await you, whatever happens to you, be a chaste and faithful wife to your husband; sacrifice everything to him; he will be the father of your children—— A father to your children!—— Stay, between you and a lover your mother always will stand; I shall be your mother only when danger threatens—— Do you see Perez's dagger? *That* is part of your dower," and she flung the weapon down on the bed. "There I leave it as a guarantee of your honor, so long as I have eyes to see and hands that can strike a blow. Farewell," she said, keeping back the tears; "may heaven direct that we never meet again," and at that her tears flowed fast.

"Poor child! you have been very happy in this little cell, happier than you know. Act in such a way that she may never look back on it with regret," La Marana added, looking at her future son-in-law.

The story, which has been given simply by way of introduction, is not by any means the subject of the following study; it has been told to explain, in the first place, how Montefiore and Diard became acquainted, how Captain Diard came to marry Juana dei Mancini, and to make known what passions filled Mme. Diard's heart, what blood flowed in her veins.

By the time that the quartermaster had been through the slow and tedious formalities indispensable for a French soldier who is obtaining leave to marry, he had fallen passionately in love with Juana dei Mancini, and Juana dei Mancini had had time to reflect on her fate. An appalling fate! Juana, who neither loved nor esteemed this Diard, was none the less bound to him by a promise, a rash promise no doubt, but there had been no help for it. The Provençal was neither handsome nor well made. His manners were totally lacking in distinction, and savored of the camp, of his provincial bringing up and imperfect education. How should the young girl love Diard? With her perfect elegance and grace, her unconquerable instinct for luxury and refinement, her natural inclinations were towards the higher spheres of society; and she could not bring herself to feel so much as esteem for this Diard who was to marry her, and precisely for that very reason.

The repugnance was very natural. Woman is a sacred and gracious being, almost always misunderstood; the judgments passed upon her are almost always unjust, because she is not understood. If Juana had loved Diard, she would have esteemed him. Love creates a new self within a woman; the old self passes away with the dawn of love, and in the wedding-robe of a passion that shall last as long as life itself, her life is invested with whiteness and purity. After this new birth, this revival of modesty and virtue, she has no longer a past; it is utterly forgotten; she turns wholly to the future that she may learn all things afresh. In this sense, the words of the famous line that a modern poet has put into the mouth of Marion Delorme, a line, moreover, that Corneille might well have written, are steeped in truth—

"And Love gives back my maidenhood to me."

Does it not read like a reminiscence of some tragedy of Corneille's? The style of the father of French drama, so forceful, owing so little to epithet, seems to be revived again in the words. And yet the writer, the poet of our own day, has been compelled to sacrifice it to the taste of a public only capable of appreciating vaudevilles.

So Juana, loveless, was still the same Juana, betrayed, humiliated, brought very low. How should this Juana respect a man who could take her thus? With the high-minded purity of youth, she felt the force of a distinction, subtle in appearance, but real and immutable, a binding law upon the heart, which even the least thoughtful women instinctively apply to all their sentiments. Life had opened out before Juana, and the prospect saddened her inmost soul.

Often she looked at Perez and Doña Lagounia, her eyes full of the tears she was too proud to let fall; they understood the bitter thoughts contained in those tears, but they said no word. Were not reproaches useless? And why should they seek to comfort her? The keener the sympathy, the wider the pent-up sorrow would spread.

One evening, as Juana sat in her little cell in a dull stupor of wretchedness, she heard the husband and wife talking together. They thought that the door was shut, and a wail broke from her adopted mother.

"The poor child will die of grief!"

"Yes," answered Perez in a faltering voice; "but what can we do? Can I go now to boast of my ward's chaste beauty to the Comte d'Arcos, to whom I hoped to marry her?"

"There is a difference between one slip and vice," said the old woman, indulgent as an angel could have been.

"Her mother gave her to him," objected Perez.

"All in a minute, and without consulting her!" cried Doña Lagounia.

"She knew quite well what she was doing——"

"Into what hands our pearl will pass!"

"Not a word more, or I will go and pick a quarrel with that —— Diard!"

"And then there would be one more misfortune," exclaimed Doña Lagounia.

Juana, listening to these terrible words, knew at last the value of the happy life that had flowed on untroubled until her error ended it. So the innocent hours in her peaceful retreat were to have been crowned by a brilliant and splendid existence; the delights so often dreamed of would have been hers. Those dreams had caused her ruin. She had fallen from the heights of social greatness to the feet of *Monsieur* Diard! Juana wept; her thoughts almost drove her mad. For several seconds she hesitated between a life of vice and religion. Vice offered a prompt solution; religion, a life made up of suffering. The inward debate was stormy and solemn. To-morrow was the fatal day, the day fixed for this marriage. It was not too late; Juana might be Juana still. If she remained free, she knew the utmost extent of her calamities; but when married, she could not tell what might lie in store for her. Religion gained the day. Doña Lagounia came to watch and pray by her daughter's side, as she might have done by a dying woman's bed.

"It is the will of God," she said to Juana. Nature gives to a woman a power peculiarly her own, that enables her to endure suffering, a power succeeded in turn by weakness that counsels resignation. Juana submitted without an afterthought. She determined to fulfill her mother's vow, to cross the desert of life, and so reach heaven, knowing that no flowers could spring up in the thorny paths that lay before her. She married Diard.

As for the quartermaster, though Juana judged him pitilessly, who else would not have forgiven him? He was intoxicated with love. La Marana, with the quick instinct natural to her, had felt passion in the tones of his voice, and seen in him the abrupt temper, the impulsive generosity of the south. In the paroxysm of her great anger she had seen Diard's good qualities, and these only, and thought that these were sufficient guarantees for her daughter's happiness.

And to all appearance the early days of this marriage were happy. But to lay bare the underlying facts of the case, the miserable secrets that women bury in the depths of their souls, Juana had determined that she would not overcloud her husband's joy. All women who are victims of an ill-assorted marriage come sooner or later to play a double part—a part terrible to play, and Juana had already taken up her rôle. Of such a life, a man can only record the facts; and women's hearts alone can divine the inner life of sentiments. Is it not a story impossible to relate in all its truth? Juana, struggling every hour against her own nature, half-Spanish, half-Italian; Juana, shedding tears in secret till she had no tears left to shed, was a typical creation, a living symbol, destined to represent the uttermost extent of woman's misfortunes. The minute detail required to depict that life of restless pain would be without interest for those who crave melodramatic sensation. And would not an analysis, in which every wife would discover some of her own experience, require an entire volume if it were to be given in full? Such a book, by its very nature, would be impossible to write, for its merits must consist in half-tones and in subtle shades of color that critics would consider vague and indistinct. And besides, who that does not bear another heart within his heart can touch on the pathetic, deeply-hidden tragedies that some women take with them to their graves; the heartache, understood of none—not even of those who cause it; the sighs in vain; the devotion that, here on earth at least, meets with no return; unappreciated magnanimities of silence and scorn of vengeance; unfailing generosity, lavished in vain; longings for happiness destined to be unfulfilled; angelic charity that blesses in secret; all the beliefs held sacred, all the inextinguishable love? This life Juana knew; fate spared her in nothing. Hers was to be in all things the lot of a wronged and unhappy wife, always forgiving her wrongs; a woman pure as a flawless diamond, though through her beauty, as flawless and as dazzling as the diamond, a way of revenge lay open to her. Of a truth, she need not dread the dagger in her dower.

But at first, under the influence of love, of a passion that for a while at least can work a change in the most depraved nature, and bring to light all that is noblest in a human soul, Diard behaved like a man of honor. He compelled Montefiore to go out of the regiment, and even out of that division of the army, that his wife might not be compelled to meet the Marquis during the short time that she was to remain in Spain. Then the quartermaster asked to change his regiment, and managed to exchange into the Imperial Guard. He meant at all costs to gain a title; he would have honors and a great position to match his great fortune. With this thought in his mind, he displayed great courage in one of our bloodiest battles in Germany, and was so badly wounded that he could no longer stay in the service. For a time it was feared that he might have to lose his leg, and he was forced to retire, with his pension indeed, but without the title of baron or any of the rewards which he had hoped for, and very likely would have won, if his name had not been Diard.

These events, together with his wound and his disappointed hopes, made a changed man of the late quartermaster. The Provençal's energy, wrought for a time to a fever pitch, suddenly deserted him. At first, however, his wife sustained his courage; his efforts, his bravery, and his ambition had given her some belief in her husband; and surely it behooved her, of all women, to play a woman's part, to be a tender consoler for the troubles of life.

Juana's words put fresh heart into the major. He went to live in Paris, determined to make a high position for himself in the administration; the quartermaster of the Sixth Line Regiment should be forgotten, and some day Madame Diard should wear a splendid title. His passion for his charming wife had made him quick to guess her inmost wishes. Juana did not speak of them, but he understood her; he was not loved as a man dreams of being loved—he knew it, and longed to be looked up to and loved and caressed. The luckless man anticipated happiness with a wife who was at all times so submissive and so gentle; but her gentleness and her submission meant nothing but that resignation to her fate which had given Juana to him. Resignation and religion, were these love? Diard could often have wished for a refusal instead of that wifely obedience; often he would have given his soul if Juana would but have deigned to weep upon his breast, and ceased to conceal her feelings with the smile that she wore proudly as a mask upon her face.

Many a man in his youth (for after a certain time we give up struggling) strives to triumph over an evil destiny that brings the thunder-clouds from time to time above the horizon of his life; and when he falls into the depths of misfortune, those unrequited struggles should be taken into account. Like many another, Diard tried all ways, and found all ways barred against him. His wealth enabled him to surround his wife with all the luxuries that can be enjoyed in Paris. She had a great mansion and vast drawing-rooms, and presided over one of those houses frequented by some few artists who are uncritical by nature, by a great many schemers, by the frivolous folk who are ready to go anywhere to be amused, and by certain men of fashion, attracted by Juana's beauty. Those who make themselves conspicuous in Paris must either conquer Paris or fall victims. Diard's character was not strong enough, nor compact enough, nor persistent enough to impress itself upon the society of a time when every one else was likewise bent upon reaching a high position. Ready-made social classifications are not improbably a great blessing, even for the people. Napoleon's "Memoirs" have informed us of the pains he was at to impose social conventions upon a court composed for the most part of subjects who had once been his equals. But Napoleon was a Corsican, Diard was a Provençal.

If the two men had been mentally equal—an islander is always a more complete human being than a man born and bred on the mainland ; and though Provence and Corsica lie between the same degrees of latitude, the narrow stretch of sea that keeps them apart is, in spite of man's inventions, a whole ocean that makes two different countries of them both.

From this false position, which Diard falsified yet further, grave misfortunes arose. Perhaps there is a useful lesson to be learned by tracing the chain of interdependent facts that imperceptibly brought about the catastrophe of the story.

In the first place, Parisian scoffers could not see the pictures that adorned the late quartermaster's mansion without a significant smile. The recently purchased masterpieces were all condemned by the unspoken slur cast upon the pictures that had been the spoils of war in Spain ; by this slur, self-love avenged itself for the involuntary offense of Diard's wealth. Juana understood the meaning of some of the ambiguous compliments in which the French excel. Acting upon her advice, therefore, her husband sent the Spanish pictures back to Taragona. But the world of Paris, determined to put the worst construction on the matter, said, "That fellow Diard is shrewd; he has sold his pictures," and the good folk continued to believe that the paintings which still hung on the walls had not been honestly come by. Then some ill-natured women inquired how a Diard had come to marry a young wife so rich and so beautiful. Comments followed, endless absurdities were retailed, after the manner of Paris. If Juana rose above it all, even above the scandal, and met with nothing but the respect due to her pure and devout life, that respect ended with her, and was not accorded to her husband. Her shining eyes glanced over her rooms, and her woman's clear-sightedness brought her nothing but pain. And yet—the disparagement was quite explicable. Military men, for all the virtues with which romance endows them, could not forgive the quondam quartermaster for his wealth and his determination to cut a figure in Paris, and for that very reason.

There is a world in Paris that lies between the farthest house in the Faubourg Saint-Germain on the one hand, and the last mansion in the Rue Saint-Lazare on the other; between the rising ground of the Luxembourg and the heights of Montmartre; a world that dresses and gossips, dresses to go out, and goes out to gossip; a world of petty and great airs; a world of mean and poor ambitions, masquerading in insolence; a world of envy and of fawning arts. It is made up of gilded rank, and rank that has lost its gilding, of young and old, of nobility of the fourth century and titles of yesterday, of those who laugh at the expense of a *parvenu*, and others who fear to be contaminated by him, of men eager for the downfall of a power, though none the less they will bow the knee to it if it holds its own; and all these ears hear, and all these tongues repeat, and all these minds are informed in the course of an evening of the birthplace, education, and previous history of each new aspirant for its high-places. If there is no High Court of Justice in this exalted sphere, it boasts the most ruthless of *procureurs-généraux*, an intangible public opinion that dooms the victim and carries out the sentence, that accuses and brands the delinquent. Do not hope to hide anything from this tribunal, tell everything at once yourself, for it is determined to go to the bottom of everything, and knows everything. Do not seek to understand the mysterious operation by which intelligence is flashed from place to place, so that a story, a scandal, or a piece of news is known everywhere simultaneously in the twinkling of an eye. Do not ask who set the machinery in motion; it is a social mystery, no observer can do more than watch its phenomena, and its working is rapid beyond belief. A single example shall suffice. The murder of the Duc de Berri, at the opera, was known in the farthest part of the Ile Saint-Louis ten minutes after the crime was committed. The opinion of the Sixth Regiment of the line concerning Diard permeated this world of Paris on the very evening of his first ball.

So Diard himself could accomplish nothing. Henceforward his wife, and his wife alone, might make a way for him. Strange portent of a strange civilization! If a man can do nothing by himself in Paris, he has still some chance of rising in the world if his wife is young and clever. There are women, weak to all appearance, invalids who, without rising from their sofas or leaving their rooms, make their influence felt in society, and, by bringing countless secret springs into play, gain for their husbands the position which their own vanity desires. But Juana, whose girlhood had been spent in the quaint simplicity of the narrow house in Taragona, knew nothing of the corruption, the baseness, or the opportunities afforded by life in Paris; she looked out upon it with girlish curiosity, and learned from it no worldly wisdom save the lessons taught her by her wounded pride and susceptibilities. Juana, moreover, possessed the quick instinct of a maiden heart, and was as swift to anticipate an impression as a sensitive plant. The lonely girl had become a woman all at once. She saw that if she endeavored to compel society to honor her husband, it must be after the Spanish fashion, of telling a lie, carbine in hand. Did not her own constant watchfulness tell her how necessary her manifold precautions were? A gulf yawned for Diard between the failure to make himself respected and the opposite danger of being respected but too much. Then as suddenly as before, when she had foreseen her life, there came a revelation of the world to her; she beheld on all sides the vast extent of an irreparable misfortune. Then came the tardy recognition of her husband's peculiar weaknesses, his total unfitness to play the parts he had assigned to himself, the incoherency of his ideas, the mental incapacity to grasp this society as a whole, or to comprehend the subtleties that are all-important there. Would not tact effect more for a man in his position than force of character? But the tact that never fails is perhaps the greatest of all forces.

So far from effacing the blot upon the Diard scutcheon, the major was at no little pains to make matters worse. For instance, as it had not occurred to him that the Empire was passing through a phase that required careful study, he tried, though he was only a major, to obtain an appointment as prefect. At that time almost every one believed in Napoleon; his favor had increased the importance of every post. The prefectures, those empires on a small scale, could only be filled by men with great names, by the gentlemen of the household of his majesty the Emperor and King. The prefects by this time were Grand Viziers. These minions of the great man laughed at Major Diard's artless ambitions, and he was fain to solicit a sub-prefecture. His modest pretensions were ludicrously disproportioned to his vast wealth. After this ostentatious display of luxury, how could the millionaire leave the royal splendors of his house in Paris for Issoudun or Savenay? Would it not be a descent unworthy of his fortunes? Juana, who had come to understand our laws and the manners and customs of our administration, too late enlightened her husband. Diard, in his desperation, went begging to all the powers that be; but Diard met with nothing but rebuffs, no way was open to him. Then people judged him as the government had judged him, and passed his own verdict upon himself. Diard had been badly wounded on the field of battle, and Diard had not been decorated. The quartermaster, who had gained wealth, but no esteem, found no place under the government, and society quite logically refused him the social position to which he had aspired. In short, in his own house the unfortunate man continually felt that his wife was his superior. He had come to feel it in spite of the "velvet glove" (if the metaphor is not too bold) that disguised from her husband the supremacy that astonished her herself, while she felt humiliated by it. It produced its effect upon Diard at last.

A man who plays a losing game like this is bound to lose heart, and to grow either a greater or a worse man for it; Diard's courage, or his passion, was sure to diminish, after repeated blows dealt to his self-love, and he made mistake upon mistake. From the first everything had been against him, even his own habits and his own character. The vices and virtues of the impulsive Provençal were equally patent. The fibres of his nature were like harp-strings, and every old friend had a place in his heart. He was as prompt to relieve a comrade in abject poverty as the distress of another of high rank; in short, he never forgot a friend, and filled his gilded rooms with poor wretches down on their luck. Beholding which things, the general of the old stamp (a species that will soon be extinct) was apt to greet Diard in an off-hand fashion, and address him with a patronizing, "Well, my dear fellow!" when they met. If the generals of the Empire concealed their insolence beneath an assumption of a soldier's bluff familiarity, the few people of fashion whom Diard met showed him the polite and well-bred contempt against which a self-made man is nearly always powerless. Diard's behavior and speech, like his half-Italian accent, his dress, and everything about him, combined to lower him in the eyes of ordinary minds; for the unwritten code of good manners and good taste is a binding tradition that only the greatest power can shake off. Such is the way of the world.

These details give a very imperfect idea of Juana's martyrdom. The pangs were endured one by one. Every social species contributed its pin-prick, and hers was a soul that would have welcomed dagger-thrusts in preference. It was intolerable painful to watch Diard receiving insults that he did not feel, insults that Juana must feel though they were not meant for her. A final and dreadful illumination came at last for her; it cast a light upon the future, and she knew all the sorrows that it held in store. She had seen already that her husband was quite incapable of mounting to the highest rung of the social ladder, but now she saw the inevitable depths to which he must fall when he should lose heart; and then a feeling of pity for Diard came over her.

The future that lay before her was very dark. Juana had never ceased to feel an overhanging dread of some evil, though whence it should come she knew not. This presentiment haunted her inmost soul, as contagion hovers in the air; but she was able to hide her anguish with smiles. She had reached the point when she no longer thought of herself.

Juana used her influence to persuade Diard to renounce his social ambitions, pointing out to him as a refuge the peaceful and gracious life of the domestic hearth. All their troubles came from without; why should they not shut out the world? In his own home Diard would find peace and respect; he should reign there. She felt that she had courage enough to undertake the trying task of making him happy, this man dissatisfied with himself. Her energy had increased with the difficulties of her life; she had within her the heroic spirit needed by a woman in her position, and felt the stirrings of those religious aspirations which are cherished by the guardian angel appointed to watch over a Christian soul, for this poetic superstitious fancy is an allegory that expresses the idea of the two natures within us.

Diard renounced his ambitions, closed his house, and literally shut himself up in it, if it is allowable to make use of so familiar a phrase. But therein lay the danger. Diard was one of those centrifugal souls who must always be moving about. The luckless soldier's turn of mind was such that no sooner had he arrived in a place than this restless instinct forthwith drove him to depart. Natures of this kind have but one end in life; they must come and go unceasingly like the wheels spoken of in the Scriptures. It may have been that Diard would fain have escaped from himself. He was not weary of Juana; she had given him no cause to blame her, but with possession his passion for her had grown less absorbing, and his character asserted itself again.

Thenceforward his moments of despondency came more frequently; he gave way more often to his quick southern temper. The more virtuous and irreproachable a woman is, the more a man delights to find her in fault, if only to demonstrate his titular superiority; but if by chance she compels his respect, he must needs fabricate faults, and so between the husband and wife nothings are exaggerated and trifles become mountains. But Juana's meek patience and gentleness, untinged with the bitterness that women can infuse into their submission, gave no handle to this fault-finding of set purpose, the most unkind of all. Hers was, moreover, one of those noble natures for whom it is impossible to fail in duty; her pure and holy life shone in those eyes with the martyr's expression in them that haunted the imagination. Diard first grew weary, then he chafed, and ended by finding this lofty virtue an intolerable yoke. His wife's discretion left him no room for violent sensations, and he craved excitement. Thousands of such dramas lie hidden away in the souls of men and women, beneath the uninteresting surface of apparently simple and commonplace lives. It is difficult to choose an example from among the many scenes that last for so short a time, and leave such ineffaceable traces in a life; scenes that are almost always precursors of the calamity that is written in the destiny of most marriages. Still one scene may be described, because it sharply marks the first beginnings of a misunderstanding between these two, and may in some degree explain the catastrophe of the story.

Juana had two children; luckily for her, they were both boys. The oldest was born seven months after her marriage; he was named Juan, and was like his mother. Two years after they came to Paris her second son was born; he resembled Diard and Juana, but he was more like Diard, whose names he bore. Juana had given the most tender care to little Francisco. For the five years of his life his mother was absorbed in this child; he had more than his share of kisses and caresses and playthings; and besides and beyond all this, his mother's penetrating eyes watched him continually. Juana studied his character even in the cradle, noticing heedfully his cries and movements, that she might direct his education. Juana seemed to have but that one child. The Provençal, seeing that Juan was almost neglected, began to take notice of the older boy. He would not ask himself whether the little one was the offspring of the short-lived love affair to which he owed Juana, and by a piece of rare flattery made of Juan his Benjamin. Of all the race inheritance of passions which preyed upon her, Mme. Diard gave way but to one—a mother's love; she loved her children with the same vehemence and intensity that La Marana had shown for her child in the first part of this story; but to this love she added a gracious delicacy of feeling, a quick and keen comprehension of the social virtues that it had been her pride to practice, in which she had found her recompense. The secret thought of the conscientious fulfillment of the duties of motherhood had been a crude element of poetry that left its impress on La Marana's life; but Juana could be a mother openly; it was her hourly consolation. Her own mother had been virtuous as other women are criminal, by stealth; she had stolen her illicit happiness, she had not known all the sweetness of secure possession. But Juana, whose life of virtue was as dreary as her mother's life of sin, knew every hour the ineffable joys for which that mother had longed in vain. For her, as for La Marana, motherhood summed up all earthly affection, and both the Maranas from opposite causes had but this one comfort in their desolation. Perhaps Juana's love was the stronger, because, shut out from all other love, her children became all in all to her, and because a noble passion has this in common with vice: it grows by what it feeds upon. The mother and the gambler are alike insatiable.

Juana was touched by the generous pardon extended over Juan's head by Diard's fatherly affection, and thenceforward the relations between husband and wife were changed; the interest which Diard's Spanish wife had taken in him from a sense of duty only became a deep and sincere feeling. Had he been less inconsequent in his life, if fickleness and spasmodic changes of feeling on his part had not quenched that flicker of timid but real sympathy, Juana must surely have loved him; but, unluckily, Diard's character belonged to the quick-witted southern type, that has no continuity in its ideas; such men will be capable of heroic actions over night, and sink into nonentities on the morrow; often they are made to suffer for their virtues, often their worst defects contribute to their success; and for the rest, they are great when their good qualities are pressed into the service of an unflagging will. For two years Diard had been a prisoner in his home, a prisoner bound by the sweetest of all chains. He lived, almost against his will, beneath the influence of a wife who kept him amused, and was always bright and cheerful for him, a wife who devoted all her powers of coquetry to beguiling him into the ways of virtue; and yet all her ingenuity could not deceive him, and he knew this was not love.

Just about that time a murder caused a great sensation in Paris. A captain of the armies of the Republic had killed a woman in a paroxysm of debauchery. Diard told the story to Juana when he came home to dine. The officer, he said, had taken his own life to avoid the ignominy of a trial and the infamous death of a criminal. At first Juana could not understand the reason for his conduct, and her husband was obliged to explain to her the admirable provision of the French law, which takes no proceedings against the dead.

"But, papa, didn't you tell us the other day that the King can pardon anybody?" asked Francisco.

"The King can only grant *life*," said Juan, nettled.

Diard and Juana watched this little scene with very different feeling. The tears of happiness in Juana's eyes as she glanced at her oldest boy let her husband see with fatal clearness into the real secrets of that hitherto inscrutable heart. Her older boy was Juana's own child; Juana knew his nature; she was sure of him and of his future; she worshiped him, and her great love was a secret known only to her child and to God. Juan, in his secret heart, gladly endured his mother's sharp speeches. What if she seemed to frown upon him in the presence of his father and brother, when she showered passionate kisses upon him when they were alone? Francisco was Diard's child, and Juana's care meant that she wished to check the growth of his father's faults in him and to develop his good qualities.

Juana, unconscious that she had spoken too plainly in that glance, took little Francisco on her knee; and, her sweet voice faltering somewhat with the gladness that Juan's answer had caused her, gave the younger boy the teaching suited to his childish mind.

"His training requires great care," the father said, speaking to Juana.

"Yes," she answered simply.

"But *Juan!*"

The tone in which the two words were uttered startled Mme. Diard. She looked up at her husband.

"Juan was born perfection," he added, and having thus delivered himself, he sat down and looked gloomily at his wife. She was silent, so he went on, "You love one of *your* children better than the other."

"You know it quite well," she said.

"No!" returned Diard. "Until this moment I did not know which of them you loved the most."

"But neither of them has as yet caused me any sorrow," she answered quickly.

"No, but which of them has given you more joys?" he asked still more quickly.

"I have not kept any reckoning of them."

"Women are very deceitful!" cried Diard. "Do you dare to tell me that Juan is not the darling of your heart?"

"And if he were," she said, with gentle dignity, "do you mean that it would be a misfortune?"

"You have never loved me! If you had chosen, I might have won kingdoms for you with my sword. You know all that I have tried to do, sustained by one thought—a longing that you might care for me. Ah! if you had but loved me——"

"A woman who loves," said Juana, "lives in solitude far from the world. Is not that what we are doing?"

"Oh! I know, Juana, that you are never in the wrong."

The words, spoken with such intense bitterness, brought about a coolness between them that lasted the rest of their lives.

On the morrow of that fatal day, Diard sought out one of his old cronies, and with him sought distraction at the gaming-table. Unluckily, he won a great deal of money, and he began to play regularly. Little by little he slipped back into his old dissipated life. After a short time he no longer dined at home. A few months were spent in the enjoyment of the first pleasures of freedom; he made up his mind that he would not part with it, left the large apartments of the house to his wife, and took up his abode separately on the *entresol*. By the end of the year Diard and Juana only met once a day—at breakfast-time.

In a few words, like all gamblers, he had runs of good and bad luck; but as he was reluctant to touch his capital, he wished to have entire control of their income, and his wife accordingly ceased to take any part in the management of the household economy. Mistrust had succeeded to the boundless confidence that he had once placed in her. As to money matters, which had formerly been arranged by both husband and wife, he adopted the plan of a monthly allowance for her own expenses; they settled the amount of it together in the last of the confidential talks that form one of the most attractive charms of marriage.

The barrier of silence between two hearts is a real divorce, accomplished on the day when husband and wife say *we* no longer. When that day came, Juana knew that she was no longer a wife, but a mother; she was not unhappy, and did not seek to guess the reason of the misfortune. It was a great pity. Children consolidate, as it were, the lives of their parents, and the life that her husband led apart was to weave sadness and anguish for others as well as for Juana. Diard lost no time in making use of his newly-regained liberty; he played high, and lost and won enormous sums. He was a good and bold player, and gained a great reputation. The respect which he had failed to win in society in the days of the Empire was accorded now to the wealth that was risked upon a green table, to a talent for all and any of the games of chance of that period. Ambassadors, financiers, men with large fortunes, jaded pleasure-seekers in quest of excitement and extreme sensations admired Diard's play at their clubs; they rarely asked him to their houses, but they all played with him.

Diard became the fashion. Once or twice during the winter his independent spirit led him to give a fête to return the courtesies that he had received, and by glimpses Juana saw something of society again; there was a brief return of balls and banquets, of luxury and brilliantly-lighted rooms;

but all these things she regarded as a sort of duty levied upon her happiness and solitude.

The queen of these high festivals appeared in them like some creature fallen from an unknown world. Her simplicity that nothing had spoiled, a certain maidenliness of soul with which the changed conditions of her life had invested her, her beauty, her unaffected modesty, won sincere admiration. But Juana saw few women among her guests; and it was plain to her mind that if her husband had ordered his life differently without taking her into his confidence, he had not risen in the esteem of the world.

Diard was not always lucky. In three years he had squandered three-fourths of his fortune; but he drew from his passion for gambling sufficient energy to satisfy it. He had a large circle of acquaintance, and was hand and glove with certain swindlers on the Stock Exchange—gentry who, since the Revolution, have established the principle that robbery on a large scale is a mere *peccadillo*, transferring to the language of the counting-house the brazen epithets of the license of the eighteenth century.

Diard became a speculator, engaged in the peculiar kinds of business described as "shady" in the slang of the Palais. He managed to get hold of poor wretches ignorant of commercial red-tape, and weary of everlasting proceedings in liquidation; he would buy up their claims on the debtor's estate for a small sum, arrange the matter with the assignees in the course of an evening, and divide the spoil with the latter. When liquifiable debts were not to be found, he looked out for floating debts; he unearthed and revived claims in abeyance in Europe and America and uncivilized countries. When at the Restoration the debts incurred by the princes, the Republic, and the Empire were all paid, he took commissions on loans, on contracts for public works and enterprises of all kinds. In short, he committed legal robbery, like many another carefully masked delinquent behind the scenes in the theatre of politics. Such thefts, if perpetrated by the light of a street lamp, would send the luckless offender to the hulks; but there is a virtue in the glitter of chandeliers and gilded ceilings that absolves the crimes committed beneath them.

Diard forestalled and regrated sugars; he sold places; to him belongs the credit of the invention of the "warming-pan;" he installed lay-figures in lucrative posts that must be held for a time to secure still better positions. Then he fell to meditating on bounties; he studied the loop-holes of the law, and carried on contraband trades against which no provision had been made. This traffic in high-places may be briefly described as a sort of commission agency; he received "so much per cent." on the purchase of fifteen votes which passed in a single night from the benches on the left to the benches on the right of the legislative chamber. In these days such things are neither misdemeanors nor felony; exploiting industry, the art of government, financial genius—these are the names by which they are called.

Public opinion put Diard in the pillory, where more than one clever man stood already to keep him company; there, indeed, you will find the aristocracy of this kind of talent—the upper chamber of civilized rascality.

Diard, therefore, was no commonplace gambler, no vulgar spendthrift who ends his career, in melodramas, as a beggar. Above a certain social altitude that kind of gambler is not to be found. In these days a bold scoundrel of this kind will die gloriously in the harness of vice in all the trappings of success: he will blow out his brains in a coach and six, and all that has been intrusted to him vanishes with him. Diard's talent determined him not to buy remorse too cheaply, and he joined this privileged class. He learned all the springs of government, made himself acquainted with all the secrets and the weaknesses of men in office, and held his own in the fiery furnace into which he had cast himself.

Mme. Diard knew nothing of the infernal life that her husband led. She was well content to be neglected, and did not ponder overmuch the reasons for his neglect. Her time was too well filled. She devoted all the money that she had to the education of her children; a very clever tutor was engaged for them, besides various masters. She meant to make men of her boys, to develop in them the faculty of reasoning clearly, but not at the expense of their imaginative powers. Nothing affected her now save through her children, and her own colorless life depressed her no longer. Juan and Francisco were for her what children are for a time for many mothers—a sort of expansion of her own existence. Diard had come to be a mere accident in her life. Since Diard had ceased to be a father and the head of the family, nothing bound Juana to her husband any longer, save a regard for appearances demanded by social conventions; yet she brought up her children to respect their father, shadowy and unreal as that fatherhood had become; indeed, her husband's continual absence from home helped her to maintain the fiction of his high character. If Diard had lived in the house, all Juana's efforts must have been in vain. Her children were too quick and bright not to judge their father, and this process is a moral parricide.

At length, however, Juana's indifference changed to a feeling of dread. She felt that sooner or later her husband's manner of life must affect the children's future. Day by day that old presentiment of coming evil gathered definiteness and strength. On the rare occasions when Juana saw her husband, she would glance at his hollow cheeks, at his face grown haggard with the vigils he kept, and wrinkled with violent emotions; and Diard almost trembled before the clear, penetrating eyes. At such times her husband's assumed gaiety alarmed her even more than the dark look that his face wore in repose, when for a moment he happened to forget the part that he was playing. He feared his wife as the criminal fears the headsman. Juana saw in him a disgrace on her children's name; and Diard dreaded her, she was like some passionless Vengeance, a Justice with unchanging brows, with the arm that should one day strike always suspended above him.

One day, about fifteen years after his marriage, Diard found himself without resources. He owed a hundred thousand crowns, and was possessed of a bare hundred thousand francs. His mansion (all that he possessed beside ready money) was mortgaged beyond its value. A few more days, and the prestige of enormous wealth must fade; and when those days of grace had expired, no helping hand would be stretched out, no purse would be open for him. Nothing but unlooked-for luck could save him now from the slough into which he must fall; and he would but sink the deeper in it, men would scorn him the more because for a while they had estimated him at more than his just value.

Very opportunely, therefore, he learned that with the beginning of the season diplomatists and foreigners of distinction flocked to watering-places in the Pyrenees, that play ran high at these resorts, and that the visitors were doubtless well able to pay their losings. So he determined to set out at once for the Pyrenees. He had no mind to leave his wife in Paris; some of his creditors might enlighten her as to his awkward position, and he wished to keep it secret, so he took Juana and the two children. He would not allow the tutor to go with them, and made some difficulties about Juana's maid, who, with a single manservant, composed their traveling suite. His tone was curt and peremptory; his energy seemed to have returned to him. This hasty journey sent a shiver of dread to Juana's soul; her penetration was at fault, she could not imagine the why and wherefore of their leaving Paris. Her husband seemed to be in high spirits on the way; and during the time spent together perforce in the traveling carriage, he took more and more notice of the children, and was more kindly to the children's mother. And yet—every day brought new and dark forebodings for Juana, the forebodings of a mother's heart. These inward warnings, even when there is no apparent reason for them, are seldom vain, and the veil that hides the future grows thin for a mother's eyes.

Diard took a house, not large, but very nicely furnished, situated in one of the quietest parts of Bordeaux. It happened to be a corner house with a large garden, surrounded on three sides by streets, and on the fourth by the wall of a neighboring dwelling. Diard paid the rent in advance, and installed his wife and family, leaving Juana fifty louis, a sum barely sufficient to meet the housekeeping expenses for three months. Mme. Diard made no comment on this unwonted niggardliness. When her husband told her that he was about to go to the Baths, and that she was to remain in Bordeaux, she made up her mind that the children should learn the Spanish and Italian languages thoroughly, and that they should read with her the great masterpieces of either tongue.

With this object in view, Juana's life should be retired and simple, and in consequence her expenses would be few. Her own woman waited upon them; and, to simplify the housekeeping, she arranged on the morrow of Diard's departure to have their meals sent in from a restaurant. Everything was provided for until her husband's return, and she had no money left. Her amusements must consist in occasional walks with the children. She was now a woman of thirty-three; her beauty had developed to its fullest extent, she was in the full splendor of her maturity. Scarcely had she appeared in Bordeaux before people talked of nothing but the lovely Spanish lady. She received a first love-letter, and thenceforth confined her walks to her own garden.

At first Diard had a run of luck at the Baths. He won three hundred thousand francs in two months; but it never occurred to him to send any money to his wife, he meant to keep as large a sum as possible by him, and to play for yet higher stakes. Towards the end of the last month the Marquis di Montefiore came to the Baths, preceded by a reputation for a fine figure and great wealth, for the match that he had made with an English lady of family, and most of all for a passion for gambling. Diard waited for his old comrade in arms, to add the spoils to his winnings. A gambler with something like four hundred thousand francs at his back can command most things; Diard felt confident in his luck, and renewed his acquaintance with Montefiore. That gentleman received him coldly, but they played together, and Diard lost everything.

"Montefiore, my dear fellow," said the sometime quartermaster, after a turn round the room in which he had ruined himself, "I owe you a hundred thousand francs; but I have left my money at Bordeaux, where my wife is staying."

As a matter of fact, Diard had notes for the amount in his pockets at that moment; but, with the self-possession of a man accustomed to take in all the possibilities of a situation at a glance, he still hoped something from the incalculable chances of the gaming-table. Montefiore had expressed a desire to see something of Bordeaux; and if Diard were to settle at once with him, he would have nothing left, and could not have his "revenge." A "revenge" will sometimes more than make good all previous losses. All these burning hopes depended on the answer that the Marquis might give.

"Let it stand, my dear fellow," said Montefiore; "we will go to Bordeaux together. I am rich enough now in all conscience; why should I take an old comrade's money?"

Three days later, Diard and the Italian were at Bordeaux. Montefiore offered the Provençal his revenge. In the course of an evening, which Diard began by paying down the hundred thousand francs, he lost two hundred thousand more upon parole. He was as light-hearted over his losses as if he could swim in gold. It was eleven o'clock, and a glorious night, surely Montefiore must wish to breathe the fresh air under the open sky and to take a walk to cool down a little after the excitement of play; Diard suggested that the Italian should accompany him to his house and take a cup of tea there when the money was paid over.

"But Mme. Diard!" queried Montefiore.

"Pshaw!" answered the Provençal.

They went downstairs together; but, before leaving the house, Diard went into the dining-room, asked for a glass of water, and walked about the room as he waited for it. In this way he managed to secrete a tiny steel knife with a handle of mother-of-pearl, such as is used at dessert for fruit; the thing had not yet been put away in its place.

"Where do you live?" asked Montefiore, as they crossed the court; "I must leave word, so as to have the carriage sent round for me."

Diard gave minute directions.

"Of course, I am perfectly safe as long as I am with you, you see," said Montefiore in a low voice, as he took Diard's arm; "but if I came back by myself, and some scamp were to follow me, I should be worth killing."

"Then have you money about you?"

"Oh! next to nothing," said the cautious Italian, "only my winnings. But they would make a pretty fortune for a penniless rascal; he might take brevet rank as an honest man afterwards for the rest of his life, that I know."

Diard took the Italian into a deserted street. He had noticed the gateway of a single house in it at the end of a sort of avenue of trees, and that there were high dark walls on either side. Just as they reached the end of this road he had the audacity to ask his friend, in soldierly fashion, to walk on. Montefiore understood Diard's meaning, and turned to go with him. Scarcely had they set foot in the shadow, when Diard sprang like a tiger upon the Marquis, tripped him up, boldly set his foot on his victim's throat, and plunged the knife again and again into his heart, till the blade snapped off short in his body. Then he searched Montefiore, took his money, his pocket-book, and everything that the Marquis had.

But though Diard had set about his work in a frenzy that left him perfectly clear-headed, and completed it with the deftness of a pickpocket; though he had taken his victim adroitly by surprise, Montefiore had had time to shriek "Murder!" once or twice, a shrill, far-reaching cry that must have sent a thrill of horror through many sleepers, and his dying groans were fearful to hear.

Diard did not know that even as they turned into the avenue a crowd of people returning home from the theatre had reached the upper end of the street. They had heard Montefiore's dying cries, though the Provençal had tried to stifle the sounds, never relaxing the pressure of his foot upon the murdered man's throat until at last they ceased.

The high walls still echoed with dying groans which guided the crowd to the spot whence they came. The sound of many feet filled the avenue and rang through Diard's brain. The murderer did not lose his head; he came out from under the trees, and walked very quietly along the street, as if he had been drawn thither by curiosity and saw that he had come too late to be of any use. He even turned to make sure of the distance that separated him from the new-comers, and saw them all rush into the avenue, save one man, who not unnaturally stood still to watch Diard's movements.

"There he lies! There he lies!" shouted voices from the avenue. They had caught sight of Montefiore's dead body in front of the great house. The gateway was shut fast, and after diligent search they could not find the murderer in the alley.

As soon as he heard the shout, Diard knew that he had got the start; he seemed to have the strength of a lion in him and the fleetness of a stag; he began to run, nay, he flew. He saw, or fancied that he saw, a second crowd at the other end of the road, and darted down a side street. But even as he fled, windows were opened, and rows of heads were thrust out, lights and shouting issued from ever door; to Diard, running for dear life, it seemed as if he were rushing through a tumult of cries and swaying lights. As he fled straight along the road before him, his legs stood him in such good stead that he left the crowd behind; but he could not keep out of sight of the windows, nor avoid the watchful eyes that traversed the length and breadth of a street faster than he could fly.

In the twinkling of an eye, soldiers, gendarmes, and householders were all astir. Some in their zeal had gone to wake up commissaries of police, others stood by the dead body. The alarm spread out into the suburbs in the direction of the fugitive (whom it followed like a conflagration from street to street) and into the heart of the town, where it reached the authorities. Diard heard as in a dream the hurrying feet, the yells of a whole horror-stricken city. But his ideas were still clear; he still preserved his presence of mind, and he rubbed his hands against the walls as he ran.

At last he reached the garden wall of his own house. He thought that he had thrown his pursuers off the scent. The place was perfectly silent save for the far-off murmur of the city, scarcely louder there than the sound of the sea. He dipped his hands into a runnel of clear water and drank. Then, looking about him, he saw a heap of loose stones by the roadside, and hastened to bury his spoils beneath it, acting on some dim notion such as crosses a criminal's mind when he has not yet found a consistent tale to account for his actions, and hopes to establish his innocence by lack of proofs against him. When this was accomplished, he tried to look serene and calm, forced a smile, and knocked gently at his own door, hoping that no one had seen him. He looked up at the house front and saw a light in his wife's windows. And then in his agitation of spirit visions of Juana's peaceful life rose before him; he saw her sitting there in the candlelight with her children on either side of her, and the vision smote his brain like a blow from a hammer. The waiting-woman opened the door, Diard entered, and hastily shut it to again. He dared to breathe more freely, but he remembered that he was covered with perspiration, and sent the maid up to Juana, while he stayed below in the darkness. He wiped his face with a handkerchief and set his clothes in order, as a coxcomb smooths his coat before calling upon a pretty woman; then for a moment he stood in the moonlight examining his hands; he passed them over his face, and with unspeakable joy found that there was no trace of blood upon him, doubtless his victim's wounds had bled internally.

He went up to Juana's room, and his manner was as quiet and composed as if he had come home after the theatre, to sleep. As he climbed the stairs, he could think over his position, and summed it up in a phrase—he must leave the house and reach the harbor. These ideas did not cross his brain in words; he saw them written in letters of fire upon the darkness. Once down at the harbor, he could lie in hiding during the day, and return at night for the treasure; then he would creep with it like a rat into the hold of some vessel, and leave the port, no one suspecting that he was on board. For all these things money was wanted in the first place. And he had nothing. The waiting-woman came with a light.

"Félicie," he said, "do you not hear that noise? people are shouting in the street. Go and find out what it is and let me know——"

His wife in her white dressing-gown was sitting at a table, reading Cervantes in Spanish with Francisco and Juan; the two children's eyes followed the text while their mother read aloud. All three of them stopped and looked up at Diard, who stood with his hands in his pockets, surprised perhaps by the surroundings, the peaceful scene, the fair faces of the woman and the children in the softly-lit room. It was like a living picture of a Madonna with her son and the little Saint John on either side.

"Juana, I have something to say to you."

"What is it?" she asked. In her husband's wan and sallow face she read the news of this calamity that she had expected daily; it had come at last.

"Nothing, but I should like to speak to you—to you, quite alone," and he fixed his eyes on the two little boys.

"Go to your room, my darlings, and go to bed," said Juana. "Say your prayers without me."

The two boys went away in silence, with the uninquisitive obedience of children who have been well brought up.

"Dear Juana," Diard began in coaxing tones, "I left you very little money, and I am very sorry for it now. Listen, since I relieved you of the cares of your household by giving you an allowance, perhaps you may have saved a little money, as all women do?"

"No," answered Juana, "I have nothing. You did not allow anything for the expenses of the children's education. I am not reproaching you at all, dear; I only remind you that you forgot about it, to explain how it is that I have no money. All that you gave me I spent on lessons and masters——"

"That will do!" Diard broke in. "*Sacré tonnerre!* time is precious. Have you no jewels?"

"You know quite well that I never wear them."

"Then there is not a *sou* in the house!" cried Diard, like a man bereft of his senses.

"Why do you cry out?" she asked.

"Juana," he began, "I have just killed a man!"

Juana rushed to the children's room, and returned, shutting all the doors after her.

"Your sons must not hear a word of this," she said; "but whom can you have fought with?"

"Montefiore," he answered.

"Ah!" she said, and a sigh broke from her; "he is the one man whom you had a right to kill——"

"There were plenty of reasons why he should die by my hand. But let us lose no time. Money, I want money, in God's name! They may be on my track. We did not fight, Juana, I—I killed him."

"Killed him!" she cried. "But how——?"

"Why, how does one kill a man? He had robbed me of all I had at play; and I have taken it back again. Juana, since we have no money, you might go now, while everything is quiet, and look for my money under the heap of stones at the end of the road; you know the place."

"Then," said Juana, "you have robbed him."

"What business is it of yours? Fly I must, mustn't I? Have you any money?—— They are after me!"

"Who?"

"The authorities.'

Juana left the room, and came back suddenly.

"Here," she cried, holding out a trinket, but standing at a distance from him; this is Doña Lagounia's cross. There are four rubies in it, and the stones are very valuable; so I have been told. Be quick, fly, fly—— why don't you go?"

"Félicie has not come back," he said in dull amazement. "Can they have arrested her?"

Juana dropped the cross on the edge of the table, and sprang towards the windows that looked out upon the street. Outside in the moonlight she saw a row of soldiers taking their places in absolute silence along the wall. She came back again; to all appearance she was perfectly calm.

"You have not a minute to lose," she said to her husband; "you must escape through the garden. Here is the key of the little door."

A last counsel of prudence led her, however, to give a glance over the garden. In the shadows under the trees she saw the silvery gleam of the metal rims of the gendarmes' caps. She even heard a vague murmur of a not far-distant crowd; sentinels were keeping back the people gathered together by curiosity at the further ends of the streets by which the house was approached.

As a matter of fact, Diard had been seen from the windows of the houses; the maidservant had been frightened, and afterwards arrested; and, acting on this information, the military and the crowd had soon blocked the ends of the streets that lay on two sides of the house. A dozen gendarmes, coming off duty at the theatres, were posted outside; others had climbed the wall, and were searching the garden, a proceeding authorized by the serious nature of the crime.

"Monsieur," said Juana, "it is too late. The whole town is aroused."

Diard rushed from window to window, with the wild recklessness of a bird that dashes frantically against every pane. Juana stood absorbed in her thoughts.

"Where can I hide?" he asked.

He looked at the chimney, and Juana stared at the two empty chairs. To her it seemed only a moment since her children were sitting there. Just at that moment the gate opened, and the courtyard echoed with the sound of many footsteps.

"Juana, dear Juana, for pity's sake, tell me what to do."

"I will tell you," she said; "I will save you."

"Ah! you will be my good angel!"

Again Juana returned with one of Diard's pistols; she held it out to him, and turned her head away. Diard did not take it. Juana heard sounds from the courtyard; they had brought in the dead body of the Marquis to confront the murderer. She came away from the window and looked at Diard; he was white and haggard; his strength failed him; he made as if he would sink into a chair.

"For your children's sake," she said, thrusting the weapon into his hands.

"IS THAT M. DIARD."

"But, my dear Juana, my little Juana, do you really believe that——? Juana, is there such need of haste?—— I would like to kiss you before——"

The gendarmes were on the stairs. Then Juana took up the pistol, held it at Diard's head; with a firm grasp on his throat she held him tightly in spite of his cries, fired, and let the weapon fall to the ground.

The door was suddenly flung open at that moment. The public prosecutor, followed by a magistrate and his clerk, a doctor, and the gendarmes, all the instruments of man's justice, appeared upon the scene.

"What do you want?" she asked.

"Is that M. Diard?" answered the public prosecutor, pointing to the body lying bent double upon the floor.

"Yes, monsieur."

"Your dress is covered with blood, madame——"

"Do you not understand how it is?" asked Juana.

She went over to the little table and sat down there, and took up the volume of Cervantes; her face was colorless; she strove to control her inward nervous agitation.

"Leave the room," said the public prosecutor to the gendarmes. He made a sign to the magistrate and the doctor, and they remained.

"Madame, under the circumstances, we can only congratulate you on your husband's death. If he was carried away by passion, at any rate he has died like a soldier, and it is vain for justice to pursue him now. Yet little as we may desire to intrude upon you at such a time, the law obliges us to inquire into a death by violence. Permit us to do our duty."

"May I change my dress?" she asked, laying down the volume.

"Yes, madame, but you must bring it here. The doctor will doubtless require it——"

"It would be too painful to Mme. Diard to be present

while I go through my task," said the doctor, understanding the public prosecutor's suspicions. "Will you permit her, gentlemen, to remain in the adjoining room?"

The two functionaries approved the kindly doctor's suggestion, and Félicie went to her mistress. Then the magistrate and the public prosecutor spoke together for a while in a low voice. It is the unhappy lot of administrators of justice to be in duty bound to suspect everybody and everything. By dint of imagining evil motives, and every possible combination that they may bring about, so as to discover the truth that lurks beneath the most inconsistent actions, it is impossible but that their dreadful office should in course of time dry up the source of the generous impulses to which they may never yield. If the sensibilities of the surgeon who explores the mysteries of the body are blunted by degrees, what becomes of the inner sensibility of the judge who is compelled to probe the intricate recesses of the human conscience? Magistrates are the first victims of their profession; their progress is one perpetual mourning for their lost illusions, and the crimes that hang so heavily about the necks of criminals weigh no less upon their judges. An old man seated in the tribunal of justice is sublime; but do we not shudder to see a young face there? In this case the magistrate was a young man, and it was his duty to say to the public prosecutor, "Was the woman her husband's accomplice, do you think? Must we take proceedings? Ought she, in your opinion, to be examined?"

By way of reply, the public prosecutor shrugged his shoulders; apparently it was a matter of indifference.

"Montefiore and Diard," he remarked, "were a pair of notorious scamps. The servant-girl knew nothing about the crime. We need not go any further."

The doctor was making his examination of Diard's body, and dictating his report to the clerk. Suddenly he rushed into Juana's room.

"Madame——"

Juana, who had changed her blood-stained dress, confronted the doctor.

"You shot your husband, did you not?" he asked, bending to say the words in her ear.

"Yes, monsieur," the Spaniard answered.

"*And from circumstantial evidence*" (the doctor went on dictating) "*we conclude that the said Diard has taken his life by his own act.* Have you finished?" he asked the clerk after a pause.

"Yes," answered the scribe.

The doctor put his signature to the document. Juana glanced at him, and could scarcely keep back the tears that, for a moment, filled her eyes.

"Gentlemen," she said, and she turned to the public prosecutor, "I am a stranger, a Spaniard. I do not know the law. I know no one in Bordeaux. I entreat you to do me this kindness, will you procure me a passport for Spain?"

"One moment!" exclaimed the magistrate. "Madame, what has become of the sum of money that was stolen from the Marquis di Montefiore?"

"M. Diard said something about a heap of stones beneath which he had hidden it," she answered.

"Where?"

"In the street."

The two functionaries exchanged glances. Juana's involuntary start was sublime. She appealed to the doctor.

"Can they suspect me?" she said in his ear; "suspect *me* of some villainy? The heap of stones is sure to be somewhere at the end of the garden. Go yourself, I beg of you, and look for it and find the money."

The doctor went, accompanied by the magistrate, and found Montefiore's pocket-book.

Two days later Juana sold her golden cross to meet the expenses of the journey. As she went with her two children to the diligence in which they were about to travel to the Spanish frontier, some one called her name in the street. It was her dying mother, who was being taken to the hospital; she had caught a glimpse of her daughter through a slit in the curtains of the stretcher on which she lay. Juana bade them carry the stretcher into a gateway, and there for the last time the mother and daughter met. Low as their voices were while they spoke together, Juan overheard these words of farewell—

"Mother, die in peace; I have suffered for you all."

PARIS, *November*, 1832.

THE EXECUTIONER.

(*El Verdugo.*)

To Martinez de la Rosa.

MIDNIGHT had just sounded from the belfry tower of the little town of Menda. A young French officer, leaning over the parapet of the long terrace at the further end of the castle gardens, seemed to be unusually absorbed in deep thought for one who led the reckless life of a soldier; but it must be admitted that never was the hour, the scene, and the night more favorable to meditation.

The blue dome of the cloudless sky of Spain was overhead; he was looking out over the coy windings of a lovely valley lit by the uncertain starlight and the soft radiance of the moon. The officer, leaning against an orange tree in blossom, could also see, a hundred feet below him, the town of Menda, which seemed to nestle for shelter from the north wind at the foot of the crags on which the castle itself was built. He turned his head and caught sight of the sea; the moonlit waves made a broad frame of silver for the landscape.

There were lights in the castle windows. The mirth and movement of a ball, the sounds of the violins, the laughter of the officers and their partners in the dance were borne towards him and blended with the far-off murmur of the waves. The cool night had a certain bracing effect upon his frame, wearied as he had been by the heat of the day. He seemed to bathe in the air, made fragrant by the strong, sweet scent of flowers and of aromatic trees in the gardens.

The castle of Menda belonged to a Spanish grandee, who was living in it at that time with his family. All through the

evening the oldest daughter of the house had watched the
officer with such a wistful interest that the Spanish lady's
compassionate eyes might well have set the young Frenchman
dreaming. Clara was beautiful; and although she had three
brothers and a sister, the broad lands of the Marqués de
Légañès appeared to be sufficient warrant for Victor Marchand's belief that the young lady would have a splendid
dowry. But how could he dare to imagine that the most
fanatical believer in blue blood in all Spain would give his
daughter to the son of a grocer in Paris? Moreover, the
French were hated. It was because the Marquis had been
suspected of an attempt to raise the country in favor of
Ferdinand VII. that General G——, who governed the province, had stationed Victor Marchand's battalion in the little
town of Menda to overawe the neighboring districts which
received the Marqués de Légañès' word as law. A recent
despatch from Marshal Ney had given ground for fear that the
English might ere long effect a landing on the coast, and had
indicated the Marquis as being in correspondence with the
Cabinet in London.

In spite, therefore, of the welcome with which the Spaniards
had received Victor Marchand and his soldiers, that officer
was always on his guard. As he went towards the terrace,
where he had just surveyed the town and the districts confided
to his charge, he had been asking himself what construction
he ought to put upon the friendliness which the Marquis had
invariably shown him, and how to reconcile the apparent
tranquillity of the country with his general's uneasiness. But
a moment later these thoughts were driven from his mind by
the instinct of caution and very legitimate curiosity. It had
just struck him that there was a very fair number of lights in
the town below. Although it was the Feast of Saint James,
he himself had issued orders that very morning that all lights
must be put out in the town at the hour prescribed by military
regulations. The castle alone had been excepted in this

order. Plainly here and there he saw the gleam of bayonets, where his own men were at their accustomed posts; but in the town there was a solemn silence, and not a sign that the Spaniards had given themselves up to the intoxication of a festival. He tried vainly for a while to explain this breach of the regulations on the part of the inhabitants; the mystery seemed but so much the more obscure because he had left instructions with some of his officers to do police duty that night, and make the rounds of the town.

With the impetuosity of youth, he was about to spring through a gap in the wall preparatory to a rapid scramble down the rocks, thinking to reach a small guard-house at the nearest entrance into the town more quickly than by the beaten track, when a faint sound stopped him. He fancied that he could hear the light footstep of a woman along the graveled garden walk. He turned his head and saw no one; for one moment his eyes were dazzled by the wonderful brightness of the sea, the next he saw a sight so ominous that he stood stock-still with amazement, thinking that his senses must be deceiving him. The white moonbeams lighted the horizon, so that he could distinguish the sails of ships still a considerable distance out at sea. A shudder ran through him; he tried to persuade himself that this was some optical delusion brought about by chance effects of moonlight on the waves; and even as he made the attempt, a hoarse voice called to him by name. The officer glanced at the gap in the wall; saw a soldier's head slowly emerge from it, and knew the grenadier whom he had ordered to accompany him to the castle.

"Is that you, commandant?"

"Yes. What is it?" returned the young officer in a low voice. A kind of presentiment warned him to act cautiously.

"Those beggars down there are creeping about like worms; and, by your leave, I came as quickly as I could to report my little reconnoitring expedition."

"Go on," answered Victor Marchand.

"I have just been following a man from the castle who came round this way with a lantern in his hand. A lantern is a suspicious matter with a vengeance! I don't imagine that there was any need for that good Christian to be lighting tapers at this time of night. Says I to myself, 'They mean to gobble us up!' and I set myself to dogging his heels; and that is how I found out that there is a pile of faggots, sir, two or three steps away from here."

Suddenly a dreadful shriek rang through the town below, and cut the man short. A light flashed in the commandant's face, and the poor grenadier dropped down with a bullet through his head. Ten paces away a bonfire flared up like a conflagration. The sounds of music and laughter ceased all at once in the ballroom; the silence of death, broken only by groans, succeeded to the rhythmical murmur of the festival. Then the roar of cannon sounded from across the white plain of the sea.

A cold sweat broke out on the young officer's forehead. He had left his sword behind. He knew that his men had been murdered, and that the English were about to land. He knew that if he lived he would be dishonored; he saw himself summoned before a court-martial. For a moment his eyes measured the depth of the valley; the next, just as he was about to spring down, Clara's hand caught his.

"Fly!" she cried. "My brothers are coming after me to kill you. Down yonder at the foot of the cliff you will find Juanito's Andalusian. Go!"

She thrust him away. The young man gazed at her in dull bewilderment; but obeying the instinct of self-preservation, which never deserts even the bravest, he rushed across the park in the direction pointed out to him, springing from rock to rock in places unknown to any save the goats. He heard Clara calling to her brothers to pursue him; he heard the footsteps of the murderers; again and again he heard their balls whistling about his ears; but he reached the foot of the cliff, found the horse, mounted, and fled with lightning speed.

A few hours later the young officer reached General G——'s quarters, and found him at dinner with the staff.

"I put my life in your hands!" cried the haggard and exhausted commandant of Menda.

He sank into a seat, and told his horrible story. It was received with an appalling silence.

"It seems to me that you are more to be pitied than to blame," the terrible general said at last. "You are not answerable for the Spaniard's crimes, and, unless the marshal decides otherwise, I acquit you."

These words brought but cold comfort to the unfortunate officer.

"When the Emperor comes to hear about it!" he cried.

"Oh, he will be for having you shot," said the general, "but we shall see. Now we will say no more about this," he added severely, "except to plan a revenge that shall strike a salutary terror into this country, where they carry on war like savages."

An hour later a whole regiment, a detachment of cavalry, and a convoy of artillery were upon the road. The general and Victor marched at the head of the column. The soldiers had been told of the fate of their comrades, and their rage knew no bounds. The distance between headquarters and the town of Menda was crossed at a wellnigh miraculous speed. Whole villages by the way were found to be under arms; every one of the wretched hamlets was surrounded and their inhabitants decimated.

It so chanced that the English vessels still lay out at sea, and were no nearer the shore, a fact inexplicable until it was known afterwards that they were artillery transports which had outsailed the rest of the fleet. So the townsmen of Menda, left without the assistance on which they had reckoned when the sails of the English appeared, were surrounded by French troops almost before they had had time to strike a blow. This struck such terror into them that they offered to surrender at discretion. An impulse of devotion, no isolated instance in the history of the Peninsula, led the actual slayers of the French to offer to give themselves up; seeking in this way to save the town, for from the general's reputation for cruelty it was feared that he would give Menda over to the flames, and put the whole population to the sword. General G—— took their offer, stipulating that every soul in the castle from the lowest servant to the Marquis should likewise be given up to him. These terms being accepted, the general promised to spare the lives of the rest of the townsmen, and to prohibit his soldiers from pillaging or setting fire to the town. A heavy contribution was levied, and the wealthiest inhabitants were taken as hostages to guarantee payment within twenty-four hours.

The general took every necessary precaution for the safety of his troops, provided for the defense of the place, and refused to billet his men in the houses of the town. After they had bivouacked, he went up to the castle and entered it as a conqueror. The whole family of Légañès and their household were gagged, shut up in the great ballroom, and closely watched. From the windows it was easy to see the whole length of the terrace above the town.

The staff was established in an adjoining gallery, where the general forthwith held a council as to the best means of preventing the landing of the English. An aide-de-camp was despatched to Marshal Ney, orders were issued to plant batteries along the coast, and then the general and his staff turned their attention to their prisoners. The two hundred Spaniards given up by the townsfolk were shot down then and there upon the terrace. And after this military execution, the general gave orders to erect gibbets to the number of the prisoners in the ballroom in the same place, and to send for the hangman out of the town. Victor took advantage of the interval before dinner to pay a visit to the prisoners. He soon came back to the general.

"I am come in haste," he faltered out, "to ask a favor."

"*You!*" exclaimed the general, with bitter irony in his tones.

"Alas!" answered Victor, "it is a sorry favor. The Marquis has seen them erecting the gallows, and hopes that you will commute the punishment for his family; he entreats you to have the nobles beheaded."

"Granted," said the general.

"He further asks that they may be allowed the consolations of religion, and that they may be unbound; they give you their word that they will not attempt to escape."

"That I permit," said the general, " but you are answerable for them."

"The old noble offers you all that he has if you will pardon his youngest son."

"Really!" cried the commander. "His property is forfeited already to King Joseph." He paused; a contemptuous thought set wrinkles in his forehead, as he added, "I will do better than they ask. I understand what he means by that last request of his. Very good. Let him hand down his name to posterity; but whenever it is mentioned, all Spain shall remember his treason and its punishment! I will give the fortune and his life to any one of the sons who will do the executioner's office. There, don't talk any more about them to me."

Dinner was ready. The officers sat down to satisfy an appetite whetted by hunger. Only one among them was absent from the table—that one was Victor Marchand. After long hesitation, he went to the ballroom, and heard the last sighs of the proud house of Léganès. He looked sadly at the scene before him. Only last night, in this very room, he had seen their faces whirl past him in the waltz, and he shuddered to think that those girlish heads with those of the three young brothers must fall in a brief space by the executioner's sword. There sat the father and mother, their three sons and two daughters, perfectly motionless, bound to their gilded chairs. Eight serving-men stood with their hands tied behind them. These fifteen prisoners, under sentence of death, exchanged grave glances; it was difficult to read the thoughts that filled them from their eyes, but profound resignation and regret that their enterprise should have failed so completely was written on more than one brow.

The impassive soldiers who guarded them respected the grief of their bitter enemies. A gleam of curiosity lighted up all faces when Victor came in. He gave orders that the condemned prisoners should be unbound, and himself unfastened the cords that held Clara a prisoner. She smiled mournfully at him. The officer could not refrain from lightly touching the young girl's arm; he could not help admiring her dark hair, her slender waist. She was a true daughter of Spain, with a Spanish complexion, a Spaniard's eyes, blacker than the raven's wing beneath their long curving lashes.

"Did you succeed?" she asked, with a mournful smile, in which a certain girlish charm still lingered.

Victor could nor repress a groan. He looked from the faces of the three brothers to Clara, and again at the three young Spaniards. The first, the oldest of the family, was a man of thirty. He was short, and somewhat ill made; he looked haughty and proud, but a certain distinction was not lacking in his bearing, and he was apparently no stranger to the delicacy of feeling for which in olden times the chivalry of Spain was famous. His name was Juanito. The second son, Felipe, was about twenty years of age; he was like his sister Clara; and the youngest was a child of eight. In the features of little Manuel a painter would have discerned something of that Roman steadfastness which David has given to the children's faces in his Republican *genre* pictures. The old Marquis, with his white hair, might have come down from some canvas of Murillo's. Victor threw back his head in despair after this survey; how should one of these accept the general's offer! nevertheless he ventured to intrust it to Clara. A shudder ran through the Spanish girl, but she recovered herself almost instantly, and knelt before her father.

"Father," she said, "bid Juanito swear to obey the commands that you shall give him, and we shall be content."

The Marquesa trembled with hope, but as she leaned towards her husband and learned Clara's hideous secret the mother fainted away. Juanito understood it all, and leaped up like a caged lion. Victor took it upon himself to dismiss the soldiers, after receiving an assurance of entire submission from the Marquis. The servants were led away and given over to the hangman and their fate. When only Victor remained on guard in the room, the old Marqués de Légañès rose to his feet.

"Juanito," he said. For all answer Juanito bowed his head in a way that meant refusal; he sank down into his chair, and fixed tearless eyes upon his father and mother in an intolerable gaze. Clara went over to him and sat on his knee; she put her arms about him, and pressed kisses on his eyelids, saying gaily—

"Dear Juanito, if you but knew how sweet death at your hands will be to me! I shall not be compelled to submit to the hateful touch of the hangman's fingers. You will snatch me away from the evils to come and—— Dear, kind Juanito, you could not bear the thought of my belonging to any one—well, then?"

The velvet eyes gave Victor a burning glance; she seemed to try to awaken in Juanito's heart his hatred for the French.

"Take courage," said his brother Felipe, "or our well-nigh royal line will be extinct."

Suddenly Clara sprang to her feet. The group round Juanito fell back, and the son who had rebelled with such good reason was confronted with his aged father.

"Juanito, I command you!" said the Marquis solemnly.

The yount Count gave no sign, and his father fell on his knees; Clara, Manuel, and Felipe unconsciously followed his example, stretching out suppliant hands to him who must save their family from oblivion, and seeming to echo their father's words.

"Can it be that you lack the fortitude of a Spaniard and true sensibility, my son? Do you mean to keep me on my knees? What right have you to think of your own life and of your own sufferings? Is this my son, madame?" the old Marquis added, turning to his wife.

"He will consent to it," cried the mother in agony of soul. She had seen a slight contraction of Juanito's brows which she, his mother, alone understood.

Mariquita, the second daughter, knelt, with her slender clinging arms about her mother; the hot tears fell from her eyes, and her little brother Manuel upbraided her for weeping. Just at that moment the castle chaplain came in; the whole family surrounded him and led him up to Juanito. Victor felt that he could endure the sight no longer, and with a sign to Clara he hurried from the room to make one last effort for them. He found the general in boisterous spirits; the officers were still sitting over their dinner and drinking together; the wine had loosened their tongues.

An hour later, a hundred of the principal citizens of Menda were summoned to the terrace by the general's orders to witness the execution of the family of Légañès. A detachment had been told off to keep order among the Spanish townsfolk, who were marshaled beneath the gallows whereon the Marquis' servants hung; the feet of those martyrs of their cause all but touched the citizens' heads. Thirty paces away stood the block; the blade of a scimitar glittered upon it, and the executioner stood by in case Juanito should refuse at the last.

The deepest silence prevailed, but before long it was broken by the sound of many footsteps, the measured tramp of a picket of soldiers, and the jingling of their weapons. Mingled with these came other noises—loud talk and laughter from the dinner-table where the officers were sitting; just as the music and the sound of the dancers' feet had drowned the preparations for last night's treacherous butchery.

All eyes turned to the castle, and beheld the family of nobles coming forth with incredible composure to their death. Every brow was serene and calm. One alone among them, haggard and overcome, leaned on the arm of the priest, who poured forth all the consolations of religion for the one man who was condemned to live. Then the executioner, like the spectators, knew that Juanito had consented to perform his office for a day. The old Marquis and his wife, Clara and Mariquita, and their two brothers knelt a few paces from the fatal spot. Juanito reached it, guided by the priest. As he stood at the block, the executioner plucked him by the sleeve, and took him aside, probably to give him certain instructions. The confessor so placed the victims that they could not witness the executions, but one and all stood upright and fearless, like Spaniards, as they were.

Clara sprang to her brother's side before the others.

"Juanito," she said to him, "be merciful to my lack of courage. Take me first!"

As she spoke, the footsteps of a man running at full speed echoed from the walls, and Victor appeared upon the scene. Clara was kneeling before the block; her white neck seemed to appeal to the blade to fall. The officer turned faint, but he found strength to rush to her side.

"The general grants you your life if you will consent to marry me," he murmured.

The Spanish girl gave the officer a glance full of proud disdain.

"Now, Juanito!" she said in her deep-toned voice.

Her head fell at Victor's feet. A shudder ran through the Marquesa de Léganès, a convulsive tremor that she could not control, but she gave no other sign of her anguish.

"Is this where I ought to be, dear Juanito? Is it all right?" little Manuel asked his brother.

"Oh, Mariquita, you are weeping!" Juanito said when his sister came.

"Yes," said the girl; "I am thinking of you, poor Juanito; how unhappy you will be when we are gone."

Then the Marquis' tall figure approached. He looked at the block where his children's blood had been shed, turned to the mute and motionless crowd, and said in a loud voice as he stretched out his hands to Juanito.

"Spaniards! I give my son a father's blessing. Now, *Marquis*, strike 'without fear;' thou art 'without reproach.'"

But when his mother came near, leaning on the confessor's arm—"She fed me from her breast!" Juanito cried, in tones that drew a cry of horror from the crowd. The uproarious mirth of the officers over their wine died away before that terrible cry. The Marquesa knew that Juanito's courage was exhausted; at one bound she sprang to the balustrade, leaped forth, and was dashed to pieces on the rocks below. A cry of admiration broke from the spectators. Juanito swooned.

"General," said an officer, half-drunk by this time, "Marchand has just been telling me something about this execution; I will wager that it was not by your orders."

"Are you forgetting, gentlemen, that in a month's time five hundred families in France will be in mourning, and that we are still in Spain?" cried General G——. "Do you want us to leave our bones here?"

But not a man at the table, not even a subaltern, dared to empty his glass after that speech.

In spite of the respect in which all men hold the Marqués de Légañès, in spite of the title of *El Verdugo* (the executioner) conferred upon him as a patent of nobility by the

King of Spain, the great noble is consumed by a gnawing grief. He lives a retired life, and seldom appears in public. The burden of his heroic crime weighs heavily upon him, and he seems to wait impatiently till the birth of a second son shall release him, and he may go to join the Shades that never cease to haunt him.

PARIS, *October*, 1820.

FAREWELL.

(Adieu.)

To Prince Friedrich von Schwarzenberg.

"COME, Deputy of the Centre, come along! We shall have to mend our pace if we mean to sit down to dinner when every one else does, and that's a fact! Hurry up! Jump, Marquis! That's it! Well done! You are bounding over the furrows just like a stag!"

These words were uttered by a sportsman seated much at his ease on the outskirts of the Forêt de l'Isle-Adam; he had just finished a Havana cigar, which he had smoked while he waited for his companion, who had evidently been straying about for some time among the forest undergrowth. Four panting dogs by the speaker's side likewise watched the progress of the personage for whose benefit the remarks were made. To make their sarcastic import fully clear, it should be added that the second sportsman was both short and stout; his ample girth indicated a truly magisterial corpulence, and in consequence his progress across the furrows was by no means easy. He was striding over a vast field of stubble; the dried cornstalks underfoot added not a little to the difficulties of his passage, and, to add to his discomforts, the genial influence of the sun that slanted into his eyes brought great drops of perspiration into his face. The uppermost thought in his mind being a strong desire to keep his balance, he lurched to and fro much like a coach jolted over an atrocious road.

It was one of those September days of almost tropical heat that finishes the work of summer and ripens the grapes. Such heat forbodes a coming storm; and though as yet there were wide patches of blue between the dark rain-clouds low down on the horizon, pale golden masses were rising and scattering with ominous swiftness from west to east, and drawing a shadowy veil across the sky. The wind was still, save in the upper regions of the air, so that the weight of the atmosphere seemed to compress the steamy heat of the earth into the forest glades. The tall forest trees shut out every breath of air so completely that the little valley across which the sportsman was making his way was as hot as a furnace; the silent forest seemed parched with the fiery heat. Birds and insects were mute; the topmost twigs of the trees swayed with scarcely perceptible motion. Any one who retains some recollection of the summer of 1819 must surely compassionate the plight of the hapless supporter of the ministry who toiled and sweated over the stubble to rejoin his satirical comrade. That gentleman, as he smoked his cigar, had arrived, by a process of calculation based on the altitude of the sun, to the conclusion that it must be about five o'clock.

"Where the devil are we?" asked the stout sportsman. He wiped his brow as he spoke, and propped himself against a tree in the field opposite his companion, feeling quite unequal to clearing the broad ditch that lay between them.

"And you ask that question of *me!*" retorted the other, laughing from his bed of tall brown grasses on the top of the bank. He flung the end of his cigar into the ditch, exclaiming, "I swear by Saint Hubert that no one shall catch *me* risking myself again in a country that I don't know with a magistrate, even if, like you, my dear d'Albon, he happens to be an old schoolfellow."

"Why, Philip, have you really forgotten your own language? You surely must have left your wits behind you in Siberia," said the stouter of the two, with a glance half-comic, half-pathetic at a guide-post distant about a hundred paces from them.

"I understand," replied the one addressed as Philip. He snatched up his rifle, suddenly sprang to his feet, made but one jump of it into the field, and rushed off to the guide-post. "This way, d'Albon, here you are! left about!" he shouted, gesticulating in the direction of the high-road. "To Baillet and l'Isle-Adam!" he went on; "so if we go along here, we shall be sure to come upon the cross-road to Cassan."

"Quite right, colonel," said M. d'Albon, putting the cap with which he had been fanning himself back on his head.

"Then *forward!* highly respected councilor," returned Colonel Philip, whistling to the dogs, that seemed already to obey him rather than the magistrate their master.

"Are you aware, my Lord Marquis, that two leagues yet remain before us?" inquired the malicious soldier. "That village down yonder must be Baillet."

"Great heavens?" cried the Marquis d'Albon. "Go on to Cassan by all means, if you like; but if you do, you will go alone. I prefer to wait here, storm or no storm; you can send a horse for me from the château. You have been making game of me, Sucy. We were to have a nice day's sport by ourselves; we were not to go very far from Cassan, and go over ground that I knew. Pooh! Instead of a day's fun, you have kept me running like a greyhound since four o'clock this morning, and nothing but a cup or two of milk by way of breakfast. Oh! if ever you find yourself in a court of law, I will take care that the day goes against you if you were in the right a hundred times over."

The dejected sportsman sat himself down on one of the stumps at the foot of the guide-post, disencumbered himself of his rifle and empty game-bag, and heaved a prolonged sigh.

"Oh, France, behold thy deputies!" laughed Colonel de Sucy. "Poor old d'Albon; if you had spent six months at the other end of Siberia as I did——"

He broke off, and his eyes sought the sky, as if the story of his troubles was a secret between himself and God.

"Come, march!" he added. "If you once sit down, it is all over with you."

"I can't help it, Philip! It is such an old habit in a magistrate! I am dead beat, upon my honor. If I had only bagged one hare though!"

Two men more different are seldom seen together. The civilian, a man of forty-two, seemed scarcely more than thirty; while the soldier, at thirty years of age, looked to be forty at the least. Both wore the red rosette that proclaimed them to be officers of the Legion of Honor. A few locks of hair, mingled white and black, like a magpie's wing, had strayed from beneath the colonel's cap; while thick, fair curls clustered about the magistrate's temples. The colonel was tall, spare, dried up, but muscular; the lines in his pale face told a tale of vehement passions or of terrible sorrows; but his comrade's jolly countenance beamed with health, and would have done credit to an Epicurean. Both men were deeply sunburnt. Their high gaiters of brown leather carried souvenirs of every ditch and swamp that they crossed that day.

"Come, come," cried M. de Sucy, "forward! One short hour's march, and we shall be at Cassan with a good dinner before us."

"You never were in love, that is positive," returned the councilor, with a comically piteous expression. "You are as inexorable as Article 304 of the Penal Code!"

Philip de Sucy shuddered violently. Deep lines appeared in his broad forehead, his face was overcast like the sky above them; but though his features seemed to contract with the pain of an intolerably bitter memory, no tears came to his eyes. Like all men of strong character, he possessed the power of forcing his emotions down into some inner depth, and, perhaps, like many reserved natures, he shrank from laying bare a wound too deep for any words of human speech, and winced at the thought of ridicule from those who do not care to understand. M. d'Albon was one of those who are keenly sensitive by nature to the distress of others, who feel at once the pain they have unwittingly given by some blunder. He respected his friend's mood, rose to his feet, forgot his weariness, and followed in silence, thoroughly annoyed with himself for having touched on a wound that seemed not yet healed.

"Some day I will tell you my story," Philip said at last, wringing his friend's hands, while he acknowledged his dumb repentance with a heartrending glance. "To-day, I cannot."

They walked on in silence. As the colonel's distress passed off the councilor's fatigue returned. Instinctively, or rather urged by weariness, his eyes explored the depths of the forest around them; he looked high and low among the trees, and gazed along the avenues, hoping to discover some dwelling where he might ask for hospitality. They reached a place where several roads met; and the councilor, fancying that he saw a thin film of smoke rising through the trees, made a stand and looked sharply about him. He caught a glimpse of the dark green branches of some firs among the other forest trees, and finally, "A house! a house!" he shouted. No sailor could have raised the cry of "Land ahead!" more joyfully than he.

He plunged at once into undergrowth, somewhat of the thickest; and the colonel, who had fallen into deep musings, followed him unheedingly.

"I would rather have an omelette here and home-made bread, and a chair to sit down in, than go further for a sofa, truffles, and Bordeaux wine at Cassan."

This outburst of enthusiasm on the councilor's part was caused by the sight of the whitened wall of a house in the distance, standing out in strong contrast against the brown masses of knotted tree-trunks in the forest.

"Aha! This used to be a priory, I should say," the Marquis d'Albon cried once more, as they stood before a grim old gateway. Through the grating they could see the house itself standing in the midst of some considerable extent of park land; from the style of the architecture it appeared to have been a monastery once upon a time.

"Those knowing rascals of monks knew how to choose a site!"

This last exclamation was caused by the magistrate's amazement at the romantic hermitage before his eyes. The house had been built on a spot half-way up the hillside on the slope below the village of Nerville, which crowned the summit. A huge circle of great oak trees, hundreds of years old, guarded the solitary place from intrusion. There appeared to be about forty acres of the park. The main building of the monastery faced the south, and stood in a space of green meadow, picturesquely intersected by several tiny clear streams, and by larger sheets of water so disposed as to have a natural effect. Shapely trees with contrasting foliage grew here and there. Grottos had been ingeniously contrived; and broad terraced walks, now in ruin, though the steps were broken and the balustrades eaten through with rust, gave to this sylvan Thebaïd a certain character of its own. The art of man and the picturesqueness of nature had wrought together to produce a charming effect. Human passions surely could not cross that boundary of tall oak trees which shut out the sounds of the outer world, and screened the fierce heat of the sun from this forest sanctuary.

"What neglect!" said M. d'Albon to himself, after the first sense of delight in the melancholy aspect of the ruins in the landscape, which seemed blighted by a curse.

It was like some haunted spot, shunned of men. The twisted ivy stems clambered everywhere, hiding everything away beneath a luxuriant green mantle. Moss and lichens, brown and gray, yellow and red, covered the trees with fantastic patches of color, grew upon the benches in the garden, overran the roof and the walls of the house. The window-sashes were weather-worn and warped with age, the balconies were dropping to pieces, the terraces in ruins. Here and there the folding shutters hung by a single hinge. The crazy doors would have given way at the first attempt to force an entrance.

Out in the orchard the neglected fruit trees were running to wood, the rambling branches bore no fruit save the glistening mistletoe berries, and tall plants were growing in the garden walks. All this forlornness shed a charm across the picture that wrought on the spectator's mind with an influence like that of some enchanting poem, filling his soul with dreamy fancies. A poet must have lingered there in deep and melancholy musings, marveling at the harmony of this wilderness, where decay had a certain grace of its own.

In a moment a few gleams of sunlight struggled through a rift in the clouds, and a shower of colored light fell over the wild garden. The brown tiles of the roof glowed in the light, the mosses took bright hues, strange shadows played over the grass beneath the trees; the dead autumn tints grew vivid, bright unexpected contrasts were evoked by the light, every leaf stood out sharply in the clear, thin air. Then all at once the sunlight died away, and the landscape that seemed to have spoken grew silent and gloomy again, or, rather, it took gray soft tones like the tenderest hues of autumn dusk.

"It is the palace of the Sleeping Beauty," the councilor said to himself (he had already begun to look at the place from the point of view of an owner of property). "Whom can the place belong to, I wonder. He must be a great fool not to live on such a charming little estate!"

Just at that moment, a woman sprang out from under a walnut tree on the right-hand side of the gateway, and passed before the councilor as noiselessly and swiftly as the shadow of a cloud. This apparition struck him dumb with amazement.

"Hallo, d'Albon, what is the matter?" asked the colonel.

"I am rubbing my eyes to find out whether I am awake or asleep," answered the magistrate, whose countenance was pressed against the grating in the hope of catching a second glimpse of the ghost.

"In all probability she is under that fig tree," he went on, indicating, for Philip's benefit, some branches that overtopped the wall on the left-hand side of the gateway.

"She? Who?"

"Eh! how should I know?" answered M. d'Albon. "A strange-looking woman sprang up there under my very eyes just now," he added, in a low voice; "she looked to me more like a ghost than a living being. She was so slender, light and shadowy that she might be transparent. Her face was as white as milk, her hair, her eyes, and her dress were black. She gave me a glance as she flitted by. I am not easily frightened, but that cold, stony stare of hers froze the blood in my veins."

"Was she pretty?" inquired Philip.

"I don't know. I saw nothing but those eyes in her head."

"The devil take dinner at Cassan!" exclaimed the colonel; "let us stay here. I am as eager as a boy to see the inside of this queer place. The window-sashes are painted red, do you see? There is a red line round the panels of the doors and the edges of the shutters. It might be the devil's own dwelling; perhaps he took it over when the monks went out. Now, then, let us give chase to the black and white lady; come along!" cried Philip, with forced gaiety.

He had scarcely finished speaking when the two sportsmen heard a cry as if some bird had been taken in a snare. They listened. There was a sound like the murmur of rippling water, as something forced its way through the bushes; but diligently as they lent their ears, there was no footfall on the path, the earth kept the secret of the mysterious woman's passage, if indeed she had moved from her hiding-place.

"This is very strange!" cried Philip.

Following the wall of the park, the two friends reached

before long a forest road leading to the village of Chauvry; they went along this track in the direction of the highway to Paris, and reached another large gateway. Through the railings they had a complete view of the façade of the mysterious house. From this point of view, the dilapidation was still more apparent. Huge cracks had riven the walls of the main body of the house built round three sides of a square. Evidently the place was allowed to fall to ruin; there were holes in the roof, broken slates and tiles lay about below. Fallen fruit from the orchard trees was left to rot on the ground; a cow was grazing over the bowling-green and trampling the flowers in the garden beds; a goat browsed on the green grapes and young vine-shoots on the trellis.

"It is all of a piece," remarked the colonel. "The neglect is in a fashion systematic." He laid his hand on the chain of the bell-pull, but the bell had lost its clapper. The two friends heard no sound save the peculiar grating creak of the rusty spring. A little door in the wall beside the gateway, though ruinous, held good against all their efforts to force it open.

"Oho! all this is growing very interesting," Philip said to his companion.

"If I were not a magistrate," returned M. d'Albon, "I should think that the woman in black is a witch."

The words were scarcely out of his mouth when the cow came up to the railings and held out her warm damp nose, as if she were glad of human society. Then a woman, if so indescribable a being could be called a woman, sprang up from the bushes, and pulled at the cord about the cow's neck. From beneath the crimson handkerchief about the woman's head, fair matted hair escaped, something as tow hangs about a spindle. She wore no kerchief at the throat. A coarse black-and-gray striped woolen petticoat, too short by several inches, left her legs bare. She might have belonged to some tribe of Redskins in Fenimore Cooper's novels; for her neck, arms, and ankles looked as if they had been painted brick-red. There was no spark of intelligence in her featureless face; her pale, bluish eyes looked out dull and expressionless from beneath the eyebrows with one or two straggling white hairs on them. Her teeth were prominent and uneven, but white as a dog's.

"Hallo, good woman," called M. de Sucy.

She came slowly up to the railing, and stared at the two sportsmen with a contorted smile painful to see.

"Where are we? What is the name of the house yonder? Whom does it belong to? Who are you? Do you come from hereabouts?"

To these questions, and to a host of others poured out in succession upon her by the two friends, she made no answer save gurgling noises in the throat, more like animal sounds than anything uttered by a human voice.

"Don't you see that she is deaf and dumb?" said M. d'Albon.

"*Minorites!*" the peasant woman said at last.

"Ah! she is right. The house looks as though it might once have been a Minorite convent," he went on.

Again they plied the peasant woman with questions, but, like a wayward child, she colored up, fidgeted with her sabot, twisted the rope by which she held the cow that had fallen to grazing again, stared at the sportsmen, and scrutinized every article of clothing upon them; she gibbered, grunted, and clucked, but no articulate word did she utter.

"Your name?" asked Philip, fixing her with his eyes as if he were trying to bewitch the woman.

"Geneviève," she answered, with an empty laugh.

"The cow is the most intelligent creature we have seen so far," exclaimed the magistrate. "I shall fire a shot, that ought to bring somebody out."

D'Albon had just taken up his rifle when the colonel put out a hand to stop him, and pointed out the mysterious woman who had aroused such lively curiosity in them. She seemed to be absorbed in deep thought, as she went along a green alley some little distance away, so slowly that the friends had time to take a good look at her. She wore a threadbare black satin gown, her long hair curled thickly over her forehead, and fell like a shawl about her shoulders below her waist. Doubtless she was accustomed to the dishevelment of her locks, for she seldom put back the hair on either side of her brows; but when she did so, she shook her head with a sudden jerk that had not to be repeated to shake away the thick veil from her eyes or forehead. In everything that she did, moreover, there was a wonderful certainty in the working of the mechanism, an unerring swiftness and precision, like that of an animal, wellnigh marvelous in a woman.

The two sportsmen were amazed to see her spring up into an apple tree and cling to a bough lightly as a bird. She snatched at the fruit, ate it, and dropped to the ground with the same supple grace that charms us in a squirrel. The elasticity of her limbs took all appearance of awkwardness or effort from her movements. She played about upon the grass, rolling in it as a young child might have done; then, on a sudden, she lay still and stretched out her feet and hands, with the languid natural grace of a kitten dozing in the sun.

There was a threatening growl of thunder far away, and at this she started up on all fours and listened, like a dog who hears a strange footstep. One result of this strange attitude was to separate her thick black hair into two masses, that fell away on either side of her face and left her shoulders bare; the two witnesses of this singular scene wondered at the whiteness of the skin that shone like a meadow daisy, and at the neck that indicated the perfection of the rest of her form.

A wailing cry broke from her; she rose to her feet, and stood upright. Every successive movement was made so lightly, so gracefully, so easily, that she seemed to be no human being, but one of Ossian's maids of the mist. She went across the grass to one of the pools of water, deftly shook off her shoe, and seemed to enjoy dipping her foot, white as marble, in the spring; doubtless it pleased her to make the circling ripples, and watch them glitter like gems. She knelt down by the brink, and played there like a child, dabbling her long tresses in the water, and flinging them loose again to see the water drip from the ends, like a string of pearls in the sunless light.

"She is mad!" cried the councilor.

A hoarse cry rang through the air; it came from Geneviève, and seemed to be meant for the mysterious woman. She rose to her feet in a moment, flinging back the hair from her face, and then the colonel and d'Albon could see her features distinctly. As soon as she saw the two friends she bounded to the railings with the swiftness of a fawn.

"*Farewell!*" she said in low, musical tones, but they could not discover the least trace of feeling, the least idea in the sweet sounds that they had awaited impatiently.

M. d'Albon admired the long lashes, the thick, dark eyebrows, the dazzling fairness of a skin untinged by any trace of red. Only the delicate blue veins contrasted with that uniform whiteness.

But when the Marquis turned to communicate his surprise at the sight of so strange an apparition, he saw the colonel stretched on the grass like one dead. M. d'Albon fired his gun into the air, shouted for help, and tried to raise his friend. At the sound of the shot, the strange lady, who had stood motionless by the gate, fled away, crying out like a wounded wild creature, circling round and round in the meadow, with every sign of unspeakable terror.

M. d'Albon heard a carriage rolling along the road to l'Isle Adam, and waved his handkerchief to implore help. The carriage immediately came towards the Minorite convent, and M. d'Albon recognized neighbors, M. de and Mme. de Grandville, who hastened to alight and put their carriage at his disposal. Colonel de Sucy inhaled the salts which Mme. de Grandville happened to have with her; he opened his eyes, looked towards the mysterious figure that still fled wailing through the meadow, and a faint cry of horror broke from him; he closed his eyes again, with a dumb gesture of entreaty to his friends to take him away from this scene. M. and Mme. de Grandville begged the councilor to make use of their carriage, adding very obligingly that they themselves would walk.

"Who can the lady be?" inquired the magistrate, looking towards the strange figure.

"People think that she comes from Moulins," answered M. de Grandville. "She is a Comtesse de Vandières; she is said to be mad; but as she has only been here for two months, I cannot vouch for the truth of all this hearsay talk."

M. d'Albon thanked M. and Mme. de Grandville, and they set out for Cassan.

"It is she!" cried Philip, coming to himself.

"She? who?" asked d'Albon.

"Stéphanie—— Ah! dead and yet living still; still alive, but her mind is gone! I thought the sight would kill me."

The prudent magistrate, recognizing the gravity of the crisis through which his friend was passing, refrained from asking questions or exciting him further, and grew impatient of the length of the way to the château, for the change wrought in the colonel's face alarmed him. He feared lest the Countess' terrible disease had communicated itself to Philip's brain. When they reached the avenue at l'Isle-Adam d'Albon sent the servant for the local doctor, so that the colonel had scarcely been laid in bed before the surgeon was beside him.

"If Monsieur le Colonel had not been fasting, the shock must have killed him," pronounced the leech. "He was overtired, and that saved him," and with a few directions as to the patient's treatment, he went to prepare a composing draught himself. M. de Sucy was better the next morning, but the doctor had insisted on sitting up all night with him.

"I confess, Monsieur le Marquis," the surgeon said, "that I feared for the brain. M. de Sucy has had some very violent shock; he is a man of strong passions, but with his temperament, the first shock decides everything. He will very likely be out of danger to-morrow."

The doctor was perfectly right. The next day the patient was allowed to see his friend.

"I want you to do something for me, dear d'Albon," Philip said, grasping his friend's hand. "Hasten at once to the Minorite convent, find out everything about the lady whom we saw there, and come back as soon as you can; I shall count the minutes till I see you again."

M. d'Albon called for his horse, and galloped over to the old monastery. When he reached the gateway he found some one standing there, a tall, spare man with a kindly face, who answered in the affirmative when he was asked if he lived in the ruined house. M. d'Albon explained his errand.

"Why, then, it must have been you, sir, who fired that unlucky shot! You all but killed my poor invalid."

"Eh! I fired into the air!"

"If you had actually hit Madame la Comtesse, you would have done less harm to her."

"Well, well, then, we can neither of us complain, for the sight of the Countess all but killed my friend, M. de Sucy."

"The Baron de Sucy, is it possible?" cried the other, clasping his hands. "Has he been in Russia? was he in the Beresina?"

"Yes," answered d'Albon. He was taken prisoner by the Cossacks and sent to Siberia. He has not been back in this country a twelvemonth."

"Come in, monsieur," said the other, and he led the way to a drawing-room on the ground-floor. Everything in the room showed signs of capricious destruction.

Valuable china jars lay in fragments on either side of a clock beneath a glass shade, which had escaped. The silk hangings about the windows were torn to rags, while the muslin curtains were untouched.

"You see about you the havoc wrought by a charming being to whom I have dedicated my life. She is my niece; and though medical science is powerless in her case, I hope to restore her to reason, though the method which I am trying is, unluckily, only possible to the wealthy."

Then, like all who live much alone and daily bear the burden of a heavy trouble, he fell to talk with the magistrate. This is the story that he told, set in order, and with the many digressions made by both teller and hearer omitted.

When, at nine o'clock at night, on the 28th of November, 1812, Marshal Victor abandoned the heights of Studzianka, which he had held through the day, he left a thousand men behind with instructions to protect, till the last possible moment, the two pontoon bridges over the Beresina that still held good. The rearguard was to save if possible an appalling number of stragglers, so numbed with the cold that they obstinately refused to leave the baggage-wagons. The heroism of the generous band was doomed to fail; for, unluckily, the men who poured down to the eastern bank of the Beresina found carriages, caissons, and all kinds of property which the army had been forced to abandon during its passage on the 27th and 28th days of November. The poor, half-frozen wretches, sunk almost to the level of brutes, finding such unhoped-for riches, bivouacked in the deserted space, laid hands on the military stores, improvised huts out of the material, lighted fires with anything that would burn, cut up the carcasses of the horses for food, tore out the linings of the carriages, wrapped themselves in them, and lay down to sleep, instead of crossing the Beresina in peace under cover of night—the Beresina that even then had proved, by an incredible fatality, so disastrous to the army. Such apathy on the part of the poor fellows can only be understood by those who remember tramping across those vast deserts of snow, with nothing to quench their thirst but snow, snow for their bed, snow as far as the horizon on every side, and no food but snow, a little frozen beetroot, horseflesh, or a handful of meal.

The miserable creatures were dropping down, overcome by hunger, thirst, weariness, and sleep, when they reached the shores of the Beresina and found fuel and fire and victuals, countless wagons and tents, a whole improvised town, in short. The whole village of Studzianka had been removed piecemeal from the heights to the plain, and the very perils and miseries of this dangerous and doleful habitation smiled invitingly to the wayfarers, who beheld no propsect beyond it but the awful Russian deserts. A huge hospice, in short, was erected for twenty hours of existence. Only one thought—the thought of rest—appealed to men weary of life or rejoicing in unlooked-for comfort.

They lay right in the line of fire from the cannon of the Russian left; but to that vast mass of human creatures, a patch upon the snow, sometimes dark, sometimes breaking into flame, the indefatigable grapeshot was but one discomfort the more. For them it was only a storm, and they paid the less attention to the bolts that fell among them because there were none to strike down there save dying men, the wounded, or perhaps the dead. Stragglers came up in little bands at every moment. These walking corpses instantly separated, and wandered begging from fire to fire; and meeting, for the most part, with refusals, banded themselves together again, and took by force what they could not otherwise obtain. They were deaf to the voices of their officers prophesying death on the morrow, and spent the energy required to cross the swamp in building shelters for the night and preparing a meal that often proved fatal. The coming death no longer seemed an evil, for it gave them an hour of slumber before it came. Hunger and thirst and cold—these were evils, but not death.

At last wood and fuel and canvas and shelters failed, and hideous brawls began between destitute late-comers and the rich already in possession of a lodging. The weaker were driven away, until a few last fugitives before the Russian advance were obliged to make their bed in the snow, and lay down to rise no more.

Little by little the mass of half-dead humanity became so dense, so deaf, so torpid—or perhaps it should be said so happy—that Marshal Victor, their heroic defender against twenty thousand Russians under Wittgenstein, was actually compelled to cut his way by force through this forest of men, so as to cross the Beresina with the five thousand heroes whom he was leading to the Emperor. The miserable creatures preferred to be trampled and crushed to death rather than stir from their places, and died without a sound, smiling at the dead ashes of their fires, forgetful of France.

Not before ten o'clock that night did the Duc de Belluno reach the other side of the river. Before committing his men to the pontoon bridges that led to Zembin, he left the fate of the rearguard at Studzianka in Eblé's hands, and to Eblé the survivors of the calamities of the Beresina owed their lives.

About midnight, the great general, followed by a courageous officer, came out of his little hut by the bridge and gazed at the spectacle of this camp between the bank of the Beresina and the Borizof road to Studzianka. The thunder of the Russian cannonade had ceased. Here and there faces that had nothing human about them were lighted up by countless fires that seemed to grow pale in the glare of the snowfields, and to give no light. Nearly thirty thousand wretches, belonging to every nation that Napoleon had hurled upon Russia, lay there hazarding their lives with the indifference of brute beasts.

"We have all these to save," the general said to his subordinate. "To-morrow morning the Russians will be in Studzianka. The moment they come up we shall have to set fire to the bridge; so pluck up heart, my boy! Make your way out and up yonder through them, and tell General Fournier that he has barely time to evacuate his post and cut his way through to the bridge. As soon as you have seen him set out, follow him down, take some able-bodied men, and set fire to the tents, wagons, caissons, carriages, anything and everything, without pity, and drive these fellows on to the bridge. Compel everything that walks on two legs to take refuge on the other bank. We must set fire to the camp; it is our last resource. If Berthier had let me burn those d——d wagons sooner, no lives need have been lost in the river except my poor pontooneers, my fifty heroes, who saved the army, and will be forgotten."

The general passed his hand over his forehead and said no more. He felt that Poland would be his tomb, and foresaw that afterwards no voice would be raised to speak for the noble fellows who had plunged into the stream—into the waters of the Beresina!—to drive in the piles for the bridges. And, indeed, only one of them is living now, or, to be more accurate, starving, utterly forgotten, in a country village! The brave officer had scarcely gone a hundred paces towards Studzianka, when General Eblé roused some of his patient pontooneers, and began his work of mercy by setting fire to the camp on the side nearest the bridge, so compelling the sleepers to rise and cross the Beresina. Meanwhile the young aide-de-camp, not without difficulty, reached the one wooden house yet left standing in Studzianka.

"So the box is pretty full, is it, messmate?" he said to a man whom he found outside.

"You will be a knowing fellow if you manage to get inside," the officer returned, without turning round or stopping his occupation of hacking at the woodwork of the house with his sabre.

"Philip, is that you?" cried the aide-de-camp, recognizing the voice of one of his friends.

"Yes. Aha! is it you, old fellow?" returned M. de Sucy, looking around at the aide-de-camp, who like himself was not more than twenty-three years old. "I fancied you were on the other side of this confounded river. Do you come to bring us sweetmeats for dessert! You will get a warm welcome," he added, as he tore away a strip of bark from the wood and gave it to his horse by way of fodder.

"I am looking for your commandant. General Eblé has sent me to tell him to file off to Zembin. You have only just time to cut your way through that mass of dead men; as soon as you get through, I am going to set fire to the place to make them move——"

"You almost make me féel warm! Your news has put me in a fever; I have two friends to bring through. Ah! but for these marmots, I should have been dead before now, old fellow. On their account I am taking care of my horse instead of eating him. But have you a crust about you, for pity's sake? It is thirty hours since I have stowed any victuals. I have been fighting like a madman to keep up a little warmth in my body and what courage I have left."

"Poor Philip! I have nothing—not a scrap! But is your general in there?"

"Don't attempt to go in. The barn is full of our wounded. Go up a bit higher, and you will see a sort of pigsty to the right—that is where the general is. Good-bye, my dear fellow. If ever we meet again in a quadrille in a ballroom in Paris——"

He did not finish the sentence, for the treachery of the northeast wind that whistled about them froze Major Philips' lips, and the aide-de-camp kept moving for fear of being frostbitten. Silence soon prevailed, scarcely broken by the groans of the wounded in the barn, or the stifled sounds made by M. de Sucy's horse crunching the frozen bark with famished eagerness. Philip thrust his sabre into the sheath, caught at the bridle of the precious animal that he had managed to keep for so long, and drew her away from the miserable fodder that she was bolting with apparent relish.

"Come along, Bichette! come along! It lies with you now, my beauty, to save Stéphanie's life. There, wait a little longer, and they will let us lie down and die, no doubt;" and Philip, wrapped in a pelisse, to which doubtless he owed his life and energies, began to run, stamping his feet on the frozen snow to keep them warm. He was scarcely five hundred paces away before he saw a great fire blazing on the spot where he had left his carriage that morning with an old soldier to guard it. A dreadful misgiving seized upon him. Many a man under the influence of a powerful feeling during the Retreat summoned up energy for his friend's sake when he would not have exerted himself to save his own life; so it was with Philip. He soon neared a hollow, where he had left a carriage sheltered from the cannonade, a carriage that held a young woman, his playmate in childhood, dearer to him than any one else on earth.

Some thirty stragglers were sitting round a tremendous blaze, which they kept up with logs of wood, planks, wrenched from the floors of the caissons, and wheels, and panels, from carriage bodies. These had been, doubtless, among the last to join the sea of fires, huts, and human faces that filled the great furrow in the land between Studzianka and the fatal river, a restless living sea of almost imperceptibly moving figures, that sent up a smothered hum of sound blended with frightful shrieks. It seemed that hunger and despair had driven these forlorn creatures to take forcible possession of the carriage, for the old general and his young wife, whom they had found warmly wrapped in pelisses and traveling cloaks, were now crouching on the earth beside the fire, and one of the carriage doors was broken.

As soon as the group of stragglers round the fire heard the

footfall of the major's horse, a frenzied yell of hunger went up from them. "A horse!" they cried. "A horse!"

All the voices went up as one voice.

"Back! back! Lookout!" shouted two or three of them, leveling their muskets at the animal.

"I will pitch you neck and crop into your fire, you blackguards!" cried Philip springing in front of the mare. "There are dead horses lying up yonder; go and look for them!"

"What a rum customer the officer is! Once, twice, will you get out of the way?" returned a giant grenadier. "You won't? All right then, just as you please."

A woman's shriek rang out above the report. Luckily, none of the bullets hit Philip; but poor Bichette lay in the agony of death. Three of the men came up and put an end to her with thrusts of the bayonet.

"Cannibals! leave me the rug and my pistols," cried Philip in desperation.

"Oh! the pistols if you like; but as for the rug, there is a fellow yonder who has had nothing to wet his whistle these two days, and is shivering in his coat of cobwebs, and that's our general."

Philip looked up and saw a man with worn-out shoes and a dozen rents in his trousers; the only covering for his head was a ragged foraging cap, white with rime. He said no more after that, but snatched up his pistols.

Five of the men dragged the mare to the fire, and began to cut up the carcass as dexterously as any journeymen butchers in Paris. The scraps of meat were distributed and flung upon the coals, and the whole process was magically swift. Philip went over to the woman who had given the cry of terror when she recognized his danger, and sat down by her side. She sat motionless upon a cushion taken from the carriage, warming herself at the blaze; she said no word, and gazed at him without a smile. He saw beside her the soldier whom he had left mounting guard over the carriage; the poor fellow had been wounded; he had been overpowered by numbers, and forced to surrender to the stragglers who had set upon him, and, like a dog who defends his master's dinner till the last moment, he had taken his share of the spoil, and had made a sort of cloak for himself out of a sheet. At that particular moment he was busy toasting a piece of horseflesh, and in his face the major saw a gleeful anticipation of the coming feast.

The Comte de Vandières, who seemed to have grown quite childish in the last few days, sat on a cushion close to his wife, and stared into the fire. He was only just beginning to shake off his torpor under the influence of the warmth. He had been no more affected by Philip's arrival and danger than by the fight and subsequent pillage of his traveling carriage.

At first Sucy caught the young Countess' hand in his, trying to express his affection for her, and the pain that it gave him to see her reduced like this to the last extremity of misery; but he said nothing as he sat by her side on the thawing heap of snow, he gave himself up to the pleasure of the sensation of warmth, forgetful of danger, forgetful of all things else in the world. In spite of himself his face expanded with an almost fatuous expression of satisfaction, and he waited impatiently till the scrap of horseflesh that had fallen to his soldier's share should be cooked. The smell of the charred flesh stimulated his hunger. Hunger clamored within him and silenced his heart, his courage, and his love. He coolly looked round on the results of the spoilation of his carriage. Not a man seated round the fire but had shared the booty, the rugs, cushions, pelisses, dresses—articles of clothing that belonged to the Count and Countess or to himself. Philip turned to see if anything worth taking was left in the berline. He saw by the light of the flames, gold, and diamonds, and silver lying scattered about; no one had cared to appropriate the least particle. There was something hideous in the silence among those human creatures round the fire;

none of them spoke, none of them stirred, save to do such things as each considered necessary for his own comfort.

It was a grotesque misery. The men's faces were warped and disfigured with the cold, and plastered over with a layer of mud; you could see the thickness of the mask by the channel traced down their cheeks by the tears that ran from their eyes, and their long slovenly-kept beards added to the hideousness of their appearance. Some were wrapped round in women's shawls, others in horse-cloths, dirty blankets, rags stiffened with melting hoar-frost; here and there a man wore a boot on one foot and a shoe on the other; in fact, there was not one of them but wore some ludicrously odd costume. But the men themselves with such matter for jest about them were gloomy and taciturn.

The silence was unbroken save by the crackling of the wood, the roaring of the flames, the far-off hum of the camp, and the sound of sabres hacking at the carcass of the mare. Some of the hungriest of the men were still cutting tit-bits for themselves. A few miserable creatures, more weary than the others, slept outright; and if they happened to roll into the fire, no one pulled them back. With cut-and-dried logic their fellows argued that if they were not dead, a scorching ought to be sufficient warning to quit and seek out more comfortable quarters. If the poor wretch woke to find himself on fire, he was burned to death, and nobody pitied him. Here and there the men exchanged glances, as if to excuse their indifference by the carelessness of the rest; the thing happened twice under the young Countess' eyes, and she uttered no sound. When all the scraps of horseflesh had been broiled upon the coals, they were devoured with a ravenous greediness that would have been disgusting in wild beasts.

"And now we have seen thirty infantry-men on one horse for the first time in our lives!" cried the grenadier who had shot the mare, the one solitary joke that sustained the Frenchman's reputation for wit.

Before long the poor fellows huddled themselves up in their clothes, and lay down on planks of timber, on anything but the bare snow, and slept—heedless of the morrow. Major de Sucy having warmed himself and satisfied his hunger, fought in vain against the drowsiness that weighed upon his eyes. During this brief struggle he gazed at the sleeping girl who had turned her face to the fire, so that he could see her closed eyelids and part of her forehead. She was wrapped round in a furred pelisse and a coarse horseman's cloak, her head lay on a blood-stained cushion; a tall astrakhan cap tied over her head by a handkerchief knotted under the chin protected her face as much as possible from the cold, and she had tucked up her feet in the cloak. As she lay curled up in this fashion, she bore no likeness to any creature.

Was this the lowest of camp-followers? Was this the charming woman, the pride of her lover's heart, the queen of many a Parisian ballroom? Alas! even for the eyes of this most devoted friend, there was no discernible trace of womanhood in that bundle of rags and linen, and the cold was mightier than the love in a woman's heart.

Then for the major the husband and wife came to be like two distant dots seen through the thick veil that the most irresistible kind of slumber spread over his eyes. It all seemed to be part of a dream—the leaping flames, the recumbent figures, the awful cold that lay in wait for them three paces away from the warmth of the fire that glowed for a little while. One thought that could not be stifled haunted Philip—"If I go to sleep, we shall all die; I will not sleep," he said to himself.

He slept. After an hour's slumber M. de Sucy was awakened by a hideous uproar and the sound of an explosion. The remembrances of his duty, of the danger of his beloved, rushed upon his mind with a sudden shock. He uttered a cry like the growl of a wild beast. He and his servant stood upright above the rest. They saw a sea of fire in the darkness, and against it moving masses of human figures. Flames were devouring the huts and tents. Despairing shrieks and yelling cries reached their ears; they saw thousands upon thousands of wild and desperate faces; and through this inferno a column of soldiers was cutting its way to the bridge, between two hedges of dead bodies.

"Our rearguard is in full retreat," cried the major. "There is no hope left!"

"I have spared your traveling carriage, Philip," said a friendly voice.

Sucy turned and saw the young aide-de-camp by the light of the flames.

"Oh, it is all over with us," he answered. "They have eaten my horse. And how am I to make this sleepy general and his wife stir a step?"

"Take a brand, Philip, and threaten them."

"Threaten the Countess?——"

"Good-bye," cried the aide-de-camp; "I have only just time to get across that unlucky river, and go I must, there is my mother in France!—— What a night! This herd of wretches would rather lie here in the snow, and most of them would sooner be buried alive than get up—— It is four o'clock, Philip! In two hours the Russians will begin to move, and you will see the Beresina covered with corpses a second time, I can tell you. You haven't a horse, and you cannot carry the Countess, so come along with me," he went on, taking his friend by the arm.

"My dear fellow, how am I to leave Stéphanie!"

Major de Sucy grasped the Countess, set her on her feet, and shook her roughly; he was in despair. He compelled her to wake, and she started at him with dull fixed eyes.

"Stéphanie, we must go, or we shall die here!"

For all answer the Countess tried to sink down again and sleep on the earth. The aide-de-camp snatched a brand from the fire and shook it in her face.

"We must save her in spite of herself," cried Philip, and he carried her in his arms to the carriage. He came back to entreat his friend to help him, and the two young men took the old general and put him beside his wife, without knowing whether he were alive or dead. The major rolled the men over as they crouched on the earth, took away the plundered clothing, and heaped it upon the husband and wife, then he flung some of the broiled fragments of horseflesh into a corner of the carriage.

"Now, what do you mean to do?" asked his friend, the aide-de-camp.

"Drag them along!" answered Sucy.

"You are mad!"

"You are right!" exclaimed Philip, folding his arms on his breast.

Suddenly a desperate plan occurred to him.

"Look you here!" he said, grasping his sentinel by the unwounded arm, "I leave her in your care for one hour. Bear in mind that you must die sooner than let any one, no matter whom, come near the carriage!"

The major seized a handful of the lady's diamonds, drew his sabre, and violently battered those who seemed to him to be the bravest among the sleepers. By this means he succeeded in rousing the gigantic grenadier and a couple of men whose rank and regiment were undiscoverable.

"It is all up with us!" he cried.

"Of course it is," returned the grenadier; "but that is all one to me."

"Very well then, if die you must, isn't it better to sell your life for a pretty woman, and stand a chance of going back to France again?"

"I would rather go to sleep," said one of the men, dropping down into the snow; "and if you worry me again, major, I shall stick my toasting-iron into your belly!"

"What is it all about, sir?" asked the grenadier. "The

man's drunk. He is a Parisian, and likes to lie in the lap of luxury."

"You shall have these, good fellow," said the major, holding out a *rivière* of diamonds, "if you will follow me and fight like a madman. The Russians are not ten minutes away; they have horses; we will march up to the nearest battery and carry off two stout ones."

"How about the sentinels, major?"

"One of us three——" he began; then he turned from the soldier and looked at the aide-de-camp. "You are coming, aren't you, Hippolyte?"

Hippolyte nodded assent.

"One of us," the major went on, "will look after the sentry. Besides, perhaps those blessed Russians are also fast asleep."

"All right, major; you are a good sort! But will you take me in your carriage?" asked the grenadier.

"Yes, if you don't leave your bones up yonder. If I come to grief, promise me, you two, that you will do everything in your power to save the Countess."

"All right," said the grenadier.

They set out for the Russian lines, taking the direction of the batteries that had so cruelly raked the mass of miserable creatures huddled together by the river bank. A few minutes later the hoof of two galloping horses rang on the frozen snow, and the awakened battery fired a volley that passed over the heads of the sleepers; the hoof-beats rattled so fast on the iron ground that they sounded like the hammering in a smithy. The generous aide-de-camp had fallen; the stalwart grenadier had come off safe and sound; and Philip himself had received a bayonet thrust in the shoulder while defending his friend. Notwithstanding his wound, he clung to his horse's mane, and gripped him with his knees so tightly that the animal was held as in a vice.

"God be praised!" cried the major, when he saw his

soldier still on the spot, and the carriage standing where he had left it.

"If you do the right thing by me, sir, you will get me the cross for this. We have treated them to a sword dance to a pretty tune from the rifle, eh?"

"We have done nothing yet! Let us put the horses in. Take hold of these cords."

"They are not long enough."

"All right, grenadier, just go and overhaul those fellows sleeping there; take their shawls, sheets, anything——"

"I say! the rascal is dead," cried the grenadier, as he plundered the first man who came to hand. "Why, they are all dead! how queer!"

"All of them?"

"Yes, every one. It looks as though horseflesh *à la neige* was indigestible."

Philip shuddered at the words. The night had grown twice as cold as before.

"Great heaven! to lose her when I have saved her life a score of times already."

He shook the Countess. "Stéphanie! Stéphanie!" he cried.

She opened her eyes.

"We are saved, madame!"

"Saved!" she echoed, and fell back again.

The horses were harnessed after a fashion at last. The major held his sabre in his unwounded hand, took the reins in the other, saw to his pistols, and sprang on one of the horses, while the grenadier mounted the other. The old sentinel had been pushed into the carriage, and lay across the knees of the general and the Countess; his feet were frozen. Urged on by blows from the flat of the sabre, the horses dragged the carriage at a mad gallop down to the plain, where endless difficulties awaited them. Before long it became almost impossible to advance without crushing sleeping men, women, and even children at every step, all of whom declined to stir when the grenadier awakened them. In vain M. de Sucy looked for the track that the rearguard had cut through this dense crowd of human beings; there was no more sign of their passage than of the wake of a ship in the sea. The horses could only move at a foot-pace, and were stopped most frequently by soldiers, who threatened to kill them.

"Do you mean to get there?" asked the grenadier.

"Yes, if it costs every drop of blood in my body! if it costs the whole world!" the major answered.

"Forward, then!—— You can't have the omelette without breaking eggs." And the grenadier of the Garde urged on the horses over the prostrate bodies and upset the bivouacs; the blood-stained wheels ploughing that field of faces left a double furrow of dead. But in justice it should be said that he never ceased to thunder out his warning cry, "Carrion! lookout!"

"Poor wretches!" exclaimed the major.

"Bah! That way, or the cold, or the cannon!" said the grenadier, goading on the horses with the point of his sword.

Then came the catastrophe, which must have happened sooner but for miraculous good fortune; the carriage was overturned, and all further progress was stopped at once.

"I expected as much!" exclaimed the imperturable grenadier. "Oho! he is dead!" he added, looking at his comrade.

"Poor Laurent!" said the major.

"Laurent! Wasn't he in the Fifth Chasseurs?"

"Yes."

"My own cousin. Pshaw! this beastly life is not so pleasant that one need be sorry for him as things go."

But all this time the carriage lay overturned, and the horses were only released after great and irreparable loss of time. The shock had been so violent that the Countess had been awakened by it, and the subsequent commotion aroused her from her stupor. She shook off the rugs and rose.

"Where are we, Philip?" she asked in musical tones, as she looked about her.

"About five hundred paces from the bridge. We are just about to cross the Beresina. When we are on the other side, Stéphanie, I will not tease you any more; I will let you go to sleep; we shall be in safety, we can go on to Wilna in peace. God grant that you may never know what your life has cost!"

"You are wounded!"

"A mere trifle."

The hour of doom had come. The Russian cannon announced the day. The Russians were in possession of Studzianka, and thence were raking the plain with grapeshot; and by the first dim light of the dawn the major saw two columns moving and forming above on the heights. Then a cry of horror went up from the crowd, and in a moment every one sprang to his feet. Each instinctively felt his danger, and all made a rush for the bridge, surging toward it like a wave.

Then the Russians came down upon them, swift as a conflagration. Men, women, children, and horses all crowded towards the river. Luckily for the major and the Countess, they were still at some distance from the bank. General Eblé had just set fire to the bridge on the other side; but in spite of all the warnings given to those who rushed towards the chance of salvation, not one among them could or would draw back. The overladen bridge gave way, and not only so, the impetus of the frantic living wave towards that fatal bank was such that a dense crowd of human beings was thrust into the water as if by an avalance. The sound of a single human cry could not be distinguished; there was a dull crash as if an enormous stone had fallen into the water, and the Beresina was covered with corpses.

The violent recoil of those in front, striving to escape this death, brought them into hideous collision with those behind them, who were pressing towards the bank, and many were suffocated and crushed. The Comte and Comtesse de Vandières owed their lives to the carriage. The horses that had trampled and crushed so many dying men were crushed and trampled to death in their turn by the human maelstrom which eddied from the bank. Sheer physical strength saved the major and the grenadier. They killed others in self-defense. That wild sea of human faces and living bodies, surging to and fro as by one impulse, left the bank of the Beresina clear for a few moments. The multitude had hurled themselves back on the plain. Some few men sprang down from the banks towards the river, not so much with any hope of reaching the opposite shore, which for them meant France, as from dread of the wastes of Siberia. For some bold spirits despair became a panoply. An officer leaped from hummock to hummock of ice, and reached the other shore; one of the soldiers scrambled over miraculously on the piles of dead bodies and drift ice. But the immense multitude left behind saw at last that the Russians would not slaughter twenty thousand unarmed men, too numb with the cold to attempt to resist them, and each awaited his fate with dreadful apathy. By this time the major and his grenadier, the old general and his wife were left to themselves not very far from the place where the bridge had been. All four stood dry-eyed and silent among the heaps of dead. A few able-bodied men and one or two officers, who had recovered all their energies at this crisis, gathered about them. The group was sufficiently large; there were about fifty men all told. A couple of hundred paces from them stood the wreck of the artillery bridge, which had broken down the day before; the major saw this, and "Let us make a raft!" he cried.

The words were scarcely out of his mouth before the whole group hurried to the ruins of the bridge. A crowd of men began to pick up iron clamps and to hunt for planks and ropes —for all the materials for a raft, in short. A score of armed men and officers, under command of the major, stood on guard to protect the workers from any desperate attempt on the part of the multitude if they should guess their design. The longing for freedom, which inspires prisoners to accomplish impossibilities, cannot be compared with the hope which lent energy at that moment to these forlorn Frenchmen.

"The Russians are upon us! Here are the Russians!" the guard shouted to the workers.

The timbers creaked, the raft grew larger, stronger, and more substantial. Generals, colonels, and common soldiers all alike bent beneath the weight of wagon-wheels, chains, coils of rope, and planks of timber; it was a modern realization of the building of Noah's ark. The young Countess, sitting by her husband's side, looked on, regretful that she could do nothing to aid the workers, though she helped to knot the lengths of rope together.

At last the raft was finished. Forty men launched it out into the river, while ten of the soldiers held the ropes that must keep it moored to the shore. The moment that they saw their handiwork floating on the Beresina, they sprang down on to it from the bank with callous selfishness. The major, dreading the frenzy of the first rush, held back Stéphanie and the general; but a shudder ran through him when he saw the landing place black with people, and men crowding down like play-goers into the pit of a theatre.

"It was I who thought of the raft, you savages!" he cried. "I have saved your lives, and you will not make room for me!"

A confused murmur was the only answer. The men at the edge took up stout poles, thrust them against the bank with all their might, so as to shove the raft out and gain an impetus at its starting upon a journey across a sea of floating ice and dead bodies towards the other shore.

"*Tonnerre de Dieu!* I will knock some of you off into the water if you don't make room for the major and his two companions," shouted the grenadier. He raised his sabre threateningly, delayed the departure, and made the men stand closer together, in spite of threatening yells.

"I shall fall in!—— I shall go overboard!——" the fellows shouted.

"Let us start! Put off!"

The major gazed with tearless eyes at the woman he loved; an impulse of sublime resignation raised her eyes to heaven.

"To die with you!" she said.

In the situation of the folk upon the raft there was a certain comic element. They might utter hideous yells, but not one of them dared to oppose the grenadier, for they were packed together so tightly that if one man were knocked down, the whole raft might capsize. At this delicate crisis, a captain tried to rid himself of one of his neighbors; the man saw the hostile intention of his officer, collared him, and pitched him overboard. "Aha! The duck has a mind to drink—— Over with you! There is room for two now!" he shouted. "Quick, major! throw your little woman over, and come! Never mind that old dotard; he will drop off to-morrow!"

"Be quick!" cried a voice, made up of a hundred voices.

"Come, major! Those fellows are making a fuss, and well they may!"

The Comte de Vandières flung off his ragged blankets, and stood before them in his general's uniform.

"Let us save the Count," said Philip.

Stéphanie grasped his hand tightly in hers, flung her arms about, and clasped him close in an agonized embrace.

"Farewell!" she said.

Then each knew the other's thoughts. The Comte de Vandières recovered his energies and presence of mind sufficiently to jump on to the raft, whither Stéphanie followed him after one last look at Philip.

"Major, won't you take my place? I do not care a straw for life; I have neither wife, nor child, nor mother belonging to me——"

"I give them into your charge," cried the major, indicating the Count and his wife.

"Be easy; I will take as much care of them as of the apple of my eye."

Philip stood stock-still on the bank. The raft sped so violently towards the opposite shore that it ran aground with a violent shock to all on board. The Count, standing on the very edge, was shaken into the stream; and as he fell, a mass of ice swept by and struck off his head, and sent it flying like a ball.

"Hey! major!" shouted the grenadier.

"Farewell!" a woman's voice called aloud.

An icy shiver of dread ran through Philip de Sucy, and he dropped down where he stood, overcome with cold and sorrow and weariness.

"My poor niece went out of her mind," the doctor added after a brief pause. "Ah! monsieur," he went on, grasping M. d'Albon's hand, "what a fearful life for the poor little thing, so young, so delicate! An unheard-of misfortune separated her from that grenadier of the Garde (Fleuriot by name), and for two years she was dragged on after the army, the laughing-stock of a rabble of outcasts. She went barefoot, I heard, ill-clad, neglected, and starved for months at a time; sometimes confined in a hospital, sometimes living like a hunted animal. God alone knows all the misery which she endured, and yet she lives. She was shut up in a mad-house in a little German town, while her relations, believing her to be dead, were dividing her property here in France.

"In 1816 the grenadier Fleuriot recognized her in an inn in Strasbourg. She had just managed to escape from captivity. Some peasants told him that the Countess had lived for a whole month in a forest, and how that they had tracked her and tried to catch her without success.

"I was at that time not many leagues from Strasbourg; and hearing the talk about this girl in the woods, I wished to verify the strange facts that had given rise to absurd stories. What was my feeling when I beheld the Countess? Fleuriot told me all that he knew of the piteous story. I took the poor fellow with my niece into Auvergne, and there I had the misfortune to lose him. He had some ascendency over Mme. de Vandières. He alone succeeded in persuading her to wear clothes; and in those days her one word of human speech—*Farewell*—she seldom uttered. Fleuriot set himself to the task of awakening certain associations; but there he failed completely; he drew that one sorrowful word from her a little more frequently, that was all. But the old grenadier could amuse her, and devoted himself to playing with her, and through him I hoped; but——" here Stéphanie's uncle broke off. After a moment he went on again.

"Here she has found another creature with whom she seems to have an understanding—an idiot peasant girl, who once, in spite of her plainness and imbecility, fell in love with a mason. The mason thought of marrying her because she had a little bit of land, and for a whole year poor Geneviève was the happiest of living creatures. She dressed in her best, and danced on Sundays with Dallot; she understood love; there was room for love in her heart and brain. But Dallot thought better of it. He found another girl who had all her senses and rather more land than Geneviève, and he forsook Geneviève for her. Then the poor thing lost the little intelligence that love had developed in her; she can do nothing now but cut grass and look after the cattle. My niece and the poor girl are in some sort bound to each other by the invisible chain of their common destiny, and by their madness due to the same cause. Just come here a moment; look!" and Stéphanie's uncle led the Marquis d'Albon to the window.

There, in fact, the magistrate beheld the pretty Countess sitting on the ground at Geneviève's knee, while the peasant girl was wholly absorbed in combing out Stéphanie's long, black hair with a huge comb. The Countess submitted herself to this, uttering low smothered cries that expressed her enjoyment of the sensation of physical comfort. A shudder ran through M. d'Albon as he saw her attitude of languid abandonment, the animal supineness that revealed an utter lack of intelligence.

"Oh! Philip, Philip!" he cried, "past troubles are as nothing. Is it quite hopeless?" he asked.

The doctor raised his eyes to heaven.

"Good-bye, monsieur," said M. d'Albon, pressing the old man's hand. "My friend is expecting me; you will see him here before very long."

"Then it is Stéphanie herself?" cried Sucy when the Marquis had spoken the first few words. "Ah! until now I did not feel sure!" he added. Tears filled the dark eyes that were wont to wear a stern expression.

"Yes; she is the Comtesse de Vandières," his friend replied.

The colonel started up and hurriedly began to dress.

"Why, Philip!" cried the horrified magistrate. "Are you going mad?"

"I am quite well now," said the colonel simply. "This news has soothed all my bitterest grief; what pain could hurt me while I think of Stéphanie? I am going over to the Minorite convent, to see her and to speak to her, to restore her to health again. She is free; ah, surely, surely, happiness will smile on us, or there is no Providence above. How can you think that she could hear my voice, poor Stéphanie, and not recover her reason?"

"She has seen you once already, and she did not recognize you," the magistrate answered gently, trying to suggest some wholesome fears to his friend, whose hopes were visibly too high.

The colonel shuddered, but he began to smile again, with a slight involuntary gesture of incredulity. Nobody ventured to oppose his plans, and a few hours later he had taken up his abode in the old priory, to be near the doctor and the Comtesse de Vandières.

"Where is she?" he cried at once.

"Hush!" answered M. Fanjat, Stéphanie's uncle. "She is sleeping. Stay; here she is."

Philip saw the poor distraught sleeper crouching on a stone bench in the sun. Her thick hair, straggling over her face, screened it from the glare and heat; her arms dropped languidly to the earth; she lay at ease as gracefully as a fawn, her feet tucked up beneath her; her bosom rose and fell with her even breathing; there was the same transparent whiteness as of porcelain in her skin and complexion that we so often admire in children's faces. Geneviève sat there motionless, holding a spray that Stéphanie doubtless had brought down from the top of one of the tallest poplars; the idiot girl was waving the green branch above her, driving away the flies from her sleeping companion, and gently fanning her.

She stared at M. Fanjat and the colonel as they came up; then, like a dumb animal that recognizes its master, she slowly turned her face towards the Countess, and watched over her as before, showing not the slightest sign of intelligence or of astonishment. The air was scorching. The glittering particles of the stone bench shone like sparks of fire; the meadow sent up the quivering vapors that hover above the grass and gleam like golden dust when they catch the light, but Geneviève did not seem to feel the raging heat.

The colonel wrung M. Fanjat's hands; the tears that gathered in the soldier's eyes stole down his cheeks, and fell on the grass at Stéphanie's feet.

"Sir," said her uncle, "for these two years my heart has been broken daily. Before very long you will be as I am; if you do not weep, you will not feel your anguish the less."

"You have taken care of her!" said the colonel, and jealousy no less than gratitude could be read in his eyes.

The two men understood one another. They grasped each other by the hand again, and stood motionless, gazing in admiration at the serenity that slumber had brought into the lovely face before them. Stéphanie heaved a sigh from time to time, and this sigh, that had all the appearance of sensibility, made the unhappy colonel tremble with gladness.

"Alas!" M. Fanjat said gently, "do not deceive yourself, monsieur; as you see her now, she is in full possession of such reason as she has."

Those who have sat for whole hours absorbed in the delight of watching over the slumber of some tenderly-beloved one, whose waking eyes will smile for them, will doubtless understand the bliss and anguish that shook the colonel. For him this slumber was an illusion, the waking must be a kind of death, the most dreadful of all deaths.

Suddenly a kid frisked in two or three bounds towards the bench, and snuffed at Stéphanie. The sound awakened her; she sprang lightly to her feet without scaring away the capricious creature; but as soon as she saw Philip she fled, followed by her four-footed playmate, to a thicket of elder trees; then she uttered a little cry like the note of a startled wild-bird, the same sound that the colonel had heard once before near the grating, when the Countess appeared to M. d'Albon for the first time. At length she climbed into a laburnum tree, ensconced herself in the feathery greenery, and peered at the *strange man* with as much interest as the most inquisitive nightingale in the forest.

"Farewell, farewell, farewell," she said, but the soul sent no trace of expression of feeling through the words, spoken with the careless intonation of a bird's notes.

"She does not know me!" the colonel exclaimed in despair. "Stéphanie! Here is Philip, your Philip!—— Philip!" and the poor soldier went towards the laburnum tree; but when he stood three paces away, the Countess eyed him almost defiantly, though there was timidity in her eyes; then at a bound she sprang from the laburnum to an acacia, and thence to a spruce-fir, swinging from bough to bough with marvelous dexterity.

"Do not follow her," said M. Fanjat, addressing the colonel. "You would arouse a feeling of aversion in her which might become insurmountable; I will help you to make her acquaintance and to tame her. Sit down on the bench. If you pay no heed whatever to her, poor child, it will not be long before you will see her come nearer by degrees to look at you."

"That *she* should not know me! that *she* should fly from me!" the colonel repeated, sitting down on a rustic bench and leaning his back against a tree that overshadowed it.

He bowed his head. The doctor remained silent. Before very long the Countess stole softly down from her high refuge in the spruce-fir, flitting like a will-of-the-wisp; for, as the wind stirred through the boughs, she lent herself at times to the swaying movements of the trees. At each branch she stopped and peered at the stranger; but as she saw him sitting motionless, she at length jumped down to the grass, stood a while, and came slowly across the meadow. When she took up her position by a tree about ten paces from the bench, M. Fanjat spoke to the colonel in a low voice.

"Feel in my pocket for some lumps of sugar," he said, "and let her see them, she will come; I willingly give up to you the pleasure of giving her sweetmeats. She is passionately fond of sugar, and by that means you will accustom her to come to you and to know you."

"She never cared for sweet things when she was a woman," Philip answered sadly.

When he held out the lump of sugar between his thumb and finger, and shook it, Stéphanie uttered the wild note again, and sprang quickly towards him; then she stopped short, there was a conflict between longing for the sweet morsel and instinctive fear of him; she looked at the sugar, turned her head away, and looked again like an unfortunate dog forbidden to touch some scrap of food, while his master slowly recites the greater part of the alphabet until he reaches the letter that gives permission. At length animal appetite conquered fear; Stéphanie rushed to Philip, held out a dainty brown hand to pounce upon the coveted morsel, touched her lover's fingers, snatched the piece of sugar, and vanished with it into a thicket. This painful scene was too much for the colonel; he burst into tears, and took refuge in the drawing-room.

"Then has love less courage than affection?" M. Fanjat asked him. "I have hope, Monsieur le Baron. My poor niece was once in a far more pitiable state than at present."

"Is it possible?" cried Philip.

"She would not wear clothes," answered the doctor.

The colonel shuddered, and his face grew pale. To the doctor's mind this pallor was an unhealthy symptom; he went over to him and felt his pulse, M. de Sucy was in a high fever; by dint of persuasion, he succeeded in putting the patient in bed, and gave him a few drops of laudanum to gain repose and sleep.

The Baron de Sucy spent nearly a week, in a constant struggle with a deadly anguish, and before long he had no tears left to shed. He was often wellnigh heart-broken; he could not grow accustomed to the sight of the Countess' madness; but he made terms for himself, as it were, in this cruel position, and sought alleviations in his pain. His heroism was boundless. He found courage to overcome Stéphanie's wild shyness by choosing sweetmeats for her, and devoted all his thoughts to this, bringing these dainties, and following up the little victories that he set himself to gain over Stéphanie's instincts (the last gleam of intelligence in her), until he succeeded to some extent—she grew tamer than ever before. Every morning the colonel went into the park; and if, after a long search for the Countess, he could not discover the tree in which she was rocking herself gently, nor the nook where she lay crouching at play with some bird, nor the roof where she had perched herself, he would whistle the well-known air

Partant pour la Syrie, which recalled old memories of their love, and Stéphanie would run towards him lightly as a fawn. She saw the colonel so often that she was no longer afraid of him; before very long she would sit on his knee with her thin, lithe arms about him. And while thus they sat as lovers love to do, Philip doled out sweetmeats one by one to the eager Countess. When they were all finished, the fancy often took Stéphanie to search through her lover's pockets with a monkey's quick instinctive dexterity, till she had assured herself that there was nothing left, and then she gazed at Philip with vacant eyes; there was no thought, no gratitude in their clear depths. Then she would play with him. She tried to take off his boots to see his foot; she tore his gloves to shreds, and put on his hat; and she would let him pass his hands through her hair, and take her in his arms, and submit passively to his passionate kisses, and at last, if he shed tears, she would gaze silently at him.

She quite understood the signal when he whistled *Partant pour la Syrie*, but he could never succeed in inducing her to pronounce her own name—*Stéphanie*. Philip persevered in his heart-rending task, sustained by a hope that never left him. If on some bright autumn morning he saw her sitting quietly on a bench under a poplar tree, grown brown now as the season wore, the unhappy lover would lie at her feet and gaze into her eyes as long as she would let him gaze, hoping that some spark of intelligence might gleam from them. At times he lent himself to an illusion; he would imagine that he saw the hard, changeless light in them falter, that there was a new life and softness in them, and he would cry, "Stéphanie! oh, Stéphanie! you hear me, you see me, do you not?"

But for her the sound of his voice was like any other sound, the stirring of the wind in the trees, or the lowing of the cow on which she scrambled; and the colonel wrung his hands in a despair that lost none of its bitterness; nay, time and these vain efforts only added to his anguish.

One evening, under the quiet sky, in the midst of the silence and peace of the forest hermitage, M. Fanjat saw from a distance that the Baron was busy loading a pistol, and knew that the lover had given up all hope. The blood surged to the old doctor's heart; and if he overcame the dizzy sensation that seized on him, it was because he would rather see his niece live with a disordered brain than lose her for ever. He hurried to the place.

"What are you doing?" he cried.

"That is for me," the colonel answered, pointing to a loaded pistol on the bench, "and this is for her!" he added, as he rammed down the wad into the pistol that he held in his hands.

The Countess lay stretched out on the ground, playing with the balls.

"Then you do not know that last night, as she slept, she murmured 'Philip?'" said the doctor quietly, dissembling his alarm.

"She called my name?" cried the Baron, letting his weapon fall. Stéphanie picked it up, but he snatched it out of her hands, caught the other pistol from the bench and fled.

"Poor little one!" exclaimed the doctor, rejoicing that his stratagem had succeeded so well. He held her tightly to his heart as he went on. "He would have killed you, selfish that he is! He wants you to die because he is unhappy. He cannot learn to love you for your own sake, little one! We forgive him, do we not? He is senseless; you are only mad. Never mind; God alone shall take you to Himself. We look upon you as unhappy because you no longer share our miseries, fools that we are!—— Why, she is happy," he said, taking her on his knee; "nothing troubles her; she lives like the birds, like the deer——"

Stéphanie sprang upon a young blackbird that was hopping about, caught it with a little shriek of glee, twisted its neck, looked at the dead bird, and dropped it at the foot of a tree without giving it another thought.

The next morning at daybreak the colonel went out into the garden to look for Stéphanie; hope was very strong in him. He did not see her, and whistled; and when she came, he took her arm, and for the first time they walked together along an alley beneath the trees, while the fresh morning wind shook down the dead leaves about them. The colonel sat down, and Stéphanie, of her own accord, lit upon his knee. Philip trembled with gladness.

"Love!" he cried, covering her hands with passionate kisses, "I am Philip——"

She looked curiously at him.

"Come close," he added, as he held her tightly. "Do you feel the beating of my heart? It has beat for you, for you only. I love you always. Philip is not dead. He is here. You are sitting on his knee. You are my Stéphanie, I am your Philip!"

"Farewell!" she said, "farewell!"

The colonel shivered. He thought that some vibration of his highly-wrought feeling had surely reached his beloved; that the heart-rending cry drawn from him by hope, the utmost effort of a love that must last for ever, of passion in its ecstasy, striving to reach the soul of the woman he loved, must awaken her.

"Oh, Stéphanie! we shall be happy yet!"

A cry of satisfaction broke from her, a dim light of intelligence gleamed in her eyes.

"She knows me! Stéphanie!——"

The colonel felt his heart swell, and tears gathered under his eyelids. But all at once the Countess held up a bit of sugar for him to see; she had discovered it by searching diligently for it while he spoke. What he had mistaken for a human thought was a degree of reason required for a monkey's mischievous trick!

Philip fainted. M. Fanjat found the Countess sitting on his prostrate body. She was nibbling her bit of sugar, giving expression to her enjoyment by little grimaces and gestures that would have been thought clever in a woman in full possession of her senses if she tried to mimic her paroquet or her cat.

"Oh, my friend!" cried Philip, when he came to himself. "This is like death every moment of the day! I love her too much! I could bear anything if only through her madness she had kept some little trace of womanhood. But, day after day, to see her like a wild animal, not even a sense of modesty left, to see her——"

"So you must have a theatrical madness, must you?" said the doctor sharply, "and your prejudices are stronger than your lover's devotion? What, monsieur! I resign to you the sad pleasure of giving my niece her food and the enjoyment of her playtime; I have kept for myself nothing but the most burdensome cares. I watch over her while you are asleep, I—— Go, monsieur, and give up the task. Leave this dreary hermitage; I can live with my little darling; I understand her disease; I study her movements; I know her secrets. Some day you will thank me."

The colonel left the Minorite convent, that he was destined to see only once again. The doctor was alarmed by the effect that his words made upon his guest; his niece's lover became as dear to him as his niece. If either of them deserved to be pitied, that one was certainly Philip; did he not bear alone the burden of an appalling sorrow?

The doctor made inquiries, and learned that the hapless colonel had retired to a country house of his near Saint-Germain. A dream had suggested to him a plan for restoring the Countess to reason, and the doctor did not know that he was spending the rest of the autumn in carrying out a vast scheme. A small stream ran through his park, and in the winter-time flooded a low-lying land, something like the plain on the eastern side of the Beresina. The village of Satout, on the slope of a ridge above it, bounded the horizon of a picture of desolation, something as Studzianka lay on the heights that shut in the swamp of the Beresina. The colonel set laborers to work to make a channel to resemble the greedy river that had swallowed up the treasures of France and Napoleon's army. By the help of his memories, Philip reconstructed on his own lands the bank where General Eblé had built his bridges. He drove in piles, and then set fire to them, so as to reproduce the charred and blackened balks of timber that on either side of the river told the stragglers that their retreat to France had been cut off. He had materials collected like the fragments out of which his comrades in misfortune had made the raft; his park was laid waste to complete the illusion on which his last hopes were founded. He ordered ragged uniforms and clothing for several hundred peasants. Huts and bivouacs and batteries were raised and burned down. In short, he omitted no device that could reproduce that most hideous of all scenes. He succeeded. When, in the earliest days of December, snow covered the earth with a thick white mantle, it seemed to him that he saw the Beresina itself. The mimic Russia was so startlingly real, that several of his old comrades recognized the scene of their past sufferings. M. de Sucy kept the secret of the drama to be enacted with this tragical background, but it was looked upon as a mad freak on his part, in several of the leading circles of society in Paris.

In the early days of the month of January, 1820, the colonel drove over to the Forest of l'Isle-Adam in a carriage like the one in which M. and Mme. de Vandières had driven from Moscow to Studzianka. The horses closely resembled that other pair that he had risked his life to bring from the Russian lines. He himself wore the grotesque and soiled clothes, accoutrements, and cap that he had worn on the 29th of November, 1812. He had even allowed his hair and beard to grow, and neglected his appearance, that no detail might be lacking to recall the scene in all its horror.

"I guessed what you meant to do," cried M. Fanjat, when he saw the colonel dismount. "If you mean your plan to succeed, do not let her see you in that carriage. This evening I will give my niece a little laudanum, and while she sleeps we will dress her in such clothes as she wore at Studzianka, and put her in your traveling carriage. I will follow you in a berline."

Soon after two o'clock in the morning, the young Countess was lifted into the carriage, laid on the cushions, and wrapped in a coarse blanket. A few peasants held torches while this strange elopement was arranged.

A sudden cry rang through the silence of night, and Philip and the doctor, turning, saw Geneviève. She had come out half-dressed from the low room where she slept.

"Farewell, farewell; it is all over, farewell!" she called, crying bitterly.

"Why, Geneviève, what is it?" asked M. Fanjat.

Geneviève shook her head despairingly, raised her arm to heaven, looked at the carriage, uttered a long snarling sound, and, with evident signs of profound terror, slunk in again.

"'Tis a good omen," cried the colonel. "The girl is sorry to lose her companion. Very likely she *sees* that Stéphanie is about to recover her reason."

"God grant it may be so!" answered M. Fanjat, who seemed to be affected by this incident. Since insanity had interested him, he had known several cases in which a spirit of prophecy and the gift of second-sight had been accorded to a disordered brain—two faculties which many travelers tell us are also found among savage tribes.

So it happened that, as the colonel had foreseen and arranged, Stéphanie traveled across the mimic Beresina about nine o'clock in the morning, and was awakened by an explosion of rockets about a hundred paces from the scene of action.

It was a signal. Hundreds of peasants raised a terrible clamor, like the despairing shouts that startled the Russians when twenty thousand stragglers learned that by their own fault they were delivered over to death or to slavery.

When the Countess heard the report and the cries that followed she sprang out of the carriage and rushed in frenzied anguish over the snow-covered plain; she saw the burned bivouacs and the fatal raft about to be launched on a frozen Beresina. She saw Major Philip brandishing his sabre among the crowd. The cry that broke from Mme. de Vandières made the blood run cold in the veins of all who heard it. She stood face to face with the colonel, who watched her with a beating heart. At first she stared blankly at the strange scene about her, then she reflected. For an instant, brief as a lightning flash, there was the same quick gaze and total lack of comprehension that we see in the bright eyes of a bird; then she passed her hand across her forehead with the intelligent expression of a thinking being; she looked round on the memories that had taken substantial form, into the past life that had been transported into her present; she turned her face to Philip—and saw him! An awed silence fell upon the crowd. The colonel breathed hard, but dared not speak; tears filled the doctor's eyes. A faint color overspread Stéphanie's beautiful face, deepening slowly, till at last she glowed like a girl radiant with youth. Still the bright flush grew. Life and joy, kindled within her as the blaze of intelligence, swept through her like leaping flames. A convulsive tremor ran from her feet to her heart. But all these tokens, which flashed on the sight in a moment, gathered and gained consistence, as it were, when Stéphanie's eyes gleamed with heavenly radiance, the light of a soul within. She lived, she thought! She shuddered—was it with fear? God Himself unloosed a second time the tongue that had been bound by death, and set His fire anew in the extinguished soul. The electric torrent of the human will vivified the body whence it had so long been absent.

"Stéphanie!" the colonel cried.

"Oh! it is Philip!" said the poor Countess.

She fled to the trembling arms held out towards her, and the embrace of the two lovers frightened those who beheld it. Stéphanie burst into tears.

Suddenly the tears ceased to flow; she lay in his arms a dead weight, as if stricken by a thunderbolt, and said faintly—

"Farewell, Philip!—— I love you—— farewell!"

"She is dead!" cried the colonel, unclasping his arms.

The old doctor received the lifeless body of his niece in his arms as a young man might have done; he carried her to a stack of wood and set her down. He looked at her face, and laid a feeble hand, tremulous with agitation, upon her heart —it beat no longer.

"Can it really be so?" he said, looking from the colonel, who stood there motionless, to Stéphanie's face. Death had invested it with a radiant beauty, a transient aureole, the pledge, it may be, of a glorious life to come.

"Yes, she is dead."

"Oh, but that smile!" cried Philip; "only see that smile. Is it possible?"

"She has grown cold already," answered M. Fanjat.

M. de Sucy made a few strides to tear himself from the sight; then he stopped, and whistled the air that the mad Stéphanie had understood; and when he saw that she did not rise and hasten to him, he walked away, staggering like a drunken man, still whistling, but he did not turn again.

In society General de Sucy is looked upon as very agreeable, and, above all things, as very lively and amusing. Not very long ago a lady complimented him upon his good humor and equable temper.

"Ah! madame," he answered, "I pay very dearly for my merriment in the evening if I am alone."

"Then, you are never alone, I suppose."

"No," he answered, smiling.

If a keen observer of human nature could have seen the look that Sucy's face wore at that moment, he would, without doubt, have shuddered.

"Why do you not marry?" the lady asked (she had several daughters of her own at a boarding-school). "You are wealthy; you belong to an old and noble house; you are clever; you have a future before you; everything smiles upon you."

"Yes," he answered; "one smile is killing me——"

On the morrow the lady heard with amazement that M. de Sucy had shot himself through the head that night.

The fashionable world discussed the extraordinary news in divers ways, and each had a theory to account for it; play, love, ambition, irregularities in private life, according to the taste of the speaker, explained the last act of the tragedy began in 1812. Two men alone, a magistrate and an old doctor, knew that Monsieur le Comte de Sucy was one of those souls unhappy in the strength God gives them to enable them to triumph daily in a ghastly struggle with a mysterious horror. If for a moment God withdraws His sustaining hand, they succumb.

PARIS, *March*, 1830.

A SEASIDE TRAGEDY.*

(*Un Drame au bord de la mer.*)

To Madame la Princesse Caroline Galitzin de Genthod, née Comtesse Walewska, this souvenir of the Author is respectfully dedicated.

THE young for the most part delight to measure the future with a pair of compasses of their own; when the strength of the will equals the boldness of the angle that they thus project, the whole world is theirs.

This phenomenon of mental existence takes place, however, only at a certain age, and that age, without exception, lies in the years between twenty-two and eight-and-twenty. It is an age of first conceptions, because it is an age of vast longings, an age which is doubtful of nothing; doubt at that time is a confession of weakness; it passes as swiftly as the sowing time, and is followed by the age of execution. There are in some manner two periods of youth in every life—the youth of confident hopes, and the youth of action; sometimes in those whom nature has favored, the two ages coincide, and then we have a Cæsar, a Newton, or a Bonaparte—the greatest among great men.

I was measuring the space of time that a single thought needs for its development, and (compass in hand) stood on a crag a hundred fathoms above the sea, surveying my future, and filling it with great works, like an engineer who should survey an empty land, and cover it with fortresses and palaces. The sea was calm, the waves toyed with the reefs of rock. I had just dressed after a swim, and was waiting for Pauline, my guardian angel, who was bathing in a granite basin floored

* A letter written by Louis Lambert.

with fine sand, the daintiest bathing-place of nature's fashioning for the sea-fairies.

We were at the utmost extremity of Croisic-point, a tiny peninsula in Brittany; we were far from the haven itself, and in a part of the coast so inaccessible that the inland revenue department ignored it, and a coastguard scarcely ever passed that way. Ah! to dip in the winds of space, after a plunge in the sea! Who would not have launched forth into the future? Why did I think? Why does a trouble invade us? Who knows? Ideas drift across heart and brain by no will of yours. No courtesan is more capricious, more imperious, than an artist's inspiration; you must seize her like fortune, and grasp her by the hair—when she comes. Borne aloft by my thought, like Astolpho upon his hippogriff, I rode across my world, and arranged it all to my liking. Then when I was fain to find some augury in the things about me for these daring castles that a wild imagination bade me build, I heard a sweet cry above the murmur of the restless sea-fringe that marks the ebb and flow of the tide upon the shore, the sound of a woman's voice calling to me through the loneliness and silence, the glad cry of a woman fresh from the sea. It was as if a soul leaped forth in that cry, and it seemed to me as if I had seen the footprints of an angel on the bare rocks, an angel with outspread wings, who cried, "You will succeed!" I came down, radiant and light of foot, by bounds, like a pebble flung down some steep slope. "What is it?" she asked as soon as she saw me, and I did not answer; my eyes were full of tears.

Yesterday Pauline had felt my sorrow, as to-day she felt my joy, with the magical responsiveness of a harp that is sensitive to every change in the atmosphere. Life has exquisite moments. We went in silence along the beach. The sky was cloudless; there was not a ripple on the sea; others might have seen nothing there but two vast blue steppes above and below; but as for us, who had no need of words to understand each other, who could conjure up illusions to feast the eyes of youth and fill the space between the zones of sea and sky— those swaddling-bands of the Infinite—we pressed each other's hands at the slightest change that passed over the fields of water or the fields of air, for in those fleeting signs we read the interpretation of our double thought. Who has not known, in the midst of pleasure, the moment of infinite joy when the soul slips its fetters of flesh, as it were, and returns to the world whence it came? And pleasure is not our only guide to those regions; are there not hours when feeling and thought intertwine with thought and feeling, and fare forth together as two children who take each other by the hand and run, without knowing why? We went thus.

The roofs of the town had come to be a faint gray line on the horizon by the time that we came upon a poor fisherman on his way back to Croisic. He was barefooted; his trousers, of linen cloth, were botched, and tattered, and fringed with rags; he wore a shirt of sailcloth, and a mere rag of a jacket. This wretchedness jarred upon us, as if it had been a discordant note in the midst of our harmony. We both looked at each other, regretting that we had not Abul Kasim's treasury to draw upon at that moment. The fisherman was swinging a splendid lobster and an adder-pike on a string in his right hand, while in the left he carried his fishing tackle. We called to him, with a view to buying his fish. The same idea that occurred to us both found expression in a smile, to which I replied by a light pressure of the arm that lay in mine as I drew it closer to my heart.

It was one of those nothings that memory afterwards weaves into poems, when by the fireside our thoughts turn to the hour when that nothing so moved us, and the place rises before us seen through a mirage which as yet has not been investigated, a magical illusion that often invests material things about us during those moments when life flows swiftly and our hearts are full. The most beautiful places are only what we make them.

What man is there, with something of a poet in him, who does not find that some fragment of rock holds a larger place in his memories than famous views in many lands which he has made costly journeyings to see? Beside that rock what thoughts surged through him! There he lived through a whole life; there fears were dissipated, and gleams of hope shone into the depths of his soul. At that moment the sun, as if sympathizing with those thoughts of love or of the future, cast a glow of light and warmth over the tawny sides of the rock; his eyes were drawn to a mountain flower here and there on its sides, and the crannies and rifts grew larger in the silence and peace; the mass, so dark in reality, took the hue of his dreams; and then how beautiful it was with its scanty plant life, its pungent-scented camomile flowers, its velvet fronds of maiden-hair fern! How splendidly decked for a prolonged festival of human powers exultant in their strength! Once already the Lake of Bienne, seen from the island of Saint-Pierre, had so spoken to me; perhaps the rock at Croisic will be the last of these joys. But, then, what will become of Pauline?

"You have had a fine catch this morning, good man," I said to the fisherman.

"Yes, sir," he answered, coming to a stand; and we saw his face, swarthy with exposure to the sun's rays that beat down on the surface of the sea. The expression of his face told of the patient resignation and the simple manners of fisher-folk. There was no roughness in the man's voice; he had a kindly mouth, and there was an indefinable something about him—ambitionless, starved, and stunted. We should have been disappointed if he had looked otherwise.

"Where will you sell the fish?"

"In the town."

"What will they give you for the lobster?"

"Fifteen sous."

"And for the adder-pike?"

"Twenty sous."

"Why does it cost so much more than the lobster?"

"Oh! the adder-pike" (he called it an *etter*-pike) "is much more delicate, sir! And then they are as spiteful as monkeys, and very hard to catch."

"Will you let us have them both for five francs?" asked Pauline. The man stood stock-still with astonishment.

"You shall not have them!" I cried, laughing. "I bid ten francs for them. Emotions should be paid for at a proper rate."

"Quite right," returned she; "but I mean to have them. I bid ten francs two sous for them."

"Ten sous."

"Twelve francs."

"Fifteen francs."

"Fifteen francs fifty centimes," said she.

"A hundred francs."

"A hundred and fifty."

I bowed. We were not rich enough just then to bid against each other any longer. Our poor fisherman was mystified, not knowing whether to be annoyed or to give himself up to joy; but we helped him out of his difficulty by telling him where we lodged, and bidding him take the lobster and the adder-pike to our landlady.

"Is that how you make a living?" I asked, wondering how he came to be so poor.

"It is about all I can do, and it is a very hard life," he said. "Shore fishing is a chancy trade when you have neither boat nor nets and must do it with hooks and tackle. You have to wait for the tide, you see, for the fish or the shell-fish, while those who do things on a large scale put out to sea. It is so hard to make a living at it that I am the only shore-fisher in these parts. For whole days together I get nothing at all. For if you are to catch anything, an adder-pike must fall asleep and get left by the tide, like this one here, or a lobster must be fool enough to stick to the rocks. Sometimes some bass come up with a high tide, and then I get hold of them."

"And, after all, taking one thing with another, what do you make each day?"

"Eleven or twelve sous. I could get on if I had no one but myself, but I have my father to keep, and the old man can't help me; he is blind."

The words came from him quite simply; Pauline and I looked at each other in silence.

"Have you a wife or a sweetheart?"

He glanced at us with one of the most piteous expressions that I have ever seen on a human face, and answered, "If I had a wife, I should have to turn my old father adrift; I could not keep him and keep a wife and children too."

"But, my good fellow, why don't you try to earn something more by carrying salt in the haven or by working in the salt pits?"

"Ah! sir, I could not stand the work for three months. I am not strong enough, and if anything happened to me my father would have to beg. The only kind of work for me is something that wants a little skill and a lot of patience."

"But how can two people live on twelve sous a day?"

"Oh, sir, we live on buckwheat bannocks and the barnacles I break off the rocks."

"How old are you?"

"Thirty-seven."

"Have you always stopped here?"

"I once went to Guérande to be drawn for the army, and once to Savenay to be examined by some gentlemen who measured me. If I had been an inch taller, they would have made me into a soldier. The first long march would have put an end to me, and my poor father would have been begging his bread this day."

I have imagined many tragedies, and Pauline, who passes her life by the side of a man who suffers as I do, is used to strong emotion, yet neither of us had ever heard words so touching as these of the fisherman. We walked on for several steps in silence, fathoming the dumb depths of this stranger's life, admiring the nobleness of a sacrifice made unconsciously; the strength of his weakness made us marvel, his reckless generosity humbled us. A vision of the life of this poor creature rose before me, a life of pure instinct, a being chained to his rock like a convict fettered to a cannon-ball, seeking for shell-fish to gain a livelihood, and upheld in that long patience of twenty years by a single feeling! How many hopes disappointed by a squall or a change in the weather! And while he was hanging over the edge of a block of granite with arms outstretched like a Hindoo fakir, his old father, crouching on his stool in the dark, silent hut, was waiting for the coarsest of the shell-fish, and bread, if the sea should please.

"Do you drink wine now and then?" I asked.

"Three or four times a year."

"Very well, you shall drink wine to-day, you and your father; and we will send you a white loaf."

"You are very kind, sir."

"We will give you the wherewithal for dinner, if you care to show us the way along the shore to Batz, where we shall see the tower that gives you a view of the harbor and the shore between Batz and Croisic."

"With pleasure," said he. "Go straight on, follow the road you are in; I will overtake you again when I have gotten rid of my tackle."

We both made the same sign of assent, and he rushed off towards the town in great spirits. We were still as we had been before, but the meeting had dimmed our joyousness.

"Poor man!" Pauline exclaimed, in the tone that takes from a woman's compassion any trace of the something that wounds us in pity, "it makes one ashamed to feel happy when he is so miserable, doesn't it?"

"There is nothing more bitter than helpless wishing," I answered. "The two poor creatures, this father and son, could no more understand how keen our sympathy has been than the world could understand the beauty in that life of theirs, for they are laying up treasures in heaven."

"Poor country!" she said, pointing out to me the heaps of cow-dung spread along a field under a wall of unhewn stones. "I asked why they did that, and a peasant woman who was spreading it said that she was 'making firewood.' Just imagine, dear, that when the cow-dung is dry, the poor people heap it up and light fires with it. During the winter they sell it, like blocks of bark fuel. And, finally, how much do you think the best-paid sempstresses earn? Five sous a day and their board," she went on after a pause.

"Look," I said, "the sea-winds blight or uproot everything; there are no trees. Those who can afford it burn the driftwood and broken-up boats; it costs too dear, I expect, to bring firewood from other parts of Brittany where there is so much timber. It is a country without beauty, save for great souls, and those who have no hearts could not live here—it is a land for poets and barnacles, and nothing between. It was only when the salt warehouses were built on the cliff that people came to live here. There is nothing here but the sand, the sea beyond it, and above us—space."

We had already passed the town, and were crossing the waste between Croisic and the market-town of Batz. Imagine, dear uncle, two leagues of waste covered with gleaming sand. Here and there a few rocks raised their heads; you might almost think that extinct monsters were crouching among the dunes. The waves broke over the low ridges along the margin of the sea, till they looked like large white roses floating on the surface of the water and drifted up upon the beach. I looked across this savanna that lay between the ocean on the right and the great lagoon on the left, made by the encroaching sea between Croisic and the sandy heights of Guérande, with the barren salt marshes at their feet; then I looked at Pauline, and asked if she felt able to walk across the sands in the burning sun.

"I have laced boots on; let us go over there," she said, looking towards the Tower of Batz, which caught the eye by its great mass, erected there like a pyramid in the desert, a slender spindle-shaped pyramid however, a pyramid so picturesquely ornate that one could imagine it to be an outlying sentinel ruin of some great Eastern town laid desolate.

We went a few paces further to reach a fragment of rock to sit in the shade that it still cast, but it was eleven o'clock in the morning, and the shadows which crept closer and closer to our feet swiftly disappeared altogether.

"How beautiful the silence is," she said; "and how the murmur of the sea beating steadily against the beach deepens it!"

"If you surrender your mind to the three immensities around us—the air, the sea, and the sands"—I answered, "and heed nothing but the monotonous sound of the ebb and flow, you would find its speech intolerable, for you would think that it bore the burden of a thought that would overwhelm you. Yesterday, at sunset, I felt that sensation; it crushed me."

"Oh yes, let us talk," she said, after a long pause. "No speaker is more terrible. I imagine that I am discovering the causes of the harmonies about us," she went on. "This landscape that has but three contrasting colors—the gleaming yellow of the sand, the blue heavens, and the changeless green of the sea—is great without anything savage in its grandeur, vast but not desolate, monotonous but not dreary; it is made up of three elements; it has variety."

"Women alone can render their impressions like that," I said; "you would be the despair of a poet, dear soul, that I have read so well."

"These three expressions of the Infinite glow like a burning flame in the noonday heat," Pauline said, laughing. "Here I can imagine the poetry and passions of the East."

"And I, a vision of despair."

"Yes," she said; "the dune is a sublime cloister."

We heard our guide hurrying after us; he wore his holiday clothes. We asked him a few insignificant questions; he thought he saw that our mood had changed, and, with the self-repression that misfortune teaches, he was silent; and we also —though from time to time each pressed the hand of the other to communicate thoughts and impressions—walked for half an hour in silence, either because the shimmering heat above the sands lay heavily upon us, or because the difficulty of walking absorbed our attention. We walked hand in hand like two children; we should not have gone a dozen paces if we had walked arm in arm.

The way that led to Batz was little more than a track; the first high wind effaced the ruts or the dints left by horses' hoofs; but the experienced eyes of our guide discerned traces of cattle and sheep dung on this way, which sometimes wound towards the sea and sometimes towards the land, to avoid the cliffs on the one hand and the rocks on the other. It was noon, and we were only half-way.

"We will rest there," I said, pointing to a headland where the rocks rose high enough to make it probable that we might find a cave among them. The fisherman, following the direction of my finger, jerked his head.

"There is some one there! Any one coming from market at Batz to Croisic, or from Croisic to Batz, always goes round some way so as not to pass near the place."

He spoke in a low voice that suggested a mystery.

"Then is there a robber there, a murderer?"

Our guide's only answer was a deep breath that left us twice as curious as before.

"If we go past, will any harm come to us?"

"Oh, no!"

"Will you go with us?"

"No, sir!"

"Then we shall go, if you will assure us that there is no danger for us."

"I do not say that," the fisherman answered quickly; "I only say that the one who is there will say nothing to you, and will do you no harm. Oh, good heavens! he will not so much as stir from his place."

"Then who is it?"

"A man!"

Never were two syllables uttered in such a tragical fashion.

At that moment we were some twenty paces away from the ridge about which the sea was lapping. Our guide took the way that avoided the rocks, and we held straight on for them, but Pauline took my arm. Our guide quickened his pace so as to reach the spot where the two ways met again at the same time as ourselves. He thought, no doubt, that when we had seen "the man," we should hurry from the place. This kindled our curiosity; it became so strong that our hearts beat fast, as if a feeling of terror possessed us both. In spite of the heat of the day and a certain weariness after our walk over the sands, our souls were steeped in the ineffable languid calm of an ecstasy that possessed us both, brimming with pure joy, that can only be compared with the delight of hearing exquisite music—music like the *Andiamo mio ben* of Mozart. When two souls are blended in one pure thought, are they not like two sweet voices singing together? Before you can appreciate the emotion that thrilled us both, you must likewise share in the half-voluptuous mood in which the morning's experiences had steeped us.

If you had watched for a while some daintily-colored wood-dove on a swaying branch, above a spring, you would utter a cry of distress if you saw a hawk pounce down, bury claws of steel in its heart, and bear it away with the murderous speed with which powder wings a bullet. We had scarcely set foot in the space before the cavern, a sort of esplanade some hundred feet above the sea, protected from the surge by the steep rocks that sloped to the water's edge, when we were conscious of an electric thrill, something like the shock of a sudden awakening by some noise in a silent night. Both of us had seen a man sitting there on a block of granite, and he had looked at us.

That glance, from two bloodshot eyes, was like the flash of fire from a cannon, and his stoical immobility could only be compared to the changeless aspect of the granite slabs that lay about him. Slowly his eyes turned towards us; his body as rigid and motionless as if he had been turned to stone; then after that glance, that made such a powerful impression upon our minds, his eyes turned to gaze steadily over the vast stretch of sea, in spite of the glare reflected from it, as the eagle, it is said, gazes at the sun without lowering his eyelids, nor did he look up again from the waves.

Try to call up before you, dear uncle, some gnarled oak stump, with all its branches lately lopped away, rearing its head, like a strange apparition, by the side of a lonely road, and you will have a clear idea of this man that we saw. The form of an age-worn Hercules, the face of Olympian Jove bearing marks of the ravages of time, of a life of rough toil upon the sea, of sorrow within, of coarse food, and darkened as if blasted by lightning. I saw the muscles, like a framework of iron, standing out upon his hard shaggy hands, and all things else about him indicated a vigorous constitution. In a corner of the cavern I noticed a fairly large heap of moss, and on a rough slab of granite, that did duty as a table, a piece of a round loaf lay over the mouth of a stoneware pitcher.

Never among my visions of the life led in the desert by early Christian anchorites had I pictured a face more awe-inspiring, more grand and terrible in repentance than this. And even you, dear uncle, in your experience of the confessional, have, perhaps, never seen a penitence so grand; for this remorse seemed to be drowned in a sea of prayers, of prayers that flowed for ever from a dumb despair. This fisherman, this rough Breton sailor, was sublime through a thought hidden within him. Had those eyes shed tears? Had the hand of that rough-hewn statue ever struck a blow? A fierce honesty was stamped upon a rugged forehead where force of character had still left some traces of the gentleness that is the prerogative of all true strength. Was that brow, so scored and furrowed with wrinkles, compatible with a great heart? How came this man to abide with the granite? How had the granite entered into him? Where did the granite end and the man begin? A whole crowd of thoughts passed through our minds; and, as our guide had expected, we went by quickly and in silence. When he saw us again, we were either perturbed with a sense of dread or overcome by the strangeness of this thing, but he did not remind us that his prediction had come true.

"Did you see him?" he asked.

"What is the man?"

"They call him the man under a vow."

You can readily imagine how we both turned to our fisherman at these words. He was a simple-minded fellow; he understood our mute inquiry; and this is the story which I have tried to tell, as far as possible, in the homely language in which he told it.

"The Croisic folk and the people at Batz think that he has been guilty of something, madame, and that he is doing a penance laid upon him by a famous rector, to whom he went to confess, beyond Nantes. There are some who think that Cambremer (that is his name) is unlucky, and that it brings bad luck to pass through the air he breathes, so a good many of them before going round the rocks will stop to see which way the wind blows. If it blows from the nor'west," he said, pointing in that direction with his finger, "they would not go on if they had set out to seek a bit of the True Cross; they turn back again; they are afraid. Other folk, rich people in Croisic, say that Cambremer once made a vow, and that is why he is called 'the man under a vow.' He never leaves the place; he is there night and day.

"There is some show of reason for these tales," he added, turning round to point out to us something that had escaped our notice. "You see that wooden cross that he has set up there on the left; that is to show that he has put himself under the protection of God and the Holy Virgin and the saints. He would not be respected as he is, if it were not that the terror people have of him makes him as safe as if he had a guard of soldiers.

"He has not said a word since he went into prison in the open air. He lives on bread and water that his brother's little girl brings him every morning, a little slip of a thing twelve years old; he has left all he has to her, and a pretty child she is, as gentle as a lamb, and full of fun, a dear little pet. She has blue eyes as long as *that*," he went on, holding out his thumb, "and hair like a cherub's. When you begin —'I say, Pérotte'—(that is what we say for *Pierrette*," he said, interrupting himself; "Saint Pierre is her patron saint, Cambremer's name is Pierre and he was her godfather)—'I say, Pérotte, what does your uncle say to you?'—'He says nothing,' says she, 'nothing whatever, nothing at all.'—'Well, then, what does he do when you go?'—'He kisses me on the forehead of a Sunday.'—'Aren't you afraid of him?' —'Not a bit,' says she; 'he is my godfather.'—He will not have any one else bring his food. Pérotte says that he smiles when she comes; but you might as well say that the sun shone in a fog, for he is as gloomy as a sea-mist, they say."

"But you are exciting our curiosity without satisfying it," I broke in. "Do you know what brought him there? Was it trouble, or remorse, or crime, or is he mad, or what?"

"Eh! sir, there is hardly a soul save my father and me that knows the rights of the matter. My mother that's gone was in service in the house of the justice that Cambremer went to. The priest told him to go to a justice, and only gave him absolution on that condition, if the tale is true that they tell in the haven. My poor mother overheard Cambremer without meaning to do so, because the kitchen was alongside the sitting-room in the justice's house. So she heard. She is dead, and the justice has gone too. My mother made us promise, my father and me, never to let on to the people round about; and I can tell you this, every hair bristled up on my head that night when my mother told us the story——"

"Well, then, tell it to us; we will not repeat it."

The fisherman looked at us both—then he went on, something after this fashion—

"Pierre Cambremer, whom you saw yonder, is the oldest of the family. The Cambremers have been seamen from father to son; you see, their name means that the sea has always bent under them. The one you saw had a fishing-boat, several fishing-boats, and the sardine-fishery was his trade, though he did deep-sea fishing as well for the dealers. He would have fitted out a bigger vessel, and gone to the cod-fishing, if he had not been so fond of his wife; a fine woman she was, a Brouin from Guérande, a strapping girl with a warm heart. She was so fond of Cambremer that she would never let her man go away from her for longer than for the sardine-fishing. They lived down yonder, there!" said our fisherman, standing on a hillock to point out to us an islet in the little inland sea between the dunes where we were walking and the salt marshes at Guérande. "Do you see the house? It belonged to him.

"Jacquette Brouin and Cambremer had but one child, a boy, whom they loved like—what shall I say?—like an only child; they were crazy over him. Their little Jacques might have done something (asking your pardon) into the soup, and they would have thought it sweetened it. Times and times again we used to see them buying the finest toys at the fair for him! There was no sense in it—everybody told them so. Little Cambremer found out that he could do as he liked with them, and he grew as willful as a red donkey. If any one told his father, 'Your boy has all but killed little So-and-so,' Cambremer used to laugh and say, ' Bah! he will be a meddlesome sailor! He will command the king's ships.' Another would say, 'Pierre Cambremer, do you know that your lad put out Pougaud's little girl's eye?' 'He will be one for the girls,' Pierre would say. It was all right in his eyes. By the time the little rascal was ten years old he knocked everybody about, and twisted the fowls' necks for fun, and ripped open the pigs; he was as bloodthirsty as a weasel. 'He will make a famous soldier!' said Cambremer; 'he has a liking for bloodshed.'

"You see, I myself remember all this," said our fisherman; "and so does Cambremer," he added, after a pause.

"Jacques Cambremer grew up to be fifteen or sixteen and he was—well, a bully. He would go off and amuse himself at Guérande, and cut a figure at Savenay. He must have money for that. So he began robbing his mother, and she did not dare to tell her husband. Cambremer was so honest that if any one had overpaid him twopence on an account, he would have gone twenty leagues to pay it back. At last one day the mother had nothing left. While the father was away at the fishing, Jacques made off with the dresser, the plenishing, and the sheets and the linen, and left nothing but the four walls; he had sold all the things in the house to pay for his carryings-on at Nantes. The poor woman cried about it day and night. She would have to tell his father when he came back, and she was afraid of the father; not for herself though, not she! So when Pierre Cambremer came back and saw his house furnished with things the neighbors had loaned her, he asked—

"'What does this mean?'

"And the poor thing, more dead than alive, answered, 'We have been robbed.'

"'What has become of Jacques?'

"'Jacques is away on a spree!'

"Nobody knew where the rogue had gone.

"'He is too fond of his fun,' said Pierre.

"Six months afterwards the poor father heard that Jacques had gotten into trouble at Nantes. He goes over on foot— it is quicker than going by sea—puts his hand on his son's shoulder, and fetches him home. He did not ask him, 'What have you been doing?'

"'If you don't keep steady here for a couple of years with your mother and me,' he said, 'and help with the fishing, and behave yourself like a decent fellow, you will have me to reckon with!'

"The harebrained youngster, counting on the weakness his father and mother had for him, made a grimace at his father, and thereupon Pierre fetched him a slap in the face that laid up Jacques for six months afterwards.

"The poor mother was breaking her heart all the time. One night she was lying quietly asleep by her husband's side, when she heard a noise and sat up, and got a stab in the arm from a knife. She shrieked; and when they had struck a light, Pierre Cambremer found that his wife was wounded. He thought it was a robber, as if there were any robbers in our part of the world, when you can carry ten thousand francs in gold from Croisic to Saint Nazaire, and no one would so much as ask you what you had under your arm. Pierre looked about for Jacques, and could not find him anywhere. In the morning the unnatural wretch had the face to come back and say that he had been at Batz.

"I should tell you that the mother did not know where to

hide her money. Cambremer himself used to leave his with M. Dupotet at Croisic. Their son's wild ways had eaten up crowns and francs and gold louis; they were ruined, as you may say, and it was hard on folk who had about twelve thousand livres, including their little island. Nobody knew how much Cambremer had paid down at Nantes to have his son back. Their luck went from bad to worse. One of Cambremer's brothers was unfortunate, and wanted help. Pierre told him, to comfort him, that Jacques and Pérotte (the younger brother's girl) should be married some day. Then, to put him in the way of earning his bread, he took him to help in the fishing; for Joseph Cambremer was obliged to work with his own hands. His wife had died of the fever, and he had to pay some one else to nurse Pérotte till she was weaned. Pierre Cambremer's wife owed as much as a hundred francs to different people on the baby's account for linen and things, and two or three months to big Frelu, who had a child by Simon Gaudry, and nursed Pérotte. La Cambremer, too, had sewn a Spanish doubloon into the flock of her mattress, and written on it, 'For Pérotte.' You see, she had had a good education, and could write like a clerk; she had taught her son to read too—that was the ruin of him.

"Nobody knew how it came about, but that scoundrel Jacques got wind of the gold and took it, and went off to get drunk at Croisic. Old Cambremer, just as if it had happened on purpose, came in with his boat; and as he came up to the house he saw a scrap of paper floating about. He picked it up and took it in to his wife; and she dropped down, for she knew her own handwriting. Cambremer said not a word. He went over to Croisic, and heard there that his son was in the billiard-room. Then he sent for the good woman who kept the café, and said to her—

"'I told Jacques not to change a piece of gold that he will pay his score with: let me have it; I will wait at the door, and you shall have silver for it.'

"The woman of the house brought him out the gold-piece. Cambremer took it.

"'Good!' said he, and he went away home.

"All the town knew that. But this I know, and the rest of them have only a sort of general guess at how it was. He told his wife to set their room to rights; it is on the ground floor. He kindled a fire on the hearth, he lighted two candles, and put two chairs on one side of the fireplace, and a three-legged stool on the other. Then he bade his wife put out the suit he was married in, and to put on her wedding-gown. He dressed himself; and then when he was dressed, he went out for his brother, and told him to keep watch outside the house, and give warning if he heard any sound on either beach, here by the sea or yonder on the salt marshes at Guérande. When he thought his wife must be dressed, he went in again; he loaded a gun and hid it in the chimney-corner.

"Back comes Jacques to the house. It was late when he came; he had been drinking and gambling up to ten o'clock; he had got some one to ferry him over at Carnouf point. His uncle heard him hail the boat, and went to look for him along the side of the salt marshes, and passed him without saying anything.

"When Jacques came in, his father spoke:

"'Sit you down there,' he said, pointing to the stool. 'You are before your father and mother; you have sinned against them, and they are your judges.'

"Jacques began to bellow, for Cambremer's face twitched strangely. The mother sat there, stiff as an oar.

"'If you make any noise, if you stir, if you don't sit straight up like a mast on your stool,' said Pierre, pointing his gun at him, 'I will shoot you like a dog.'

"Cambremer's son grew mute as a fish, and all this time the mother said not a word.

"'Here is a bit of paper that wrapped up a Spanish gold coin. That coin was in your mother's mattress. No one knew where it was except your mother. I found the bit of paper floating on the water when I came in. Only this evening you changed the piece of Spanish gold at Mother Fleurant's, and your mother cannot find the coin in her mattress. Explain yourself.'

"Jacques said that he had not taken his mother's money, and that he had had the coin at Nantes.

"'So much the better,' said Pierre. 'How can you prove it?'

"'I did have it.'

"'You did not take your mother's coin?'

"'No.'

"'Can you swear it on your salvation?'

"He was just going to swear, when his mother looked up and said—

"'Jacques, my child, take care; do not swear if it is not true. You can repent and mend; there is still time,' and she cried at that.

"'You are a So-and-so,' said he; 'you have always tried to ruin me.'

"Cambremer turned white, and said, 'What you have just said to your mother goes to swell your account. Now, come to the point! Will you swear?'

"'Yes.'

"'Stop a bit,' said Pierre, 'was there a cross on your coin like the mark the sardine merchant put on the coin he paid me?'

"Jacques grew sober at that, and began to cry.

"'That is enough talk,' said Pierre. 'I say nothing of what you have done before—I had no mind that a Cambremer should die in the market-place at Croisic. Say your prayers, and let us be quick! A priest is coming to hear your confession.'

"The mother had gone out of the room that she might not hear her son's doom. As soon as she went out, Joseph Cambremer, the uncle, came in with the rector from Piriac. To him Jacques would not open his mouth. He was shrewd; he knew his father well enough to feel sure that he would not kill him till he had confessed.

"'Thanks. Pardon us, sir,' Cambremer said to the priest when Jacques continued obstinate. 'I meant to give my son a lesson, and I beg you to say nothing about it. As for you,' he went on, turning to Jacques, 'if you do not mend your ways, next time you go wrong shall be the last, and shrift or no shrift, I will make an end of it.'

"He sent him off to bed. The young fellow believed him, and fancied that he could make things right with his father. He slept. His father sat up. When he saw his son fast asleep, he covered the young fellow's mouth with hemp, bound it tightly round with a strip of sailcloth; then he tied him hand and foot. He writhed, he 'shed tears of blood,' so Cambremer told the justice. What would you have! His mother flung herself at the father's feet.

"'He is doomed,' said Cambremer; 'you will help me to put him into the boat.'

"She would not help him, and Cambremer did it alone; he fastened him down in the bottom of the boat, and tied a stone round his neck, put out of the bay, reached the sea, and came out as far as the rock where he sits now. Then the poor mother, who had made her brother-in-law take her over, cried out in vain for mercy; it was like throwing a stone at a wolf. By the moonlight she saw the father take the son, towards whom her heart still yearned, and fling him into the water; and as there was not a breath of air stirring, she heard the gurgling sound, and then *nothing*—not an eddy, not a ripple; the sea is a famous keeper of secrets, that it is! When Cambremer reached the place to silence her moans, he found her lying like one dead. The two brothers could not carry her, so they had to put her in the boat that had carried her son, and they took her round home by way of the Croisic channel.

"Ah, well! *la belle Brouin*, as they called her, did not live the week out. She died, asking her husband to burn the accursed boat. Oh! he did it; yes, he did it. He himself was queer after that; he did not know what ailed him; he reeled about like a man who cannot carry his wine. Then he went off somewhere for ten days, and came back again to put himself where you saw him; and since he has been there, he has not said a word."

The fisherman told us the story in a few minutes, in words even more simple than those that I have used. Working people make little comment on what they tell; they give you the facts that strike them, and interpret them by their own feelings. His language was as keenly incisive as the stroke of a hatchet.

"I shall not go to Batz," said Pauline, when we reached the outer rim of the lake.

We went back to Croisic by way of the salt marshes, the fisherman guiding us through the labyrinth. He had also grown silent. Our mood had changed. Both of us were deep in melancholy musings, and saddened by the mournful story which explained the swift presentiment that we had felt at the sight of Cambremer. We had each of us sufficient knowledge of human nature to fill in the outlines of the three lives that our guide had sketched for us. The tragedy of these three human beings rose up before us as if we saw scene after scene of a drama crowned by the father's expiation of an inevitable crime. We did not dare to look at the rocks where he sat, the fate-bound soul who struck terror into a whole country-side. A few clouds overcast the sky. The mist rose on the horizon of the sea. We were walking through the most acrid dreariness that I have ever seen; the earth beneath our feet seemed sick and unwholesome in these salt marshes, which, with good reason, might be called a cutaneous eruption on the face of the earth. The ground is scored over in rough squares, with high banks of gray earth about them; each is full of brackish water; the salt rises to the surface. These artificial hollows are intersected by raised pathways, on which the workmen stand to skim the surface of the pools with long scrapers; and the salt, when collected, is deposited to drain on circular platforms set at even distances, till it is fit to lay up in heaps. For two hours we skirted this dreary chessboard, where the salt stops the growth of any green thing; occasionally, at long intervals, we came upon one or two *paludiers*, so they call the men who work among the salt marshes. These workers, or it should rather be said, this race apart among the Bretons, wear a special costume, a white jacket rather like those that brewers wear. They marry only among themselves; a girl belonging to this tribe has never been known to marry any one but a *paludier*. The hideous desolation of those swamps where the boggy soil is scraped up into symmetrical heaps, the grayness of the soil, from which every Breton flower shrinks in disgust, were in keeping with the sadness within us. We reached the spot where you cross an arm of the sea, the channel doubtless through which the salt-water breaks in upon the low-lying land and leaves its deposits on the soil, and we were glad to see the scanty plant-life growing along the edge of the sand. As we crossed it, we saw the island in the lagoon where the Cambremers once lived, and turned our heads away.

When we reached our inn we noticed a billiard-table in the room on the ground floor, and when we learned that it was the only public billiard-table in Croisic, we made our preparations for departure that night, and on the morrow we went to Guérande.

Pauline was still depressed, and I myself felt a return of the burning sensation that scorches my brain. I was so grievously haunted by the visions of those three lives that I had conjured up, that Pauline said, "Write the story, Louis, and the fever may take a turn."

So, dear uncle, I have written the story for you; but our adventure has already undone the good effects of repose, the result of our stay here and at the Baths.

PARIS, *November* 20, 1834.

www.ingramcontent.com/pod-product-compliance
Lightning Source LLC
Chambersburg PA
CBHW022118290426
44112CB00008B/715